Louise Meintjes

SOUND OF AFRICA!

Making Music Zulu in a South African Studio

Duke University Press   Durham & London   2003

© 2003 Duke University Press

All rights reserved

Printed in the United States of

America on acid-free paper ⊗

Designed by C. H. Westmoreland

Typeset in Trump Medieval by

Tseng Information Systems, Inc.

Library of Congress Cataloging-in-

Publication Data appear on the last

printed page of this book.

TO FRANK XE MAGNE

for your love, your voice, your play.

AND ALSO FOR

JANET DUDU DLAMINI

ebunganini bakhe, nobuculi, nogqozi ekwenzeni kwakhe,

for friendship, song, performance.

Contents

Illustrations

Color Plates (between pgs. 208–209)

Notes to the Reader

On Zulu Pronunciation

Click consonants are represented as follows.

q—palatal alveolar (e.g., middle to front part of the palate)

c—dental

x—lateral

Each may be radical (e.g., "q"), aspirated (e.g., "qh"), voiced (e.g., "gq" or "ngq"), or nasalized (e.g., "nq"). *Mbaqanga* is thus spoken with a radical palatal alveolar click consonant and *isigqi* with a voiced palatal alveolar click consonant.

Lateral alveolar fricatives, in which the edges of the tongue press against the front part of the palate and breath is forced around it, are represented as follows.

hl—radical

dl—voiced

An "h" following a consonant indicates aspiration. *Mahlathini* is thus spoken with a radical lateral alveolar fricative and an aspirated "t."

A word-initial "m" or "n," when followed by a second consonant, indicates nasalization of that consonant. *Mbaqanga* thus sounds with a nasalized "b."

Vowels, broadly described.

i—high, as in *see*

a—low and well back in the mouth

u—fairly high and back, as in *fool*

e—lower "e," as in *get*

o—pronounced with fully rounded lips, as in *or*

Stress generally falls on the penultimate syllable.

On Zulu Noun Prefixes

In English I follow popular convention by dropping the prefixes of Zulu noun stems that refer to ethnic groups and languages. For example, Zulu people are *amaZulu* and their language *isiZulu;* I refer to both simply as *Zulu* except where clarity demands otherwise.

On Zulu Orthography

I follow the revisions noted by J. Khumalo in his preface to the English–Zulu/Zulu–English Dictionary of Doke et al. 1990. Thus, implosive "b" is recorded as "b," explosive as "bh." In orthographic practice the placement of capital letters in compound proper names varies. Some capitalize concords and others word stems. "Izintombi Zesimanjemanje" also appears in print as "Izintombi Zesi Manje Manje," "Izintombi zesiManjemanje," and "Izintombi Zesimanje-manje." I capitalize concords except when reproducing a name as it appears on an album cover or in a print citation.

On the Name of the Principal Band in the Text

The group named Isigqi Sesimanje at the time of my principal research in 1991–1992 had formerly been called Izintombi Zesimanjemanje and subsequently Izintombi Zesimanje. I follow the musicians by referring to their group in abbreviated form as Zesimanjemanje, Zesimanje, Sesimanje, Simanje, Simanjemanje, or Isigqi. In 1994 some members split from the frontline and formed their own group, taking the name Isigqi Sesimanje with them; in the text, however, I use this name to refer to the 1991–92 band, unless otherwise stated.

Acknowledgments

I gratefully acknowledge the financial assistance and endorsement of the National Research Foundation (South Africa), National Science Foundation, Wenner-Gren Foundation for Anthropological Research, the Charlotte W. Newcombe Foundation, and the Arts and Sciences Research Council, Center for International Studies, and Oceans Connect project at Duke University. I am also grateful to the executives and employees of Gallo Africa, especially of Gallo Music Productions and Gallo Music Publishers, who facilitated the research for this book. Any opinions, findings, and conclusions expressed herein are those of the author and do not necessarily reflect the views of these agencies or of Gallo Africa.

The participants in my research and writing produced the sociability that made me want to stay. They are, in a sense, the *Sound of Africa!*

First, I thank the music-makers at Downtown Studios—musicians, sound engineers, and producers—who shared their takes on South African music production with me in passing moments, in extended sessions, and even in times when I disrupted their work. I especially thank the artists of Isigqi Sesimanje (now Izintombi Zesimanjemanje again), their backing vocalists Abashayi Bengoma, and their backing band for sharing their expertise, concerns, and fun. It was a privilege to engage with producers West Nkosi and Hamilton Nzimande, all the sound engineers at Downtown Studios, and John Lindemann at Audiolab. I am also grateful to those music-makers whose voices and sessions do not appear explicitly on these pages though their ideas, performances, and work inspire and inform the book. Those whom I characterize in this account I thank for the liberty to do so. I hope my representations have been faithful to the complexity of each individual with whom I have worked. If in any instance I have failed, the responsibility is mine. I hope, too, that readers will join me in recognizing the artfulness and necessity of the trickstering rhetoric of some of those documented in the text.

I warmly acknowledge Koloi Lebona and Monty Bogatsu for their support of my project. They were my guide vocals in recording and key critics at playback. Gallo archivist Rob Allingham and royalty officer Albert Ralulimi were generous and stunningly encyclopedic. Without them, the documentation of South Africa's recorded music history would be impoverished. I am also grateful to the public relations, marketing, and administrative personnel of GMP/GRC and Downtown Studios. Their willingness to entertain my research in their midst as well as their assistance in many practical ways was indispensable.

For a way of working the beat that made for memorable joint ventures, I thank photographer TJ Lemon, whose captivating images add a dimension to *Sound of Africa!* I could not have come close to delivering on my own. For assistance in transcription and translation and for the passionate politicizing stories evoked in the process, thanks go to Mpumelelo Ncwadi and to Siyazi Zulu, who was poetic and precise with the same task. James Harkins lent his superb ear and computing skills to the musical transcriptions. Susan Lepselter taught me to appreciate good scholarly writing. Those parts of my text that enjoy organizational and theoretical clarity have been subjected to the editorial finesse of Purnima Bose, David Samuels, Jairo Moreno, Helen Meintjes, and Paul Berliner. Three reviewers for Duke University Press offered stimulating critique in a tone that made it easy to hear, and Tim Taylor kindly checked the whole manuscript with his reassuring and uncompromising eye. I appreciate the remarkable efficiency, attention to style, and intellectual energy of Ken Wissoker and his assistants at Duke University Press.

The project began as a dissertation at the University of Texas. My dissertation committee members—Steve Feld, Katie Stewart, Veit Erlmann, and Barbara Harlow—shaped my thinking for the project and convinced me of the enduring politics and pleasures of doing anthropology. Greg Urban and Charles Keil prompted some of my best thinking. My fellow graduate students and friends at the University of Texas provided sustaining spirits, snappy irreverence, and helpful ideas. Steve Feld found a skillful balance between warm support, critical input, and scholarly independence.

For convivial and persistent debate I also thank Tom Porcello, Aaron Fox, Patricia Sawin, Angela Impey, Jonathan Kramer, Chris Waterman, Ellen Gray, Georgiary McElveen, Christina Gier, Marc Faris, and my colleagues at Duke University. Ethnomusicologists, Africanists, anthropologists, and musicologists at other institutions challenged me constructively after presentations of sections of the book: Vassar College; Universities of Natal, Tennessee, Wisconsin, and Tromsø; UNC–Greensboro and UNC–Chapel Hill; Iowa, Northwestern, Columbia, York, and Humbolt Universities; and the Norwegian University of Science and Technology.

My family offered patient and good-humored support, as did my friends outside the academy. Thank you to Helen Meintjes and Paul Berliner who through their own writing processes encouraged and supported me with mine.

Demo Tape

About *Sound of Africa!*

Setting Up   *Some Moments Inspected, Some Worlds Observed*

19 November 1991

In the top right-hand corner of the main recording console, a board is punctured by a grid of holes: a patch bay. Chord jacks sit in the numbered holes. Red, yellow, green, blue, gray, and black chords spray out of the board like a fireworks display. They link microphone and MIDI lines to recording channels on the console. This is the nerve center of the electronic system.

Peter, an engineer, sets up for the second recording session. He mutters to himself. Engineer Humphrey half looks on, distracted in his early morning daydream.

"I'm wondering if I shouldn't just start again—patch everything in again," Peter mutters.

"Why?" asks Humphrey.

"Well this has been undone . . . this is coming from there."

Peter prods another hole with another jack, linking up console channels with microphone lines, keyboards with batteries of effects, MIDI lines, and electronic modules.

"Nine. See, that's been unpatched. What's this?" Peter asks himself.

Humphrey mumbles.

"Uh," thinks Peter aloud, "we don't need that, we only need the DX7 to drive the, uh, that thing."

His eyebrows point to a sleek machine stacked on a trolley.

"The DX7 is driving the modules. We're not using the DX7 at all. Tell you what—let me redo all this shit quickly," he says.

He yanks out all the patch chords.

"I'm getting really annoyed." He tugs at his hair. "Okay, there's the DBX. These are the URIS which should go across the desk. Where's this? Haven't seen this. Six! I wasn't using six. SCAMPS . . . which go across the guitars."

He sucks in his lips, creases his eyebrows together.

"What?! Four . . . five, six. Okay."

He patches five and six in methodically.

"Okay. Vocal is going into thirty three . . . nine. Guitar, eleven and twelve—and it's going to GTR thirteen and fifteen?"

Humphrey answers him, "Ja, thirteen and fifteen guitar."

Peter links holes eleven and twelve to thirteen and fifteen, numbering them aloud as he does so. Their chords loop and bury their ends like luminous earthworms discovering compost.

"Fifteen. Bass is in thirteen, fourteen, . . . going to ten and eleven."

Musicians, singers, producer, engineer, and anthropologist busy themselves in the studio. Listen: hear the talk in the control room around the consoles; whispers on the couch at the back; discussion in the recording booths; laughter, playback from the tape; pre-recording monitoring of the booth, sound as it's laid onto tape; sound checked pre-mixing desk; sound flipping from big monitors mounted high on the wall to middle-sized monitors to the boombox imitation on the console ledge; single tracks inspected one moment, multiple tracks blaring the next; instruments punched in, punched out; timbres blended, boosted, mixed and matched; lines tested dry, listened to with effects; talk piped in from the booths, musicians mouthing or shouting through the double-paned windows; the producer pressing the talk button to instruct artists in the booth; speaking over singing; practicing over storytelling; laying fresh tracks; overdubbing new sounds onto backing tracks; dropping in moments to recorded micro mistakes; rehearsing. Record cut four take one. Redo as take two, while talking in the control room. Erase it. Take two, again. Try a third take. "Tape rolling!" The producer gestures to the artists to sing again.

In the studio's fragmenting and circuitous practice lie openings for poetic innovation, for social and professional repositioning, and for empowering moves. *Sound of Africa!* illustrates how these possibilities work themselves out, dialogically, through music and talk, during moments in the studio process. Moments emerge out of studio sessions, which organize the process of music production, which happens within the music industry, headquartered in the buzz of Johannesburg, where South Africa's transitional politics spill out onto the street.

Musicians arrive in town in taxis and head down to the studios. Witness their recording sessions: setting up mikes, getting sounds, programming rhythm tracks on the drum machine, laying down guide vocals and basic backing tracks; rechecking a song on the demo tape; double- or triple-tracking vocals, overdubbing percussion, keyboards, flutes, accordion; slipping in a solo, cutting out a break, copying a chorus, retuning the guitar, bumming cigarettes, changing the lyrics, rehearsing on the spot, experimenting. "Do we now have a working mix?" They go back to reprogramming percussion. They call in another session musician, rehearse between sessions upstairs. There are cancellations, late starts, transportation troubles from the townships, a labor stayaway; postponements, no-shows, a funeral. They do takes, playbacks, and retakes: track by track, instrument by instrument, effect by effect, sound by sound, voice by voice, break by break, phrase by phrase, song by song or cut by cut, session by session, day by day. Rewind. Retake that. Give us a heavier groove. Change the lyrics, shift the arrangement, improvise. There are mixing sessions: a rough mix, remixing; playback again. A final mix happens, eventually, late into the night. It gets transferred from two-inch tape to DAT. Then Peter heads down to the editing suite with the DAT cassette slipped into his pocket. He prepares a final tape for cutting, pressing, and cassette duplication.[1]

Consider the state of the industry. "It's a melting pot at the moment, anything could happen. It's bloody exciting!" reckons sound engineer John Lindemann. "I mean eighteen months ago we were in the total grip of sanctions—*total* grip—so we actually knew where we were going because we knew what the limitations were. I had fixed ideas as to how music should be." But now that the cultural boycott has disintegrated, handshaking foreigners make forays into the domestic scene, hooking up here, bypassing there, gazing across the crowds in the jazz clubs. "We have lots to learn, but if there's a flood of foreigners we'll have to be helluva careful." Striking media workers want better black representation: let's remember South Africa, let's promote local talent, we must care for our homegrown economy. Give South African music broadcasting airtime quotas! We are with you, reply some producers, performers, the musicians' alliance, music rights organizations, and a managing director or two. And where are the festivals? Which are the halls? Producers bring guns to the stadiums. Unionized musicians meet over property rights.

Few products go platinum anymore.[2] Cassette costs rocket while salaries slump and payola runs on unabated. Some indies go under. Studios close. Music-makers shuffle between corporations. Some fly overseas; they return or they don't. And still, new labels emerge, signings are celebrated, new subsidiaries hope for new sounds. BMG enters, Sony waits, and EMI pushes its product. Gallo manufactures its first CDs, updates its studios, opens an international marketing wing. Gallo moves its headquarters to ritzy Rosebank.

For downtown Johannesburg taunts white suburbia at the dawn of a new South Africa. It flaunts the promises and exposes the risks of fast change, slow change, wrong change, no change. Suited professionals hurry with briefcases; workers crisscross their paths. Taxis stop here, there, anywhere, and line up for blocks on Bree Street. Motorbiked messengers zigzag through traffic; lorries unload mid-lane; brash Mercedes tailgate Hondas; pedestrians cross on the orange. Cramped fabric stores bustle against bargain shops, appliance centers, hawkers' warehouses; CityLab graphics, the mirrored Carlton Centre, the pillared post office, the domed court; shoe shops, tatersalls, butchers, record bars, corner cafes; and the mosque. Mrs. Precious' Antiques has left for the suburbs; an herbalist sells roots in her place. Sirens, police. In Joubert Park lovers meander, muggers cruise, and photographers pose families against the fountain. Inner-city residents lean over balconies. High-rises crumble and ache. School pupils queue to study at library desks. The art gallery curates Africa in Wood. The city hall advertises Wednesday's symphony program. Did you see Tokyo Sekwale lunching at Kapitan's curry house, Hugh Masekela hanging near Kiepies jazz club? A car alarm. No one bothers. Movie theaters screen action films. Actors rehearse at the Market Theatre. A beggar sings gospel tapping a beat with his cup. Singing, dancing protesters move up President Street. "No to Value Added Tax!" their banners proclaim. Onlookers, police. Aged graffiti decorates underpasses; festival posters peel on railway bridges. "Welcome home baba Thambo." "Fun Valley festival: Senyaka, Platform One, Bekumuzi, more!" Security guards stand ready with machine guns while their colleagues carry cash to a bank. On a double-decker bus a granny in white gloves travels upstairs at the front. Homeless people camp out on pavements: men, women, white and black. Ten year olds sniff glue in doorways. In a huddle they heave. Vendors galore, vendors everywhere, vendors selling matches, onions, tapes, umbrellas, sunglasses. On a corner a barber shaves his customer; a daydreaming flower seller waits. A BMW pulls up to buy tiger lilies.

Imagine Johannesburg, think of the nation, 1991–1992. An all-white countrywide referendum supports the replacement of the racist government. The first Convention for a Democratic South Africa (CODESA I) is set up as the forum to negotiate the transformation to a national constitution and democratic election. CODESA I fails. CODESA II happens. Residents of hostels massacre residents of the nearby Boipatong squatter camp. CODESA II falters. Inkatha Freedom Party (IFP) supporters protest and picket. Why is Zulu King Zwelethini barred from the negotiating table? The white right wing pickets, withdraws, splits, threatens, rejoins the noisy negotiating. Workers strike. Miners fight. Political prisoners are released, or not. Which prisoners are the political ones? Some homeland leaders sit tight uneasily; others leap into new public alliances. Money moves under and around. The Congress of Traditional Leaders of South Africa convenes long meetings. Rallies and protests turn into rampages and riots. Ban the carrying of traditional weapons in public, shouts the African National Congress (ANC). Some squatter camps get devastated; some hostels get demolished. People die by bullets, pangas, axes, knopkieries (round-headed clubs), knifes, AIDS, and on the road. The ANC and IFP sign a peace accord. An upsurge of violence foments in its wake. The Pan African Congress refuses to participate in CODESA. Tension in the ANC's alliance with the South African Communist Party gets debated. A National Peace Accord papers over it. The government's "truth commission" investigates police conduct and military corruption.[3] ANC detention camp atrocities hit the headlines. Facts and figures of defense force and Inkatha collusion erupt. CODESA continues. It falters. CODESA tries again.

Studio process, industrial politics, civic organization, and state negotiations produce a context within which the sounds of the record *Lomculo Unzima* (This music is heavy/weighty/potent) take on particular characteristics. Recorded by Isigqi Sesimanje in November 1991 and March–April 1992, produced by West Nkosi under executive producer Ali Mpofu, programmed and engineered by Peter Pearlson and Neil Kuny at Gallo's Downtown Studios located in Johannesburg's city center, *Lomculo Unzima* was released in May 1992 as a domestic product of RPM—a subsidiary of Gallo Africa, which is a holding of the Johannesburg Stock Exchange and is listed as CNA Gallo Ltd.[4] It was promoted on SABC-TV and radio and through live performance, and sold in record bars and at taxi ranks. Three hundred and thirty cassettes were purchased in the first six months of its release.

Lomculo Unzima was distributed on cassette and LP, the LPs pressed primarily as promotional copies. CDs were not locally manufactured at the time of this recording. The targeted consumers were Zulu-speaking, mature urban dwellers, migrants, and men and women located in the rural areas of the KwaZulu "homeland" and the Natal province.[5]

The production comprises eight songs, all composed and performed by members of the group. They are sung in Zulu, although "South Africa" includes some English. Three songs are "traditional" *mbaqanga*, three are wedding songs, one is reggae-inflected, and one a slow ballad. They were recorded with the addition of session musicians called in by West, the producer: Lemmy Special Mabaso overdubbed a saxophone part onto the ballad; Mandla Nene joined the backing male chorus on some songs; Hansford Mthembu added acoustic guitar; and Mzwandile David played some of the bass lines.

Band members and session musicians were paid session fees, while the frontline singers and composers were contracted with royalty payments. These musicians lived sparsely, usually with no official form of income other than their earnings in the music business. While most had family members who were employed in some capacity, none of the musicians themselves worked full time. Occasionally, when they could find them—and they were always on the lookout—the musicians worked temporary part-time jobs. For example, Jane Dlamini, the lead of the frontline singers, worked for six weeks at a driving school, then as a temporary tea lady in a bank. Her partner, once a miner, worked in a tavern in Soweto until it closed, but has been unemployed since.

Mbaqanga is popularly characterized by a choreographed female close-harmony frontline, a garage band (guitar, bass, drumset, keyboard) backing them up, and a strident bass solo voice pitted against them. In the early 1990s, mbaqanga music constituted a small part of the domestic market, which was dominated by township pop, an electronic keyboard–based dance music directed at the youth. Many of mbaqanga's local consumers also listened to styles marketed as Zulu traditional music, such as a cappella male choral *isicathamiya*, singer-songwriter *maskanda*, and choruses of young women singing wedding songs to programmed instrumental backing. Along with these Zulu "traditional" musics, mbaqanga offered steady and reliable local catalog material to the companies that produced it. Internationally, mbaqanga—recognized as a form of Afropop, which is marketed under the World Music rubric—figured prominently among South African styles on the export market. Mbaqanga material available in foreign CD bins comprised re-releases of older recordings made into compilations and select contemporary star performers. The emergence of the World Music marketing category was one of the marked features of the international popular music industry of the 1980s and 1990s (T. Taylor 1997; Feld 2000). Developed first around popular African dance musics, World Music came to encompass musics of many ethnic minorities, remotely located peoples, and "third world" nationals as well as cross-cultural musical collaborations. Within the large scheme of global music production, World Music was but a small slice of the pie. But in the 1980s and 1990s musics in this category captivated audiences around the world to a degree unprecedented in their recorded history.

The production of *Lomculo Unzima* epitomized the hopes and pressures brought on by a newly opened international market for musicians, production teams, and the local industry at large. On the one hand, there were expanded horizons for South African products; on the other, fierce competition over local resources and in the marketing of South African cultural goods had developed in the later 1980s.

Isigqi Sesimanje's vision of what was available to them was linked to the kind of music they played and the position they occupied in the industry. They were veterans of an "old style" freshly revived on the international market; they had about two decades of repertoire to draw on; they had no independent capital and no access to the world stage except possibly through key contacts they had in the domestic industry; lacking recent hits, they had little bargaining power within the local industry.

Take I Music Making as Mediation

Sound of Africa! concerns the politics of Zulu music production in the South African music industry in the early 1990s. Mbaqanga music recorded in state-of-the-art studios played a significant part in the popularization of Zuluness, that is, in the shaping and circulation of particular images of the Zulu at the height of the Africa-centered World Music boom and in the transition period from apartheid to democracy. Such images were shaped dialectically: they embodied "deep Zulu" cultural values but were constructed interactively by collectivities and interest groups that were professionally, politically, economically, and/or artistically invested in Zuluness.[6] These individuals and collectivities included those who identified themselves as Zulus, black and white South Africans, and locals and foreigners involved in the World Music industry.

In South Africa of the 1990s the construction of racially and, in particular, ethnically based images had acute ramifications in the political arena and in the professional lives of black South African musicians. These images presented participants in the music business with a means to engage with and stake a claim within pluralistic South Africa and the World Music market.

Deep Zulu values informed a popular image while being molded by it. Zulu-identified musicians mobilized traditional values and beliefs—such as being the embodiment par excellence of Africanness—as a means of engaging the contemporary world. Through this, and through the process of interactively (re)shaping those values and beliefs, they affirmed their cultural sensibility and personhood and carved out a social position within South Africa at the time of transition from apartheid to democracy. Others in the Zulu music field (African producers and performers, white sound engineers, promoters, and company management) simultaneously interjected their values and ideas about Africans, South Africans, and Zulus, as well as about "tradition" and "culture" to further their own programs. Their aestheticizing take on Zulus circulated back to those who identified as Zulus themselves, into the political arena, and into the struggles of everyday life.

Sound of Africa! posits that the recording process enabled the popularization of figures of Otherness, Africanness, and Zuluness through music because of how different modes of mediation overlap, interpenetrate, and comment on one another in the production process. At its simplest, *mediation* refers to that which is both a conduit and a filter—it transfers but along the way it necessarily transforms. Mediation is a process that connects and translates disparate worlds, people, imaginations, values, and ideas, whether in its symbolic, social, or technological form. In the recording studio, these forms interact to help shape mbaqanga style; here, too, the struggle over the shaping of style also converges with economic and political struggles in the music industry. Local practices interface with perceived national and transnational musical trends. Domestic institutional controls, the transnational drive of the music industry, and the music-makers' efforts to find professional, political, and personal voice converge. Musical imaginaries collide with market forces, style jostles with stereotype (Keil 1985), innovation meets repetition, labor meets artistry, image meets sensibility. All these tensions are represented and negotiated in the process of in-studio sound mixing itself, and are literally and figuratively played out in the interaction of sound engineers, producers, and musicians.

In-studio sound mixing is a process of negotiation for control over the electronic manipulation of style. If style is conceived as a performed and multilayered sign that expresses, constructs, and reproduces the sensibilities of the artists (Feld 1990; Feld 1988; Urban 1985; Urban 1991, among others), then recording and mixing is a dramatized struggle over signs embodying values, identities, and aspirations. In their struggle, studio music-makers rework or reaffirm their sociopolitical and professional positioning in relation to one another. These negotiations concern the creative use of the studio's technological resources even as they happen through it.

The studio represents a microcosm of the society within which it exists. As such, it offers a prism into late capitalist, late apartheid experience and into how global popular culture flows are activated within the context of local politics. This prism is a keen one in the case of South Africa, where the historically repressive state of apartheid exerted its hegemony as much through cultural institutions as it did through bureaucratic civil and military ones (Gramsci 1971). In the studio, the complexities of race politics are present but play out implicitly through other means. The space of the studio is a seemingly neutral political ground, in which the primary endeavor is the production of aesthetic and exchange value, not of political positions. Any investment in shaping the proceedings is usually a heightened personal one for the participants, for they are making their art, building their professional reputations, and generating their principal incomes. Given this, studio practice intrinsically brings national political debates into immediate contact with aesthetic ones in a situation in which artist-citizens are actively engaged and deeply invested. In contrast to the many South African spaces that are acutely racialized and overtly politicized, the studio reveals how South Africa's ruthless politics are infused with feeling and embedded in the struggles of daily living and in expressive forms that on the surface appear to have little to do with race.

In *Sound of Africa!* I integrate two domains of social theory, one concerned with power relations and the other with the symbolic aesthetic realm. I do so to think through how the same expressive and technological resources are manipulated toward various specific ends by individuals occupying different sociopolitical positionings and holding different value systems (Meintjes 1990).

Three axioms ground my analysis. The first states that while formal musical elements define a style, that style derives its meaning and affective power primarily through its association with the sociopolitical positioning and social values of music participants (Keil and Feld 1994) and through the sensuous experience of those who encounter it (Seremetakis 1998; J. Taylor 1998; Feld 1996b). Style is conceived as a complex sign pointing to and embodying values understood and experienced through multiple steps of interpretation (Urban 1985; Urban 1991; Feld 1984). With respect to the second axiom, signs can be variably interpreted and are therefore subject to manipulation in the interests of a social group. Expressive culture, as a composite sign of values represented, felt, reproduced, and emerging through style can be appropriated for specific purposes or by various social groups (Hebdige 1979; Averill 1997; Erlmann 1999). In South Africa, commodified traditional music is significant to various fractions vying for political voice and socioeconomic control. In addition to presenting a means of molding the values and beliefs of potential constituencies and of regulating the content and flow of communication, traditional music also provides forms for personal expression, an arena in which to organize, and a potential opportunity to communicate beyond local communities through the media (T. Taylor 1997). The struggle between these interests creates a complex middle ground that plays itself out by contesting the meaning of signs (Hall 1979). Since signs are compact, concrete tokens manifest in style, contestation over the shaping of styles and products is a struggle over competing values and ideas.

To explicate these dynamics and thereby argue for an integrated theory of mediation, I start with interpretive symbolic anthropology applied to music systems and with class conflict and resistance models. I develop the connections between them by drawing on anthropology of the senses, especially as applied to sound. Analyses of global cultural flows, of technology consumption, of commodity fetishization, and of the colonial and apartheid state's participation in the construction of ethnicity also inform my thinking.[7]

In the past, interpretive symbolic anthropologists for the most part have examined small-scale society coherence systems and focused on the intellection of symbols. In contrast to these studies, work that draws on class conflict models has prominently addressed issues of hegemony and tropes of resistance. Scholars have attended peripherally to the coherence of these systems and to how individuals and collectivities make sense of the contradictions of contemporary life. In the process of making sense, as expressed in the symbolic representation of social life, individuals and collectivities simultaneously maintain their dignity and strive to reshape their material conditions in ways that increase their autonomy (Comaroff 1985; Coplan 1994; Erlmann 1996b; James 1999; Muller 1999).

I integrate these approaches by focusing on style itself as a site of hegemonic contestation. The effect of technology, politics, and the market can be analyzed not only in the organization of cultural production (Becker 1982; Wolff 1981), but also in the sound itself, artfully manipulated, affectively articulated and understood, and experienced through the body (Feld 1996a; Feld 1996b; Buchanan 1997; J. Taylor 1998). In the case of *Lomculo Unzima*, value systems are embedded in the commodified traditional music of a pluralistic society stratified by class and race. This pluralistic society is ravaged by violence tied to heightened ethnic consciousness, at the same time as the country is dramatically reintegrated into an international culture market.

The third axiom informing *Sound of Africa!* states that control over black expressive cultural production and ethnic identities has been a crucial feature of South African sociopolitical contestation (Spiegel and McAllister 1991; Hamilton and Wright 1993; Dlamini 2001; Frescura 2001). When other aspects of social life are severely repressed, expressive culture becomes a strategic persuasive tool for all factions and a means to open up new spaces for the disempowered. Then, with a dramatic transition to a new state through negotiated settlement, expressive culture becomes a means of generating collective celebration and of convincing constituencies of the legitimacy and effectiveness of their leadership. In both the oppressive and transitional scenarios, mediated expression is crucial, for it links local communities and concerns into national and international communication networks and simultaneously brings national and global power structures to bear on local communities.

By integrating these three axioms in a studio context during the course of this work's six chapters, I show how global and national dynamics interface with local and individual struggles to reshape social life by reworking expressive forms. While race, ethnicity, class, gender, and generation are all significant components of the struggles around identity politics in the studio, *Sound of Africa!* focuses primarily on issues of race and ethnicity, for these are self-consciously styled into the songs. During the production of *Lomculo Unzima*, the ways in which race and ethnic dynamics operate in relation to class, gender, and generation unfolded. Apartheid's social patterns intersect with the professional divisions of labor between engineers, producer, and "traditional" musicians in the process of making stylistic decisions about mbaqanga sound in the studio.

A focus on style as the site of contestation predetermines that performance be the central object of analysis, for the making of style must be captured on the move. Drawing on the legacy of the ethnography of speaking and of Bakhtinian dialogism (Bakhtin 1981), I therefore apply to studio music practice and musical sound the discourse-centered approaches taken to poetics and the sign (e.g., Bauman and Sherzer 1989; Bauman 1984; Bauman and Briggs 1990; Urban 1991; Briggs 1993; K. Stewart 1996). Thus I work outward from the performed utterance, paying attention to its form as well as to the politics of the moment of performance. My approach is not to dissect the architecture of songs as putatively complete musical forms but rather to focus on musical gestures within them. These emergent gestures represent the larger musical processes at work while they also index social and political practices. I trace the significance of these gestures out into the sociopolitical world to which they speak rather than primarily focusing on a structural explanation of their coherence within the song.

I afford some songs on *Lomculo Unzima* more attention than others, in particular those songs that Jane Dlamini, frontline lead of the group, identified as the strongest of the production: the title track "Lomculo Unzima" (This music is heavy/weighty/potent), the wedding songs "Hamba kahle" (Go well) and "uMakoti onjani" (What kind of a bride [is she]), and the song "South Africa." These were the songs that she anticipated would touch the imaginations of their target audiences.[8]

I work in sound. I listen principally at the level of timbre, taking my cue from recording studio participants. The auditory acuity and atomic listening of sound engineers and producers are phenomenal. The amount of studio time and the attention they give to the manipulation of sound and textural change at the microlevel is often greater than they lend to designing the arrangement and harmonic and melodic patterning of a song. Historically, ethnomusicology has focused on genre analysis, treating formal parameters like tune, scale, and rhythmic mode as the distinguishing features of a genre. These patterns exist at an analytic level that ethnomusicologists have been able to describe and discuss using variations on Western notation, whereas the depiction and thus analysis of timbre remains undeveloped.[9] Though understudied, timbre is becoming recognized as the carrier of much more of the affective, generic, and social significance imputed to musical expression than music scholars had previously considered. Paul Théberge has called attention to the integral role sound quality plays in the production and recognition of musical "languages" and genres (Théberge 1997). Using spectral analyses, Cornelia Fales has gone beyond the constraints of listening and conventional notation to examine the psychoacoustic properties of *inanga chuchotée* whisper songs in Burundi (1998; 2002) as well as the timbral components of electronica music (forthcoming). Timbral elements are also featured prominently in the ethnographic work of scholars such as Fox (1995, 1999), Porcello (1996, 1999), Samuels (1998, 1999), Groesbeck (1999), Averill (1999), and Willoughby (2000).

I pay particular attention, then, to the timbral dimensions of the performed utterances on which I focus. Each of the central chapters of *Sound of Africa!* isolates and tracks the ways in which artists and producers manipulate a particular mbaqanga sound in the studio. Chapter 3 focuses on a particular quality of keyboard and bass sound; chapter 4 takes up unique guitar sonorities; chapter 5 tracks a drum sound; and chapter 6 works outward from the singing bass voice. Together, these micro sound analyses point to the significance of timbre in the production of feeling, an essential ingredient in linking politics to aesthetics.

Writing outward from the musical gesture, attending especially to its timbre, and connecting musical to spoken utterances, I link issues of power and ideology at multiple levels: the sensuous evocative power of artworks, the micropolitics of personal interaction, and the politics of the music industry, state, and global economy. I bring into mutual relief the poetic, performative, emergent, and invested qualities of both sociopolitical life (its practices and institutions) and expressive forms. In other words, I am arguing for a focus on symbolic and technological mediation in order to understand the production of social difference.

With its particular historical trajectory, its political ambiguity, and its style, mbaqanga music offers an exemplary set of conditions with which to argue these positions. Stylistically, it is thoroughly integrated with technological procedure. A studio-produced music from its outset, it has shifted from foregrounding an ethos of modernity, urbanity, and "blackness" to celebrating an increasingly "traditional" and "Zulu" sensibility. Not overtly political, it has endured oppressive censorship, fostered links with African American sounds, and its practitioners have waged social struggles in the guise of professional negotiations in the studio. In mbaqanga production, artists bridge the worlds of commercialism and resistance politics. Since scholars have historically embraced the "live" music event as "authentic" and a potential site of politics, in contrast to "mass-mediated" forms, mbaqanga challenges us as theorists and activists to reevaluate notions of oppositionality in relationship to the media, to aesthetic form and feeling, to contingent interests, and to personal voice.

Take 2 Ethnography as Mediation

Sound of Africa! is as much a mediation as it is about mediation.

In order to portray and to deepen the appreciation of comparable processual features of music studio production, I privilege a nonlinear structural organization. In the studio, musicians constantly replay the sounds they have already programmed and captured on tape in order to interrelate new parts and develop the piece. I similarly reintroduce earlier sections of the text to reconsider and reintegrate them with new material.

Each chapter is entitled a "cut," borrowing the studio term for a song when it is being recorded. Some "cuts" are subdivided into two or three "tracks," which together build up the argument of the chapter. This writing procedure follows the manner in which each instrumental or vocal part of a song is recorded separately, track by track, each new track being added to the previously recorded ones until the whole song has been constructed. First, basic rhythm tracks are laid down by the drummer or drum programmer, guided by a temporary solo vocal. Then, for example, the bass, the guitar, the keyboard lines, the actual solo voice, and the backing chorus are each recorded. Next additional percussion tracks might be added. At each stage of the process, the artists who are recording the new track perform with the already recorded parts piped into their headphones.

My "cuts" and "tracks" are further subdivided into multiple "takes," which present different perspectives on the central issue of the chapter. These "takes" replicate the practice of recording the same musical material (such as a solo, a backing track, or a chorus) several times in succession in order to generate multiple options for consideration as the final product. Each take realizes the nuances and potentialities of the repeated musical material in a unique way.

I discuss the interrelationships among these various perspectives in "mixes" of the "tracks" and of "takes." These interrelations are reconsidered from different angles much as studio artists provide different interpretations of a recorded song by mixing and remixing its elements. Mixing takes place once all parts of the song have been recorded. During the process of mixing, studio practitioners shift musical elements in sonic space. For example, they might bring one instrument into the foreground, while shifting another further into the background. They also tweak the qualities of the sounds themselves. Having reconsidered the song after listening to it as a whole, they might decide to alter the reverberation on one sound or to change the volume on the middle frequencies of another. They might try softening the attack of one percussive sound and lengthening the decay on another. They also might create composite versions from multiple recorded performances. For example, they might select the best keyboard solo from all the recorded takes and combine it with the best rhythm tracks. Similarly, they might select different parts of a solo from different takes and blend them into a final rendition. Together, these kinds of micromanipulations change the song's aural focus and feel. A song can be mixed multiple times with each mix bringing different musical features of that song to attention.

Here and there, I tweak the text in the margins, in the manner in which engineers constantly manipulate the console controls to make subtle changes to the sound quality during each stage of the recording process.

Of the kinds of source materials from which I write, I privilege transcriptions of taped interviews and studio sessions. Transcriptions have long been upheld as the authorial material of ethnographic research for their seeming transparency. Yet the recording of an event and its subsequent transcription, translation, editing, and final representation in analysis involve multiple steps of mediation and forms of interpretation (Briggs 1986). Aware of the transformation of others' voices in the process, I use a variety of strategies in my text to clarify my sources. Direct quotes excerpted from my tapes are presented in double quotation marks. Translations into English of taped voices are also marked in this way. When I reproduce dialogue written down after the event in my fieldnotes, I put it in single quotes. In a few instances, when I recreate verbal interactions from memory, I present the voices without direct speech punctuation. I merely index the speaker as a character in a story, a performer on a textual stage.

Using the transcripts, I work outward from performed utterances, musical gestures, and storied moments. For the most part, the latter are written in the present tense, but they do not appear in chronological order. I am looking for ways to give significance to concrete compact instances in my representation, without giving the impression that such concreteness implies that interpretations and values are fixed. I am also looking for ways to represent the idea of the local as a slice through a moment in a system always on the move. The moment, the gesture, and the utterance capture the emergence and indeterminacy of the processes by which values are embedded in material conditions and sound events. At the same time, such processes are necessarily incomplete and based on contingencies. These interrelated issues are keys to understanding and effecting empowering moves and creative innovation.

Ethnography is a form of mediation between reader and event, story and explanation, and poetics and analysis (Clifford 1983; White 1987; Thornton 1992). By borrowing aspects of studio practice for the organization of the materials in *Sound of Africa!*, I extend into ethnographic and narrative domains the idea of art as a form of production (Wolff 1981; Becker 1982; Attali 1985; Minh-Ha 1991; Keil and Feld 1994; Marcus and Myers 1995). The dynamics of creative expression are thereby placed in dialogue with those of cultural and theoretical production, a move that exposes the analytic limitations of dichotomizing production and consumption, poetics and analysis, and politics and aesthetics. Drawing correspondences between the production of music, local imaginaries, forms of knowledge, and scholarship brings into mutual relief the poetic, performative, indeterminate, emergent, and invested qualities of them all. I am arguing for the centrality of aesthetic expression to the production of knowledge and power, and of forms of power to the production of expressive culture.

Mix

Cut 1 chronicles the intertwined professional lives of the central characters of the book, namely music producers Hamilton Nzimande and West Nkosi, and mbaqanga artists Isigqi Sesimanje and Mahlathini, the Mahotella Queens, and the Makgona Tsohle Band. As their biographies unfold so, too, do the characteristics and practices of mbaqanga.

Cut 2 concerns the studio as a social, creative, and rarefied space, focusing on how studio technology mediates the creative process and how it brings the sociopolitical and ideological world of apartheid into the heart of the production process.

Cut 3 begins a discussion of the striking emphasis in mbaqanga studio sessions on a musical and linguistic discourse about social types. Sound images based on various social types (a "Zulu" organ, a "whitey" song, a "sound of Africa," and so forth) are crucial to the shaping of a local aesthetic in the encounter with global commodity production. Similarly, the preoccupation with social types both characterizes and is a product of the struggle with issues of new identities in South Africa.

Cut 3 also foregrounds the relationship between blackness and Africanness, understood at once as ideas, sounds, sensualities, and rhetorical positions. It presents local mbaqanga perspectives on how the idea of sounding "live" is played out as the epitome of Africanness and as a trope of authenticity in recorded music. The converging of these domains in the idea of "liveness" enhances the expressive and rhetorical power of contemporary mbaqanga sound.

Cut 4 explores a moment of disintegration of the studio session in order to analyze whiteness, Africanness, and South Africanness as discourses and sound images that music-makers elaborate as they maneuver creatively through the network of power relations within the mbaqanga studio and as they feel their ways through the complexities of identity politics in voicing their own senses of personhood.

Moving analytically between the studio, staged events, and party political strategy, cut 5 explores the concept of Zuluness. I document the paradoxical relation between an aesthetics of liveness cultivated by the music industry for the World Music market and a politics of destruction and death fostered by the Inkatha Freedom Party of South Africa (an ethnic nationalist movement) in the early 1990s. Processes of mediation between Zuluness as a political position, an everyday experience, and a poetic form play a role in the production and consumption of ethnicity and violence. TJ Lemon's photo essay in the center leaf presents a visual take on the same issues.

Cut 6 analyzes local ideas about "overseas," an influential concept in South African music production. I look at how global and local spheres intersect and refract in the artists' imagination, as realized in sonic choices made during recording. International experiences and stories about overseas co-produce both local artists' visions of the world out there and their sound as it is recorded onto tape.

In the conclusion I review the expansive and diverse forms of mediation that come into play in the studio. It is in the convergence of these forms of mediation that social difference is produced and variously made powerful.

Playback

May 1992

I admire Jane, Joana, and Janet posing on the jacket front of Isigqi Sesimanje's completed album.

'Eyi! We are too fat these days!' exclaims Joana.

'The record is finished,' delights Jane. 'Now you will see what will happen, like before.'

Completion is not closure. A released product is a moment of dispersion, a renewal of fantasies, a node of recollection. It is the casting out of a net for the gathering of goods, ideas, mobility, and reputation (Barber and Waterman 1995). Released songs resonate with their promise, reverberating out there.

cut 1

Mbaqanga

Is mbaqanga a set of formal characteristics that are rendered in performance? Is mbaqanga a quality of experience? If I list generic traits in order
to work outward from a definition of a prototype, I miss the shifts in interpretive communicative praxis that make mbaqanga into what it is. Such a
list would sidestep the social, historical, political, biographical, and many
of the performed and sonic relationships by means of which mbaqanga is
constituted, imputed with significance, transformed, and reinstantiated.

This cut considers, in three main parts, the problem and significance
of genre in relation to agency, voice, and the formation of institutions.
Track 1 offers versions of mbaqanga as it is presented by performing artists. Track 2 situates their soundings within a history of personal and
industrial relations that co-construct mbaqanga as a marketing category,
artistic canon, and a set of social practices. A mix of the tracks proposes
that a focus on the utterance brings significance to the process of definition rather than to the definition of mbaqanga itself. Genrefication is
intimately tied to the self-making rhetoric that elaborates artistic reputations.

Track 1 Mbaqanga as Sound, Performance, and Image

take 1 : Izintombi Zesimanjemanje

Johannesburg, February 1991

"Eita!" drummer Michael calls, announcing his arrival to the musicians
already assembled for rehearsal. As he swivels to greet me, I notice
"Africa" emblazoned across the back of his jacket in bold yellow letters.
He's decked out in an outfit tailored like military camouflages, black fabric splattered with a yellow leopard-like design. He clutches the Sowetan

newspaper between his elbow and bottom rib. A plastic shopping bag dangles from one hand, a Kleenex and Ugwayi snuff box bought from a street vendor nestles in the other.

He prepares for rehearsal while the keyboardist, bass player, and guitarist warm up on their instruments. First, his Africa jacket gets neatly hung on a coathanger. Underneath he is wearing a tourist T-shirt from Mauritius. This layer he peels off. He's elegant, lithe. He replaces the T-shirt with an old rehearsal shirt. He sits down behind the drums. Then he sets about tightening the hi-hat screw just right, adjusting the position of the bass-drum pedal, propping up the leg of the tom-tom stand, resting the snare drum on an old kick drum with a split head. He scruffles through his shopping bag to find his drumsticks, snorts his tobacco, settles the position of his wobbling chair, and drum rolls himself into the already moving groove.

By all means, producer Hamilton Nzimande had offered, visit my group downtown in my rehearsal room on the third floor of RPM House;[1] they're practicing every day. He'll let them know to expect me.

Michael, for one, has dressed for the meeting.

I'm squeezed into the rehearsal room, dense with sensation. Bass sounds batter my ribcage. The distortion grating out of the amp speaker feels like mango hairs between my teeth. Michael hits the crash cymbal. I hear a hubcap rolling off a taxi. Keyboard chords wheeze. A guitar sears the thick air.

No one can breathe but everybody does. Soon RPM House's remodeling will be complete and the air-conditioning will be operational on the rehearsal floor, they say. Despite the heat, the door stays closed because beats and basses and screaming guitars are bursting out of other rooms along the passageway.

Michael drums from the farthest corner of the slender room. Opposite him, Bethwell boosts his bottom end, turns down his tops, and shoots up the neck of his bass.[2] His left-hand fingers stop the strings then slide down to their next position while, with a plectrum in his right hand, he cuts and clicks onto new notes. A waiting singer-dancer youth slumps in a scruffy office chair wedged in between Michael and Bethwell. Mkhize the guitarist and Tefo the keyboard player squeeze in beside them. Tefo's fingers, hands, and wrists spin around the keyboard like he's tatting lace. He plays a Korg CX-3, an old single-manual electronic keyboard encased in a wooden box like a coffin. An updated digital Yamaha DDX7 double manual stands beside him. Mkhize's fingers run across the higher strings of his electric guitar. He twists and turns his sound patterns in balletic circles. Still with the distortion swirling around me, the bass rattling my ribcage, I'm breathing in heat, I can't really hear.

Onlookers are pressed up against stacks of clunky leaden equipment lining the long wall. Piles have accumulated on top of these old speakers and amps: instruments, the rehearsers' street clothing, shoes, colored plastic shopping packets waiting to be taken home at the end of the day, a liter bottle of water periodically refilled in the bathroom, each person's towel to be grabbed in a pause.

More people fill the chairs packed in tight against the third wall. Someone next to the door gets up and leans into the corner to make space for a newcomer.

Eight singing dancers—four women, four backing men—line the long wall facing the jumbled equipment. They dance doubled-up steps into the body of the narrow room. I strain to hear the details of their close-harmony vocals against the throbbing garage-band sound.

Between songs Jane Dlamini shakes my hand and smiles. 'Welcome,' she gestures. She introduces Janet, Joana, and Joanna, her frontline co-singers called Izintombi Zesimanjemanje (The Modern Girls). They run through four more songs for me.

Sweat shines. The women swivel intricately, tiptoe or flatheeled. They scoop toe to heel with their ankles, quiver their wrists, flick their arms, jostle their hips, raise their knees, and stamp lightly. Pause. Shuffle backwards. They dance in their old T-shirts, sweatpants, and scrubbed unlaced *takkies* (canvas tennis shoes). The women know their songs and movements like they know their pulses. They are full, contoured, present women, in their late thirties to late forties.

The men—lean and youthful Muhle, Oscar, Phatiswe, and Mdlolo—are learning by repetition. (They are a three-week-old addition to the lineup, Jane informs me later.) They pass through the women's line and shuffle forward for their vocals. Drawing their shoulders up to their cheeks, they sing into imaginary microphones, lips to electronic diaphragms. They retreat after their verse; the women shuffle-swivel forward again.

After Zesimanje, the onlookers take to the floor to display their skills. They are a new, young, "Zulu traditional" group called Abavithizi, yet to be produced. Hamilton found them playing around in the black townships in the Johannesburg area, Joana explains while the young maskandi (Zulu guitarist) opens his song with a virtuosic flurry of notes, introducing the key and scale to the band. He sways his guitar neck to the slow, heavy beat of the drum and the bass as they enter and set the groove; then he glides into nasal vocals. Tefo punches "accordion" into the Yamaha

DX7 keyboard and adds the "Zulu trad" concertina part. The hi-hat rasps away consistently. Three singer-dancers interject chorus lines. During an instrumental break they flick their legs up, then stamp down on the heavy beats.

They are waiting to record their first album, after Zesimanje's is completed, they say. That will be soon, they say.

After rehearsal, while their fellow performers tidy up, Michael and Joana show me photos from their tour to Mauritius in October 1990. In the glossy black-and-white 8" x 10" promotional picture, the three women in the group pose in a deserted late afternoon Johannesburg street, dead center on the asphalt. I recognize the city center, somewhere close to this studio and rehearsal building. The women wear beaded headbands and beaded haltertops. Their midriffs show. Beaded aprons and layered beaded belts overlay their short, fringed skirts. They all wear crocheted and tasseled white wool arm and leg garters, white canvas tennis shoes, black hose. They pose as if captured in dance in a fast-shuttered snapshot. Three congas stand hip high alongside them. A saxophonist waves his instrument half out of the frame of the picture. Four bare-chested dancer-youths pose in the background in skins. I recognize some of the rehearsers in the shot. Ripped strips of cloth are wrapped haphazardly into men's headbands and garters. The angles of the dancers' raised, bent elbows and their raised right knees zigzag through the center of focus. Nineteen fifties high-rises stacked along the pavement disrupt the frame of the photograph. Litter lies forgotten in a clump.

I look at the photos, then am told the first of the many stories I will hear: Izintombi Zesimanjemanje toured Mauritius. It was beautiful. But very, very hot. They played two shows at a hotel in the capital city. The people loved them. When the singers and musicians left the stage, "The people they say, 'no, how come?'" Jane recounts. "We tell them, 'We're finished, we'll sing again tomorrow.' People, they stood there!" Jane looks at me with the determination of the crowd she remembers standing there demanding more music. "Everyone in the audience said, 'No, we are not leaving!' We went to the hotel. They came and fetched us from the hotel to go back and play again. It was the best!"[3] The Mauritians wanted the group to visit their country again.

"At the hotel, people said, 'We saw you on the TV!' Same time!"

"More than ten thousand people! Oh, it was very good!" remembers Joana.

"Like in the Ivory Coast, those people support our shows!" exclaims Jane.

In fact they've performed this mbaqanga music all over Africa, adds Michael, and they were very, very popular—Ivory Coast, Botswana, Zambia, Malawi, Zimbabwe, Swaziland, Namibia. His snuffbox-and-Kleenex hand sweeps a flourish over the map. Lesotho, adds Joana, and all over South Africa, everywhere. And Michael has played what's the club in New York called again—yes, s.o.b.s, and the Apollo in Harlem. He was drumming for Zulu guitarist Sipho Mchunu when he toured overseas.

They tell me Hamilton Nzimande says he will be booking their session time in the studio downstairs very soon. Then they can go on the road again, promoting. At which time Hamilton will buy them some new equipment.

They want to go to Paris. And America. Joana reckons they'll be overseas within the year. God willing. They hear I have a brother in America.

"West's group" is "that side" right now, Joana says. They were neck to neck with us, she says while rubbing her forefingers against each other to show me how fiercely Mahotella Queens and Zesimanjemanje had run against each other at the peak of their popularity in the 1970s. In fact, two of the old Zesimanjemanje are now touring as Mahotella, that side, Jane says.

I want to catch Hamilton in rehearsal. Jane says he pops in to check on them, maybe about twice week, but really he takes up their time with his talking.[4] Jane, Joana, Janet, and Joanna are changing back into street clothes to catch a minivan taxi back out to Soweto. They've all lived there for years, though they come from the KwaZulu-Natal province.

take 2 : Mahlathini and the Mahotella Queens

Austin, Texas, April 1993

Roadies push, lift, shove, trundle, and clunk at the back of Liberty Lunch. Mahlathini, guitarist Marks, and bass player Joseph Makwela snap and flick aces, queens, hearts, and clubs onto the counter in their luxury bus. Drummer Phillemon, sax player Teaspoon, and keyboardist Ralph hang out with other men in the parking lot taking a breather from their cooped-up long-distance traveling. Together these instrumentalists form the Makgona Tsohle Band, which backs Mahlathini and the Queens. The Queens bustle about in and out of the bus. I greet them. Why did I wait until now to talk to them about mbaqanga, reprimands singer Hilda, backed up by Mildred—because, after all, they are the ones who are the real mbaqanga, and in South Africa they are not busy like they are here. Singer Nobesuthu quips that Zesimanjemanje most probably told me not to. Not so, I protested, I had been tied up and busy, and you renowned Queens had been touring overseas much of the time.

"M—ba—qa—nga!" calls Teaspoon Ndelu after the band's opening number has brought the clubgoers crowding up to the edge of the stage. He is the band's pennywhistler, saxophonist, and chief emcee on this tour. "M," he taunts the audience through his handheld microphone "m . . . m," till we say "m" back at him. "Ba!" he calls. "Ba!" we throw back. "Qa!" he calls. Titters in the crowd. "Qa!" he shoots at the microphone again. His alveolar-palatal consonant click and low "a" resound like a cork rocketing out of a fizzy bottle. "Qa! . . . Qa!" he repeats. He laughs, holding his microphone out into the crowd, and waits. The audience tries. "Qa!" teases Teaspoon again, "Mbaqanga! Mbaqanga! Mbaqanga!" The audience chants with him as best they can as he struts across the stage.

He signals to Ralph Mahura the keyboardist, who launches a synth piano line into the electric air. The crowd hushes. Phillemon Hamole drumrolls a two-beat pick-up. Full trap set, bass, and rhythm guitar enter on beat one: clockwork sound from the Makgona Tsohle Band. A hard bass drum pelts every beat at the bottom of the mix. Sixteen-note hi-hat patterns tickle the tops. A hard and punchy bass guitar dumps itself equally onto the first and second beats, then treats the pick-up to each measure just as seriously. Phillemon sets the snare against the heavy front of the riff by thwacking the offbeats of the half and full measure. Marks Mankwane slips into the layered groove with his rippling signature high-necked guitar notes. He flicks up the ends of his licks, as if singeing the sound. The classic harmony rocks through blues progressions in a major key. The soundman somehow mixes air and spaces into this busy texture. What aural clarity for this style in a half-outdoor club venue. I want to dance.

Old Mahlathini stomps about the stage as if petulant. Suddenly he grabs the microphone stand. He blurts out the story of the band's self-acclaimed history. "Sawuqala umbaqanga, sawutshala kulolonke, nanamuhla sisawutshala," he sings, with "q"s popping at us, rasping attacks on syllables placed on the strong beats, and percussive exhalations as the phrases expire, fading in volume and drooping in pitch. 'We started mbaqanga, we sowed it all over the place, even today we're sowing it.' In the next line, twice as long, he draws out the later syllables, then pulls the verse to its final vocal descent. That voice: strident, deep, rough around the edges. Joseph Makwela's limber bass riff dances under Mahlathini's musical ranting. On Mahlathini's last two phrases of this first verse Joseph slips in an upward flick on his bass and an octave drop onto the beginning of the riff. He knows mbaqanga.

Then the three Queens enter royally, repeating Mahlathini's lines in close harmony. Every note is equally blended, perfectly placed. They round the verse off with a downward glide, as if ending it with a caress. Mahlathini enters: "Sawuqala umbaqanga, sawuqala kulolonke," he repeats. This time he notches up the grittiness of his rasp, widens his vowels a little, extends the phrase, stretches the second-to-last phoneme sung at the peak of the melodic contour and spills on into the second line. His vocal dryness and seeming unpredictability is again set off by the oiled precision and blending of the trio of the women's frontline, singing, swiveling, gesturing the meaning of the lyrics.

Ralph throws a synthesized flute motive into the mix.

As the women take the vocal lead, Joseph shifts his bass riff to parallel their voices. Mahlathini interjects his own comments, his own phrase, overlapping their story. Teaspoon's sax and Ralph's synth horns punch the end of the verse. They do it again. Ralph's flute motive flies over the top again. Joseph picks it up on his bass. Bass and flute talk in passing. The groove intensifies. "Sinjenje sizwe sakithi, siya ziqenya ngani kuwo wonke umhlaba; sinjenje kungenxa yenu, baladeli bethu, siya siqenya ngani," the women sing. 'We are like this, our nation, we shine all over the world; we are like this because of you, our followers; we shine because of you.' They flutter their hands above their heads, then point to their audience.

Joseph plays a stepped three-note pick-up (get ready for the drop way down onto the tonic) while Phillemon drum rolls into the next section. Joseph lands back in his opening riff. "Ladies and gentlemen," calls out Hilda Tloubatla in English as the backing pulses on, "This group was formed in 1964 and has been together since then! They are the creator of mbaqanga. Ha!" she exclaim-sings breathily and triumphantly, thrusting her fist into the air. "Come on now, everybody," she beckons as she begins to move her voice and body into rhythm with the groove. "Come on, let's do mbaqanga!" she sings.

"We do mbaqanga," answer Nobesuthu Shawe, Mildred Mangxola, and Mahlathini in densely layered harmonies.

"Ye ye ye," sings Hilda over their repeating phrase. Her full vibrating alto sound travels out over the crowd: "Mbaqanga, -ga, -qanga, let's do mbaqanga! Together, let's be happy!"

"And join mbaqanga!" emphasizes the chorus while Hilda pops more "q"s off her palate and hoists "g"s out from near the back of her throat.

"Mbaqanga, -ga, -qanga!" Hilda sings.

"Join mbaqanga!" calls the chorus.

The synth flute and the bass resume their contrapuntal conversation. Marks extends his guitar licks. The keyboard injects offbeats into the middle register and middle of the mix. Rhythm guitar and sax riff and pulse in the groove while the women dance an instrumental break. Hips register the syncopations, footwork describes the beat. Steps to the left and a lift of the left knee, forearms swiveling; pause; steps to the right and a lift of the right knee. Bodies in close-fitting leopard-skin tank tops rotate buoyantly. Flicks of their buttocks complete their rotation. Pause again. The crowd cheers. They repeat the sequence. Beaded aprons, woolen fringes fastened around their waists, and short grasslike shredded fabric skirts shiver, swing, and jitter as they pick up the rhythm of the Queens' infectious hips.

Meanwhile Mahlathini struts about, flaunting his *ibheshu* (men's rear hide apron) and his headdress. In his Zulu sandals cut from car tires he stamps hard on the offbeats. He stops suddenly and glares at the crowd. "Wo! Wo! Wo!" he interjects in the middle of his vocal range. He dance-kicks a second sequence.

"Siyagiya noma sesibadala, emculeni akugugwa sesihlala sitshakadula njalo," enter the Queens. 'We dance even in our old age, but in music there is no getting old, we are still as frisky as calves.' Mahlathini affirms their sentiment as he takes over the tune. 'We imbibed music from the breast, we grew up on it, we eat and sleep it, we awake to it and go everywhere with it,' he sings in Zulu: "Sancela umculo, sakhula ngawo, sidla umculo, silala ngomculo, sivuke ngawo, o, sihamba ngomculo."

The Queens return to their earlier Zulu verse, "Sinjenje. . . ." 'We are like this, we shine all over the world.' Hilda solos. Mahlathini throws in a line against hers. Joseph playfully anticipates the groaner's vocal line with upward offbeat glides on his bass just before the groaner's characteristic final downward vocal glissando.

The Queens repeat their call to the crowd: "Come on, come on, come let's do mbaqanga! Mbaqanga, -ga, -qanga! Mbaqanga, -qanga! Let's be happy and join mbaqanga!"

Phillemon strikes his cymbals, rolls on his drums. "Mbaqanga!" they call as the crowd cheers for more. The band gives them but a moment's break before Marks ripples into the next song at the top of his guitar range.

For this and the next set they perform songs from their internationally released CDs.

take 3 : West Nkosi

'Meintjes?' producer West Nkosi quips in the passageway as a way of noting my Afrikaans surname. 'And you're from Pretoria?'[5]

'Yes, but we met in Austin, Texas. Liberty Lunch, May 1990, when you were gigging on sax with Mahlathini,' I remind him.

We enter his office at Gallo Music Productions in Johannesburg's ritzy Rosebank suburb. LPs are stacked on the cabinets, on the floor, next to the record player. The sound system power is on. His inbox pile teeters precariously. Huge photographs cover the walls. He dumps his black leather briefcase on the floor, gestures me to a seat, and sits down behind his sprawling desk. From there he checks me out. His eyes dance. His skinny, three-inch dreads flicker around his moon-face now and then. He is wearing a New Orleans Jazz Festival T-shirt, a round Afrika pendant edged in bulky leather stitching, and over this a knitted jacket boldly patterned and half zipped up despite the heat outside. I feel like I am facing a large man.

He launches forth: "Here in our country, we made this mbaqanga music through one thing [in response to a particular sociopolitical situation]. In 1955 the government divided the blacks. Blacks used to live together— as different tribes. But the government decided to split them and divide them."

My heart sinks, for I don't want a history lecture in my first interview with West. Does he suspect that as a scholar I would omit mbaqanga's political significance, or is he giving me the mbaqanga-as-indestructable-beat line the international popular press probably elicit? Or is he thinking of me as a young, white, local woman, naïve enough not to know about the history of the homeland policy, the backbone of the nationalist party's "separate development" divide-and-rule strategy? When black South Africans were shafted onto 13 percent of the country's land, they were forcibly relocated on the basis of ethnic groupings as defined by the state. These arid "homelands" were designed as semiautonomous regions under local leadership, which was of course to be puppeteered by the state. The homelands were planned in the 1950s and legally institutionalized in 1960. Only those Africans with employment could legally reside in urban areas. At that time, a youthful West had already moved from the rural northeast to the city—Pretoria—where he was working as a gardener in the suburbs and playing in a street band with his friends.

"Now we were still teenagers, but we could see that there were some problems. Now what can we do? So we took little bits from all these different tribes—rhythms, their traditional [music]—and we put it all together. We made one good solid rhythm that could appeal to all these different tribes. And it worked out very well. People could come together and start respecting one another—not like today. Today we're battling to get the people to understand that they should respect one another, for the New South Africa. It's a very big problem." He pauses, looks for his cigarettes, repositions the miniature saxophone paperweight on his desk, and stretches for his dish of an ashtray. "It's a very big problem."

I have to agree. In the late 1980s and into the 1990s, the escalation in property theft and destruction, personal injuries, and ghastly murders in and around Johannesburg was alarming. However hard progressives argued in and out of the media, explanations for South Africa's social pathologies came to rest too easily in ethnic terms such as "black on black unrest," "Zulu and Xhosa prejudices," "age-old tribal animosities." The concept of tribes raised its ugly head repeatedly in the suburban conversation of citizens searching for the roots of the distress around them. Even among those who recognized that the concept was propagated by the apartheid apparatus in justifying its homelands, there were some who in fearful moments nevertheless still called on the concept. Swiveling in his padded chair and checking me out, West puts a positive spin on tribes. Before the government, blacks lived together peacefully as different tribes. He takes another puff and continues.

"But in those [apartheid] days, it was very easy for us [musicians] to cool the people down a little bit. You know there was no riots, as such."

My mind races to the turbulent early 1960s when the multiple strategies of the liberation movement were met by intensely repressive countermeasures. He's conveying an image of black living in the 1950s and 1960s as a singular front against the apartheid regime, an image of committed order and tranquil reasoning. Is he nostalgic for a 1960s resistance, which he depicts as sustained and united by artistic expression, in contrast to the seemingly chaotic, factional, dangerous present?

"And when a record was released, people would all go for it and listen to it carefully because we use some of their traditional rhythms. It reminds them what type of people they are. Have they forgotten their respect [for themselves]? Do they remember who they are? Then they start thinking to respect one another. That worked out very well."

He shifts tack a little. He's earnest.

"Some of the politicians also used this music to get the people together, you know. But we put it in a way that the government could not stop, because it was simple. We had to put a message across to the people in our style. All these blacks have got their terms that they use. You won't understand what they mean. It's only the blacks who understand. That has helped us a lot. It has made me feel very important to our society for the job that I'm doing."

He stubs out his cigarette and shovels its ashes into a little heap in his ashtray. I am facing "the former herdboy" who, according to the magazine *Blackchain Today*, had in 1982 "made history by becoming the first and only black director of Gallo Records" (Mahlaba 1982).[6] I look to Nkosi's office walls, quilted with framed gold discs and gigantic photographs. Gold sales discs awarded to Amaswazi Emvelo and Ladysmith Black Mambazo hang opposite a local black-and-white photo of Mahlathini and the Mahotella Queens receiving the 1987 OKTV award. A few international color shots fill the rest of the wall: Mahlathini and the Mahotella Queens glitzed under Tokyo show lights; Mahlathini and the Mahotella Queens jiving on stage in Central Park, NYC, in front of a jumbled and jubilant crowd dancing in the sunshine; Mahlathini and the Mahotella Queens posing in a promotional poster from a Japanese tour with red swabs of paint rushed across the top of the poster, the Mahotella Queens in red *izigqoko* (headdresses), red T-shirts, beads, *izidwaba* (skirts), leaning backward, sideways, together, right feet raised and hands poised at shoulder height as though captured in a moment of dance. From the wall behind West, above his large swiveling office chair, gazes King Sobuza II of Swaziland in a portrait painted of him as a young man.

take 4 : Hamilton Nzimande

Johannesburg, March 1991

He's here at Gallo, Rosebank. He vanishes in a blink. He's downtown at the studios, he's just left, he's coming later, he's in Durban looking in on the Radio Zulu DJs, he's just out, not even his wife in Soweto knows where to find him. Secretary Betty shrugs. He said he had a meeting in Market Street. Try downstairs, she says. Or next week.

About two weeks later: A pale blue shirt, a demure gray suit, an impeccably knotted tie. Cuff links. A briefcase stands upright close beside his desk. His desk calendar is as empty as a stage waiting for a performance.

Hamilton Nzimande, producer at Gallo Music Productions, is superbly versed in the promotional interview process. He affirms my questions, often by repeating my words as if by rote. Then he stops, more or less, and waits, smiling the eloquent smile of his gentlemanliness. You have to be impressed with the discreet control with which he handles an interviewer, even while you sit in the hot seat yourself.

I want an interview that won't reproduce the promotional gloss that most musicians expect. Rather, I want Nzimande to tell me stories about his own experiences in the music industry and about his galaxy of recording artists from his point of view. I let him know that I know he's an important figure in the history of black South African music—a star in his own right, whose shimmering goes unnoticed in the dazzle of the artists he has catapulted into the limelight.

Hamilton and I watch each other attentively across his desk as the interview sputters into life. I explain again how I want to learn and eventually write about "traditional" and mbaqanga music as experienced, remembered, and narrated by music-makers themselves, and I want to know more about his own contribution. I tell him I'm not a journalist, a foreigner, or an expert. I remind him I'd witnessed a session of his a year ago in the old Gallo studio. I am researching a thesis. As he politely sizes up my purpose and my person, story snippets trickle out. They are cued by me, by the intensifying of my tone, the rise in my pitch, the mms and silences. But my cues were often prompted by his performance. Hamilton is a master.

First he slips a yellowing brochure out of his top drawer and slides it across his desk—a souvenir program of his mbaqanga group Izintombi Zesimanjemanje from a 1979 Zambian tour. I am delighted with this prize historical document and by the fact that Hamilton has figured it would be of significance to me. He has more paraphernalia at home, he promises.

At my request, he then lays out his professional history, from its beginning.

"Ja, I can tell you. Music, it was something that was in my blood. I started to have my own choir—that was early 1957—at school. We used to perform for raising funds for schools, for churches, and all that. Immediately when I left school, I joined EMI as a rep [record sales representative]. I was the first rep—black rep. It was only whites. So they said, 'Let's try a black rep, because he understands more about mus—black music; he can explain and do all that.' Well, they tried me as a rep, I think for three years. So there was a gentleman from Holland, Mr. Wyngaard, who was running EMI production. He said, 'No, I would like you to come to the studio and do something for me.' I went to the studio, I found the groups were rehearsing. And then I was interested. He said, 'Do you think you can do something about this producing?' I said, 'Well, I've had my own group at school, I don't think it will be difficult.' So he said, 'Can you form a group, and then you can buy instrument[s] for your rehearsal room.'[7] Then I formed Izintombi Zesimanjemanje, which you've got on your booklet there."

On the front cover the five women singers of Izintombi Zesimanjemanje pose at a fishpond. Peach-colored, fluted, semicircular chiffon tunics drape over their long peach-colored gowns. They stand graciously at arm's length from one another, holding hands, shoulder high. The scoops of their arms reproduce the scallops of their chiffon, elegant 1970s mollusks strung together in a necklace. They reflect in the still water. Water lilies grow in a cluster. I spot Hilda Tloubatla and Nobesuthu Shawe—later to become Mahotella Queens—under their Afro hairdos. I think of Aretha in gospel garb; I think of her performing in flowing pastel blue chiffon. I think of the early Supremes.[8]

Two additional color photos decorate the back cover. The first photo shows the five women being presented with framed gold discs. They are dressed in slacks and polo necks. Jane Dlamini wears matching white bell-bottoms, hip-length jacket, and wide-brimmed hat. Her feet are chopped out of the frame, but she must be standing in platform shoes coordinated with her outfit in the then fashionable 1970s African American soul style. Nobesuthu gloriously displays her disc above her head.

In the second photo, the group is performing with groaner Mthunzi Malinga. Bare-chested Mthunzi wears traditional skins and garters and a headdress. The women wear black bras. Beaded aprons and belts overlay their fringed skirts. They all wear cowtail arm and leg garters. They sing into mikes.

"Eh, and then I formed another group, Bra Sello, a saxophone group with a backing Abafana Bentuthuko. That was recorded 1967.[9] It was a hell of a success! The record just went like that—platinums! [Mr. Wyngaard] was surprised. So from there on I continued to be a producer. I only recorded, eh, local music—I mean I'm talking about traditional, mbaqanga, soul, pop, different music, up to now."

I fill his long, smiling pause with an exclamation.

"So now I'm almost twenty-five years producing the music."

mix : on reputation

They show me their promotional photographs for their Mauritius tour. They say they've toured all over Africa—Ivory Coast, Zambia, Botswana, and so forth. Yet those tours happened before all but two of them were members of group. "Ladies and gentlemen, this group was created in 1964 and has been together ever since!" calls Hilda Tloubatla from the stage. Yet she and Nobesuthu, now Mahotella Queens, were once part of the frontline of Izintombi Zesimanjemanje. She's from New York, Joana, re-ferring to me, tells a young singer she's trying to impress, even though I have just explained to her that I am studying in Texas. "Platinums!" exclaims Hamilton Nzimande about the 1967 success of Izintombi Zesi-manjemanje, Bra Sello, and Abafana Bentuthuko. Yet platinum awards were instituted in about 1978.[10] He tells me that he prefers to recruit female vocalists from rural KwaZulu-Natal, "because the local girls that we've got here [in Johannesburg] don't want to sing that type of music. They want to [do] disco." You find good singers by word of mouth, he stories—at weddings in the rural areas, for instance—and then you bring them up to Johannesburg. Yet his current mbaqanga frontlines are made up of thoroughly urban women who have lived in or around Johannes-burg for many years. In a subsequent interview he elaborates a similar story authenticating the origins of one of his "Zulu traditional" artists, claiming he'd recently discovered Caiphus Dlamini playing guitar in a Zulu migrant male hostel in kwaMashu, a satellite township to Durban, the industrial center of KwaZulu-Natal. Yet the real Caiphus lives and works a few blocks from Gallo's studios in Johannesburg. Hamilton is a master.

"Sometimes I use an echo plate," trickster West confides in an inter-view when we were talking about his 1980s productions of Mahlathini et al. "I specialize on the echo plate most of the time myself. I don't use the [digital] reverb from R7 or AMS. I use a plate direct. You know there is this echo plate built in the studios, very big ones, and then they supply the echo into the control room? So I use that. It is a very nice clean echo that one; it is not artificial." Yet there has not been an echo plate available for use in the studio for a number of years. He says, when "I was discovered by a French jazz promoter in France who asked me if I'm the real West Nkosi, he wanted to have the group [Mahotella Queens]. So I left the Graceland tour to come back to South Africa to regroup the singers and band." Yet while West has traveled professionally many times and indeed was included in a Gallo executive entourage that attended the Graceland concert in London, he was not part of the Graceland tour in 1987.[11]

West says it was 1955 that the government—that is, the Christian National Party—divided the blacks. But the Nationalists came to power in 1948, and the homeland policy was written into law in 1960. Why 1955? He says that blacks used to live together as different tribes before the government split them up, as though the apartheid era and early colonialism were the same historical moment.

When West says he specializes on an echo plate to add artificial reverberation in the studio, he discursively borrows a piece of studio equipment that is highly valued, expensive, and almost obsolete in the world of sound engineering. In his story, he uses this unit as an icon of originality in order to present his contemporary productions as authentic.

When Nzimande exclaims "Platinums!" he translates Zesimanjemanje's early success into the idiom of the 1990s. He moves into an ethnographic present to tell me that they received the highest sales accolade at the time of this hit release. Sales of twenty-five thousand units were commemorated with gold disc awards in 1967. The platinum category was only added above the gold a decade later when quantities of hit record sales escalated exponentially. Nzimande's use of the ethnographic present poetically intensifies the impact of that moment since platinum refers to much higher sales in numerical terms than gold does. Nzimande's implication for the present is that Zesimanjemanje undoubtedly will win platinums today again.

By means of obfuscation, omissions, and chronological elisions these mbaqanga music-makers mobilize the past and the imagined in their narratives to serve the present. By narrating in glittery and grand rhetoric the histories of their professional advancements while keeping their personal sociopolitical struggles against apartheid regulations present in the conversation, they account for both their stardom and its limited success. By constructing logical continuities that bring their acclaimed pasts into the present, they manage their images and argue for the significance and authenticity of their current work and for their artistic caliber.

Used in concert, such trickstering discursive moves enhance the status and aura of the speakers. The individuals become more and more enigmatic as they play their front (Goffman 1959), telling stories artfully and finely timing each nuance of the telling. In the stories they elect to tell and in how they recount them, these artists work at elaborating their professional reputations.[12] By building up their status on the one hand, they gather authority; by cultivating their enigma, they keep themselves unknowable, slipping out of the frame. Together, this gives them ways and means of maneuvering through a system bent on keeping them in control. Enhanced status and an enigmatic aura helps them to carve out a space within which they can continue to create their art and to cultivate a market for their product.

Their stories also serve the moment of utterance—that is, they satisfy what they anticipate are my expectations as an interviewer and ethnographer while they figure out my reputation, history, politics, intentions, and potential usefulness. They hear I have a brother in America. "Meintjes? And you're from Pretoria?"

remix : on genre

The poetics employed in the process of elaborating musicians' reputations necessarily implicates talk about music and performance. Something called mbaqanga is dialogically shaped with the images of the artists and with the histories of the music that they and others recount. "Mbaqanga? It's our music," Jane informs me.

Mbaqanga has slipped in and out of its own definitions over the course of five decades of performance for varying audiences in many places. It appears as a musical descriptor around 1950 when it stood as a synonym for African jazz (Ballantine 1993, 61). It subsequently shifted its designation as a term of value and style a few times. During the 1950s, drawing on its meaning in Zulu cuisine as a staple maize dumpling, upwardly aspiring jazz critics, journalists, and fans employed the term to deride local popular music as "homemade" and unsophisticated (Allingham 1999, 642).[13] This "popular commercial African jazz" of the 1950s "developed from *kwela* and blended African melody, *marabi,* and American jazz" (Coplan 1985, 267).

In the 1960s the term came to reference "a new style that combined urban neo-traditional music and *marabi* (not jazz) and was played on electric guitars, saxophones, violins, accordions, and drums" (ibid.). The music and its label "mbaqanga" came to be widely celebrated. Jazz fans then began to use the term *msakazo*—essentially, "radio music"—as a derogatory synonym for mbaqanga (ibid., 268). Activists, scholars, and progressive journalists likewise dismissed it. From their point of view, the music naïvely promoted the interests of the state by complying with the broadcast media's censorship regulations (Ballantine 1993, 8).

Meanwhile, substyles and related styles emerged. For example, simanjemanje by David Coplan's definition was "a style of *mbaqanga* usually featuring a male lead singer and a four-member female chorus, performing blends of urban neo-traditional and *marabi* vocal music backed by Western instruments at stage shows and on records. It [was] directed specifically at urban workers, migrants and rural Africans" (1985, 272). This was also known as vocal mbaqanga and in the later 1960s and 1970s as *mgqashiyo*. Allingham lists distinctive traits of this style of the 1970s: a five-part close harmony (a second tenor part was added to the four-part harmony derived from African American quartet singing to form the women's choral frontline); a loud electric bass, played with a plectrum, as the foundation of the sound; an "ultra-bass male vocal that contrasted dramatically with softer, all-female harmonising"; electric guitar rapidly picked with high neck work; simple repeated melodic fragments; and rhythms that were heavy and elastic (1999, 642).

In the 1960s, 1970s, and early 1980s *jive* (vocal jive, sax jive, accordion jive, and so forth) was sometimes substituted for any of these terms in music journalism and promotional materials. In other instances, jive referred specifically to the instrumental version of the style, most often lead by saxophone, with a horn section replacing a vocal frontline.

In the 1970s, as simanjemanje enjoyed massive attention, an equivalent style emerged, fronted by a male chorus and a solo male, sweet, soft-style vocal rather than the rasping bass groan. This style was referred to as "soul," "soul jive," "soul vocal," "vocal jive," "mbaqanga soul." These terms, along with such features as highly florid organ playing, a stronger presence of the horn lineup, and the integration of the sweet male lead vocal, folded back into the women's simanjemanje style, so that records came to be fluidly marketed under these descriptors.

While a recounting of mbaqanga's sonic heritage and definitional usage assists an aural and political interpretation of contemporary sounds, practitioners don't necessarily account for the style in the various terms discussed above, for these are not necessarily the terms of their conversation or of their investment in the sound or of the politics at the moment of (re)definition. For example, setting me right in 1992, Albert Ralulimi says 'No, msakazo simply means to broadcast.' He is Gallo Music Publishers' royalty administrator, a former pennywhistler and sax jiver, and a man renowned in the industry for his memory of South Africa's music history. 'The right word for the history is *mbaqanga*. We musicians never called the music msakazo, and neither did the record companies.'

Like Mahlathini and the Mahotella Queens on stage in Austin, Texas, in 1993, Gallo in 1991 actively promoted an idea of mbaqanga appropriate to the terms of an international World Music market. The following appeared as a sleeve note on *Mbaqanga:*

> MBAQANGA (oom-bah [click] ung'ah) n. Zulu
>   1. A homemade multi-grained bread popular in South Africa.
>   2. A South African musical recipe mixing growling male vocals and female harmonies, spiced with guitars, saxophone and penny whistle, baked under intense, heated drumming. Noted for its mood uplifting effects, causing smiles and promoting non-stop dancing. First prepared in 1964 and still being served by Mahlathini and the Mahotella Queens.
>   See also: PARTY (Mahlathini and the Mahotella Queens 1991b)

> *M—ba—qa—nga!*
>   *Mbaqanga! Mbaqanga! Mbaqanga!*

With their dictionary definition of mbaqanga, Gallo promises foreign consumers of Mahlathini and the Mahotella Queens' recordings that the music is different yet accessible enough (just follow the recipe). It is a special version of the familiar—sensually intoxicating, apolitical, global party music rendered particular by its local accent ("n. Zulu").

"Mbaqanga? It's our music," Jane informs me. For her and other band members in the early 1990s, mbaqanga is not maskanda music like Abavithizi's music in the rehearsal I visited. Nor is it Zulu traditional music like Umzansi Zulu Dance. Nor is it the local pop music that the youth in the townships want to listen to. Nor is it like those traditional wedding songs that Platform One has popularized as electronically programmed arrangements. For Jane, mbaqanga sometimes *includes* jive—the saxophone lead instrumentals that follow the same basic form as vocal mbaqanga—while at other times jive *contrasts* with mbaqanga. Sometimes she calls the Soul Brothers's style mbaqanga, recognizing the Soul Brothers as the male frontline equivalent to Zesimanje's lineup; at other times she distinguishes the group's music from mbaqanga by its beat.

Mbaqanga in the 1990s is at once a presentation of one South African sound, a display of South African or African spirit on a foreign stage, an exotic experience, and a marketing category. It is to an equal degree a loosely held collection of formal properties, instrumentations, principles of arrangement, and dance moves. It is also a set of performance practices geared around staged shows promoting recorded music. For aficionados and practitioners, mbaqanga is both the pleasure of remembering, sometimes re-feeling, a glittering heyday that took place in the dark era of apartheid and a revival of that spirit and sound in response to the contemporary moment. It is constituted by means of a fluid and shifting network of artistic and professional relationships that flow through and around sonic form.

playback

I think of the 1970s in the cities' white suburbs, where African men and women socialize in the shade of tree-lined pavements during off-hours from their domestic work. On the streetcorner, betting onlookers lean over their companions who squat low to play board games. Women in aproned uniforms embroider and crochet while they rest on the edges of clipped lawns. Someone shouts across the way; a couple ambles; agile youths kick a tennis ball, one to the next, without letting it bounce on the ground. Others camp around a radio whose frenetic DJ narrates a soccer match. When the soccer match ends, they turn up the radio, blaring radio, to hear the latest mbaqanga hit. A guitar *wah-wah*s an introduction. Then everything is happening at once. The lead guitar tickles with strident timbre and rapid picking, another scratches rhythmically, the hi-hat ticks furiously, the drums carry a four-beat rhythm, a comping organ inserts florid spurts into tiny textural cracks. Women's voices enter. Short sung phrases in smooth five-part close harmony repeat in the treble register. Punchy, whining horns take a turn at a chorus with a simple, catchy phrase and answer. The groaner comments. A huge, heavy bass guitar drives the motion, with articulated attacks and thick sustain distorting the sound of the little wireless. A gardener in faded overalls dances with fast, lacy footwork. Others whistle at his artful display.

Hamilton Nzimande in a Johannesburg Studio, 1972(?).
Courtesy Jane Dlamini.

Track 2 *Mbaqanga as Institution and Social Practice*

take 1 : Hamilton Nzimande

Hamilton Nzimande entered the music industry as a record packer for Teal, originally a subsidiary of EMI. He moved to Phillips Radio for a couple of years, then joined EMI itself in 1964. At EMI he promoted the artists of producer Rupert Bopape. In 1966 he was recruited by CBS to start a black recording division for the local subsidiary, Gramophone Record Company (GRC) (Allingham 1999, 640). Here he came into his own as a talent scout and producer and built up a formidable production house, Isibaya Esikhulu (The big kraal).

At the peak of his career in the early to mid-1970s, Isibaya Esikhulu included a host of mbaqanga, soul, jive, Zulu traditional, and choral artists. The list of supporting personnel gives some indication of the scope of his house and the impressiveness of his managerial skills. Moses Dlamini worked as Isibaya's public relations officer, in addition to being employed as a sales rep at GRC. Two road and stage managers, Isaac Luvuno and Zebulon Duma, painted banners, hung posters, and managed venues. Four drivers transported the hectically touring artists in two twenty-six–seater buses and a minivan, purchased with company loans by Hamilton. The musicians promoted their own recordings by performing all over the subcontinent, up as far as Zambia and Malawi. "If one group is going this direction, the other is going that direction," exclaims Moses, with both his hands flaying around his head. In 1982 Isibaya artists even toured to the Ivory Coast.[14] The musicians gigged on equipment belonging to Hamilton—amps, guitars, a trap set, and keyboards.

In his long-standing involvement in the industry, Nzimande has made formative creative contributions to South African music. He "discovered" and produced a broad range of artists and spearheaded numerous stylistic innovations (see Allingham 1999, 640). His most successful musicians included Phuz'ushukela (Drink sugar), the Zulu traditional guitarist who established maskanda as a commercial genre; mbaqanga female vocal frontlines Izintombi Zesimanjemanje (The modern girls) and Amatshitshi (The teen girls); sax jive and backing band Abafana Bentuthuko (The boys of increasing influence); mbaqanga male "groaners" Saul Mshengu Tshabalala and Bhekitshe Tshabalala; and soul bands the Inn-Lawes, the Movers (briefly), the Soul Brothers, and the Beaters.

In the early to mid-1970s, with these musicians as the kernel of Isibaya Esikhulu, Nzimande's enterprise at GRC rivaled Rupert Bopape's outfit at Gallo, Mavuthela, and earned him the nickname "Vala Nzimande" (Close Nzimande [Zulu]) for "closing" everyone else out of the market.[15] Allingham celebrates Nzimande for being "the first producer to take 'soul' music seriously and make it massively successful" (1999, 640). Nzimande's soul mbaqanga sound derived from his addition of sweet male vocals—imitating a style of Shona music popular in what was then Salisbury—to the instrumental lineup of the Inn-Lawes (ibid.). The sound marked the beginning of a musical trend that came to dominate the market from the mid-1970s into the early 1980s.

Nzimande also made a significant contribution to choral music production. He was in the forefront of making *cothoza mfana*, the stylistic predecessor of isicathamiya, commercially available and popular in the late

1960s through the 1970s. His a cappella Zulu choir the Kingstar Brothers, who recorded commercially with him from 1967, paved the way for the success of Ladysmith Black Mambazo (Erlmann 1996b, 360). Throughout his career, he has also maintained a steady religious choral music catalogue. And, following his soul music successes, Nzimande launched the career of a township pop band, Splash, whose music largely defined a new market category, township pop.[16]

GRC was incorporated into the Gallo group of companies as Gallo–GRC in 1985. In practice, this buyout amounted to a corporate amalgamation of South Africa's two foremost rival production houses—Nzimande's Isibaya Esikhulu and Bopape's Mavuthela. In a subsequent reshuffling internal to Gallo Africa, the then six in-house producers of Gallo–GRC were moved into the new Gallo Music Productions.[17] With the exception of two cursory forays into the world of independent production, Nzimande remained with Gallo until 1996 when the company again restructured.[18] Nzimande then started his own production company, again called Isibaya Esikhulu, with a distribution deal with GMP.

take 2 : West Nkosi

Unlike Hamilton who has never recorded or performed as a professional artist himself, West coupled his production work with a career on the stage and behind the studio microphone. In fact, it was as a performer that he first earned a reputation in the music industry. He began playing pennywhistle in the streets of Pretoria, where he was employed as a domestic worker when he was a young man. Next he joined a local band, the Bon Accord Brothers, who played in shebeens and township halls. He made his first recording in 1958 with the Pretoria Tower Boys, a band of domestic workers who gigged outside soccer stadiums and at the Pretoria train station. The success of this recording drew him to Johannesburg permanently and into the music industry professionally.[19] He moved to Gallo, where he played under Reggie Msomi in Msomi's Hollywood Jazz Band, then began recording under his own name on Gallo's black music labels, such as the USA label. Because Gallo was not showing good returns on their black music production, they poached producer Rupert Bopape from EMI in 1964. He formed the Makgona Tsohle Band that came to be the core of the massively productive Mavuthela production house. Gallo's success began to turn.

West was included in Mavuthela as a saxophonist in the Makgona

Tsohle Band. Makgona Tsohle was not only the main backing for Mavu-thela groups but was also a massively popular instrumental jive band in itself. West fronted the group and composed much of its repertoire. This was the sound and name that made him famous. His renown eventu-ally even reached "overseas" to African music fans and aficionados. In France he was discovered by a promoter in 1987 "who knew my name and had some of our old records with him. He asked me if I'm the *real* West Nkosi."

It was as a Mavuthela artist that West began to produce in 1972. He and others assisted Bopape sporadically until 1979 when Bopape retired and Mavuthela fragmented.[20] West then became a full-time producer at Gallo.

As a producer he has led a host of artists to media success. Isica-thamiya choir Ladysmith Black Mambazo was his first success. Having been tipped off about Mambazo's excellence by a Radio Zulu announcer in Durban, where the group had made transcription recordings, West "discovered" and produced them for Mavuthela in 1972.[21] He continued to work as a session musician, sax jiver and band member, and part-time producer. In the 1970s he talent-scouted and recorded for Gallo in what was then Rhodesia and made his name there by producing mul-tiple hits with the Green Arrows. When Bopape retired in 1979, Marks Mankwane and West Nkosi both became full-time producers.[22] Mavu-thela's roster was divided between them. Marks Mankwane became pro-ducer of the Mahotella Queens, and West became producer of the male mbaqanga/soul lineup Abafana Basequdeni.

The artists West developed and produced in the 1970s and especially in the 1980s include most notably Zulu guitarist Philemon Mchunu, the group Amaswazi Emvelo, soul singer Mpharanyana (1975–1979), soul lineup the Shoelaces (briefly), and township pop singer Patience Africa. From the early 1980s until 1991, when he left the Makgona Tsohle Band altogether and Mankwane became producer again, West managed and produced Mahlathini, the Mahotella Queens, and the Makgona Tsohle Band.[23] During that decade, he produced nine albums for these groups.[24] From their 1987 release *Thokozile*, they were catapulted onto the world stage.

Once he had left the Queens, West focused on domestic production. In the early 1990s he envisioned his task as building up new local tal-ent to follow South Africa's big stars, such as reggae artist Lucky Dube, onto the international stage. West's attention was primarily devoted to fashioning a young reggae group, O'Yaba, who had begun to tour inter-nationally with his help. His production work ranged from conventional

West Nkosi, Downtown Studios, 1997. *Photo by TJ Lemon.*

domestic projects to "traditional" groups like Umzansi Zulu Dance and Amadoda Ahlangene, which he projected could have foreign appeal, to new experimental recordings for the local market, including an American soul recording with ex-mbaqanga singer Walter Dlamini and his own sax jive compositions. CDs that featured his own playing and composition he intended principally for international release.

As a performer and producer he also succeeded in being integrated into executive positions. He was promoted to the company's board of directors in 1982 (Mahlaba 1982). In 1987 he was one of the initiators in the establishment of Shisa International, Gallo Africa's then international marketing subsidiary, on the board of which he served. Like Nzimande, he continued to be employed as one of the in-house producers at Gallo Africa's subsidiary Gallo Music Productions until the company restructured itself and producers became freelancers in 1996.

West's work and biography as a performing artist lent him legitimacy as a power broker in the music industry. His ability to play enhanced his authority in other spheres of music industry work. Musicians and sound engineers voiced confidence in his decisions as a producer in the studio on the grounds that through his experiences in performance he knew intuitively and technically what making music is about. He had it in his feeling. "When you're onstage it's different: you sort of get a different feel, you know, the whole body—you get tuned in to what you're doing. And then you, you, you"—West gesticulates while he searches for words—"become a victim of what you do." He lands on the word *victim* like a mbaqanga bass player dropping down onto the first beat of his riff. "And then it's just a feeling that comes. It's difficult when you are off the stage, to explain why you did that and that. You say, 'Well, it was just a feeling that came in because I was taken in this song.' There's nothing special. It's how you feel that song, that time. It comes automatically." He looks at me. "Now, once it is over, the feeling is gone also. It's not like a dream that you can always revise. If it was a dream, it was going to be easy, you know." He chuckles, shakes his head, raises his eyebrows, chuckles on, and waits for me to ask him another question.

His performance career also generated and sustained a public presence for him domestically, distributed his name and sound internationally, and provided opportunities to meet foreign industry contacts and negotiate deals for himself as a producer, for bands he managed, and for Gallo.

His biography also garnered him authority as the "genuine item" in another way. His press biographies, for example, note conspicuously that he was a herdboy who worked his way to town and into the studio via streetcorner busking, and that in later years his fame as a saxophonist opened doors to him to connect with foreign promoters on behalf of the record company at large. In his own narration as well as in official narrations given out to the press, his rural childhood ties, his urbanization into the working class, and his experiences of social struggle authenticate his identity as local, African, and politically credible, despite his exploitation, one might say, of apartheid state and capital apparatuses in order to realize his success. Moreover, as in the biographies of early blues and jazz musicians, such narrations imply that his music is "genuine"—a sincere personal expression of his South African experience of struggle against race and class prejudices. It made him important to South African society for the job he was doing.

take 3 : Izintombi Zesimanjemanje

Izintombi Zesimanjemanje were Nzimande's first artists to be successful enough on singles to warrant an LP release, their eponymously titled *Izintombi Zesi Manje Manje* (1967b).[25] They went on to enjoy massive popularity in the early and mid-1970s, even outstripping the Mahotella Queens.[26] So famous were they, that in popular discourse across the subcontinent their name—simanjemanje—was lent to the women-lead mbaqanga style more broadly.

Zesimanjemanje came to be used as an emblem of Nzimande's production house at the peak of its glory. Their photograph graced the covers of some Isibaya Esikhulu LPs on which the women did not sing at all, such as *Jacaranda Bump Jive*, an instrumental jive LP (Nzimande All Stars 1976). When Nzimande started to experiment with a male chorus, he introduced the men as backing vocals for Zesimanjemanje on some of their recordings. *Ujabulisa Abantu*, for example, featured Zesimanjemanje on side A together with a male chorus provided by the Soul Brothers, some sweet wavering-voiced solos sung by Soul Brothers' lead David Masondo, and the prominent horn section of Abafana Benthuthuko. However, the record's cover and credits bore only the name of the women's group (Izintombi Zesimanjemanje 1978).[27]

As fabulous as they were in themselves, Zesimanjemanje's renown cannot readily be extricated from the success, management, and recording and performance practice of Isibaya Esikhulu as a whole. Two important connections spring to mind. First, Zesimanjemanje were backed by a pool of excellent musicians who were essentially treated as uncredited in-house session musicians. Though the house bands remained consistent in name, and these names (Abafana Benthuthuko, Nzimande All Stars) were each associated with a specific frontline, the instrumentalists themselves were interchangeable. They substituted for one another in supporting the mbaqanga and soul vocal choruses, sax jivers, and Zulu guitarists. Isibaya's male groaners likewise sang interchangeably for Zesimanjemanje and Isibaya's other female frontlines.[28]

Second, as Zesimanjemanje's popularity waned and the Soul Brothers gathered sizzling acclaim, the Soul Brothers helped to sustain interest in the female group by continuing to share the stage and the studio with them. For example Zesimanjemanje's *Zenda Zangishiya* (1983) includes songs in which the male and female vocal choruses back and front each other or alternate singing verses.

The inverse changes in Zesimanjemanje's and the Soul Brothers's popularity rating was linked to the dynamics of the broader music market, specifically to the import of disco into South Africa (see Hamm 1988). By changing the bass and drum patterns of mbaqanga to a disco beat and giving the keyboard greater prominence in their music, the Soul Brothers drew a younger audience that was also tuning in to the latest disco imports (Allingham 1999, 648). This new local soul and disco-inflected soul, as well as disco imports, drew South African ears and cents away from the mbaqanga styles of Zesimanjemanje and others like them, so that by the early to mid-1980s, women-led mbaqanga frontlines were struggling to maintain a market and a number of groups disintegrated. Zesimanjemanje tried their hand at the new disco style, but with little success.

1985. Zesimanjemanje sing to a disco beat. Stereoed toms counter a comping keyboard. An electronic drum roll and bell-like glissando sweep the synth piano into a two-bar pentatonic tune. The piano sets the tune up by repetition, then backs into a comp as a synth marimba elaborates, then repeats the melody, dead in time, clean in articulation, consistent in tone. The bass offers a countermelody. It is a local bass sound with a punchy attack, though it's relatively subdued within the mix.

"Come everybody join me, come everybody join me, its the biggest day in Africa," sing Zesimanjemanje airily over the groove. "Come everybody join me," they repeat to the tune of the opening keyboard, exactly on pitch, paralleled by the keyboard. No vocal glides. A drumroll ends the verse. Back to the marimba and bass exactly as before. Their break repeats with some bass thumb-slap ornamentation. "Everybody's singing, everbody's dancing, singing all the songs of Africa. Up in the mountains down in the valleys you hear the music of Africa," swoops Thandi Seoka in her high voice. "Come everybody join me, come everybody join me," sings the Zesimanjemanje chorus. (Izintombi and Seoka 1985)

After a break with Nzimande and a disappointed disbandment in 1988 —a time when Isibaya Esikhulu was also struggling to maintain its glory—Jane resurrected Zesimanjemanje with some new instrumentalists and vocalists. Returning to Nzimande and Gallo, they experimented with reggae, which was enjoying local currency. But even with its topical celebration of Namibia's independence as theme, their reggae LP/cassette *Namibian People* (1990) did not turn their luck.

By now, the Mahotella Queens were captivating audiences overseas. Ex-Isibaya jive violinist Noise Khanyile, recorded and promoted by a small local independent company, has been overseas with his mbaqanga women's frontline. Zesimanjemanje goes back to mbaqanga and back to rehearsing in anticipation of a studio booking. They want to go to Paris. And America. Joana reckons they'll be overseas within the year. God willing. They hear I have a brother in America.[29]

Jane Dlamini

Jane Dlamini was born near Durban in the township of Newclare, although her family originally lived in the mountainous Paulpieterburg area of northern KwaZulu-Natal. As a young women, she moved to Johannesburg, where she worked, attended night school, and sang. She began her professional singing career with the Soweto Queens in 1965. Two years later she joined the Sweet Sixteens along with Irene Mawela who went on to become one of the Mahotella Queens. When she met Hamilton Nzimande in 1969, Izintombi Zesimanjemanje had already been active in the studios for two years and were gathering a fan base.[30] Jane joined the frontline. As constituted in 1971 by Lindiwe Mthembu, Nobesuthu Shawe, Hilda Tloubatla, and Ruth Mafuxwana, Zesimanjemanje became serious competition for the Mahotella Queens for the top position in the popularity ratings.

Woven into Zesimanjemanje's success, decline, and transformation is the personal dimension of Jane's story. She accumulated special celebrity status as the young beauty of the group who developed a romantic association with Hamilton. Five years after Jane had joined Isibaya Esikhulu, Nzimande completed customary bridewealth payments and they were married according to Zulu custom. In 1979 they married by state law. Jane was feted in the public eye by her husband and in the earlier years of their association she was treated royally. He flew me to Durban for lunch on my birthday, she cheers. Oh, in those days! However, Nzimande pressed increasingly for control not only over her sound, image, and career but also over her personal friendships, daily conduct, and her movements. They separated in 1988. Jane recognizes Nzimande as a valuable producer and good person with whom she now has an amicable and mutually respectful relationship.[31]

The failure of Jane and Hamilton's marriage coincided with the demise of Zesimanjemanje as a group. However, as an artist with special status and with striking dignity and social grace, she had come to count journalists, DJs, promoters, musicians, singers, and live-show sound technicians in her social and professional circles. On the basis of her experience with Isibaya Esikhulu and the relationships in the music industry that she had fostered as an artist, she soon resurrected the group under her own authority, gathered together a backing band, and managed them. She continued as one of the principal composers and choreographers of their repertoire. She organized festivals, negotiated mine gigs and other per-

Hamilton Nzimande and Jane Dlamini photographed at the Lilongwe
airport, Malawi, while on tour, May 1972. *Photo by C. Mwenda.
Courtesy Jane Dlamini.*

formances, pushed for record deals, broke their GMP recording contract when it was yielding no fruit and negotiated another, and eventually produced a low-budget cassette for Izintombi Zesimanjemanje (1994, with Mzwandile David as co-producer) and later a CD (1999).[32]

Joana Thango

Surname: Thango
Name: Joana
Address: 3236 Orlando East 1804
Star: Leo
Hobby: music, reading, churchgoer
Menu: fruits and soft drinks
Occupation: musician

Joana Thango was born in Vryheid in the district of Natal. I attended school at Vryheid Junior School. In 1956 I moved to Inkamana Training College where I passed Form Three. I had started singing while I was doing my lower classes. I sang for my church and school choirs. In 1969 I joined the group called Izintombi Zokuqina. We won first prize at the Pinacolada music festival and moved to Johannesburg in 1972. I joined Izintombi Zesimanjemanje under the production of Hamilton Nzimande. Not long after that, I became very sick for about five to six years. I got better in 1985 and joined a TV drama series and I did commercials for only three years. I went back to Izintombi Zesimanjemanje in 1988, but things didn't go well until we moved to Downtown Studios, from Gallo Music company. We've decided to change the name Izintombi Zesimanjemanje to Isigqi Sesimanje. We have recorded under West Nkosi and we hope and promise that our album will be very successful. (Joana Thango's 1992 press autobiography, modeled on celebrity features in local monthly magazines)

Janet Dudu Dlamini

I, Dudu Dlamini, was born in Durban in the location called Umlazi. I attended school at inanda. My father, Richard Dlamini, liked music. He had instruments and a group called Izintombi zempophoma. I joined them even though I was so young in those days. I knew that there is a talent inside my body. I met the late Roxy Buthelezi [SABC radio broadcaster Alexius Buthelezi]. He was managing a group called the Lillies. He took me to Johannesburg to work with him. After a short time he passed away. I went and joined Amagugu under the management of Titus Masikane. When the group split my sister, Jane, fetched me from there and I joined her with Izintombi Zesimanjemanje. That was 1987. In 1988 the group split for a short time. My sister, Jane, decided to rebuild the group again. The group is now called Isigqi Sesimanje. We're singing together with Abashayi Bengoma. I'm very happy with them. (Janet Dlamini's 1992 press autobiography.)

Michael Mpholofolo

I started singing in June 1970. I joined Mahlathini and Mahotella Queens and we formed a group called Mngungundlovana Kids. We toured Swaziland and Durban and we had indoor shows in town.

Later I joined John Moriri and the Mthunzini girls under Mavuthela Music Company at Gallo. In 1972 John Moriri quit Gallo and formed a new group called John Moriri and Manzini Girls under the company called Satbel Company. The records we made there were selling like hot cakes. We had hits like "Wegogo," "Wendoda Mazibuko," "Ngwana," "Malo we," and "Nyale."

In 1976 I joined the company called Isibaya Esikhulu, and our producer was Hamilton Nzimande. There I joined Nzimande All Stars, the background of Izintombi Zesimanjemanje. We also formed a group called Gold Fingers. I also recorded my album called *Tumulang ka dia tla* in Setswana. The popular album was *uMagumede, Sipho kwa Dabeka*.

In 1986 I won a competition run by Radio SeSotho. We were in the Standard Bank Arena, and the show was of an international standard.

I'm a good dancer and I play drums. I'm very good on vocals, I can sing any part. I also do choreographing. I've worked with Sipho Mchunu and Nothembi Mkhwebane and I've toured America and London. [From 1988 to 1993 he worked with Izintombi Zesimanje/Isigqi Sesimanje under Jane Dlamini. Initially he was the drummer, then he joined the frontline to sing the lower middle part.]

Now I am with Isigqi Sesimanje [formed in 1993 by Joana Thango]. We recorded a few songs and I composed some of the hits like "Mmasetshaba" and "Kgano." We are still busy doing promotions and indoor shows.

I have also toured France with Noise Khanyile and Amagugu AseAfrika. There was a festival in Denmark and we had an indoor show in Helsinki. In 1994 I went to Holland to help [South African returnee singer and children's rights advocate] Thoko Mdlalose. We recorded and we went to Germany to perform on a show. We had a big show in Holland and we helped the people of Rwanda with some cash. I also recorded with Humphrey Campbell and his wife Ruth Jacobs. The title is "Buseruka," which is selling very well in Holland. (Michael Mpholofolo's 1999 press autobiography.)

Bethwell Bhengu

Bass guitarist Bethwell Bhengu has performed and recorded as a mbaqanga artist for many years. He started his career in Durban in the mid-1960s playing lead guitar for the Banana City Queens. His first studio experience came in 1966, when the Queens recorded for Gallo under Roxy Jila. After touring with them, Bethwell moved to Johannesburg in 1970. He joined Almon Memela's Amajuba at EMI in 1973. A year later he joined Hamilton Nzimande's Isibaya Esikhulu at GRC. For three years he worked as lead guitarist for their jive band Amatayitayi. Then in 1977 he transferred to CCP Records to join the Jive Boys who backed the Rainbow Fairies. From being a Jive Boy he moved on to being a Zombie. The Zombies worked with soul band the Movers under David Thekwane at Teal record company. Despite their hits like "Bazali khuzani abantwana" and "Amakhehla asezola," the musicians reaped little reward. Thekwane's corrupt ways sent Bethwell on his way again, this time to play with Zakes and the Boots, one of the first bands aired on TV2. In 1984, back in Nzimande's fold as a member of the band Abathakathi, Bethwell played the bass guitar professionally for the first time. After a year with Abathakathi, he joined Abavakashi—a move from GRC to RPM and from Nzimande to Attie van Wyk. Abavakashi's two releases promised an energetic future. However, Attie left the company and the group soon dropped their name. Bethwell remained at RPM as a session musician. In 1991 he joined Abashayi Bengoma, the backing band of Izintombi Zesimanje which has now changed its name to Isigqi Sesimanje. His steady, energetic bass lines keep dancers on their feet. (Edited version of Bhengu's spoken biography, 1992.)

Tefo Mqoqo Sikhale

Tefo Mqoqo Sikhale was born in Bloemfontein and came to Johannesburg in 1962 with his parents—a Sotho mother and Xhosa father. They lived in Diepkloof, Soweto. He started playing the accordion in 1976 and by 1978 was playing the organ—a Tisco—in a Tsongan traditional band called the Time Keepers. This group was produced by Bra Sello, sax jive star of Isibaya Esikhulu fame. In 1980 still playing Tsongan music—both traditional and disco—he joined the Poppy Special Band. They were produced by Moses Dlamini, originally Nzimande's assistant. In Poppy Special Tefo performed on a Farfisa organ, owned by Poppy, but he recorded on a Hammond in the studio. The title song on the group's 1985 hit record, *Swilo Yim'*, was composed by Tefo. The next year he formed his own group, Moving Guys, which played straight disco, using the Yamaha DX7 and Roland Jupiter-Four as keyboards. In 1986 he joined Izintombi Zesimanje, now Isigqi Sesimanje. He played a Yamaha DX7 and other keyboards favoring the old Korg. "It's exactly like the Hammond but with fewer sounds." (Edited version of Sikhale's spoken biography, 1992)

take 4 : Mahlathini and the Mahotella Queens

Mahlathini and the Mahotella Queens began their collective performing and recording careers round the same time as Izintombi Zesimanjemanje. They first recorded in 1964, under Rupert Bopape as part of Mavuthela. When Bopape resigned, they were produced by Marks Mankwane, at the time in-house producer at Gallo Record Company, along with West. Marks was the original guitarist in the backing band, the Makgona Tsohle Band, and played with them until 1998. Until 1990 West was their sax player.

The main composers of Mahlathini and the Mahotella Queens's releases were Simon Nkabinde (Mahlathini), Hilda Tloubatla (one of the Queens), Rupert Bopape, Marks Mankwane, and Shadrack Piliso. West composed much of the Makgona Tsohle Band's music.

The group was immensely popular and productive from the 1960s to the mid-1970s. In the later 1970s Mahlathini left Gallo and recorded with a new frontline under the name Mahlathini and the Queens. He also recorded with the Mahlathini Girls. The original Mahotella Queens likewise resigned from Gallo, but the company replaced them with other singers. Marks Mankwane continued to produce them and released a number of Mahotella Queens albums, without a male groaner, although Gallo had replaced Mahlathini with Robert Mbazo Mkhize.

With the upsurge of domestic disco from the late 1970s, all these musicians' success declined. The Mahotella Queens abandoned their singing careers; Makgona Tsohle Band disbanded, although all but one of its members continued to work in some capacity in the music industry.

Mahlathini's recording career waned along with the general decline in mbaqanga's popularity.

A series of events in the early 1980s led to the reestablishment of the group at Gallo, this time under West's direction. First, Makgona Tsohle regrouped in 1983 to back a two-year local TV series, releasing two albums, *Mathaka*, Volumes 1 and 2 (Makgona Tsohle 1983) to coincide with the series. Second, Mahlathini returned to the Gallo fold to record with West's popular "Swazi traditional" group, Amaswazi Emvelo. West had ideas about reviving the original triumvirate—Mahlathini, the Mahotella Queens, and the Makgona Tsohle Band. He was probably inspired by signs of foreign interest in mbaqanga as evidenced in four releases: Harry Belafonte's *Paradise in Gazankulu* (1986), which used some members of the Makgona Tsohle Band; Paul Simon's massively successful *Graceland* (1986); and *Putting out the Light* (Mahlathini and Mahotella 1984) and *Phezulu Eqhudeni* (Mahotella 1984), both international compilations of old mbaqanga material that prominently featured Mahlathini and the Queens and others.

West reassembled the group, cut a demo, and shopped it around to Gallo executives. GMP's Geoff Paynter recognized their spirited talent and convinced them to volunteer to play at a couple of functions. The second of these was a Gallo in-house party on a late Friday afternoon, to which two Frenchmen were invited. Gilbert Castro from Celluloid Records and Christian Mousset from the Anguileme Festival were both in town scouting for South African talent. The musicians' performance thrilled the gathered Gallo group and the foreigners. From this hearing, Mahlathini and the Makgona Tsohle Band were invited to Anguileme. The festival's budgetary constraints prevented the then five Mahotella-Queens from participating on the first trip, but a second tour including three Queens soon followed.[33] With the recording of *Paris–Soweto* (Mahlathini and Mahotella 1990b) in Paris on this trip, the foundation for the band's second lease on life was in place.[34]

Exposure in two massive events catapulted Mahlathini, the Mahotella Queens, and the Makgona Tsohle Band into an international touring routine. First, their performance at the Nelson Mandela Birthday Concert at Wembley Stadium in 1988 was broadcast to about sixty countries. Then a performance in Central Park, New York, drew a crowd of five hundred thousand in 1991. For the next few years, the group toured annually, playing in Europe, the United States, the Caribbean, Australia, and Japan. This international attention somewhat revived the popularity of the singers and the band at home. More to the point, however, it provided them with a new professional arena abroad and a small new crossover market in South Africa.

Under West, the group released eight recordings between 1983 and 1990.[35] Three releases since West's departure from the band were produced by Marks, a fourth by Moses Ngwenya of the Soul Brothers, and a fifth by Christian Mousset and Philippe Teissier du Cros in France.[36] The group has been distributed internationally through Celluloid, Rykodisc, Earthworks, Shanachie, Sterns, Polydor, and Polygram, under license from Gallo Music Productions.[37]

overdub : the women's frontline

While women have been heralded as mbaqanga singers and dancers since the late 1960s, as yet there have been no female mbaqanga instrumentalists or producers. Historically women have had little say in the process of recording and mixing. However, they have written lyrics, composed and arranged songs, designed their dance sequences, largely had control over the process of rehearsing in the absence of the producer, and they have enjoyed public celebrity status as frontlines for fabulous backing bands.

These women's choreographed close-harmony vocal frontlines took their local precedent from 1950s female vocal jazz quartets, which were closely modeled on American jazz singing. As Allingham has chronicled, the first black South African artists to achieve domestic stardom in the postwar era was a close-harmony male vocal jazz quartet named the Manhattan Brothers who drew their appeal from urban as well as rural audiences (Allingham 1992; Allingham 1999; Erlmann 1996b). While numerous other groups followed their success in the early 1950s, the solo vocal jazz limelight belonged to the women at this time. Dolly Rathebe and Dorothy Masuka, who modeled themselves on the likes of Ella Fitzgerald and Sarah Vaughan, and who recorded for competing companies, were the stars. Throughout the 1950s, female soloists and groups appeared on the scene. They were present in virtually all domestic record companies and cornered a major part of the market (Allingham 1992; Allingham 1999).

At Troubadour Records, Mabel Mafuya followed in Masuka's footsteps. She was supported by an exceptional group of session musicians and backing singers, including Ruth and Doris Molifi and Mary Thobei (Allingham 1992).

At Trutone Records, where Rathebe recorded, the Quad Sisters were making a name for themselves. Trutone housed the by then massively popular Manhattan Brothers, to whom the Quad Sisters formed a counterpart. The label also benefited from having Nancy Jacobs and Her Sisters in their ranks. Under producer Strike Vilakazi, these women cut multiple singles, including "Meadowlands," one of the biggest hits of the era and now a South African jazz standard (ibid.).

Popular close-harmony groups dominated the market. Competition among them was fierce. Lo Six at Gallo countered the Manhattan Brothers at Trutone. Soon after Lo Six signed beauty queen Thoko Tomo to their group, the Manhattans added a young Miriam Makeba.[38] Makeba went on to form her own all-women group, which recorded as the Sunbeams at GRC and as the Skylarks on the Gallotone label. By the end of the 1950s, the Skylarks were the most popular black vocal group in South Africa. Before leaving the country in 1959, Makeba was South Africa's biggest star (ibid.).

By the end of the 1950s, women had carved out a prominent space in the local industry. Though no stars dominated the early 1960s market as the Skylarks had in the 1950s, a host of vocal soloists and groups continued to record. Troubadour, for one, released a number of successful recordings by their salaried studio singers who recorded under various names, such as the Sweet Sixteens and the Radio Stars (ibid.). It was not until the later 1960s, with the work of Bopape with Mavuthela and Nzimande with Isibaya Esikhulu, that female groups made their next major breakthrough in terms of style and popularity (ibid.).

mix : Hamilton, West, Zesimanjemanje, and
the Queens as a collective enterprise

The 1970s Izintombi Zesimanjemanje dressed in brand-new attire when they came to the studios to record. A shirtwaist with a sheen and pleats, high heels with ankle straps, hose, and a wide-brimmed hat stood out as elegance supreme. The five women shopped together at import stores like Matts and EVoy in Bree street, and Nzimande checked on their choices. Dress simply, he said, but smart. He sent the women to clothing stores so fancy you could buy shoes, handbags, and dresses all in the same place, and then he'd send them to lunch at the best restaurants in town open to black people, like Kapitan's curry house. If a woman from the Amatshitshi group appeared in an outfit that Jane Dlamini also owned, Jane would have to discard it from her wardrobe—because Zesimanjemanje were the queens of Hamilton's stable, Amatshitshi only princesses.

Nzimande never wanted a disgraced artist. He wanted them noticed at the taxi rank and tittered and talked about in the townships. He sent them home if they arrived in town untidy. The men in his bands lined up their shoes for regular polishing by Bra Whisky, also the production house's banner writer, and Nzimande inspected them. Nzimande was class itself, they said. He drove an Impala and the men in the street checked out his turn-ups, his speckless lace-ups, the tip of his hat brim, the glint on his sunglasses, his cuff links, the razor-edged ironing of his shirt.

When Nzimande saw the Mahotella Queens of the Mavuthela stable swishing down the street in pleats, he'd send Zesimanjemanje shopping again for a fresh pleatless look, because the Mahotella Queens were, after all, their rivals.[39]

In the studio the producers each exercised control in different ways, generating various perks and struggles for the engineers and performers. During recording sessions in the early days—the late 1960s and 1970s—Hamilton didn't allow his performers to join him in the studio control room, except for Jane and Moses, Isibaya Esikhulu's public relations officer.[40] "That's how Hamilton (had) his way," explains Peter Ceronio, who engineered most of Hamilton's productions at the time. "When you came in to the studio, the thing was rehearsed and it was ready." When Hamilton went to the live shows, "He would find himself a certain corner somewhere, where he is not going to be seen by anybody. He just sits there alone, and watches," remembers Moses. Hamilton's enigma entices quizzical wondering. "He's just that type of a person," Moses smiles and delicately shrugs a shoulder.[41]

But "on the other side [Mavuthela] you had plenty of argument!" Ceronio recounts, telling me studio stories from the 1970s. "You used to put maybe six sides down a day. Whereas Hamilton put forty-eight, maybe, or thirty-six—that was the difference: the discipline, you see. Also, in the ranks, Rupert Bopape was there and West Nkosi was there. You basically had two producers already in the control room. Rupert Bopape will go out into his office, and he's sitting trying to get a song right. And then they change lyrics; and then somebody says, 'No, but we must put this in!'

"But Hamilton was never like that. When you came in there, the thing was rehearsed and it was ready.

"Now Mavuthela would have rehearsed and say, 'Well, it's ready!' and then finally West says, 'This is it!' Jis! [Jeez!]—and you're just halfway through the take and Mr. Bopape walks in: 'No, no, no, no, no!'—just walks right through the studio ( )—'No, no, this song must have this.'—

Izintombi Zesimanjemanje in Doornforntein, Johannesburg, 1973. Left to right: Jane Dlamini, Hilda Tloubatla, Windy Sibeko, Ruth Mafuxwana, Zodwa Mnguni, Lindiwe Mthembu. *Courtesy Jane Dlamini.*

Okay, now we go back; now he changes. Three quarters of an hour later we can do the song.

"In those days it used to aggravate us sometimes. But in actual fact, if you think about it today, they were right, basically, because they were creating and that's what it's all about."

In talking about the 1980s and 1990s, engineer John Lindemann clenches his fist to show me that West is "a producer's producer. He rules with an iron hand." West instructs me that with contemporary studio technology, "You can just take voices, play around with them when [the singers] are not there. You can make them sound like Mickey Mouse. You can make them sound anyhow you want them to. That is a producer's job." The performing artist's sound is West's raw material in the studio.

Jane says West doesn't come to the rehearsals. "He just comes when he's going to the studio. He listens and says, 'Ready girls, let's go down to the studio.' And when we enter the studio, he changes it. He wants to hear what is happening on the desk [console], and then he'll come back to you. He finds something he likes on the desk and he changes you to go with that thing. He's like that. His arrangement was good. We are not used to the way he changed things, but it is good. He has very, very good ideas. But you just have to have a long heart, because he will change and change and change. But at the end, you will hear that he was doing something that was very good.

"Now Hamilton leaves you to be free. You do anything you want to with the song. He'll tell you if something is wrong. He'll say, 'Just take out that word, it's not right, just put something else.' He will say this from the rehearsals."

By November 1991, tired of waiting for a studio booking, Izintombi Zesimanje has broken from Nzimande and GMP, changed their name to Isigqi Sesimanje, contracted to RPM records (another Gallo subsidiary), and convinced West to produce them.[42]

In the studio West leans back and lights up again. Engineer Peter is working the console. Jane, Joana, Janet, and Michael bustle back into the control room to hear their backing vocals. Working in the studio again generates memories and optimism. They're poised at an edge, once again anticipating a new hit.

West launches into his bulldozer explanation about their songs. 'You have to go with the market, you have to go with what's happening now. You'll never make it with this old stuff. You have to do wedding songs. Yes, the whole album.'

But these are "noisy" women, to use West's phrase. Unpleasing changes happen only with protest. Today they intervene with caution, for the production is only just under way. They are pleased to have West producing them—they chose him because he is a man of action, they respect his musical and marketing ear, he knows mbaqanga from Mavuthela's side, they think he's the one with the best contacts (overseas). Okay, they agree, they'll try one or two. Out of his earshot they grumble: wedding songs are not their thing, not what they are known for, not what they have rehearsed, and not what they want to do. And besides, now suddenly they have to compose new songs over lunchtime and overnight. No, the success must come overnight, not the preparation for it.

The next morning they are back in the studio, singing a wedding song. Joana has composed two new ones, and they have changed their mbaqanga song "Phumani" to fit the wedding genre.

The phone rings like a summer cricket, piercing Lemmy Special
Mabaso's sax overdub. West drops the monitor level way down to
answer.

"General Hospital. Ja, Peter's here, just hold on. . . . I'm telling
you, you want patient Peter?" West chuckles. "No, he's in
hospital, he's in bed now." Chuckling merrily, he passes the phone
to sound engineer Peter. "It's Steven."

Decisions about appearance, rehearsal procedures, modes of working in the studio, personnel, and repertoire are idiosyncratic to the personalities involved and to the timing of the events. Such choices are made by musicians in the process of reaching for professional advancement, creative authority, and financial benefit. What is crucial here, peculiar to South African musicians, and critical to the outcome of mbaqanga as sound and social practice is that these mbaqanga musicians and others like them had to mold their individual styles within the context of a struggle against apartheid.

By the early 1990s, Hamilton, West, Zesimanjemanje, and the Mahotella Queens had been active in music production for three decades during which state policies directly impinged on their work. Because they relied on live performance and on broadcast media for promotion throughout these decades, those policies that curtailed their freedom of movement and freedom of expression were especially significant.

At the time when Hamilton, West, Zesimanjemanje, and the Mahotella Queens entered the music industry, the day-to-day freedom of movement of black South Africans was restricted by petty apartheid regulations as well as by laws of influx control and the Urban Areas Act. They could not live in or travel to places outside the ethnically determined rural "homelands" to which they were designated by the state, except where they were granted authorization for reasons of employment.[43] They could only eat, sleep, and perform in locations designated as black.

Even as petty apartheid regulations slackened through the 1970s and 1980s, other apartheid rulings stiffened in response to intensifying popular resistance within the country. Freedom of gathering was vigilantly and violently curtailed, including by means of new curfews, when in 1976 the Soweto Uprising signaled a new and volatile era of resistance strategies designed to render the townships ungovernable. In 1985 and again from 1986 to 1990 the declaration by the government of a state of emergency further reinforced these restrictions. These policy changes were accompanied by an escalation, on all fronts, of multiple forms of violence, making live performance increasingly difficult and dates and venues increasingly unstable.[44]

At the end of the 1980s, the lifting of restrictions such as the Urban Areas Act and influx control laws, along with implementation of the international cultural boycott that led up to the unbanning of the African National Congress and other organizations within the liberation movement in 1990, opened up more space for artists and other black South Africans to conduct their professional lives with increased mobility, greater authority, and better opportunities for promoting their products. However, this time of transition was coupled with an escalation in violence and with strained national and personal economics, so that live performance was still severely hampered, except perhaps in the urban club scene and at flagship festivals. Mbaqanga was not part of the club scene, except for the 1990s Mahotella Queens with their new crossover audience, and had to share the city festival stage with a wide range of musics.

Struggling against the changing constraints apartheid regulations imposed on their freedom of movement for three decades, mbaqanga musicians nevertheless promoted their music through live performance. They were also able to reach a massive listenership through the broadcast media, to which they gained access because they had a product useful to the state. A state set on a policy of divide-and-rule (so-called separate development) of course needed a propaganda machine to assist in the policy's implementation. State-run media facilities, especially in the form of radio, were charged with the task of morally and politically edifying South Africa's white citizens via the English and Afrikaans language stations, and of promoting the ideology of separate development among black South Africans via its Radio Bantu stations (see Allingham 1999; Coplan 1985; Hamm 1991; Tomaselli, Tomaselli, and Muller 1989). Radio Bantu, established in 1960 under a Bantu programming control board, had begun a transition to FM transmission within two years of its inception and had expanded into seven language-specific broadcasting stations with a listenership estimated to be six-and-a-half million by 1970 (Hamm 1995, 226).[45] By 1974, according to a market research survey, radio penetration of the black population had reached 97.7 percent; that is, that percentage of the population had access to a radio and listened to it (ibid., 228). All these stations required a hefty dose of local musical product that would bolster the ideology of separate development as well as attract listeners. While this was a boon for the industry and for recording artists, in order to get played over the state airwaves, musical recordings had to pass through heavy censorship regulations that stipulated appropriate ideological content as well as criteria for accessibility and formal attractiveness. Censorship laws were rigorously upheld by the SABC (Hamm 1991; see also Coplan 1985, 194).

It is thus in conjunction with the needs and stipulations of the state that the music industry expanded exponentially in the 1960s and 1970s. The industry geared its product to exploit Radio Bantu's promotional potential and ably fulfilled the SABC's three major musical programming needs: traditional, choral, and popular (Hamm 1995, 230). Mbaqanga of this era came to fit perfectly—or almost perfectly—with SABC regulations. It generally stuck to a single language for each song, its lyrics were mostly without direct reference to the political milieu, and it was widely popular among black South Africans.[46]

Black producers at that time had professional opportunities like never before. They were crucial figures on whom the industry depended in order to effect its expansion within the framework of apartheid. The all-white owners of domestic and foreign music industry capital were ignorant about African musics, languages, musicians, lifestyles, traditions, tastes, and concerns. Furthermore, white people's movements and business relationships were also at times restricted by changing apartheid policies. Music executives therefore could not but rely on their black employees to find and select material, and to promote and distribute products among black South Africans, their major market.

Thus, in establishing their domestic recording facilities, all the major record companies hired black talent scouts-cum-producers (Allingham 1999, 640). The energetic scouting and promotional drives of these men brought artists into the studio and product to the right consumers. Within the company, these men also had to manage the gulfs between artists and studio personnel, as well as between artists and company executives.

Five major producers who ran "virtual African fiefdoms within the companies" became formative figures in the industry (ibid.). The "big five" (which included Hamilton and Bopape) were caught in a paradoxical situation.[47] On the one hand, they were given enormous power to make artistic/repertorial decisions and to direct the flow and character of the overall product. On the other hand, they were constrained and disempowered by draconian racist legislation and rampant prejudice. The key artists in their production houses (West, Jane, and others) likewise worked within this paradox, under the patronage of their producer.

How to find room to maneuver: that must have been an automatic preoccupation for all who were artistically motivated and ambitious. Hamilton and West's styles were distinctly different, though both developed during this grand era. Hamilton constantly danced out of the center. He played the wings and backstage. He worked in the rehearsal room. He managed the on- and offstage presentation of his artists. He reigned outside Gallo headquarters, outside his office, away from the console controls, and outside the studio. West used all his resources to work himself steadily from the margins into the industry's centers. He progressed from the street into the boardroom, from playing as a session musician to calling the shots as a producer, from sporadic chances at directing studio sessions to international renown as one of South Africa's premier producers. In accumulating power, his linchpins were his ability to perform and his reputation as an artist. As he moved into new positions, he continued simultaneously with his former tasks, playing the authority of one against the other.

"*Paris–Soweto* was done in Paris."

"All of it?" I ask West.

"We [Mahlathini, Mahotella Queens, and the Makgona Tsohle Band] were on tour, and I made a deal with Celluloid Records immediately, while we were on tour. Then I communicated with our company [Gallo] that 'Look, we've got a company here who is very interested in releasing some of our records—they are able to pay for everything.' So then we went into the studio and recorded the whole album." (*Paris–Soweto* was co-produced by West and Philippe Groux-Cibial at Harry Son Studios in Paris in 1990.)

"And then I get a phone call to check on these songs, for copyright registration," Gallo's encyclopedic royalty administrator, Albert Ralulimi, recounts. "West isn't good at remembering who does what, I don't know why, he doesn't care about getting history right—and there he is far away in Paris, so he gave an old song composed and registered by other people a new name, with himself as owner. That had to be put right."

The ways in which Hamilton and West played the legislated system and institutional networks from the 1960s to the 1990s positioned them uniquely among South African producers in the 1990s. West captured the contemporary moment in a way that enabled him to play the global field like no other South African producer has been able to do and to make the best of the power a producer could have in the studio. In the 1990s he produced music for both the international and domestic markets. Though he never learned to operate the console independently, he understood the procedures and the extent to which sound could be manipulated, and he used his authority as producer to get it done his way. As a performer he recognized how his forms of artistic control converged at the console, and he moved away from the stage almost entirely. Having left the Makgona Tsohle Band in 1991, his own performance and composition returned to instrumental sax jive with musicians mostly from the old Mavuthela and Isibaya rosters. While he did make occasional live guest appearances, his band was conceived as a studio band, recording principally for the international market.

Hamilton is the last of the "big five" still active in the music industry. He has maintained his autonomy and some of his former authority by concerning himself primarily with local consumers, lower budget recordings, and, in the later 1990s, with the vast black church music industry. He has not developed much of an interest in the workings of the electronic console, nor has he established much contact with foreign music industry personnel. 'It doesn't help you to get one of your groups overseas,' Hamilton once observed. 'You build them up till they make it overseas and then they dump you and leave you with nothing.' He leaned at me across his wide desk as if to make sure I'd heard him right. True, West and Ladysmith Black Mambazo had just parted ways. And not long before this, West and Mahlathini and the Mahotella Queens had done likewise.

The biographies of Izintombi Zesimanje, the Mahotella Queens, Hamilton Nzimande, and West Nkosi intersect critically with the changing patterns of South Africa's apartheid eras, the institutional and market openings it provided them as well as the strictures they suffered under its rulings. Mbaqanga as an institution and a set of social practices is critically linked to the biographical paths of the people who made it and to the histories of political institutions within which they lived and worked.

playback

7 January 1993

Jane and Mkhize, a mbaqanga keyboardist, are again seeking gigs on the mines for their groups. Thousands of migrant laborers live in hostels adjacent to the shafts they work in. They spend most of their leisure hours on the mining premises, for they are some fifty kilometers west of the city and some distance from the nearest townships and small white towns in this right-wing Conservative Party constituency. Jane knows the Lebanon mine has a good entertainment hall and an amiable compound manager. She also knows the social organization of the mining system, for her partner was once a miner, and she has played many shows in mining arenas and halls throughout her career.

Inside Lebanon, we cruise past the clipped militarist lawns of the main buildings and the housing of the white chiefs and their families, past the pewter gravel mountains tossed out from the tunneled depths of the ever-grinding Shaft Number Four. We greet the guard who lifts the boom, and we park. Workers stride to or from their shifts down in the earth with flashlights strapped on their sun-yellow helmets and slush on their gum-boots. Other men just sit, sit in the shade, play cards in a cluster, queue for the pay phone. Here and there a hot bicyclist dawdles. A radio plays from a shoulder or from where it's propped up on a stone with an external battery dangling from delicate red wires.

Jane, Mkhize, and I are an odd sight at the midweek, midmorning mine. Jane is dressed for business, in pleats, with handbag and hose. Mkhize is sleekly styled in black from top to toe and sporting broad sunglasses. I am wearing my ladies' shoes and earrings, a skirt. Mkhize and I follow Jane as we are ushered into the office of the compound manager, who is reputed to be an amiable man. He's out. Temporarily out, back soon. We wait. Nobody important comes, so Jane is advised to see the head clerk in the building across the way. Our eager advisees express pleasure that Izintombi Zesimanjemanje want to perform at Lebanon. They treat Jane with serious respect.

As we cross to the other building, miners greet us. They enthuse at the prospect of a mbaqanga show and laugh incredulously when Jane accounts for me as her sister-in-law. Then she turns to remind me that since Afrikaans is midnight to her, I am their band manager today. Once we enter the main office, I should act accordingly.

Inside we get shuffled through the ranks of clerks with rubber stamps and ledger books on their desks. The head clerk frowns his doubt at us but herds us along the pastel-green passage to the office of Mr. Fourie. We sit upright in a row outside his office. Jane chuckles. We have made it to the portal of the big white compound boss. She cheers that my presence oiled the way, even though I have yet to open my mouth and Fourie is the first white person we are to encounter.

We wait and wait until Fourie steps into the air conditioning, back from the blazing athletic fields. I introduce us in Afrikaans. Jane makes the pitch. All we request is a venue, some advertising over the intercom, permission to put up posters, and a show date that doesn't fall at month-end just before payday.

No, he replies. There's too much unrest on the mines to sanction a commercial entertainment venture. He pronounces in his gritty South African tongue. These are violent times, you know.

These artists have been performing on other mines in the area recently without causing disruptions, I reassure him. Has trouble erupted during or after musical entertainment here?

No, he says, not to his knowledge on his mine.

I reiterate that these veteran performers continue to enjoy a wide following, across ethnic lines. (Here I consciously elaborate their reputation.) Their music is not about politics, and they don't have links with the trade unions. The mines used to be one of their principal fan bases and performing venues in the 1970s and early 1980s.

But Fourie doesn't care about that. He informs us that they have their own dancing on the mine and that miners don't really go for this modern pop stuff.

These performers include traditional dancing in their show, I say—gum boot dancing, jive, mbaqanga—it's fantastic!

Jane coaxes him with the assurance that the compound manager is willing to work with them. The people on your mine know us, she tells the boss.

He can't give us an answer without putting it to the board, whose members won't take the risk this year. Because of the violence factor.

Surely you would agree, Mr. Fourie, that entertaining the masses keeps them out of trouble?

He agrees but recommends we make our request in writing.

As we file out from Fourie, the head clerk hopes we were well enough helped. We exchange muffled greetings with the underling clerks. We wave to miners outside in the sun.

While rasping off to the next mine in my Volkswagen Beetle we lose power. The Beetle goes up in flames. A speeding white dude screams to a halt, busts out of his Corvette, shakes a Coca-Cola, and sprays it over our engine. He shouts at the roadworkers for interfering. The blackened little engine sizzles. Two ruddy young mechanics in oily overalls come and hitch my Volkswagen to their monstrous tow truck. They say I can sit in the cab with them.

Tracks Mixed *The Constitution of Mbaqanga*

31 March 1992

Peter Wium, studio technician, walks into Studio 3 with engineer John Lindemann. He couldn't have expected the rant: Segal left the air conditioner on last night, it's frozen over this morning, so we are sweating and suffocating in this box of a control room. West demands that Peter relieve our discomfort, that he serve the studio's client.

Peter defends himself. Segal is, luckily, safely back at Gallo headquarters doing his artists-and-repertoire (A&R) work. John notices my Sony MDRV2 headphones lying on the console ledge.

"Whose cans are those?" he asks curiously. "Those are nice, hey!"

"Ja, beautiful—probably West's," muses Peter. West owns good-quality items—a fine leather jacket, a beautiful acoustic guitar, a large Mercedes-Benz.

John wants definition. Did Segal forget his cans as well, in the early hours of the morning?

I claim them nonchalantly.

"Jeez, they're nice!" nods John to me.

"Expensive, those Sony's," adds Peter.

"Sony's?" notices engineer trainee Lance, who has just joined the hub-bub. "Whoa! Those are nice!"

West is sitting with his arms folded, waiting for the AC's ice to melt, waiting for someone to do something about it.

He casts his discursive net over the prized belonging and over the engineers' talk by asserting himself in an impatient voice, "Those are mine."

Peter joins the play. "No, she said they're hers, so you've got two owners now." Peter laughs, but West persists.

"I'm owning both—the owner and the headphones," he teases. John leaps in and grants West the land and nation with a sweeping gesture. "Listen," he orders us as if for real, "West owns this country, I'm telling you!" West laughs loudest. He cracks again, "I'm owning both of them!"

We take an early lunch break while waiting for the AC to edge its way back to life.

Just as Hamilton, West, and the artists have negotiated through the institutional and political power structures both in the past and at a macro-level, so have they skillfully elaborated their own reputations to effect professional and creative gains both in the moment and at a microlevel. Mbaqanga as a form of performance, a set of images, and a sound is critically linked to Hamilton's, West's, Zesimanjemanje's, and the Mahotella Queens's individual professional achievements as artists and producers. Furthermore, their achievements have been interdependent and their reputations co-storied. This is especially so given that their storying and their careers have largely been generated in comparison and often in competition.

Image and self, stance and sensibility: in creatively building their reputations, these music-makers blur the boundaries between public and private, "real" and story, past and present, frontstage and backstage, market strategy and creative inspiration, deception and sincerity. By moving through these zones of ambiguity, the self becomes entextualized through performance while the self-consciously staged text is saturated with the self. In South Africa, music-makers like those I have introduced manage their ways through these zones particularly by means of a strategic understanding of and participation in the politics of gender and race.

In an industrial institution geared around the production and distribution of black artistry but regulated by historically white capital, which was constrained in some ways and supported in others by an apartheid state, black music-makers have of necessity developed a virtuosic play with doubleness and irony as the basis of a self-making rhetoric. She's my sister-in-law; you're our band manager. As artists subject to apartheid oppression and its legacy of everyday racism, they must take license to perform themselves through the gaps in the system in its everydayness in order to counter or simply manage the constraints of the system at large.

West's, Hamilton's, and the artists' professional authority—and hence their access to resources by means of which they can realize their creative potential—is predicated on the reputations that they build up through their narratives and activities, as well as on the material contributions they have made to the history of a music style, to the development of a repertoire, to the accumulation of a catalogue, and to the production of soaring hits. Their biographies and creative output are inseparable from the changing politics of apartheid lived in and outside the industry and inseparable, too, from the poetics of mbaqanga.

To list a set of generic mbaqanga traits and to trace their social and musical lineages tells one story. Though, like all stories, it is selective, it is an important and persuasive one. It holds some sway over the continuing production of mbaqanga, for it provides some conventions, patterns, and expectations to which contemporary artists are compelled to cohere to varying degrees when they represent and think of themselves as mbaqanga artists. Though each mbaqanga artist's biography is unique to her or his historical circumstances, their retellings are elaborated in ways that downplay their situational variability in order to fit a received story of mbaqanga. Sometimes this requires that the "facts" be obscured or reinterpreted. When speaking *to* tales rather than *about* them, as the musicians by their example insist we do, the binary opposition between knower and known, subject and truth, self and other is broken (Minh-Ha 1991). "Truth is not attained here through logocentric certainties," Minh-Ha claims (13). Instead, with the boundaries of lie and truth incessantly multiplied, the potency of utterances and the authority of the speakers reside in the skill and patterning of the unwinding and multiplying. Herein, in part, lies the enigma of the speakers.

Are all speakers enigmatic? Are performers who are reaching for stardom, elaborating public personae, and staging artistic sensibilities especially enigmatic? Is this trickstering a particularly South African mode of being, artfully developed in order to slip through gaps in an apartheid system, or is it one shared with others faced with a denial of access based in particular on race? Are these modes of cultivating enigma exclusive to mbaqanga practitioners whose music is tied to apartheid state practices and global media practices?

Mbaqanga is best known in performance. In that moment when a multiplicity of musical events happen together as a musical utterance unfolds, mbaqanga, like other music, can simply feel right. In a densely layered, compact instance of performance, mbaqanga can be experienced as a deeply personal, socially saturated, immediate, and substantive "thing." Its significance is concretized into form and felt with clarity. At that moment, mbaqanga makes sense as mbaqanga to its performer or listener, because it "gets into your feeling." It is "not a dream which you can revise." In such moments it is as if you know mbaqanga. But the moment and feeling pass—and promise to return again, for mbaqanga, like other music styles, is a set of gestures that are never complete, never reducible to singular significance, and never fully or finally fixed. That is the enigma of musical style. In saying that style is enigmatic, I am suggesting that the attraction and the unpredictability of a performed utterance—and hence its power—lie in the formal play between the effort to re-present a genre (understood from a particular point of view) and its irreproducibility in new situations.

Is mbaqanga a set of formal characteristics that are rendered in performance, or is mbaqanga a quality of experience? If I list generic traits in order to work outward from a definition of a prototype, I miss the shifts in interpretive communicative praxis that make mbaqanga into what it is. Such a list would sidestep the social, historical, political, biographical, and many of the performed and sonic relationships by means of which mbaqanga is constituted, imputed with significance, transformed, and reinstantiated in the moment. While a 1970s performance event in a township hall outside Johannesburg and a 1970s radio broadcast that captivates domestic workers in the suburbs share some stylistic traits with a 1993 Liberty Lunch performance in Austin, Texas, the enduring features are not necessarily the defining features of the music for mbaqanga artists or for the different sets of dancing listeners. Similarly, mbaqanga at Liberty Lunch is not just a more polished version of mbaqanga heard in the local preproduction rehearsal room or of mbaqanga performed in an arena at a mine shaft—it is a somewhat different "thing." The Mahotella Queens on the stage in Austin isolate and articulate mbaqanga's metacultural markers, and they frame them in a way that coheres—or coheres well enough—with the fantasies, expectations, tastes, and knowledge of their foreign (English-speaking, American) audiences. Is this less or more "the real thing" in the early 1990s than Izintombi Zesimanje's version? They are equally but somewhat differently mbaqanga, though each group might contest this statement of mine in some contexts.

The refinement of the Mahotella Queens's sound is made possible by the support of multiple wings of the record company to which they are contracted and is made necessary by the contexts in which they perform and to which their product is directed. Is this refinement a corruption of the mbaqanga aesthetic or its crystallization? Its critical evaluation in these terms can only be spoken from socially and musically situated vantage points. It is one version of a mbaqanga aesthetic. Is Zesimanje's mbaqanga just "half-baked" or "rough" mbaqanga? It is mbaqanga realized within the local financial, industrial, and political constraints experienced by a different set of artists. Some of Zesimanje's artists have talents and artistic imagination of the caliber of the Mahotella Queens and the Makgona Tsohle Band, whereas others have less professional experience and lesser talents. There is certainly more mbaqanga rendered like Zesimanje's than like that of the 1990s Mahotella Queens.

Mbaqanga is constituted by a particular set of artists who not only have knowledge of one another's sounds but have intricate social ties, within bands, across bands, and among performers, composers, arrangers, producers, band managers, instrumentalists, singers, black and white musical personnel, men and women. The early 1990s sound arises from the history of these relationships as well as from their ongoing evolutions. The particular relationships recounted in this book are crucial to the constitution of contemporary mbaqanga. Other South Africans also write and perform this kind of mbaqanga with a women's frontline, such as the

Super Queens, Amagugu, and Thoko Mdlalose. However, without the relationships articulated here around the most celebrated and financially supported band and the two reigning remaining producers of women's mbaqanga, 1990s mbaqanga would have turned out to be something different.

Mbaqanga also comes to be what it is through the metacultural and metamusical discourse that articulates and defines mbaqanga's substance within the context of specific forms of utterance. In the studio artists, producers, and engineers are engaged in the process of telling a story to one another about what they think mbaqanga is. In their studio discourse, they co-construct their version of mbaqanga. The musicians and producers also represent their work, their selves, and their professional personae and artistic reputations to me in demonstrations, conversations, and interviews, as I look for ways to represent myself and my work to them through the glaze of apartheid's social constructions and political tensions, within the male-dominated industry, and by means of the research techniques with which my training has equipped me. We are all, in a sense, elaborating what we hope are appropriate and productive reputations in the circumstances in which we locate ourselves. In this process, mbaqanga is given a particular kind of life and life story.

Metadiscourse about mbaqanga intersects with metadiscourse about the artistic self of mbaqanga musicians. "Genre" and "reputation" are co-constructed emergent categories. Each provokes the other in performance; each prompts the other to shift in form.

Playback

12 March 1992

It is the biennial Gallo Gold Awards night at the Carlton Hotel. Hamilton is one of the personalities to be honored with a lifetime-achievement award. The embossed invitation stipulates black tie or African attire. Hamilton wears a sleek suit. West wears an ornate, brightly patterned African shirt, pants, and cap. The Elite Swingsters entertain us with their African jazz between hors d'oeuvres and entree. An old group of Hamilton's, they have recently revived and released a new CD, with 1960s hit singer Dolly Rathebe. Hamilton produced them. West assisted on a remix in an effort to bring the production quality to international standards, the sound more in line with an international ear, and—mostly—to cover up some tuning too "off" for the world to hear.[48] Tonight West joins the Swingsters onstage as a guest to play an old pennywhistle number. Spotlighted centerstage blowing his tin whistle, he jives alongside the lead sax while stewards with white napkins folded over their forearms top off the wine glasses of the music biz.

The Recording Studio as Fetish

Hamilton has called Dingane back into the music business. He wants to revive Dingane's music. Dingane, veteran mbaqanga singer and bass groaner from Hamilton's old production house, dreams that he might follow Mahlathini and the Mahotella Queens's recent international success. He has grouped Lindiwe, Gugu, and Connie together as his backing vocalists. Like Dingane, Lindiwe and Gugu have returned to the studio, beckoned by the promises of this comeback recording.

8 June 1992

Engineer Neil Kuny is laying down the women's backing vocals in Studio 4.

The women huddle around the mike in the recording booth, waiting attentively to lay down their part and then to doubletrack it.

Neil holds down the talkback button on the mixing console and speaks naturally, into the air, to instruct the women. There are no visual signs of the microphone that picks up his voice to transmit it to the artists in the soundproofed recording booth, for the microphone is set flat into the console. When the talkback function is held down, it activates the circuit. "Can you hear me?" Neil asks, holding down the talkback button. Silence. He checks their headphone lines. "Can you hear me?" Pause. "Can you hear me?" Oddly, Neil's console faces the back wall in this cramped and gawky space. He communicates visually with the women in the booth by means of a mirror suspended above the console and facing the recording booth window. The women hear his question and reply, gesturing through the glass at the mirror. They don't speak directly into the mike as they would were they recording, but nevertheless—by their positioning around it—they talk in its basic direction. Their mike lines are open, so we hear their voices through the monitors mounted on the control-room wall.

Some of the band's musicians are hanging around in the control room.

"Heyi!" notes one to the others in casual Zulu conversation, "but white people are experts!" He looks towards Neil and continues. "He just talks here and it's heard on the other side, even though we don't have mikes [in the control room]!" Hamilton joins in wryly. "When whiteys want to say something to Jesus, they simply talk and He hears."[1]

"Up above [in heaven]," agrees another, chuckling.

"Bra Ham is right!" they laugh.

"Right now, it looks like they want to leave us on this earth," speculates Fakes seriously. "They're going off with Apollo, they're battling to go and live up there [on the moon]." His idea is tossed aside. "No, never ( )!"

"Do they really want to go and live there?" interrupts Thami skeptically.

"Ja, they want to via straight," asserts Fakes.[2] Thami laughs a little. "They don't want to hear about living here [with us] anymore!" Fakes continues. The implausibility of the project gets another laugh rolling out from the corner of the studio. "It's true!" Fakes persists.

"Heyi! I don't believe it!" another replies as if adamantly.

"Heyi! White people have been around a long time [so they are knowledgeable]." Hamilton enters the fray again. "Once they stayed [on the moon] . . ."

"For days!" Thami remembers.

"For days," Hamilton affirms. "They raised a flag, stuck it into the ground, and then came back—"

"They stayed on the moon, with the flag," interrupts Thami.

"Just so they could say, 'We were here!'" affirms Fakes.

"You're right," announces Thami, acting out the planting of the flag. "'We were here!'" Fakes takes up the story again. "Now they're building an aeroplane so that when Sputnik takes off, it can transport people, you see . . ."

"Mmh," agrees a listener.

". . . and take them there when they leave [the earth]," Fakes continues.

"So that if you have a ticket, you can just follow on there," says Thami.

"And remember that they say they are still building on the moon so that it can be a station they'll pass by—they're going to Mars. That's where they're going! And it's the things on Mars that they want! Ah!" Fakes slaps his palms together and shakes his head in a bemused, dumbfounded gesture.

The loose end of the tape that Neil has been rewinding flaps against the empty reel as it spins round and round. Neil gets up to change the reel.

"There it is, gents!" exclaims Hamilton, anticipating the imminent playback of the backing tracks of the next song and drawing the musicians' attention back to their music. "Let's hear where we're going."

The musicians' talk sparkles with the promise of success. They praise one another's mastery captured on the backing tracks.

"As soon as we've finished this ( ), and then we go to TV. We'll make another video," anticipates Thami.

"Hey, brother, you really played the bass well on this last number!" Fakes congratulates Mloi. If they can keep up this fire in the studio, their energetic excitement seems to say, then they, too, will go places.

In this cut I follow the example of these music-makers by looking at the poetic links between the studio and other spaces in order to understand the studio's formal particularities, the kinds of experiences it makes possible, and the kinds of creative and political power it makes available to music-makers. I start from the pragmatics of instructional communication into and out of a soundproofed room and work outward into the complexities of technological operation and into the seeming esoterica of composition. I hold down the talkback buttons that make spaces live in order to hear what the artists have to say. I name technological objects, place them within discursive contexts, then thrust them further into ideological or theoretical spaces. I return repeatedly to the spinning tape reel on which sounds are registered as magnetic flux, where songs are captured in the process of composition, where music making is moving through a step in the production process. It is from here that music-maker's poetics travel through conversation to God, to the moon, to Mars, and back into their sound. And it is from this tape reel that the lives of music-makers might spin off into new places.

The cut comprises three main parts. First, in Setting up the Session, I situate the studio in Johannesburg, within the history and corporate structure of the music industry, and in the studio's architectural space.

The four takes of the second part look at how the quality of the space can come to be constructed and experienced as magical and as a fetish by music-makers who work within it. By typifying the space as magical, I mean that it is remote from the ordinary and that through the art of illusion and the capacity of the imagination, it seems to house a natural force (the presence of something Walter Benjamin would have called "an original") that when tapped produces compelling art. By thinking of the studio as a fetish, I reify it into an object that can procure for those who have earned access to it the services of that force, or "spirit," lodged within it.

The studio's power of rarefaction is salient for both professionals inside the studio and consumers, who come to know the studio through the rhetoric of the popular media, the promotion of recordings, and advertising of electronic wares. Music-makers are, of course, also consumers—these categories are neither mutually exclusive nor analytically distinct. My focus in this cut lies with the professionals as they come to think about the workings of a studio through their participation in recording practice.

In the third part, the Mix and Remix take opposing positions on how the image of hidden potency in the studio plays into the creative process. The Mix treats the magic as a creative resource available to all who work in the studio, and I detail those structural properties of the space that facilitate its fetishization. The Remix takes account of the studio's positioning within postapartheid South Africa and of professional hierarchies in the control room. Metadiscourse in the control room rarefies the value of the studio masking difference, marking closures, and in many ways limiting access. In efforts to partake in the South African studio's power lies a struggle for dignity, voice, future, and wealth.

Setting Up the Session

Johannesburg, 1991

I'd come whizzing into the city center on my bicycle. Past the taxi rank where vendors sell oranges, Lux soap, cassettes, and haircuts; past the dilapidated Georgeson Mansions where Isigqi Sesimanje's Joana overlooks the noisy taxi rank from her sixth-floor flat; past record bars blasting the latest house-music out into the sunshine; past the previous Gallo building and the isicathamiya hall above the parking garage opposite it; past musician-dancers Muhle and Mdlolo's room on the corner of Kerk and Bree, just a block west from where musicians Siyazi, Msawetshitshi, and Nogabisela live and a block east from Gallo's 1940s-to-1960s headquarters, where records are sculpted like cherubs high up on its concrete walls. I hurtle past Shandel Music, down past Soul Brothers Music. Musicians cruise in and out up to the Soul Brothers' rehearsal rooms. David Masondo, one of the famous Brothers, parks his gold Mercedes. At the next intersection, the corner-shop barber greets me from his spot in the sun (his is not a frenetic business).

It is a dingy part of town here. The roaring overpass loops the city center nearby, while minivan taxis and sealed suburban cars race up thorough-fares to the heart of the city. Messengers on motorbikes weave through the traffic and around pedestrians who move slowly through the district. Along the sidewalks, corrugated warehouse doors alternate with battered burglar-proofing that protects budget stores. Tired business banners peel or flap; luminous posters scream out from cluttered store windows ad-vertising P.A.Y.E., pay as you earn. Take-away cafes serve up slap chips [French fries], *ipapa nenyama* [porridge and meat], and bunny chow [bread and curry]. Outside the fabric store with bright blankets and frocks hang-ing from the eaves, the old Indian owner smokes his stubby cigar. On the corner a woman sells oranges and tomatoes stacked in pyramids on blue plastic plates. A limping man hobbles by with a stick. Snot splotches the pavement, and sometimes last night's dark, sticky blood.

Downtown Studios stands out from its surroundings on this side of the town, near the bottom of Fox Street, half a block from the barber. A mauve-and-purple awning juts out over the entrance like a winking eyelid from its freshly painted face. I stop on the sidewalk.

When the sun is warm and toasty, musicians and their groupies will be hanging out in its brightness. If it's blazing, they'll be in the shade across the road talking about how hot it is, making arrangements for a rehearsal or a gig, or waiting for loosely promised arrivals. Bra Steve, building super-visor and receptionist, might be sweeping a dawdler off the front steps. 'Regulation,' he says. Gallo wants a clean, always penetrable professional entrance. Cars honk at the side entrance to the garage. *Clatter clatter*, up scrolls the security door, and tightly down again. Engineer Lee has arrived in his zooty BMW or Neil in his brown job or a client or someone from the Gallo headquarters in ritzy Rosebank. I catch a glimpse of Hamilton's minivan—his nickname, Vala Nzimande, stenciled in an arc across its tail—as he slips into the garage.

In front of the building, parking is a mess. Incessant traffic officers sporting clipboards and paunches dutifully return on every shift. A truck is backed into the loading entrance, packing equipment in or out. Per-haps building-cleaner David is polishing a car. A personalized minivan or two are sure to be parked—Lucky Dube's, the Dalom Kid's, Peta Teanet's, or Splash's with its peacock logo—people packed in, or people piling out, waiting to go to a gig, returning from a shoot. Sipho arrives with his key-board slung over his shoulder, Harare with his slim sling bag of drum-sticks. "Irene," "irene," "irene," they greet everyone, knocking clenched fists top to bottom, bottom to top, knuckles to knuckles, thumb to thumb with a twist. West's minivan blocks the road, idling. "Here Comes Your

Partner In Music" is painted on its front, "There Goes Your Partner In Music' " on the back. West gesticulates, laughs, shouts, organizes from the driver's seat. A late musician leaps down the hallowed entrance stairs, squeezes into the front seat, slams the door. An outsider motorist honks from behind. West finishes his conversation first, drives off quipping to Dumi on the corner. I spot Joana and Janet idling a block away, en route to the studios. Nhlanhla is quietly leaning against the wall, waiting for them, and for the others. Fakes, decked out in his shades, is bumming a cigarette and chatting up Ebony's backing female vocalists. A dude with a briefcase and a rocker's haircut passes into the building. Engineer Peter follows with his candy bar and his cigarettes. Mandla wants to borrow my "Porsche" to cycle all the way to Soweto, but instead he carries it inside and into the elevator, and we cruise up to Downtown Studios on the second floor.

Of the multitude of recording studios in contemporary Johannesburg, Downtown Studios is unmatched in terms of its historical lineage. Its heritage is partly mapped onto the city as landmarks. It is also scattered through the city and through rehearsal rooms and studios in the stories of veteran musicians and producers. "Gallos," they call the company. (The studios are subsidiary to Gallo Africa.) "When old Gallos. . . ." This lineage, memorialized in bits and pieces, lends to the studios a significance that no other studios in the city can equal.

At the 1992 Gallo Gold Awards dinner that honored musicians, producers, and engineers, a compilation CD was presented to each guest. It was specially issued to commemorate the sixty-fifth anniversary of the founding of the Gallo company. The CD is as sleek as a tuxedo—gold and silver print embosses the black disc. Its glossy, twenty-page booklet devotes six thousand words to the early history of the company (1926–1965), meticulously recorded by Gallo Music Publisher's archivist, Rob Allingham (Allingham 1992). It is largely an in-house address: most dinner guests were directly associated with the Gallo group; others attended as valued clients, business partners, and supporters. The narration instills a sense of awe at the company's historical achievements, tracing Gallo's expansion from a tiny local startup in 1926 into the major domestic industry power, from an enterprise dependent on shipping musicians overseas for recording to the owner of the largest state-of-the-art studio complex in South Africa by the end of the 1960s.[3]

Allingham masterfully weaves together strands of corporate history with the history of music styles, personalities, labels, and production process. He chronicles the significant advances in Gallo's studio operations and maps the various studio premises onto the layout of the city center. By dwelling on studio details, he etches the significance of the studio into the history of the Gallo enterprise at large, and he invigorates that history's citywide presence by pointing out its contemporary landmarks: a spot around the corner from the Rissik Street post office where Gallo built the first sub-Saharan African studio in 1928; 160 Market Street, where a better version replaced it in 1929; the corner of Troye and President Streets where a larger and fancier upgrade was installed in 1938 (Allingham 1992).

This studio remained Gallo's recording facility until 1969 when the company moved to the Newkirk Centre on the nearby corner of Kerk and Goud Streets, where there was room to expand the studio, build a second one, and upgrade the equipment.

With the shift of premises to the Newkirk Centre, the company had become the leading music enterprise in Johannesburg, with the best studio in town and satellite studios in Nairobi, Kenya, and Bulawayo, Southern Rhodesia. Gallo's basic corporate structure and character as it stands today was established (Allingham 1992). Here ends Allingham's celebratory narration.

Standby, I'm dropping this in. Two, three, four, rolling.

Short, round, radiant, Eric Gallo stands up. Like a loose pearl button on a velvet bow tie, he nods a gracious thanks. He nods again. The diners add whistles to their ovation.

The later 1960s and 1970s were marked by radical innovations in studio technology that challenged record companies to upgrade and expand their facilities in order to keep ahead of their rivals. Most notably the development of multitrack recording devices set new studio standards. Gallo's move to the Newkirk Centre had included the replacement of four-track consoles with sixteen-track ones, which in turn were superceded by twenty-four-track ones.

Furthermore, throughout the 1970s the domestic market for African music expanded enormously. This meant increased recording activities for existing studios as well as the entry of new studios into the busy recording market. Most of the newcomers—SATBEL, RPM, Takk Studios, and others—were independent of a wholesale record company. All were locally owned. In fact, the only multinational to have had direct holdings in a studio is South Africa is EMI, which had constructed a studio in Johannesburg in 1951.[4]

Of all the studios active during the 1970s and 1980s, RPM's and EMI's came to bear most significantly on the Gallo studio's profile. Gallo, RPM, and EMI studios produced the bulk of the local African product. They rivaled one another in size, sophistication, and productivity during two decades of intensely active recording business in South Africa.

EMI's studio flourished so well that in the early 1980s the company relocated its facility into industrial Johannesburg and expanded it into a then state-of-the-art, two-studio complex. With mounting pressure from the anti-apartheid movement to withdraw from South Africa's cultural and economic life, EMI renamed its facility Powerhouse Studios and established a new subsidiary, CCP Records, which would continue recording and marketing local black music.

RPM recording company, established in 1968, had constructed a large and grand studio complex in the late 1970s. It housed three studios conveniently located in downtown Johannesburg at the corner of Fox and Goud Streets, close to Gallo's Newkirk studios, in a building named RPM House. Like EMI's studios, RPM's were busy. In 1985, when Gallo acquired a hundred percent of RPM, it shifted most of its studio production over from the Newkirk Centre to these facilities, though they continued to use the Newkirk studios for some projects until the end of the decade.

In 1989, while retaining the studio facilities downtown at RPM House in easy reach for musicians, Gallo moved its offices from the Newkirk Centre out to the northern suburb of Rosebank. Two years later, in the midst of RPM House's exterior facelift, interior redecoration, and the revamping and updating of its studios to international standards of the time, up went a deco-like mauve-and-purple awning over the entrance and a new sign splashing out across the building's face: "Downtown Studios."

If multitrack innovations and a burgeoning local market for African music marked the 1970s and earlier 1980s, digital audio innovations and the opening up of a global market shaped South Africa's studio developments in the later 1980s and 1990s.

Digital recording technology prompted change in both low- and high-end sound production. On the low end, small studios with the facility to produce a competitive sound quality mushroomed in backyards, garages, offices, flats, and houses. They popped up in the suburbs as well as in city center high-rise spaces. Most of them were independent ventures offering eight- or sixteen-track and/or digital programming facilities for demos, jingles, soundtracks, budget albums, and wholly programmed projects. Most in the early 1990s were white owned and white managed.

In high-end production, digital innovations enhanced the sound quality and the efficiency of recording. However, the overhaul of studio equipment and the redesign of analog studios to accommodate new digital gear put significant strain on studio budgets.

The demise of the apartheid regime and transition to a nonracial democracy likewise had positive and negative repercussions for the local studios. These political developments reopened the international market to South Africans and South Africa to foreign interests, raising the competition for securing the best musical talent. At a time at which South African studios found themselves at critical political and technological junctures, they were caught by severe budgetary constraints. The South African music industry, like the economy at large, suffered (and suffers) severe financial stress in the late- and postapartheid eras. For the music industry, this happened at the very moment at which South Africa shed its pariah status and fully reentered an internationally competitive market.

Different enterprises made different decisions in the early 1990s. Gallo's closest competitor, Powerhouse Studios, decided to close down in 1993 rather than invest in the upgrade that would enable it to compete with digital studios worldwide. Outside the city, about a four-hour drive away, the broadcasting corporation of then "independent homeland" of Bophuthatswana had a superb R54 million (U.S. $17.8 million) studio complex.[5] It was the newest in the country and unrivaled in terms of acoustic design and electronic sophistication—at least until Downtown installed its SSL console. But in the early 1990s booking fees were higher than at Downtown and the studio was inconveniently located for everyday productions.[6] While the studio in Bophuthatswana moved to close, Gallo upgraded. In addition to being the first to establish a CD-manufacturing plant (CDT) in 1991, the company poured money into new studio recording gear.

From the 1960s to the 1990s, Gallo's studio facility had remained highly visible in a vibrantly competitive market. It had retained its profile through the talent it recorded, its drive to maintain a technological edge on its competitors, as well as through the voracious acquisition strategies of its mother company. Today Downtown Studios still stands out among the city's scattered facilities for its lineage, its size, its alignment with the largest music manufacturing and distribution enterprise in South Africa, its array of contemporary electronics, and its decision to upgrade its technology to internationally competitive standards.

While Gallo also owns Videolab, a smaller studio complex in Randburg, a satellite city just northwest of Johannesburg, the bulk of its recording takes place at Downtown Studios.[7] Videolab is a long taxi ride from the city center, from the corner of Goud and Fox, from Downtown Studios in the newly painted building, where we are riding in the elevator to the second floor.

I buzz at the studio's locked glass door. It could be any Johannesburg business entrance, save for the company logo tattooed on the door. Receptionist Florence or Liza lets us in. The reception area is couched, ashtrayed, potplanted, and hung with framed disc awards advertising the achievements of the engineers, the excellence of studio product, and the prestigious clientele they attract. Among the frames hang a couple of Scotty Awards won by past recording teams (engineer, producer, and artist), reminding the public that these studios have a history of excellence and of good creative relationships. Florence and Liza sit at a high semicircular desk that separates the professional studio space from the public. A door adjoins the desk. Music-biz professionals, visitors, and clients lean on the high desk while they wait to be let through the doors or for a worker to be summoned out of the studios. On the other side of the semicircular desk, on the other side of the adjoining door, workers chat, use the phone, check studio bookings, and talk over Florence and Liza to the professionals, visitors, and clients waiting on the public side.

Usually Florence or Liza lets me saunter through as I wave a greeting. Sometimes I slip by like a worker. Other days they check on my purpose before granting me entrance.

On the nonpublic studio side, resting artists lounge on the couches dotted about in the general thoroughfare area. More discs and LP jackets of successes that have recently come out of the studios decorate the walls. Periodically the jackets of new releases replace the older. Circulating the names and faces of their prominent clientele, they promise the possibility of similar stardom to their newer artists. Two first-timers on a session break check out the display. They mimic Bhekumuzi's stance on the cover of his LP, then break their pose and laugh.

To the right a kitchenette, with a coffeemaker, tea bags, and an invariably empty sugar basin is flanked by an eating area. On a crowded graffiti wall in the eating area, artists inscribe their aspiring names in glamour. We've made it into the studios! We'll please our fans and pervade new faraway places! We've recorded alongside the big stars on this wall—Lucky Dube, Splash, Stimela. During lunch on Isigqi Sesimanje's first recording day, Tefo clambered onto a chair and stretched tiptoe to reach the empty far corner of the wall. With Janet's scarlet lipstick he inscribed their name

for *hours* and *days* doing horoscopes and tarots and medical lines and now, now I'm doing Indian [horoscope] lines. All it is it's finger PT [physical training]—hey, that tape machine. . . ." He pecks repeatedly at his thigh with one finger while rolling his eyes and contorting his mouth. "Play and record—they make a mistake—rewind, drop them in, carry on. It's hideous! It's crazy! It's a total jungle!"

The bulk of the studio's income comes from recording "black stuff," as I heard many an engineer and white person in the music industry call the stream of low-budget productions geared toward the mostly regional, sometimes national market that provides most of studio's bookings.[13] Such productions usually take up to a week of studio time and use programmed rhythm and percussion tracks. They are worked by one sound engineer, though he is often interchangeable with the others. Trad, mbaqanga, gospel, and "bubblegum" (township pop) music generally fall into this category. Session musicians are frequently called in on the spur of the moment to do an overdub. The musicians are often not present during mixing. Sometimes even the producer is absent for some or almost all of the mixing. The engineer is usually not informed until the beginning of the first session about the particularities of a production.

The production of Isigqi Sesimanje's *Lomculo Unzima* fits squarely and clearly with the bulk of its genre as a run-of-the-mill studio project. It was recorded, mixed, and edited in seven days, 18–21 November 1991 and 30 March–1 April 1992. (Not all days were full.) Different production tasks were assigned to appropriate studio spaces: the basic backing was laid down in Studio 2; the overdubs and mixing happened in the smaller Studio 3. The editing was completed in the editing suite, downstairs, as is the procedure for all studio product. Peter Pearlson was assigned to engineer the project, with producer West Nkosi's approval. Neil Kuny substituted for him for some sessions. In the course of engineering, Neil also played some of percussion overdubs, such as the steel drum (on an electronic drum pad) on the title song, "Lomculo Unzima." Session musicians were called in midsession a couple of times to overcome hitches in the band's performance.

Standby . . . rolling. . . .
The backing male chorus resorts to one by one practice in front
of the microphone in the studio. Right—on. No, it's off. Again. It's
still out of tune. Again, three, four. "Where's Mandla?" asks
West, getting bored. "He'll sing it right quickly." He calls him up

at old Gallo's in Kerk Street while Bheki runs downstairs to check
if he's hanging out in the sun outside, with Fakes and Ebony's
backing singers and Harare.

The somewhat haphazard organization of *Lomculo Unzima*'s studio production—an extended intercession, shifts in location, and engineer and musician substitutions midproduction—would be far less likely to occur during the course of prominent projects. Musicians had minimal input during mixing; few were even present. They were, of course, all present and on time the morning of the first day of recording.

Take I The Studio as Fetish

Open the door to the left of Florence and Liza's reception desk. Head down the tunnel-like passage for the double doors at the end. Unless the red "session in progress" light above the double door prohibits interruptions, enter the black box that is Studio 3.[14] It is an enclosed space, a dark-bounded interior, a private space with a secret life. Its physical placement in the company's floor plan and its architectural design separate the studio from the outside world.

Inside, the studio's decoration and the specialized objects and their arrangement within the space lend it its distinction. Black walls, low black ceiling, and overhead lighting make the small, square control-room space close in on itself. The previous sessions' cigarette smoke sits invisibly on your eyebrows. The electronic equipment reflects in the double-paned, vacuum-sealed windows connecting/separating the control room and the two recording booths. The reflections cast more techno images into the multiply machined studio space. Technology fills the floor area and stacks up against the walls. "U sho ukuthi yonke le'mishini uma kurekhodwa iyasebenza? Yonke le'mishini?" (Are you sure all these machines work when something is recorded? *All* these machines?) asks guitarist-producer Hansford Mthembu. The machines gleam magnificently. Their newness and sophistication seem to balance the space on the edge of the sonic future. Is this a mirror image of Apollo and Sputnik with their cramped and awesome technical interiors?

Iconicity is there to be noticed in the look of the studio. Panels of instruments—as in cockpits, luxury cars, rockets, and space stations—situate the studio alongside similar developments of the military-industrial complex. Music-makers' talk about the studio in terms of space research metaphorizes a particular relation of subjects to instrumentation and subjects to time. That space capsules take precedence over luxury cars and cockpits as the metaphorical reference is due to the way space has historically been presented to the public as the site of the future and how space scientists have been presented as the leaders preparing the way to that future through their technological design and operation.[15]

Phenomenological links between space travel and other kinds of movement enabled by the studio are also there to be sensed and elaborated by those who work in its space. Indeed, by means of successful recording, music-makers may well rocket upward through the star system, just as they may travel out to new places in the listening, dancing, sociopolitical world. And while working within the confines of the studio itself, they may be propelled into inner worlds, expressive worlds—art worlds—in the process of composition and production.[16] All right, gents, let's see where we're going.

Inner worlds? Elements of the studio's design and decoration point to the existence of interiors within interiors in the physical enclosure that they make and mark. The presence of these complex interiors play a part in generating an atmosphere of mystery and hidden potency, for they can be revealed—always only in part—to those who know how to access them, while they are hidden from ordinary view.

I'm isolating that track.

Master maskandi Thembinkosi Ntuli is overdubbing his own backing vocals on his self-produced recording. His singing style is taut and nasal. When in top form, he glides on and off tones like a swinging acrobat in an extravagant circus. But tonight he's struggling with the tuning, for the chorus lies awkwardly in his upper vocal range.

Take. Erase. Take. Erase. Lee directs and advises from the engineer's chair. He gets up and dims the lights in Ntuli's booth. 'Let's get some atmosphere in here!' he quips. He darkens the edges and back of the control room. The world outside disappears; the extremities of the studio hide in shadow. Now only Lee listening piercingly, and the mixing console, will be illuminated.

Around the black walls of Studio 3's control room dances an airsprayed luminous yellow, pink, and green path. Scattered graffiti-like lines depict the scientific transformation of sound from airwaves through the recording process to magnetic flux. It is as minimalist a representation of the recording process as a look at the studio is of its intricate sonic workings or as a dissection of its electronic workings is of its artistic expressive activity.

It is day one, session one, of Isigqi Sesimanje's recording.

In Studio 2 engineer Peter Pearlson and West are laying backing tracks with the instrumentalists and the drum box. Mkhize and Mzwandile, the guitar and bass players, are stuffed into the smaller sound booth with their amps. The women—Jane, Joana, and Janet—and Michael sing along in the larger booth, rehearsing into the microphone. They each cover one ear with a headphone cup. The second cup hangs open on their necks, leaving their other ear free for in-booth communication. The singers and players watch one another through the glass door partitioning their booths.

A plate bored with holes for mike and amp chord jacks is set into the front wall of the recording booths, ready to transmit audio lines into the control room. The space is carpeted, air conditioned, double-doored. Soundproofing pads the walls in sophisticated patches, visually drawing attention to the sonic difference of the space. On the ceiling, panels slant at odd angles to enhance the acoustics.

In the control room, West leans his elbows on the mixing console, listening, watching the musicians through the wide double-paned and vacuum-sealed windows that separate the control room and the booths. Peter sits alongside him listening, watching likewise, gesturing an entry to the musicians. He reaches across the enormous desk spread with knobs and buttons and sliding sound-level controls to tweak a button on the far side. He hawkeyes the lit gauges of the VU meters. He flips a switch.

The pair are seamed in between the mixing console in front, the outboard effects rack behind, the telephone, the ashtray, the remote control for the tape deck, the MIDI rack holding the drum synthesizer machine, the MIDI clock/tape synchronizing converter, a trigger converter, a sequencer or two perhaps, a thru box or a patcher. These loose components are all stacked on wheeled trolleys, drawn in close enough for Peter to swivel and reach. Signal-processing devices are sleekly stacked, floor-to-rib height, in the outboard effects console, hierarchically ordered in terms of the frequency of their use: echo, decay, delay, and reverberation machines; limiters, expanders, compressors; phasing and flanging units; exciters and pitch shifters; graphic and parametric equalizers and noise gates. The multinationals are wired into the studio system. They name their indelible presence—Lexicon, Roland, Yamaha, Korg, Technics, Amcron—on the faces of their products.

Along the side wall of the studio are more pieces of equipment, more lights, more dials. The latest Dolby SR/A noise-reduction machines are packed into a rack as tall as Peter. Alongside, at waist height, sits the mastering tape recorder and the multitrack recording deck. Two-inch tape wound onto a large, fat reel snakes around tension levers, past the recording head, onto a second reel. If the new portable Tascam DAT recorder is used instead, it is placed on top of the outboard effects console along with any keyboard in use.

Jane, Joana, Janet, and Michael's voices, Mkhize's guitar, Mzwandile's bass, and the MIDI-ed rhythm tracks rain down from the huge speakers mounted high on the wall in front of the console. The speakers are angled downward. On the ledge of the main recording console, middle-sized monitors mimic the large ones. Between them sit two tiny ones that replicate the sound of a cheap ghetto blaster.

My two microphones, perched below the little monitors, face West and Peter. I hang over the desk, facing them too. Sometimes I move to the back of the studio and lean on the rib-height console with the keyboard players and any cruising visitors. Sometimes I perch on West's or Peter's shoulders like a parakeet.

Mandla, the drummer; Bethwell the band's regular bass player whom West has replaced with Mzwandile for some of the sessions; and Phatiswe, Oscar, and Bheki, the backing vocalist dancers, lounge on the couch against the back wall. They watch, they listen, they chat, they read the Sowetan newspaper.

Stand by, I'm dropping this in.

West and his musical colleagues from the old days are recording a sax jive CD for the international market.[17] *West is the producer and principal artist. I want to listen in one day. West hesitates. He defers to the others sitting around the canteen table, lunching on goat's head and stiff maize porridge. 'Why, of course she can come in,' answers Hansford. 'She's part of the family!' Hansford turns to tease me: 'Do you like ipapa nembuzi [stiff porridge and goat's meat]?'*

The studio is remote and exclusive. It is closed to outsiders except for haphazard, enticing ingressions like mine and those of friends of the music-makers who might drop in for a session or a moment. 'If the studios had their shit together, you'd never have got in!' Wry engineer Neil half laughs, warning that 'overseas your story would be different, hey!' As Michael Taussig writes about the image of Cuna women, their very inaccessibility to outsiders (foreigners), which is controlled by mediating figures (Cuna men in Taussig's case, studio workers in this case) who make access tauntingly erratic, invests them with aura (1993, 182). Cuna women and recording studios are invested with something potent, unknowable, and desirable.

What is this something? In the words of Susan Stewart writing on miniatures, a "thing" with a "secret life," if opened up, can reveal "a set of actions and hence a narrativity and history outside the given field of perception" (1993, 54).

Take 2 The Studio's Technology Fetishized

It is not a long leap to link Apollo and Sputnik and a space station on the moon to the studio via the look of things. But the studio's awe emanates not only from the spatial encapsulation and glossy technics that promise travel, discovery, excellence, and accumulation in their design. Housed inside its machines are the fetishized worlds of science and sound. Just as the studio's technology plays a part in fetishizing the sound it produces, so do the complexity and beauty of the sound in turn intensify the aura of the technology.[18]

Fast-forward to day five, session five of Isigqi Sesimanje's recording, on 30 March 1992: In Studio 3 engineer Neil Kuny and West have just triple-tracked the backing male vocals on the first chorus of the song "South Africa Is on Fire." The backing singers—Phatiswe, Oscar, and Bheki—cluster around their microphone, listening through their headphones for further instruction from West and Neil, and watching through the window for their gestures. The women, Bethwell, and Michael hang around the control room. West decides to check the newly recorded section. They listen through the huge speakers up on the wall.

Joana enthuses, "Uyezwa ukuthi bayicula kamnandi njani? Imnandi!" (Can you hear how nicely they sing it? It's nice!)

West and Neil discuss how they will sequence this chorus of the male voices to insert wherever it's needed in the song, rather than recording it anew each time. Joana chats on. She stands alongside the MIDI rack.

"Eyi! Lento"—she loosens her folded arms and points at the MIDI clock on the top deck—"ungaze uyibone incane, iphethe yonke inhlobo yento ezakurekhodwa manje sikulekwaya." (Eyi! This thing, you might see it small as it is, [but] it is carrying all different types of things in it, which are going to be recorded. Now we are on this choir.)

With the choir triple-tracked, nine men's voices are captured in that small machine. But Joana implies more than this: nine men's voices, plus twelve women's voices (their verses also being triple-tracked), a solo voice, and all the instrumental backing now reside in that small machine.

Neil and West move on with the session. They turn to the weak bass drum sound. West wants more weight in it. They extract it from the small box to change its frequency profile and perhaps to add effects.

The MIDI clock does not actually house the sounds to which Joana refers. Rather it is a central node for entering information into the MIDI system. It synchronizes the digitally processed sounds with the sounds recorded on tape. However, its positioning for quick and easy access right next to the console at Neil's right hand and its constant use readily give it the appearance of being the central housing unit for the recorded sound, from Joana's point of view. For her, there is a whole sonic world packed into that sleek machine, which registers the presence of its precious contents only as digitized figures in a tiny control window and as a steady, red "power on" light the size of a pinhead. It is a world to which Joana can point, but that she cannot enter herself. This sonic world encoded in complex electronics is more extensive than the object within which it resides. It is invisible but sensed to be of enormous proportion. The mathematical and electronic processes that encode it are as sophisticated as the face of their component's casing is simple. This interior world—the extensive and ephemeral residing in the complex and mathematical, yet presented as the small, intact, and simple—imbues the technology with an affecting presence. Its presence is further enhanced by the complex user interface that surrounds it. The multiple steps required for its operation (and these steps are far from transparent) and the elaborate lexicon that accompanies them inhibit contact with the object by all but the specialist. Technical lexicons enshroud objects and already opaque processes in mystery.

Standby.
  "There's the DBX. These are the URIs, which should go across the desk. Six! I wasn't using six. SCAMPS—which go across the guitars. What?!"

Peter sucks in his lips, creases his eyebrows together.
"Okay. Vocal is going into thirty-three."

Take 2 interrupted in favor of a third more similar to Take 1.

Take 3 Studio Sound Fetishized

Open the door to the left of Florence and Liza's reception desk. Head down the tunnel-like passage. The carpet creeping up the walls muffles your footsteps. You can hear music stopping and starting, stopping and starting behind those double acoustic doors at the end of the passage. Enter the music box that is Studio 3. It is a space of sonic control, clarity, and separation, a space in which you notice yourself hearing and you miss the everyday reverb on your voice.

The acoustics mark the studio as a space out of the ordinary. But its distinction is not only derived from its focus around a sense other than the eye, the sense privileged in the metalanguage of the everyday (Stoller 1989; Minh-Ha 1991; Taussig 1993; Feld 1996b). The studio also draws enchantment from the very quality of the sense it privileges. For "sound is a very special modality. We cannot handle it. We cannot push it away. We cannot turn our backs to it. We can close our eyes, hold our noses, withdraw from touch, refuse to taste. We cannot close our ears though we can partly muffle them. Sound is the least controllable of all sense modalities" (Jaynes 1976, quoted in Alten 1986). In their notion of musical groove, Keil and Feld extend this idea of sound as an uncontrollable modality to one of an infusing, embodied social sensibility (Schutz 1967; Keil and Feld 1994). Because sound as groove is participatory, feelingful, and experiential, its power is essentially unpredictable, unprogrammatic, in a sense, uncontrollable. Both the purely physiological uncontrollability of sound that Jayne recognizes and its social and sensual unboundedness, which Keil and Feld discuss, imbue sound with a particular—and heightened— quality.

The studio both houses and (re)produces sound's physiological, social, and sensual dimensions. The material structure of the studio seals the space acoustically; studio technology can open up and shut down the sounds within it. Engineers control and manipulate the science of sound in order to release and play with that social/sensual uncontrollability. Their function is to harness and fix sounds momentarily in new combinations in order to create new grooves and thereby, eventually, to prompt new social and sensual experiences for those who listen (see Bendix 2000).

Studios regulate and optimize the physical and physiological conditions of listening in multiple ways. They are designed to isolate the internal sonic environment from the noise of the outside world.[19] The hubbub of the vicinity is dampened or extinguished. The world out there sounds far away.

I'm dropping this in. . . .
The telephone shrieks like a panic-stricken cricket noticing it's crouched near the console. "Hello?" Peter flicks down the master fader to hear the faint telephone voice. His takeout chicken-and-cheese has arrived at reception.

Inside the studio, the facility is insulated as tightly as possible from the noise of its own operation, for both recording and monitoring purposes. Clean sound separation is an ideal in studio design, from the overall structure of the rooms down to the minute electronic circuitry. Ambient sound from such sources as the ventilation is minimized through design and specialized insulating materials. Soundproofing in the booths and control room blocks out as much external sound as possible and absorbs unwanted internal frequencies. Specialized double-paned acoustic windows visually connect booths and the control room, while blocking the sound. Additionally, in a booth large enough to record more than one source at a time, movable, acoustically insulated baffles partition the area to limit leak-through from the sound source of one microphone into another.[20] To further minimize the effects of ambient sounds and leak-through, gating circuits are installed on microphone lines. These amplifier circuits cut out all signals below a selected threshold, thereby cutting out low-level noise. They are controlled from the outboard effects rack behind the engineer.

In addition to isolation and insulation procedures, other structural and technological features reproduce and monitor sound with minimal sonic disturbance. Music studios are designed to be acoustically dry.[21] An ideal control room is one that is itself acoustically neutral and uniform, so that there is as small a discrepancy as possible between a sound as it is laid onto tape and as it is heard through the monitors. Acoustic uniformity ensures that the quality of the sound is not affected by the spatial positioning of the listener or the live sound source. Sounds produced within this acoustic space can be isolated and listened to for and in themselves with minimal intervention, interruption, contamination, or transformation. Individual high-end headphones can further isolate external noise. The sound piped into each set can be individually mixed to accommodate a single listener's aural balance and volume needs.

Within this fantastically regulated sonic environment, by means of more technology, the infinitely "secret life" of sounds inside space, space inside sounds, and sounds inside sounds can be revealed. The studio becomes a space of sonic virtuosity, of movement, of experimentation, of creative expression let loose through the seemingly mad science of electronics. That is to say, by means of electronic processes that seem as impenetrable as sound itself, one voice is turned into many or into Mickey Mouse; dry sounds echo like a cavern; real becomes more than real; matter is transformed into something more than matter, into symbol, feeling, and aesthetic form.

"You can just take voices," West says. "You can make them
sound like Mickey Mouse — you can make them sound anyhow
you want them to. That is a producer's job."

Composite or single sounds seemingly fixed on tape or captured in computers can be minutely manipulated. Peter can control every sound parameter by means of the electronic technology available in the studio. He can manipulate the sound as a whole, or he can dissect and change it track by track or motive by motive. He can erase, shift, add, or precisely repeat any musical feature within the backing. In the mixing process, he can position each track acoustically in any given relation to the other tracks by cutting or boosting their relative volumes, channeling them to the left and/or right farther or nearer from the center for a stereo playback, and adding effects to and shaping the individual complex waveforms of their component tones in order to give a particular sense of dimension, color, and form to the overall sound.

"I like space in music," he tells me. "When I produce I try to create as much space as I can, in the tracks, because I find that you get a lot of relief from a track that is enormous and then just breaks down into absolutely nothing — there's all this space there, and it just gives you a chance to feel what is happening in the track." Peter can manipulate the wave components of a tone in multiple ways. He can play with its shape in time to effect textural features such as the attack and decay of tones. He can alter its fundamental frequency and hence its pitch. He can play with the composite frequency profile in order to shape timbre. He does so by extracting particular frequencies or frequency bands from within the composite signal or by increasing or diminishing their prominence. He can add effects to a tone or series of tones. He has at his electronic fingertips multiple versions of multiple effects programmed in the outboard gear—the signal processing devices—and linked through the MIDI systems into the programmed and recorded tracks.

With this facility, the life within a single sound can be revealed to an extent impossible outside in the everyday. With the studio's scientific precision, the technical skills of its engineers and the aural sophistication of its artists (including the engineers), sounds can be teased out of their surrounding sounds. From the macro to the micro, they are separated out for analysis, reworked, then reinserted in a transformed whole.

Studio music-makers with their superior aural competence can imagine composite sonic wholes, new sound worlds, and set about creating them with the technical expertise of their sound engineer. They can hear the details of complex sounds and set about reshaping them.[22] They can manipulate waveforms in order to give the impression of weight, density, movement, and space. That is to say, they can manipulate scientific technological processes and sound for metaphysical effect. I like space in music. Space here, inside the tracks, is at once a material band on a magnetic tape, a metaphor of that tape band extended to describe digital "space" in a computer, and an illusion and feeling of space.

By its function and the quality of its form, the studio marks sound as privileged, fantastic, enchanted, and enchanting.

Take 4 Studio Artistry Fetishized

Like the patchbay to the board, the studio is the nerve center of the creative process, the mad scientist, the head of the industry, which 'you'll never be able to figure out by observing.'

Sometimes I irritated engineer Neil, just staring at what he was doing, this face always there, in front of him, behind him, over his shoulder, squeezed into an unused space. Not that I was in the way, he reassured me. 'But I reckoned that however much you watched you'd never know what's *really* going on. You could never know what's in my head when I make adjustments on the desk.' I would never be able to detail the creative thought of an artist scientifically analyzing the sound components of what he hears on the monitors, choosing from multiple options for how

Neil Kuny, Music Master Studios, Johannesburg, 2002. *Photo by TJ Lemon.*

to improve it, and registering the changes through microelectronic ana-log or digital adjustments on the equipment in front of him. What does he hear? How does he translate it into science? Why does he boost the upper mids on the DI (direct input) bass line, change the vocal-plate settings on the solo voice, at this moment, in this combination, to these degrees?[23]

I cannot know his head. It is another unknowable, illimitable interior present in the studio and essential to music production. It is a significant phenomenological studio space, similar to the physical and metaphysical realms I have described. His head is a Cuna woman, to whom he grants me, as ethnographer, some alluring access until it appears I might claim to know and describe his creative self.

While I can account for and measure some of the adjustments he makes on the sound gear and console, I cannot necessarily anticipate or explain his choices. Neil is so deeply immersed in a set of engineering practices that his hands can race intuitively across the outboard gear. Much of his manipulation of the controls is felt, learned but not or no longer rational-ized. He plays, improvises, and experiments with the technical options his instrument offers, much as performers do with their skills and sonic materials.

Though I cannot know his head, nor systematize his musical-technological body knowledge, I can link him as agent and voice into the creative process and trace the pathways of composition through him as through the other studio realms I have characterized. The sound passes through his artistic sensibility into the technology of the mixing console; transformed into magnetic flux, it passes onto studio tape, then off it, out again through the monitors mounted on the wall, and back into the body. I like spaces in music. There's all this space there, and it just gives you a chance to feel what is happening in the track. While each space is of a different order since each resides in a different kind of material body, they are all similarly imagined in terms of their formal qualities and spatial dimensions. The musical shape of the sound is transformed in the course of flowing.

The merging of these sites for moments and the flows between them are present in the conversation of music-makers, in their perceptions of what it is they do, and their presentations of how they do it.

Fast-forward again.

It is the seventh and last day of Isigqi Sesimanje's recording, 1 April 1992. West and Peter are mixing.

Peter reaches for the logging chart to set up the board for "South Africa is on Fire."

"Heyi! It's very difficult, this one. It's not easy!" comments West as he anticipates the work ahead.

Peter agrees. They have already programmed and overdubbed the song extensively. Janet's original song, titled "Omhlaba wonke," has been translated in part into English, retitled, and transformed lyrically, rhythmically, and in its arrangement during the recording process.

"I've changed the drums, everything, you know. I've changed a lot of things," West begins to explain. *His mind is in the song.* "Now we must start putting them back together. The problem is I did not have the whole cassette for these things, to work out lines."[24] *The song is on the demo cassette, in its tracks.* "So I had to work out lines every night, you know, by thinking, you know, imagining the whole thing." *The song is in West's mind. It exists in his creative sensibility as an ephemeral entity.*

He chuckles a little. Peter is still transferring information from the logging chart onto the console controls. He's not really listening to West's patient rambling.

"So, I'm not sure where we're going!" West muses on. "But I'll pick it up. . . . And then also this one we need to pick a spot [vacant recording track] again."

"What? To clear?" asks Peter, suddenly alerted.

"Ja, to clear."

"Okay," replies Peter, "maybe we use the computer, let's see."

The song also exists in the recording tracks and in the computer. They will empty out some of its sonic clutter to make way for new signals, for new ideas. Increasingly, the computer is becoming the mind of the studio; it controls the sound-shaping tools and stores and manipulates creative ideas. However much you observed, you'd never really be able to figure out what's going on.

While Peter leaves the studio for a moment, West turns to talk to me.

"This one is very difficult!" he says again.

"'South Africa on Fire'?" I ask.

Then in Zulu he repeats the same story to Jane, Michael, Joana, and Janet.

Reshaped each night by the thoughtful inspiration of an artist churning over forms and ideas, the song eludes him in the daylight of everydayness, returning to him only in the interior presence of the studio with its technical facility to realize the nuance of his ideas in sound.

"Yes, it's difficult! The problem is I never had a cassette to set it up, you see," he explains to the musicians.

Hansford who is hanging around in the studio backs his friend up with intermittent sounds of agreement as West continues.

"Now I was building it up every night. When I get home, I try it, I work on it. Now some things I forget, and [then] remember when I'm here. Eyi! But to put them together—I've laid them down—but to put them together, it's difficult, I'm telling you! This thing is very difficult! It's not easy! Because now I have to open it up [in order to change the patterns again]. And I don't know which spot I'm going to find."

Jane is thirsty. She diverts the conversation and goes to get a cup of tea.

West presents his own creativity as interiorized, elusive, as unending, as part of his artistic personhood, and as an essential part of the production process. As Howard Becker writes, those activities that are regarded as gifted, as requiring an artistic sensibility to conduct them with excellence, are the "core activities" that are taken to distinguish an artwork from industrial product or natural object within the ideology of capital. This distinction is accompanied by certain status and privileges awarded to the artist (Becker 1982, 16). The charisma of the gifted persona, when present in the studio, lends its quality also to the space(s) of artistic production.

West's story notices distinct spaces occupied in the process of creating and producing expression—his head or imagination, the tape, the form of the song itself, which must be opened up again, the interior of the technology. There are tensions that at times fracture these spaces: "it is very difficult" to hold them together and to negotiate the moves between them. For example, West says it would be easier to rework the song in conjunction with hearing the cassette, albeit a demo of poor recording quality. He has to work with Peter "to find a spot," using the computer. This pull between the self-sufficient interiorized personhood of the artist and factors external to him or her that need to be negotiated is always present in the production process.[25]

Stand by, I'm dropping this in. . . .
I want to listen in in the studio one day. West hesitates.
'Because we are composing,' he says. As if by witnessing his
compositional process I would intrude too far into his creative
interior; as if I then might expose and disseminate his artistic
secrets and thereby publicly deconstruct his aura, lay him open to
imitation, and diminish his uniqueness.[26] *He defers to the others*
sitting around the canteen table. 'Why of course she can come
in,' answers Hansford. 'She's part of the family!' 'Do you like
ipapa nembuzi?'

It is in the momentary merging of these spaces—the mind roving into the song, the song into the mind or into the figurative and literal spaces in the machine and on the tape—as well as in the fracturing of these spaces and in the movement between them that creativity resides.

Mix

Downtown Studios's historical lineage, its size, its position in the industry, its array of contemporary electronics, and the hits produced there, all bring renown to the facility, for professionals and outsiders alike. That history is celebrated, documented, and disseminated by Gallo Africa itself.

In addition, the studio is made to feel special by the people who make music within it. For them, it is more than a functional physical space: creative agents work it into another status that derives from and contributes to the aesthetic and symbolic value of the sounds they produce.[27]

The structural design of the studio and music-makers' discourse about it together constitute the space as magical and as a fetish. The basis for the depiction of the studio in this way arises from the idea that there are complex interiors housed within it. The interior of the place itself, the internal workings of electronic machines, the components of sounds, and the interiority of the artist are each enchanting in and of themselves. Together, they enhance the aura of the studio as a whole while they are mutually enhanced.

Once inside, the specialness of the artists and of artistry itself is made palpable for being set in the studio's rarefied atmosphere. In turn, the magic of the studio space is dialogically animated by the enigma of the artists. West considers excluding me from his studio session in order to preserve the studio's aura. The studio's creative processes would be disclosed, the studio's aura would be unsettled, and West's compositional processes would be demystified by the intrusion of an outsider. He protects his own mystique as a musician as well as the symbolic value of the studio by closing it to outsiders. Similarly, it is to infuse the atmosphere of the studio's space into the sound of Ntuli's singing that Lee dims the recording booth and control room lights when Ntuli is struggling to lay down fine vocals. He wants the feeling of the darkened room to inspire focus and quality in Ntuli's performance.

The lure of the studio, like that of the fetish, lies in the coupling of the promise of the revelation of its secrets with the knowledge of their infinite unknowability (Taussig 1993). Within the material body of the studio and of the bodies within it—its technology, its artists, and its sound— there is a wealth of ever-discoverable pathways. The boundaries of the creative possibilities in the studio are unfixed, unknown, and unending. There is always another possible way to change the sound. This is both a physical and metaphysical condition.

In these four takes, I have presented the mysteriousness of the studio as a phenomenon. There is a set of conditions that renders it possible to experience the space in this way. But is the studio only mysterious to people who don't have better knowledge? Is it mysterious because people in power make it that way? Or does it only appear to be mysterious?

Remix

Control-room silence is punctuated by the patter of fingers pecking at electronic pads. Neil is searching for the right electronic coordinates on the MIDI clock/tape sync converter. He needs to program a flute line from the Yamaha DX7 keyboard to repeat through the song "Lomculo Unzima" in selected places. West, sax veteran Lemmy Special Mabaso, and guitarist-producer Hansford Mthembu—old buddies from the sax jive and mbaqanga heyday times—hang out in the control room. Hansford produces for Rainbow Records, a small independent company that markets trad, mbaqanga, jive, isicathamiya, and gospel on small budgets usually in small studios for the domestic market, and he has toured internationally as a guitarist.[28] He stares at the gear in this freshly revamped control room.

"Are you sure," he asks in Zulu, "that all these machines work during recording? *All* these machines?!"

Since the mid-1960s, Hansford has recorded in many a studio on his guitar and directed many a studio session. Behind his ironic questioning response to this studio glitz lurks perhaps—likely—a critique of the way the excess of contemporary technology exacerbates the power discrepancies in studio practice.[29] Note that West and Hansford are differently positioned in terms of their authority and status as producers in the music industry and also therefore in terms of their material and cultural capital.

So, while Hansford listens from his figurative distance, West takes up the cue to casually display his technological competence and familiarity with the recording procedure in this up-to-date control room, thereby enhancing his own status and that of the studio.

"Ja, [we use all these machines] during mixing," says West. He starts to name them didactically. He names one (inaudible on tape) then he points to the MC500. "You cue the drums here, then here." He points to another machine, but Lemmy interrupts him.

"I don't think there are any studios like the ones here [at Downtown Studios], where I am now!" exclaims Lemmy. He expresses amazement at the new facility, but in so doing he brings attention to the fact that he is familiar with other studios with which he can compare this one. His remark reminds his listeners that, like West, he is professionally experienced in the studio world.

"Ja, you see, these ones are the leaders [in the field]!" replies West, and Lemmy agrees with him.

West continues his authoritative assertions, gesturing toward the outboard gear rack nearest him, stacked up with effects units. "This is the place for the echo."

On the side, Janet grumbles to Jane that with all this chatting
[among the men], no work will get done.

The triumvirate continues their naming play, waiting for Neil to settle the flute line.

Now Lemmy and Hansford join West in a jostle for the positioning as expert, or at least for a share in that status. Lemmy points to the limiters and reverb components. "This is the place for the vocals," he asserts.

West's affirmative response overlaps with Lemmy.

"Ja, the vocals, you see—" West starts to explain. And Hansford, specifying a programmable function on the reverb machine, overlaps with them both, adding "vocal plate."

West continues "—all these things, all these things, you see. The instruments are individuals there, which means your instrument must play into here—." Gesturing from stack to stack of electronic gear, he elaborates on his list. He heightens the rarefied presence of the studio by implying in his performance that the list is inexhaustible. At the same time, he distinguishes himself from an awestruck outsider and firmly claims a place among the wizard experts on the inside by his passé rolling off of names.

Neil fast-forwards through the flute line. Synth flute notes tumble over the talk.

December 1991

Engineer Lee Short is becoming exasperated. He's going cold turkey on cigarettes, and the evening is fraying a little at the edges. This Zulu trad session threatens to drag on into the depths of the midweek night.

Master maskanda and GMP producer Thembinkosi Ntuli is producing his own album of his own songs (with assistance from Makhosonke Mhlongo, as a rather silent co-producer).[30] He's overdubbing his own backing vocals, triple-tracking each of the three voices on these choral interjections. His singing style is taut and nasal. When in top form he glides on and off tones like a swinging acrobat in an extravagant circus.

But tonight he's struggling with the tuning, for the chorus lies awkwardly in his upper vocal range.[31]

Take. Erase. Take. Erase. Rehearse cold. Rehearse with the backing. Take. No, it's out. Cut, rewind, try again. Better. Not good enough. Rehearse. Take. Playback. Next. Take. Erase. Lee sighs. He directs and advises from the engineer's chair. He mumbles that he's not hired on as a producer. The tuning's still out, second time around on the same vocal part.

Lee gets up and dims the lights in Ntuli's booth. He blackens the edges

100 Sound of Africa!

and back of the control room. 'Let's get some atmosphere in here!' he quips to whoever is listening. Now only his mixing console is illuminated from above, as if to draw Ntuli's focus. As if to re-mark the special quality of the studio, to regenerate its distinction by highlighting its distinctive features—its interiority and its electronics—at a moment in which poor performance within the space threatens to dissemble its aura. As if to re-mind that it is a domain reserved for trained, rehearsed, expert insiders. As if to assert his own presence.

'OK, I'm dropping you in again,' Lee instructs Ntuli. 'Rolling! One, two, three.'

18 November 1991

Coordinating the guitar, bass, organ, and MC500 entries on the introduction of "Lomculo Unzima" is proving difficult. Peter starts recording but cuts whenever an entry is sloppy. They rehearse or take again. The stopping and starting is confusing. Tefo stands behind the outboard gear. His fingers are poised anxiously on the keyboard, which rests on the top of the outboard console. He mumbles to Makhosini, "Asisayiboni ipanya-panya—bavele bayipanya-panya bona" (We don't see the blinking [of the controls]—they are the ones who can see the blinking). Peter and West check on the blinking; Tefo's mumble passes by unnoticed.

Once the voice of Joana (and those of her co-singers) has been recorded into that "small machine," it takes on a life of its own. Though delighted by the sound she hears and awed by the machine encapsulating it, she is now separated from this instance of her own voice and distanced from the controls over it. Drawing on their experience and knowledge, Peter and West could conceivably manipulate her recorded voice electronically until it is no longer recognizably hers. Such play is sanctioned by the roles they hold in the studio. Though her voice is there (somewhere inside the small machine), it is no longer accessible to her without the assistance of that machine's technician, Peter. For all music-makers in the studio, the internal workings of the machine and the look of the figurative world it holds are, of course, equally invisible. But immediate access to the sound world is differentially available.

The magician-like status of the studio's technicians increases concomitantly with the expansion of aura of the studio and its technology. This is measured differentially according to the training and experience of the music-makers and the division of labor during production. Those most awed and alienated by the studio environment are the musicians, particularly those with less recording experience. Tefo, paid as a session musician, criticizes his producer and engineer from the bottom of the labor hierarchy. Though they are counted among the performing elite of their generation, West, Lemmy, and Hansford vie amongst themselves for the authorial advantage on the grounds of their recording studio experience. Jane and Janet are tangled in a triple disadvantage: their gendered status maps onto their spatial position (they are shut off at this moment in the recording booth) and onto studio labor differences, where they are artists, not producers. They wait for the producers to finish their talk. Joana, a vocalist rather than an engineer, has none of the knowledge or the authority required to manipulate the electronic controls to play back her voice on her own accord.[32]

Direct access to technology is determined by the division of labor and experience within the studio. But these professional asymmetries are exacerbated by other social divisions. Lack of technical knowledge, technical lexicons, and English competence, as well as the absence of shared poetic reservoirs or listening repertoires to draw into the conversation, place additional barriers between music-makers and their studio interiors and between experts, laborers, and capital. These asymmetries are symptoms of a race and class history. "I've never recorded a Sotho band who could speak one word of English," explains engineer Peter to me in an interview. "They come straight from the mine or straight from the hills or straight from the *kraal*, in their blankets and with their big sticks.[33] They walk into the studio and they *do* not have a *clue*—not a clue—it's like an average person walking into a spaceship. It is that foreign to them, because they come from the hills and they herd cattle and they chisel coal from a rock face, and that is what they know. And they've got their music—a very, very simple people. So they are told to sit there and play. And when the engineer or the producer says, 'rolling,' they play, and when the hand is put up, they stop. That is it, and then they go home. Then they will hear the album—they don't know how it works, they don't know how records are made, they don't know how the signal is transferred through electronic transducers into electrical signal and stored as magnetic flux on tape and that is transferred onto disc in terms of vibration or transferred onto cassette—that doesn't mean a thing, as long as it kicks ass."

Punch in
> "They stayed on the moon, with the flag—," Thami recounts.
> "—just so they could say, 'We were here'!" affirms Fakes.
> "And remember, they're going to Mars—it's the things on

By imagining the Sotho musicians he works with as black, rural workers, Peter imagines his self and his own positioning in the social and professional world. He separates 'traditional' African musicians from the world of technology and machines (even from mining machinery, in his image of coal-chiseling natives), from the world of language (they neither say anything nor can communicate in English, the studio lingua franca), from the world of logic (the recording process is unknowable to them), and from the world of modern authority (they function in the mechanical, modern world by following studio orders). They are images of a knowable and singular primitive (Torgovnick 1990).

Peter speaks in good faith, with respect for Sotho musicality, and out of frustration over the professional and creative constraints placed on his own engineering excellence by the kind of recording projects and technologically inexperienced clientele on which a South African studio necessarily depends. Nevertheless, his essentializing discourse perpetuates inequality in everyday social interaction in and out of the studio and exposes the social, especially racialized, mechanisms through which studio practice is rarefied. In explaining the musicians' professional ignorance and studio inexpertise in terms of their race, class, and ethnicity as constructed by apartheid, he justifies and stultifies the divisions of labor and authority in the studio. (Peter does not condone apartheid ideology. He describes this studio situation as a consequence of the history of apartheid.)

Punch in
*"Heyi! These are white people's things!" exclaims keyboardist
Tefo in Zulu, when engineer Peter punches buttons, gauges
flicker, and the DX7 whips through the timbres in its sound bank.
Punch out*

Further, Peter erases individual distinction between musicians in his talk. They are culture-bearers, not artists. Their sound, being "traditional," never changes; "what they want doesn't change." This discursive combination of African as primitive and as studio laborer enables the first stage of abstracting the artist and cultural owner from the sonic product and image that circulates globally, accruing cultural and economic capital for the owners of production as it circulates, and constantly increasing the gap between the fragmentary, complex, and diverse voices of the musicians and the singular, unitary image of those voices in sound with each successive circulation (Feld 1994; Feld 1996a).

Musicians who are black, working class, and, though multilingual, not necessarily well-versed in English experience the studio from the least-empowered position of all studio music-makers. The layering of technological mystification onto the South African social matrix in fact empowers white men in the mbaqanga studio. It propagates the idea that technology and technological expertise is differentially accessible to music-makers on the basis of their class and color. From the point of view of women artists, studio possibilities are also constrained on the basis of gender: electronic technology is considered to be the domain of men. It is unusual to find women with experience with electronic technology in the studio.

Access to interiors inside interiors will remain graded and preferential. Entry will be influenced by factors external to the space into which such entry is desired. Something will always be obscured from view or concealed from hearing. These kinds of barriers, grounded in apartheid practices and ideology, superimpose South African social differences onto the professional divisions of labor within the studio, thereby heightening an already heightened system of inclusion and exclusion, distanced wonder and desired entry and contact.

Fakes, Dingane, Hamilton, and Thami set an example by linking issues of knowledge of a particular kind—technological experience— with power and ownership, and by linking resonances in the micro-acrobatics of the recording process with the processes of colonization. The poetic links between the movement of sound through the studio, the transmission of thought between mind and deity or earth and heaven, and human travel through the galaxy are discursively forceful because of their formal iconicities as well as their relationship (on some level) to practice and to the experience of the moment. By means of these poetic resonances, the music-makers not only recognize the structural parallels between colonial and studio relations, but they articulate a position on them. They express something about their quality of experience. These linkages emerge from and embed the experiences of the political configuration of the material world of the studio and of the postcolonial world within which the studio is positioned. The musicians' material experience of apartheid's hierarchy in and out of the recording studio brings laughter rolling out over the idea of whiteys having a direct line of access to God (or, as one of Hamilton's ironic subtexts would have it, the idea that whiteys think they have a direct line to God), while it simultaneously instills awe, distance, and respect for the sound engineer's expertise.

Celebratory studio discourse posits that the workspace is free of power discrepancies based on anything other than authority gathered in the process of music making. This coupled with the capabilities of state-of-the-art audio electronics can "augment musical potential" (Keil and Feld 1994, 158). But another view of the studio reveals it as a space that encourages the "thinning out" of musical potential (ibid.). This version focuses on the impact of external constraints and inhibitions on participation. Professional and personal limitations—the production budget, the skills of the engineer, the investment of the production team (or its members) in perfecting a particular project, the communicative and managerial skills of the producer to effect his musical ideas into sound through the engineer, the pressure of the market—limit the possibilities of perfecting the sound.

These constraints draw not only the professional and corporate world into the studio but also the world of sociopolitics with its specifically local forms and ideologies of difference. In the mbaqanga studio, race and class differences carry with them differences in culture, language, and education. These expressive means and domains of knowledge generate additional complexity by adding layers of obfuscation, interpretation, and translation to the metacultural discussion of the recording process, as well as by adding steps between the musicians and their ability to interface with the recorded sound through the studio's technology.

The dialectic between the studio as a space of creative elaboration and as a space of commodity standardization manifests itself in the sonic interplay between the augmenting and thinning out of mbaqanga style. Such interplay produces a unique authenticity: on the one hand, mbaqanga is black music made within the context of a power-contested (white) state; on the other, it is a circulatable, repeatable, sensuously flowing icon of blackness, embodied in voices, languages, and grooves and in their concomitant material signs.

Apartheid as a system of denial and privilege echoes and exacerbates the system of creative access and critical constraint in the studio. It also offers a vantage point from which to deconstruct the empowerment of aura and the production of authenticity. "Are you sure that all these machines work during recording?" asks Hansford, whose class position and experience garnered as a producer somewhat brokers his experience of race. "*All* these machines?!" he exclaims in Zulu with an ironic tempering. "When whiteys want to say something to Jesus, they simply talk and He hears," joins in Hamilton wryly, from his similar class position.

"Up above in heaven!" agrees a chuckling musician.

On day one, session one, 12 February 1992, maskanda guitarist Nogabisela is warming up in his booth. He has set a stinging sound on the amp alongside him, just the way he likes it. Dumi is slapping and pounding on his bass in the adjoining booth. Msawetshitshi warms up his breathy, rolling concertina the other side of the soundboard. Ntuli is getting settled in the control room. He is to produce the session. Lee is trekking in and out of the recording booths, moving microphones. In passing, he cuts Nogabisela's amp settings to zero, dry. Then he returns to the control room to set initial sound levels and EQs on his console, isolating each musician's warm-up runs to get the sounds just right.

While Lee is preoccupied, Nogabisela turns his mix back up on his amp.

"What's going on?" puzzles Lee as he listens to his guitar settings. He asks Nogabisela not to tamper with the amp so they can maintain a consistent sound.

When the tape is rolling and the song is beginning to groove, Ntuli hears a mistake. He stops the musicians. "You're touching two strings near the end of the intro," he points out to Nogabisela in Zulu. "Let's do it again." Take. Erase. Take. No, listen nicely. Cut, rewind to try again. Nogabisela sneaks in a little change on his amp.

"Sorry, give me a second. There's something going on," puzzles Lee again. He listens. He isolates the guitar.

"Lets play the last bit before we go further," Nogabisela says to his fellow players.

"And let's try to imitate exactly," suggests Msawetshitshi. "It's not easy —you signal for him when to come in," he tells Ntuli.

Lee is fiddling about on the controls to finesse the guitar sound.

"Don't worry, brother," Ntuli reassures Nogabisela from the control room. "I'll guide you in. I heard you touching [your amp controls] where he doesn't want you to. I'm looking after your interests."

Msawetshitshi calls for another take. Dumi chirps in with his opening bass riff.

"Stand by!" announces Ntuli.

"How're their headphones? Can they hear everything?" intercedes Lee, getting ready to roll the tape again.

The gap between creative expert and studio laborer is an increasing gap, widening both inward into the inner worlds and outward beyond the studio—except when music-makers interrupt and divert this trajectory. They do so constantly. Some musicians work at improving their own technological skills and acquiring their own electronic equipment. Others, like mbaqanga musicians, sometimes argue against the authority of technology and its exponents. They do so in multiple ways. First, the musicians can undermine the kinds of knowledge valorized on the production side of the glass simply by brilliant performance. While Peter sees the Sotho musicians' lack of understanding of electronic processes as a shortcoming, in the end, jargon, obfuscation, and studio glitz count very little if the music "kicks ass." Second, the musicians can argue against the authority of the control room more explicitly by bringing into the studio's hallowed arenas other discourses over which they themselves claim mastery—a cultural authority for example. They also play with the linguistic advantages that are present in the studio. They both exploit the engineer's inability to understand local languages for the exclusive discursive space it opens up, and they use their own incompetence at communicating verbally with the engineer in English as a pretext for taking action without consultation. Nogabisela resets his own amp. These local dynamics unsettle the conventional social and professional hierarchies of studio practice.

The studio is given definition as a creative and social space by the music-makers who use it. It is fetishized by means of the luring inaccessibility of its interiors. The layering and overlapping of this trope of interiority in various domains internal to studio production amplifies and excites the affecting presence of the studio as a whole. That affecting presence is both a form of creative symbolic power and means of social control. Spoken otherwise, the affecting presence is the source of the studio's efficacy as well as of its exclusionary and alienating potential.

Playback

Alton Ngubane leads, manages, and co-produces Special Five, a mbaqanga/soul/pop group. Although they had a hit a few years back, they are, like most bands of their genre, a struggling, low-budget group. We chat on the studio's sidewalk as the late afternoon grays into grimy city shadows. Alton advises that I should set up my own studio. He guarantees that Special Five would support me with their business and that they could produce special quality recordings if they used my studio.

I brush him off. 'Ha! Where would I find such money!'

'Just a small studio,' Ngubane reassures me. 'A sixteen-track with keyboards. You could get money from the government. It's easy for you,' he says. 'Aren't you even from Pretoria, nê?'[34]

My parents live in Pretoria; I grew up in this bosom city of the apartheid state apparatus; my father is an Afrikaner and my last name is Afrikaans. It is these things that Ngubane implies give me easy access to capital. He imagines that my race, class, and ethnicity grant me a privileged entry into the domains of the apartheid state power that he knows to be fundamentally tied to capital. And having personal capital, he suggests, is one way to bypass the barriers that limit one's access to the plenitude of the studio's inner worlds—a plenitude that he believes would propel him and his group "out there" again and upward. Now, there it is, let's see where we're going.

Producing Liveness

Guide Vocal

In the first session, West, Peter, and the musicians are working on a song called "Umhlaba lo" (This world), which came to be titled "South Africa" on the album. They are laying a track on the "organ," as the artists call the keyboard.

West says he wants a sequenced synth or clavi bass riff.[1] He sings the riff. Peter programs the basic sound on the studio's DX7 keyboard. But West wants a warmer version of it. So while West chats to the singers, Peter alters the coordinates on the keyboard and EQs the sound a little at the recording console.

"Okay, let's try one more time," Peter instructs Makhosini, who is playing the riff on the Yamaha DX7 keyboard. Peter starts the click track and counts the keyboard entry for Makhosini, who then plays along with the rhythm tracks. The synth bass sound vibrates the studio with its deep and gritty repeated sixteenths. It hits me in the chest. Sixteen pulses on the first tone (tonic) are followed by sixteen on the second (dominant). This pattern is repeated throughout the song.

"Heyi!" exclaims Tefo in township Zulu. "Peter is putting down hot stuff!" This is one of the few times during the production that a musician refers to Peter by his name. He is usually spoken about in terms such as the whitey (*umlungu*), the Boer (*iBhunu*, Afrikaner, though he isn't one), Jesus (his hair is long and curly), that boy or young man (*lo'mfana*). Peter is usually unaware of these names in the context in which they are used, since he understands little Zulu or other African languages.

Singer Janet agrees with Tefo about Peter's raspy synth bass sound.

"Kodwa ushayile!" (He's really hit it!) she cheers, using the same Zulu verb she would use to describe a dynamic performer.

Then Michael pronounces triumphantly (in Sotho), "Moribo wa Afrika! Afrika!" (The sound of Africa! Africa!)

Peter continues working on this "sound of Africa! Africa!" warming and fattening it up until West is satisfied with it. He zips through options in the DX7's sound bank for West to choose from. "That one? . . . That one?"

"These are white people's things!" exclaims a musician as he listens to the DX7's florid display of sounds and watches the flickering studio dials and gauges set in motion by Peter's button punching.

"These are white people's things!" echo other musicians in Zulu.

Then Mzwandile remarks that the synth bass riff "sounds like a bull-dozer." That is exactly right, I think to myself—it sounds like road-building machinery or a heavy construction drill.

Mkhize and Michael reiterate the same, overlapping with Mzwandile and each other as they eagerly agree, "It sounds like a bulldozer!"

Bethwell expands the idea with flourishing grandeur. "It sounds like all machines do!" he exclaims.

The tape rolls. "Cut four," calls Peter on the tape before the song plays back to the artists, who eagerly listen for their new, pulsating bass that drives the mix from underneath.

Why do these musicians select this riff as the "sound of Africa! Africa!"? How does Africanness come to be located in a single sound? While the idea of an Africanness is essentializing, ahistorical, and a gloss of a diverse geopolitical region, it takes on a particular form in the local context and performs in ways specific to its music-makers' personal and social investments, ideas, and ambitions. Africanness emerges as an utterance out of a stylistic and social history and from a locally constituted consciousness concerned with race, national citizenship, and ethnicity.

Race, citizenship, and ethnicity are figured in the context of this mbaqanga case as Africanness, South Africanness, and Zuluness respectively. They are, at one level, one and the same thing: that is, they are an essentialized Other to the whiteness of apartheid ideology, to the "West" of the postcolonial world, to the "First World" of late capitalism, and to the cosmopolitanism of the informational age. Together, the nuances of Africanness, South Africanness, and Zuluness collaborate in the production of difference. Their layering makes denser the feeling of Otherness and distances it from the familiar.

But, at another level, or in other moments, blackness, Africanness, South Africanness, and Zuluness are ideas/sensualities/rhetorical posi-

Peter Pearlson, KD
Studios, Johannesburg, 1997.
Photo by TJ Lemon.

Michael Mpholofolo, Johannesburg, 2002. *Photo by Brett Eloff.*

tions that each play against one another. Each essentialism marks distinctive investments, aesthetic sensibilities, and politics; and they are configured and reconfigured in relation to one another as sounds and in relation to the sociopolitical significances those sounds project.

My broad theoretical interest here is one common to ethnomusicology, namely, a consideration of the way in which the phenomenon of sound is a prism into sociality. Specifically, I wonder how and why we might get at seemingly indefinable, provisional, and deeply felt notions like Africanness, Zuluness, and so forth, through something equally elusive, provisional, and deeply felt: sound. Underlying this query is a critical dilemma. How does the absence of adequate language to describe the nuance and sensuality of sound both constrain and liberate our experiences of music? How does this elusiveness as well as its inevitable reduction into discourse enable politicization of the aesthetic domain, and vice versa? And why turn primarily to an analysis of timbre to investigate the links between the agency of individuals, shifting social praxis, and political movements?

Track I *Liveness as a Trope of Authenticity*

Liveness is an illusion of sounding live that is constructed through technological intervention in the studio and mediated symbolically through discourses about the natural and the artistic. To sound authentically African is to sound live. This is an ideological position sustained by the promotional engine of the music industry, and it is kept alive by African and non-African South Africans in the studio.

There are multiple versions of liveness available to be resourced in the 1990s studio, a range of reasons for doing so, and differently argued positions on the matter.

take 1 : liveness as an African aesthetic

"He's really hit it!" cheers Jane. "Moribo wa Afrika! Afrika!" answers Michael. When Michael, Mzwandile, Mkhize, Tefo, and Jane collectively celebrate the pulsating, gritty bass organ riff as the sound of Africa! Africa! and as the sound of a bulldozer, they compact ideas and sensibilities about race, ethnicity, and class into a single feelingful utterance.

By relating the sound of the riff to the experience of labor and mechanics, they characterize it in terms of a working-class position. This contrasts starkly with the race and class position of the sound engineer and his electronics. The description types the African as a worker, a heavy laborer. The sound's production by means of "white men's things" types the white person in contrast as expert, sophisticate, technician, electronic wizard. This iconicity of race and class distinction is reproduced and reasserted when Peter punches buttons, gauges flicker, and the DX7 whips through the timbres in its sound bank to the awe of the musicians. For the musicians in the control room during this session, the class identity voiced in the sound of the bulldozer/Africa arises from direct experience. They are all working class, and they all have social contact with construction laborers, miners, and factory workers.

An image grounded in manual labor—indeed, linked to working the earth—has bodily experience as its referent. This is a key reason for the potency of the image when it is rendered in sound, for sound also registers as bodily experience. In the case of the sound of Africa! Africa!, the pulsations of the sound, the way the beat is accentuated, and the strength of the bass register all serve to accentuate the riff's associations with the body. These musical features register in the listener in part as a physical experience of pulse and vibration. Bodily participation is of course present across the frequency range, but it is in the bass that issues of body, power, and pulsation converge in their most exaggerated acoustic and physiological forms.

Let me take you out on this track.

Black South African, particularly Zulu aesthetic preference is distinguished by the weight, melodic participation, and drive at the bottom of a musical mix.[2] Paul Simon noticed it.

Ellis Park Stadium, Johannesburg, 10 January 1992.

"You can call me Al, call me Al," sings Paul Simon over the hopping popping backing to Graceland's hit song. On cue Bakithi Khumalo and the second bass player break out of the ranks and jump downstage, one left, one right. Spotlights cross over and blaze down onto them. Furiously, together, they double the bass line of the instrumental break. The stadium in Johannesburg erupts.

Jane notices it. "It guides the song. You can do anything, but don't leave the bass out, because it controls the sound," she says.

Bethwell notices it. He says the synth bass epitomizes an African feel because it is so heavy and powerful. Like a bulldozer, it is the strongest of its kind. "You can't break it," he says. Joana agrees. She says "*inesigqi*" (it has power,) because "all instruments are combined in the sound." Its timbre is heavy and complex.

The sound engineers notice it. "Well, the bass was clicky and clear, because they [musicians] wanted to hear the notes," engineer John Lindemann explained to me. Drawing on his involvement in studios since the late 1960s, he explained, "One of the problems was that half the time the guy was playing bass patterns that went to the top end of the neck. So not only did it have to be clear and clean, it had to have some weight to it. The top end of the neck has no real sort of bottom end to keep it going—thump or depth. So you had to get a good round sound, but it had to be clean. And it had to have a sort of a click on it, to make sure that it cut through. The black producers we mix with want everything right up there. They want to hear the works. And they want to hear every guitar line, they want to hear every vocal line, they want to hear everything else that's going on— not like a white approach to music where there are a lot of holes, a lot of different levels—they want it all there. It used to be quite difficult to get all of this lot to mesh, and to get it in there all at one level, and be able to hear everything without losing the drive of it."

He thumps his fist into his palm, driving his point home. "It's a different approach, a totally different approach," he says.

Earlier we had been talking about the sound of the Mahlathini productions he and West had done in the 1980s. I asked him to compare the approach on *Paris–Soweto*, the album West recorded with a French production team.

"The French mix—it was a typical European mix—too much echo—I felt there was too much echo—and it was too clean. It didn't have that drive."

He thumps his fist into his palm again, and again, and again.

"It was very clean and it was lighter. You know we try—I mean, for instance there's a guy Thomas Motswane who produces Thomas Chauke, who is a Tsongan traditional artist, one of the biggest sellers. He gave me *such* a hard time when I mixed that album.[3] I just couldn't believe how much bottom he wanted, how much bass end he wanted, and yet he still wanted to hear everything else! And I had to push more bass . . ."

He thumps again.

". . . and push *more* bass."

He thumps yet again.

"It was almost fighting, you know. All the elements were fighting with each other. And it had the drive that he wanted and it was a huge seller. It was a fantastically big seller!

"I think what it's got to do with is that I think that the average black person is listening through a cassette player through lousy little speakers. And I think the bottom line is that it's all very well if it sounds great on big hi-fi speakers, but you've got to somehow get some drive into that thing so that when that person listens through their little ghetto blaster or whatever it is, it's got to work. And I think it's that bottom end they want there, to cut through and get the drive, because they dance. We go to disco—I mean, so do the blacks go to discos—but I'm thinking of the more traditional rural areas. They get their music brought to them on radios, and through tiny little speakers."[4]

I think of the 1970s in the cities' suburbs. Here and there radios play in the shade of the tree-lined pavements while African men and women socialize after work or during their lunch hour. Men play board games on the streetcorner; women embroider and knit; someone shouts across the way; another watches the afternoon pass by in silence; young men kick a luminous tennis ball deftly one to the next, or they camp around a radio whose frenetic DJ narrates a soccer match. Sometimes they dance to the latest mbaqanga hit. I think of Saturday afternoons in the 1970s suburbs, when radios blare out from servants' quarters in backyards, and men and women socialize until it's time to pre-pare beans and creamed broccoli and to roast potatoes again.

Lindemann continues, "And I think what these black producers are looking for is that when it gets heard on these things it's got that drive. So that they can dance to it. I think that's why they want so much weight on their recordings. It gives the cutting engineers endless problems because the records jump. It was always a big problem because we were putting so much bottom end, so much thump on it to get it to drive, that you had problems with the groove. And it was *always* a problem. I can remember in the earlier days, I mean, that was the main thing, boy! If the record jumped, it was a sure-fire seller. Definitely!"

Jumping, as ex-engineer Peter Ceronio explained, was the consequence of recording a bass sound so heavy that parallel record grooves merged into one another. "We always had problems with cutting the black records in those days, because first of all it was very boomy, so when we used to cut records—I used to be a cutting engineer before I became an engineer—

we used to get a lot of swing. The heavier your bass is the more it swings. That means grooves used to cut into each other. So in the old days those portable record players they used to use, by doing this the record would suddenly jump—that's from the bass cutting into each other.

"So [as a sound engineer] I used to cut that bottom out to create that clicky mid-type sound on the bass. Also they used to play a lot of cymbals. Everything was high-pitched. I removed that. Because that also created a lot of sibilance, which those record players didn't like. Eventually what I created was a loudness on the record, by using about around 4.8 [Hz], which used to give me a lot of mids. And somehow it worked."

The consumption practice—dancing, listening to the radio—is imagined right at the moment of production. The necessary technological intervention is used to boost, not only to accommodate, the bass aesthetic. And that black aesthetic—the heavy dancing beat with a percussive, clicky attack—is physically engrained and affirmed by the technological jump of the record player's needle. The physicality in each step of the performing-recording-reproducing-listening process connects a performing musician to radio and record listeners. The engagement of the body in the physicality of sound is of crucial significance in the generation of a feeling of liveness. That physiological experience of the listener out there is imagined by music-makers in the studio when they succeed in creating the "Sound of Africa! Africa!"

Liveness is also fundamental as an ideological discourse to the idea of Africanness produced in the studio. During Isigqi's production, West chided Mkhize the guitarist for sloppy timing by saying in Zulu, "No, man, this thing is easy. Can't you feel it? This is traditional music. I mean, if you were a white person, I would understand."

By comparing Mkhize's feel for music and his rhythmical ability to that of a white person, West challenges Mkhize's very selfhood as an African. Contrasting his own musicality with Mkhize's poor performance, West demonstrates that he himself is deeply African. He exhibits his easy feel for the beat. In this moment he celebrates an African essence while he employs it as a rhetorical strategy to get Mkhize to deliver a disciplined guitar track.

While timing problems raised discussion of race and ethnicity among black producers and musicians, issues of pitch never did. Intonational discrepancies they tended to approach as an issue of professional skill irrespective of color. For example, mbaqanga musicians regarded backup singing as something anyone could do, unlike dancing, which was a privileged talent of black people, among whom there were dancers of differing levels of ability. When Isigqi auditioned young men as backup singer-dancers, they selected them on the basis of a display of their dancing skills, not on the basis of their voices. An iconic link between the capacity for dance and an African sensibility is likewise present in the huge, independent African Church of the Nazarites in South Africa. For its members, dance is the highest form of worship precisely because dance is regarded as indigenous (Bongani Mthethwa in Coplan 1993, 320; see also Muller 1999).

When Michael exclaims, "The sound of Africa, Africa!" referring to a sound produced on "i-organ" as the musicians still often call the keyboard, there is also embedded in his remark a comment about the Africanness of dance. It is present by way of a historical reference. He is referring to an electronic keyboard sound—indeed, to a specific riff—heard in mbaqanga in the 1970s, which was the time when mbaqanga enjoyed an energetic performance practice and fabulous stage display. Choreographed dance was a highlighted feature, and the organ was a featured instrument during the instrumental breaks to which the frontline danced their routines. Similarly, later in the session, when Tefo voices his preference for the "right" mbaqanga "organ" sound on another keyboard riff, he is calling for the sound of his instrument as it was in the 1970s. Two decades earlier mbaqanga musicians would probably not have thought of the organ sound as "African." This characterization is a phenomenon of 1990s studio discourse. Tefo in fact refers to the organ as "Zulu" (that is, an epitome of Africanness) during another session.

Differences in timing or tuning abilities among African and non-African studio participants are also sometimes accounted for in terms of a lack of physiological ability; sometimes such a discourse is deployed in argument for rhetorical effect. For example, West reminded mbaqanga musicians to be patient with Peter when he was programming the rhythm tracks, for Peter does not have "the beat in his blood; it takes him time to understand what kind of a thing this is." He has to learn the beat. Similarly, Tom Mayberry, who engineered at a studio outside the Gallo group, accounted for the discrepancies between his own and black studio performers' aesthetic preferences in terms of physiological differences in hearing. He interprets the situation through a set of assumptions about African naivete about technology and lack of rational scientific perspective, while he downplays the significance of sensual bodily experience in "white" and sound engineers' listening processes.

"The chaps rehearse at very loud volumes and quite often in confined spaces. So what happens is that their ears become numb. These guys practically sit inside their bass amps, and it's at full blast. The kind of bass amp they're probably using is double-folded. Basically what that means is that when the sound comes out it has to travel a few feet before it becomes loud. . . . Now they're sitting right next to it, so they're not getting the full benefit of it. The better thing to do is to turn the volume down and sit a reasonable distance away from it, then you will hear. But they don't know that, and when you explain it to them it doesn't make any sense to them. Basically, they're used to playing everything at high volumes until their ears become numb. Bass sound is no longer a clear bass sound, it's sort of a throb you can feel through your whole body.

"Now you can't have that situation in the studio, because you can't hear clearly what is going on record. Whether you like him or he likes you or anything like that, that's all inconsequential. It's the end result that matters. So they play at ear-shattering level, their ears become numb and damaged after a certain period of time. And then they start talking to you about a certain sound. Now if your ears are not numb and damaged, you can't hear that certain sound they're talking about. You're hearing a different sound. You're hearing what is actually the true sound. . . . They're missing probably a lot of the high frequencies. Because the first thing that goes when your ears start getting numb is the high frequencies. You find yourself putting in more and more tops. Soon you land up with this very trebly mess. So the whole trick of recording is to actually listen, not to have it so loud that you don't have to listen, which is what these guys do. It's just like this presence around them, a wall of sound—that's what turns them on. Now you can achieve that same sound effect on record and have a really big, punchy-sounding record, but if you haven't been able to hear what you're recording, it'll just be a big mess. There'll be no sort of clarity, no definition, there'll be no mix to it. It will just be a wall of sound. That's the difference. Again it's basically because they haven't got enough knowledge, you know, and perhaps we haven't got enough knowledge of them—let's be fair about it. I mean, I try, I really do. I sit down and talk for hours with these guys. I really try to know what is going on inside their head."

Africanness as an embodied sensibility has an extremely long history in Western thought. It has been thoroughly critiqued (e.g., Mudimbe 1994; Appiah 1992; see also Torgovnick 1990) but has also been thoroughly far-reaching in its effect. In music scholarship the argument has historically been refracted through disciplinary debates about the evolution of musical systems and the varying complexities of musical parameters. Broadly spoken, in early musicological, ethnological, and ethnomusicological writings the Cartesian split between body and mind, intuition and rationality was replicated in the musicological distinction between tone and rhythm, where tonal systems were taken to be rational, logical, and mathematical, while rhythm was viewed as intuitive, known through the body, and felt through movement. The Western harmonic system and the tempered scale on which it was based were considered to be signs of the most sophisticated of all music systems the Europeans had encountered across the globe.[5] African tonal systems, on the other hand, have on the whole been characterized as simple; very little analytic attention has been given to issues concerning pitch in African music scholarship across the decades. The rhythmic complexity of African music has been consistently noted, admired, studied, discussed, and analyzed. Juxtaposed against a perceived simplicity of African tonal systems, the focus on rhythm has facilitated the characterization of Africans in terms of a primacy of body and intuition.

These views (variously nuanced through the decades by a wealth of fine Africanist scholarship in tune with the theoretical tenor of their times) have by now been thoroughly critiqued and countered with painstaking documentation, ethnographic and music analyses (Nketia 1974; Berliner 1978; Arom 1981; Erlmann 1996b; Charry 2000; and others). Their point—also variously inflected—was not to refute the claim that rhythm is felt through the body but to recognize that its rendition into sound, as well as the experience of elite listening, also involves thinking, learning, and highly developed skills. The original distinctions are nevertheless energetically sustained in a lot of World Music promotional materials and fan discourse. Africanness continues to be fervently circulated and enjoyed as an idea about beat, embodiment, and naturalness.

Peter Pearlson likes recording traditional Sotho musicians in the studio. "You've got a single vocal on top, normally doing some sort of chant or shout. It's not a musical vocal, the guys just do a sort of long, fast rap, from beginning to end, with the odd scream interjected here and there. The rhythm sections are normally really, really good. I just like the Sotho rhythms."

The African essence of beat, embodiment, and naturalness is rendered in the physicality of playing, in dancing, in an emphasis on percussion, and in the participatory ethos of African music making. These are the features that support the idea of Africanness being about liveness. No wonder, then, that African music is so often presented as synonymous with

dance music and that drumming and percussion playing, with their visually dramatic realization of the beat, have come to epitomize the continent's musicality and musical traditions for consumers of African music
as well as for some mbaqanga music-makers in the studio.

When Tefo calls for the "right" organ sound on his riff, he wants to play
an organ part rich with percussive effects and small melodic and timbral
variations for which he would have the musical control at his fingertips.
He wants to play on the old Korg cx-3 on which he can set and vary the
timbre of his notes by means of the instrument's drawbars. When backing
the vocal parts, he wants to punctuate his riffs with screaming glissandi
and quick bursts of notes in the mid- and upper registers of the keyboard.
He imagines that his instrument will be treated much like the voice in
terms of its prominence in the mix and its interaction with the voices and
other lead instruments like the guitar and bass.

But his organ sound quality, prominence, and playing style undergo
a marked reshaping when he loses out to the decision of the producer.
West changes the second organ line from the florid idea Tefo had rehearsed to a sequenced, synthesized marimba. This demands changes in
the organ line's timbre, pitch range, and melody to match the timbre and
playing style of the imitated instrument. The degree of variation in the
organ's timbre, range, and melodic ornamentation is severely limited by
the change in concept. Its improvisational potential is curtailed by the
use of sequencing to repeat the riff. In turn, these changes trigger changes
in other sounds and riffs, ultimately effecting the balance and contour as
a whole.

To match the marimba, West makes changes in the rhythm tracks. He
wants what he calls an 'East African beat.' 'This,' he tells the artists, 'is
what the people want these days.' He shifts the bass drum to the off beat,
and he keeps the rim-shot hitting every beat, so that the marimba and
rim pull against the bass. He changes their straight, uninterrupted hi-hat
(eighth-notes right through) to a more elaborate offbeat pattern. Conga
fills are programmed in later in the production.

A percussion bank with heightened cross-rhythm effects replaces the
organ's elaborate, varied, percussive playing style. The sound of wooden
mallets and skin drum heads replaces electric vibrato. West shifts a lot of
the textural interest—in terms of timbre variation, fills, body (i.e., how
much space is filled), balance (i.e., what is foregrounded)—away from the
organ onto programmed percussion and reorganizes the backing rhythm
tracks to create more complex cross rhythms. Here, a stereotype is fash-

ioned from a stylistic feature and in the process potentially reinvigo-
rates mbaqanga style (Keil 1985). Percussiveness, a fundamental aesthetic
quality in African music (Roberts 1972; Nketia 1974; Keil 1979; Waterman 1990), comes to be almost solely located in the rhythm and percussion tracks, thereby fusing the idea of percussiveness with the image
of drums and percussion. Drumming and percussion playing become an
icon of Africanness. Africanness moves toward becoming naturalized as
unmediated, tribal, performed beat.[6]

*Rose-pink rayon shirts shimmer under the stage lights as Isigqi's
male singers shuffle forward for their vocals. As they quiver their
hands, their blouson sleeves ripple and glint. They swivel on their
shoe soles and shake their trousered hips. Fans in the mining hall
whistle at them.*

*No. "The kind of music that they sing necessitates that they
wear* amabheshu," *instructs West in the studio one day.*

*When the singer-dancers shuffle forward at the next show, the
tips of their cowskin aprons swing from side to side behind them.
The fiber tassels of their loin aprons pick up the rhythm of their
swiveling hips. Bared chests ripple with movement. Fiber
pom-poms fly outward from their headdresses.*

While the discourses of African music as drumming, dance, and
rhythm, and of African performance as embodied and intuitive are enduring and pervasive, they are not fixed or closed discourses. Their stability
is undermined in rendering them into practice.

18 November 1991

Laying the marimba and percussion tracks down on tape is not progress-
ing fluently. The musicians are having trouble fitting their overdubbed
parts with the new rhythmic feel of the song. West and Peter count out the
measures, clapping the beats emphatically. Rewind. They clap it again.
West points out the keyboard/marimba's beat of entry and which instrument on the tape Makhosini should listen for in order to position
himself.

"Heyi! Bra West has put down a locust!" quips Tefo, as he starts to get
the feel of the cross rhythms jumping all over the place.

The naturalization of beat and polyrhythm as African is shown here to be a discursive distinction, which is not upheld in everyday practice. The essentialized self in discourse does not cohere directly with the practicing self at work in the studio.

The stability of Africanness is also undermined in the process of enlisting it for political gain. The claim to inherent African musicality is naturalized as an embodied phenomenon at the same time as it is recognized as a political position. At the microlevel, West's appeals to inherent rhythmicality organize studio relations in specific moments. When he appeals to Mkhize's identity as an African by criticizing his rendering of the beat, West can accrue an unchallengable professional authority with musicians and sound engineers. Other African musicians witnessing Mkhize's reprimand are pressed to align themselves with West—or at least not to voice disagreement—for a position that counters West is in effect an alignment with whiteness. The musician's authority as creative participant is destabilized. The net effect is to consolidate the producer's authority and the musician's wage-laborer status.

Another political level: in an instance that stands as an example of the "strategic use of positivist essentialism" (Spivak 1988, 13)—I argued vehemently with Sowetan singer Monty Bogatsu that a physiological claim to musicality was a racist one internalized under years of colonial oppression. "Now you want to take that away from us as well!" he retorted.

For the ease and regularity of dichotomizing African and non-African sensibilities in the studio, these categories do not map consistently onto the racial differences of studio workers. This too keeps Africanness on the move. At the moment when Peter gets the sound of Africa! Africa! programmed right, Tefo refers to him by his first name. Janet recognizes him as a music-maker instead of a mere technician when she describes his action with the Zulu verb she would use for a good performer. Having delivered the sound of Africa, Africa! for Isigqi, Peter is acknowledged as a team participant. Their professional and artistic status is momentarily shared, for he has constructed an African sound.[7]

Finally, the juxtaposition of one version of Africanness with other versions holds open the options of what form Africanness might take. The old "right" organ sound that Tefo wanted but lost to the sound of the marimba is not deleted from the album entirely. Though it is subdued in timbre and playing style, it evokes another kind of liveness through its outdated form. On Isigqi's recording as a whole, various markers of black cultural identity are present. They are drawn from local and diasporic black music styles. For example: in addition to the inclusion in places of the "right" organ sound, the title track, "Lomculo Unzima," has a reggae beat and reggae keyboard, flute and steel pan overdubs; the album's ballad has a gospelly organ chordal bed with a wide vibrato; the wedding songs include traditional ululations, among other local features. These sometimes contradictory, sometimes mutually enhancing positions coexist within the production. Their presence within the same song can be a source of aesthetic potency.

West wants an "East African beat" on the song "South Africa." Hansford calls it "the Swahili song." Both associate the idea of polyrhythmic complexity with central/east Africa. Bethwell says, "The song is mixed." He celebrates it as a manifestation of the power of Africa as supranation, not only as essentialized place: "There's something from the Zimbabweans in the sound, something from Malawians, from Tanzania and Kenya, even from Mozambique. When you mix them into a sound, it becomes very, very heavy. *Inesigqi!* It has mighty power! When they all come together, the sound could never be flimsy, because it grows out of all the states. It's the sound of Africa!"

take 2 : liveness as a studio aesthetic

The synth bass sound vibrates the studio with its rough and raspy repeated sixteenths. After sixteen pulses of the tonic, the riff drops down to throb on the dominant, before striding back up to the tonic to repeat itself, over and over. "Heyi!" exclaims Tefo, "Peter is putting down hot stuff!" The synth bass is a sequenced program on the DX7 keyboard. Its raspiness arises from the dense overlay of the complex waveform's overtones. The overtones in the mid- and upper frequency range are well out of phase with one another, basically causing microdistortions of the sound. This effect is exaggerated from the console by EQing. Peter boosts the mids to fatten the sound, thereby also exacerbating the distortion. The resulting hypermediated quality makes it sound like outdated technology. Specifically, it simulates a sound that was available on earlier synthesizers and that typifies the sound of 1970s audio electronics. It draws the ear back to a technologically primitive era in which the electronic keyboard was less sophisticated than it is today.

A connection of this instrument to the 1970s era is drawn through the timbre imitated in the sound of Africa! Africa! For those who know mbaqanga repertoire, this backward glance is also achieved by means of the actual riff it colors. In the later 1970s, pulsing bass riffs similar to the sound of Africa! Africa! underpinned a number of mbaqanga songs. Given the melodic simplicity of the riff, its position in the 1970s mixes is striking. The riff was given equivalent presence to the voices. It was a sound particularly associated with Isibaya Esikhulu through songs such as Izintombi Zesimanjemanje's "Boraditaba" (1979a) and "Lensizwa" (1993a [re-release]), the Soul Brothers's "Bayeza" (Marabi 1994 [re-release]) and "Ogandaganda" (Tefo Sikale personal communication), and Sibusiso Mbatha Nabangani's "Ngigibel' ipayoni" (Tefo Sikale personal communication). The Soul Brothers subsequently carried the sound into their soul/disco of the 1980s, in such songs as "Disco machine" and "Akanindaba" (Tefo Sikale personal communication).

The riff Peter is working on in the studio is harmonically and rhythmically identical to that in Zesimanjemanje's "Boraditaba" from 1979, though it eventually comes to be placed differently in the mix. Peter's version of it, however, plays up the noise, roughness, and clunkiness of the sound in comparison to the 1970s originals. He makes the riff sound superindustrial and technologically primitive. There is not a trace of acoustic feeling about it.[8]

The sound of old technology like that of an old synthesizer paradoxically generates liveness by referencing old recording techniques. In our era of sequencing, sampling, and MIDI programming, it draws the ear back to a time when the recording process was much more mechanical than it is today and the ideology behind recording was to transmit the sound of the moment of performance as accurately as possible within the limitations of the equipment of the time (Frith 1986; Porcello 1991).

The technological constraints of earlier studio production necessitated recording procedures more similar to live performance procedures. Performers recorded together, at the same time, usually in the same recording booth. Singers crowded around one microphone. Guitarists and bass guitarists were miked at their amps, whereas today they usually plug directly into the console and bypass the amp. The drummer playing on a standard drum kit was directly miked, whereas drummers are rarely recorded in "traditional" and mbaqanga sessions today. Instead, their parts are electronically programmed on drum boxes by the engineer.

In comparison with what studio technology was to become, the sound-processing devices in the early 1970s were primitive. Multi-tracking was certainly available—it had become a feature of major studios in the mid 1960s—but it was still in its infancy. Consider that by the 1980s, 49 track consoles were in use, and by the end of the decade, 64 track capacity was not uncommon (Clark 1999).

Technological facilities in South African studios resembled state-of-the-art facilities in good studios around the world, though they may have lagged a little behind in integrating new innovations. White South African recording artists had access to everything the studios offered. But in black music production the most updated technology was not necessarily used. Most mbaqanga cuts were just recorded on two tracks, simultaneously, straight onto quarter-inch tape in one, two, or three takes. Even when four- and then sixteen-track facilities became available in the 1970s, mbaqanga did not enjoy the privilege of its use. So, for black South African artists, the lag behind the latest overseas studio sounds and techniques was distinctly greater than it need have been were it not for local race and class prejudices.

Peter Ceronio: "Guys like West Nkosi and Rupert Bopape of Mavuthela started getting involved [in the control room procedure]. You see they were very involved with the Gallo company and with the Ivor Haarburgers and the Peter Gallos [company executives] who always tried to get the Mavuthela guys to record on sixteen track."

But independent producer Koloi Lebona recounts how he and his assistant had to insist on their professional entitlement to use all the facilities studio technology offered, or not to use them. "Some producers were afraid of telling a white engineer, 'But this is not right, I don't want this.' Now because we were doing that, we came across as 'the people who need to be watched because they are so militant.' But it's not that I was being militant—I know what I want and we should actually try my way before the engineer imposes."

Ex-engineer Peter Ceronio recalls how the Soul Brothers literally performed in front of the microphone when they were recording organ-based mbaqanga in the 1970s: "To me, the most amazing thing was that [their] beat just was always strong, from day one, every album. Those guys used to go out, rehearse—the whole album—we used to get a sound balance, and that's how we used to run them off." It was standard studio practice at the time to set the sound balance at the beginning of a studio session and then record numerous songs one after the next. Peter Ceronio remembers recording three or four groups a day when working with Hamilton's artists. "We used to put like forty-eight songs down a day! We used to run sometimes two albums in a morning and two in the afternoon."

"You were running them on a four-track?" I ask, trying to quickly tally up the time that would be allocated to each song if forty-eight were recorded in a day and they were using the studio's full facilities.

"Two-track—straight two-track—nothing fancy. The four-track that was in the studio we used to use as an echo machine. We wanted to go straight two-track because when we were finished, that was it—it was finished! . . . During lunchtime I used to edit the albums so the next day they could go to the factory and they were ready."

A decade or more later, the principle was still in place. For example, John Lindemann compared the sound and recording process of his and West's productions of Mahlathini, the Mahotella Queens, and the Makgona Tsohle Band in the 1980s to earlier recordings: "The technique didn't really change. We did some tracks with live drums, so we still tried to— West still tried to keep that live feel. Obviously equipment has improved, but there wasn't a vast direction in Mahlathini. It was just good, good mbaqanga. And, I mean, the girls—the Mahotella Queens—they probably haven't changed, you know. They must have got better—they were always good—but there were no new fancy techniques and no fancy gimmicks. Mahlathini is mbaqanga. It's good mbaqanga."

John and West were not adhering to simpler recording procedures because it would be faster to do so, or because they didn't care about the musicians, or because they thought the music deserved nothing better. No, their artistic vision for this style required of them that they make invisible the 1980s studio as the space of performance. Nostalgia for sounds, styles, and production techniques that don't appear to have changed went along with a particular interpretation of the idea of authenticity.

In this view, authenticity is both an illusion of nonmediation concerning the sound and an illusion of disengagement from technology on the part of the performing musicians. Artists are imagined to be detached from technology. They do not exploit the studio's sound facilities. They contaminate their authenticity if they actively embrace the idea of sound manipulation. No new fancy gimmicks, just good mbaqanga. Popularization through production and its fancy gimmicks is judged as vulgar; it is lamented as a loss of authenticity (Keil and Feld 1994, 284). African and other "World Music" artists also get critiqued by consumers when they become too "popular," sound too produced, and try to cross over out of the World Music market niche. For these consumers, African music must remain marginal to the mainstream market if it is to retain its authenticity (T. Taylor 1997).

In the 1990s mbaqanga's "live feel," the sense of collaborative on-the-spot performance and face-to-face communication, is attained through multiple and elaborate electronic interventions and interpretive links. These interventions and links serve to bring to the listener a sense of contact with the performer. The electronics make the face-to-face imaginable by reproducing the acoustics of such an encounter.

All the examples thus far in take 2 iconically relate the actual acoustic properties of sounds to an imagined recording or listening situation.[9] There are other instances that take the preoccupation with liveness into the realm of the hyperreal and into a discourse about a different kind of naturalness. These instances demonstrate that liveness is a value that might shape a production process even when it does not register a change in the shape of the sound itself. For example, West's championing to me of the huge obsolete echo plate, used not for his reggae productions but "especially for ethnic music," is rhetorical. To my knowledge an echo plate has not been available for use at Downtown Studios for years; I have never witnessed anyone using one in Johannesburg nor heard any requests for its use during a session. He stories to me in the present tense as though he is telling me about his practices in the 1990s as a way of claiming authenticity for his projects. It has little to do with the sound as it materializes but rather with imparting a value about that sound.

He talks about the echo plate being more natural than an echo-plate setting on an R7 or other reverb machine, for the physical vibrations of its actual plate are triggered by an audio signal from the voice. By means of an indexical process, the echo plate brings the presence of the actual performer into the sound on tape. The vibrations of the vocal chords excite the movement of the air, which sets the vibration of the metal plate in motion, which in turn replicates the resonance of the voice with its micro-variations as it would be heard in a live performance setting. The vibrations of the one come to stand in for the vibrations of the other. For West, the production of an echo effect with an echo plate is grounded in a physicality, unlike its digital imitations. Here he transposes the value accorded the physical presence of performers onto the machine.

The hyperreal is trumped by more hyperreal circulating in studio discourse. On another occasion West champions the original drum machine as unsurpassed in terms of the accuracy of its signal production.

There's a special drum box called Linn drum 1000.[10] That thing is amazing! That thing has got wonderful sounds! It's not the latest equipment, you see, it's old. But all the sounds they make from the new drum boxes can't beat that one. It's the first one—the first thing is always accurate. When they did the second one, they lost it. They did the Linn 9000.[11] The sound is not good. Now, on the original, the cowbell and cabasa [beaded gourd hand-percussion instrument] sound natural. And the bass drum and the snare, it's like somebody's playing there. In the meantime, it's actually a machine.

West carried this machine, the LM-1, under his arm to Paris for the 1990 remix of Mahlathini and the Mahotella Queens song "Kazet" (*Paris-Soweto*, 1990b). He also used it to program the percussion on Isigqi's project.[12]

There are three models of Linn drum machines, all of which are obsolete. The first one—West's preference—is a pre-MIDI, programmable drum machine, manufactured between 1980 and 1983. It has twelve tunable sampled sounds: hi-hat, kick, snare, two congas, two toms, cowbell, cabasa, handclap, tambourine, clave (Vail 2000, 290). A clumsy box with programming buttons the size of postage stamps, it sticks out like an old clunker in the midst of the studio's sleek new MIDI rack units.

Downtown Studios owned the Linn 9000, the third Linn model, which is a MIDI workstation, but West rarely chose this over the original. In addition to these Linn models, there were, of course, subsequent designs manufactured by other companies that West could have selected. But he chose the original model of the Linn drum machine—the first drum machine to use sampled sounds and the prototype for all subsequent drum machines. Though West considered the LM-1 to reproduce the sound of percussion instruments more accurately than later models have, Peter and other engineers refute this claim, arguing on the grounds of electronic logic.

The Linn drum machine was not available in the heyday mbaqanga era. West is not replicating the recording procedures of that time, when full drum kits were used in the studios. Neither is he imitating the sound of mbaqanga heyday recording technology. By using sophisticated electronics, he is trying to get beyond sounding studiolike at all. He wants to get closer to the actual sound of the hand beating on a drum and of a wooden stick beating on an iron bell. By choosing the original Linn to do this, he is using primitive technology for the sake of its own authenticity.[13]

The exchangeability in discourse of different kinds of authenticity makes ambiguous their referents—but usefully so, for together they come to represent a feeling and express a value about it. The "natural," that is, scientifically accurate sound or the physically registered signal can stand in for the material presence of acoustic instruments or performers; just as stories about these forms of liveness heaped on top of one another sustain the practices that realize some of them into sound. The live is infused into the process of sound production.

In evoking the sound or the idea of early studio production, these mbaqanga music-makers are engaging in a debate about mediation that is transnational in its issues and scope. Although South African music-makers, especially engineers and producers, consider themselves to be working in the backwaters of the international music industry, they are firmly engaged with the aesthetic and industrial issues carried in recorded sounds around the globe. They envision themselves as participants in an international musical dialogue about the aesthetics of studio production. They listen for the technical sophistication of a recording as well as for the artistic integrity of its production. Their talk and productions actively refashion the always fluid meanings and forms of studio authenticity. For example, when engineer Richard Austen categorizes "black traditional," local white (Afrikaner), and British folk-music recording under one rubric, he evaluates the one (black traditional, here) in terms of the others. He explains to me with some frustration at the limitations of his job that black traditional music production is "not so-called trendy or modern production—it's a folk standard, production has been around for about twenty-five, thirty years! There's nothing special, it's just nice songs, played nicely by good musicians, and that's it. . . . [You] come in, play the parts, mix it, mess with an echo here or there, and then it goes out." At the same time as he criticizes contemporary "traditional" music for its outdated production process, he highlights the parallels concerning the issue of liveness and mediation in the three genres of music. In these genres, "nothing special" should be done to them in the studio, because they are meant to sound unmediated. They should sound sincere, disinterested in the market and in technology, and intimately connected to their listeners. No gimmicks, just good mbaqanga.

The notion of authenticity as sincere, unmediated musical experience also shows itself in other musical situations that are, in fact, intricately hooked into electronics. To sound live is part of the ideology of early rock recording (Frith 1986; Frith 1996) and is especially noted by fans of what has now come to be earmarked as "classic rock." Here the reference is not to sounding acoustic but to sounding as if captured in the moment of performance. Music categorized as World Music shares this ideology. Liveness is also privileged in "unplugged performance" in 1990s arena concerts and acoustic MTV shows, for which super high-tech electronics are used to minimize the visual markers of sonic mediation (Porcello 1994).[14] Here, the trappings of stardom are seemingly stripped away to put the rehumanized star in touch with the audience and to represent his or her expression of sincerity (ibid.). Digitally sampled keyboard patches imitating old sound equipment (e.g., the Hammond sound), old recording equipment (e.g., vacuum tube amps and other "warm" analog gear), and renowned old studio spaces also participate in this ideology. Here, like the rasping synth bass, face-to-face collaborative recording and performing are usually referenced. All these studio practices striving for liveness are tied up with music-makers' and consumers' fantasies about participatory music making and with critiques of the alienated condition in which, as West says, "We record piece-piece—every individual plays alone, and he doesn't hear the other one."

Liveness, then, is a trope of authenticity in a number of technologically mediated musics. Liveness is key to music-makers and to consumers of these musics (scholars, journalists, critics, listeners, and music-makers alike), for the sincerity of the artists and the integrity of their art is seen to be called into question by their engagement with seductive market forces and alienating technology. As Frith wrote in the pre-electronica music era, mediated sound is given the dubious quality of being somehow false or fake on the grounds that its mode of production is fundamentally tied into hegemonic institutions (Frith 1986).[15] At the least, this demands that artists relinquish control over their expression to a larger or lesser degree as they enter into commodity production. At the most, artists are considered to sell out to the market and thereby abandon their soul, their heart, their freedom, their spontaneity, their inspiration, their individual creativity. For all these reasons, studies of pre-electronica popular culture have tended to treat mediation with suspicion and to hold on to the idea of authenticity as residing in the human, the performed, the spontaneous, the unmediated, that is, in sounding live.[16] It is important to look at this tension between the "authenticity" of performance and the "falsity" (ibid.) of mediated sound as a discursive tension that fundamentally organizes and evaluates the placement of microphones, the exploitation of available technological processes, the degree and kind of attention given to technical details, the selection of electronic gear, the programming of effects, and the sounds on tape.

takes mixed : politics, technology, and authenticity

Some liveness is laid to tape. It is sounded as in the sound of Africa! Africa!, and it reverberates out into the world beyond the studio. Some liveness is located in the process of recording. It determines technological decisions, such as the use of the LM-I drum box. It is implicated in the sound, though not necessarily sounded. Some liveness is located in talk, such as that about the echo plate and the "right" organ sound and the "naturalness" of preset percussion sounds. It is not laid to tape or made into music, but it resonates in the studio and it configures the imaginings and sensibilities of the participating musicians. All these domains together produce mbaqanga's authenticity.

This authenticity is dialogically conceived. It is shaped through negotiations within the studio that are informed by the music-makers' experiences outside of it and by their perceptions of what a marketable sound will be.

'Play the old songs. They want the old stuff overseas,'
Hamilton advises his rehearsing musicians.

The transnational negotiation over the meaning and form of authenticity in mediated music is questioned and refashioned dialogically with local debates about the meaning and form of authenticity in African music, which in turn is fashioned as a mimetic encounter, "with itself in the eyes . . . of its Others" (Taussig 1993, xv).

In the South African studio, the transnational privileging of live performance and nonmediated-sounding recording is reasoned out, positively or negatively, in relation to discourse about race and essential difference. The local success of the transnational folk/rock recording ideology—or the local necessity for that particular ideology—is accounted for in terms of African types of musicality. For instance, Peter Ceronio attributes the success of "recording straight two-track" to the fact that the Soul Brothers' "beat just was always strong." It is precisely because they are "African" that the Soul Brothers could reproduce in live takes the garage-band aesthetic and the folk-recording ideal that Peter prizes in music production in general and that enables him as an engineer to reproduce the international dialogue about good sound production. The Soul Brothers could fulfill this aesthetic standard because, according to Peter, their rhythmicality is a given.

Moses Dlamini, a black record-company public-relations officer who spent many hours in the studio in mbaqanga's heyday, interprets the recording simplicity of the day from a different race and class position than Peter Ceronio's. But he speaks through the same essentialized image. Because African musicianship is superior, he said in conversation with me, Africans could overcome the technological constraints that white and international musics did not suffer to the same extent. He noted how an aesthetic that limits technological creativity in production served local discriminatory studio practices. Seen from his perspective in the 1990s, black musicians in the early 1970s were limited in the recording techniques, time, and budget by both the folk-recording ideology and the ideology of apartheid. Describing a Zulu guitarist of the time, Moses explained how this guitarist would go to the studio and "sing right through the complete album, you know, without any hiccups, nothing—guitar this side, singing at the same time—amazing. It's amazing, really!" He pauses, checks that I'm tuned in to his sentiment, and continues. "It was amazing! Unlike nowadays, you know—nowadays you put down all the backtracks, then you start singing after that. If you make a mistake, you go back, you erase, you do it until it is correct. Those days it was straight into the quarter-inch. That's it—straight and correct, and the sound was fantastic."

Whereas Moses accounts for success residing in Africanness, some white engineers express the necessity of using folk recording techniques because African musicality requires nothing more or nothing less than live-sounding reproduction. For example, engineer Darryl Heilbrunn so treasures instruments he considers to be traditional that he will go to elaborate sophisticated technological ends to render his technological intervention as invisible/inaudible as possible. "I did an album with [Manfred Mann] where he got some guy from Swaziland who had calabashes on sticks, and he pulled these strings," he explained, "and I miked up this thing with seventeen microphones. That was a *real* traditional instrument! And it sounded great, you know."[17] But there is a flip side. His regard for the "authentic" is embedded in a complaint about "traditional" music as it is usually recorded and about "traditional" musicians. He implies that mediated black music is contaminated culture—it is neither good music nor authentic; it is "the sign of the permanent wound inflicted by history, the sign of waste, degeneracy, and thwarted narrative" (Taussig 1993, 142). Traditional black musicians who choose to engage creatively with available technology lose their selfhood and mask their musicality. "True" traditional artists are understood to be inherently divorced from the culture represented by the mode of production (Wallis and Malm 1984; Goodwin and Gore 1990). Darryl's explicit stand exemplifies this position.[18]

"[Zulu trad artists] use drum machines more than they should; they should actually be using live drums. You see, the whole irony of it is they come in and say 'We're a traditional Zulu band, record us.' But did their fathers have drums like we use in the studio? Did their forefathers have DX7s that does *whirrp, whirrp*? Did their forefathers have all these fancy machines that we use to create their music? No! So therefore they are not really traditional artists. Traditional Zulu band is animal drum skins, finger-piano, guitars made out of tin cans, okay, natural percussion, and a group of people standing around and singing and chanting.[19] *That* is traditional music. I have yet to record a traditional band that way. If they came in that way, I'd then have the respect for them. I'd say, 'Right, this is the real McCoy, I'm not using a modern Ludwig drum set here.'" Peter Pearlson does not go that far, but he struggles with the constraints placed on his own creativity in the studio by the Africanness he attributes to some of the musicians he records. In an interview he explained, "A lot of the black stuff I do—I don't need a producer. I can just take a band and do it and they will be happy with it. Because I know what they want and what they want doesn't change. It's traditional music. I mean, all the engineers have tried to add modern effects and put big reverbs on the drums and get it sounding a little bit closer to what we're hearing on international radio, and the guys are not interested. The people don't want to hear that, they want to hear raw traditional music. It's what they're used to hearing and they won't change."

As a "folk" music, mbaqanga requires less production time than other studio-produced musics. As "formulaic, churned out, catalogue" music, it deserves little production attention. As an "ethnic" music, as "black stuff," its listeners are imagined not to be discriminating in terms of studio aesthetics. As a working-class music, hi-fi production quality is considered wasted on low-fi playback equipment. These are certainly impassioned and debated positions infused with larger South African struggles over moral accountability, social status, and conceptions of difference. They are positions that have developed within the experience of a society that historically excluded and promoted on the basis of race.[20]

playback

"Moribo wa Afrika! Afrika!" celebrates Michael. The synth bass sound vibrates the studio with its rough and raspy repeated sixteenths. After sixteen pulses of the tonic, the riff drops down to throb on the dominant, before striding back up to the tonic to repeat itself, over and over.

"Kudumo ogandaganda!" (It sounds like a bulldozer!), exclaims Mzwandile.

Mkhize and Michael reiterate the same, overlapping with Mzwandile, "Kudumo ogandaganda!"

"Kudumo ogandaganda!"

"It sounds like all machines do!" flourishes Bethwell.

The tape rolls. "Cut four," calls Peter on the tape before the song plays back into the control room. The thick and heavy synth bass sound drives relentlessly under Mkhize's screamingly bright guitar and Tefo's punchy organ and the women's close vocal harmonies, answered in overlapping interjections by the men. The synth bass sits down there at the bottom of the mix, with the drum thumping hard and dry [thump thump] and with Bethwell's bass guitar riffing on a simple repeated melody. I imagine the phonograph needle. I wait for its jump. With the distorted edge to the synth bass sound, I hear the sound of the sidewalks in the 1970s suburbs.

Track 2   Liveness as Historically Constituted

Mbaqanga's stylistic history exemplifies the ironies in the idea of liveness as unmediated performance and brings attention to the fact that Africanness is a contemporary discursive position inflected in specific ways within the context of local conditions. There is no live mbaqanga sound separable from studio production and virtually no performance practice outside the promotion of recordings. That is, there is no tradition of acoustic performance behind mbaqanga, and there never has been. Neither is there much historical connection to rural South African modes of living and expression in which the idea of Africanness is rooted.

Mbaqanga's development through the mid-1960s and its heyday in the early 1970s is linked to political and technological developments of the time. The domestic political happenings that directly impinged on mbaqanga's development include the repression of the vibrant street and club life that jazz and other black, urban, politicized, popular expression had enjoyed; the exodus of many artists around the time of the banning of the African National Congress, the South African Communist Party, and aligned organizations; the expansion of state-owned media institutions to promote the ideology of separate development; increased productivity in the music industry; unionization and rapid proletarianization in urban areas through the 1970s; intensifying internal resistance and critique of ethnicity as an apartheid construct; and increased deployment of state force.

International happenings also affected mbaqanga, though less directly. In particular, mbaqanga musicians monitored the civil-rights movement in the United States with avid attention. The South African, black-produced *Zonk* magazine, directed at urban black South Africans through the 1950s, covered African American musical figures, sports stars, and some political leaders and events as much as it covered local issues. *Zonk* advertised lists and reviews of the latest American records available in South Africa alongside the same of new local hit singles. Tips on how to wear your tie or your porkpie hat to be in style with African Americans appeared alongside advertisements for fashionable clothing. After *Zonk*, *Drum* took up the flag, promoting black-is-beautiful commodities, performing artists, sounds, events, figureheads, sportsmen and -women, and beauty queens. Among nonactivist citizens in urban black South Africa, much of the success of the civil-rights struggle was gauged through the prominence of African American music stars and athletes.[21]

Mbaqanga musicians and their fans flocked to hear Jimmy Smith, Otis Redding, Ray Charles, Millie Jackson, Percy Sledge, Two Tons of Fun, Timmy Thomas, Isaac Hayes, the Tavares, and Clarence Carter when they performed in the country in the 1970s. They also listened to Jimmy McGriff, Jack McDuff, Richard "Groove" Holmes, Booker T. and the MG's, James Brown, Aretha Franklin, Diana Ross, the O'Jays, and Billy Preston. They read about them in local black magazines and newspapers and listened to their music on radio and records. With these men and women as representatives, South Africans looked to African American wealth and to African Americans' public prominence and prestige as signs of their having advanced further in the struggle for civil liberties (Hamm 1988). On this basis, mbaqanga took the African American soul movement as its predominant model in terms of style and ethos (Hamm 1988; Coplan 1985).

The Hammond organ coupled with a Leslie cabinet-speaker was distinctly associated with the sound of soul. Early in the 1970s mbaqanga musicians imported it into their lineup. Its use and playing style was directly inspired by Jimmy Smith and his Philly sound, along with other Blue Note and Prestige jazz organists of the time, and by soul and R&B bands that subsequently incorporated the organ into their lineup. "The sound of the Hammond—that's the original keyboard—was the sound of Jimmy Smith. That was the sound that also worked for mbaqanga," Bethwell explained as nonchalantly as though he were talking about the transparency of sunlight. "Of course, Black Moses [the Soul Brothers organist] didn't rob Jimmy Smith, he played the sound in his own way."

The Hammond was massively popular among mbaqanga musicians and fans. "I had to put wheels on the B3 to shunt it from studio to studio and session to session. They loved that thing!" recounts engineer John Lindemann. Where a B3 wasn't available, the C3 stood in for it. On the stage, the lighter transportable Farfisa took its place. As the Farfisa went out of fashion, the single and double manual Korgs (CX-3 and BX-3)—which have drawbars like the Hammond—replaced it. Then came the Roland Jupiter Four synthesizer, which had a Hammond sound preset, and after that, the Yamaha DX7 (loved for its pitch-bend wheel).[22]

In the later 1970s and early 1980s, the organ mediated the domestic transition from identification with soul to disco and opened the way into a keyboard-based disco sound that eventually became the sound of the township youth. The Soul Brothers were key figures in this shift. They expanded and modernized their keyboard base, although they never crossed over solidly into township disco as a marketing category themselves. While there were countless organists, none could claim as much distinction as the Soul Brothers for making organ an indelibly South African sound with overt transatlantic links and an ever-modernizing thrust. For heyday mbaqanga musicians and fans, a link to the African American soul movement and thereby into a discourse about blackness and modernity was embedded in the sound of the organ.

The organ also provided a point of entry into the world of synthesized and electronic keyboard-based music and thereby into the global community of technologically engaged popular-music producers. By its very makeup, keyboard music demanded more technological attention for black musicians in the domestic studio. As engineer John describes it, "[Musicians] used to come in and play everything live. And then slowly as the technology got more involved and better, we started getting into multitrack. Black music moved with multitracking, though not quite as fast as white music. In other words, white music was far more intricate. We were still laying them down live—but on multitrack—and then mixing them afterwards. So the product was getting better. But it was still basically live . . . until, gee, I don't know, right up till about 1975 or somewhere round there.

"But then they really started using the technology. That's when disco was very prevalent in white music. Of course the blacks cottoned on to disco also. And you can't do disco that way—it's a multitrack medium. Disco music was created by multitrack. So black music got into disco, and that's when they started learning the technology and using the technology and putting in all the extra bits and pieces. That's when it really started evolving. And they started adding more things, and double-tracking, and their sound got bigger and bigger and bigger till eventually black music was at the level of white music—sound-wise, not necessary playing-wise or performance-wise.[23] They went through the disco period, and they really got into the multitracking story, so there was no more of this coming in [to the studio just for] one day. It was taking just as long to do a black album as it was to do a white album. They sort of caught up and got on that same sort of par, although it was different music—still their own style.

"Then the synthesizer sounds started coming out and everything started becoming electronic, and they started using drum boxes and the typical synthesizer sounds. So less and less actual live playing was being done. There was only live singing and live guitar work. They really cottoned on—so much so that they are actually behind the rest of the world now [1989], because they are really getting into this synthetic music now. I think they're reaching their peak. That's basically how it has evolved: now they're right up with modern technology."

Musicians developed styles that required the use of the latest studio technology. They therefore needed more studio time and bigger studio budgets. From heyday mbaqanga, through soul and disco, then into township pop, the drive for the same kind of access that white musicians had to the studio space, technological facility, and company budget was an innovative component of black studio-music styles. The struggle on the part of local black musicians to receive the same respect and attention that white musics and musicians were granted in the studio resonates with the struggles that were being waged in the streets, though the studio dynamic was not necessarily articulated in overtly political terms of resistance and liberation. Studio contestation was argued in the racialized terms of apartheid, but it was equally much a struggle to be recognized as modern subjects and as participants in international popular culture production.

Mbaqanga inserted itself into South Africa as modern black radio music in the mid- to late 1960s and flourished for about a decade. It expressed its modernity in two ways. First, it celebrated technology and exploited the media facilities of the SABC and the recording industry. Second, it forged symbolic links with a black diasporic struggle that had advanced further elsewhere in the world. The African American style that mbaqanga musicians chose to emulate and reinterpret provided tools and terms for reaching and expressing these modernities.

In the later 1980s and early 1990s, various turns of events offered music-makers motivations to newly articulate African-centered identities, as opposed to identifying with a global black sociopolitical condition. The boom in the World Music industry following Paul Simon's *Graceland*, the rise in ethnic nationalism in South Africa, the opening up of the African continent to South Africa after the release of Mandela and the unbanning of the organizations of the liberation movement in 1990, and the sense of a pending "African renaissance" (to borrow Thabo Mbeki's coinage) in South Africa all presented music-makers with new reasons to embrace their heritages. Within this context, mbaqanga came to articulate a specifically African sensibility. To typify the synth bass as an African sound would have been unlikely in the 1970s, yet in the 1990s it is transparently African to the musicians in the studio. Mbaqanga's ethos had shifted from foregrounding an idea of blackness to Africanness. This is a shift from sounding modern to sounding traditional, from an aesthetic of sounding mediated to one of sounding live.

playback

Jane smiles with the detachment of gazing back nine years at their 1983 LP cover. She, Janet, and the three other then Izintombi Zesimanjemanje members are seated around a glass-topped coffee table. Poised and elegant in tailored jackets and straight skirts, they perch on the edges of their seats, ankles and knees together, pointing off to the side. Janet pages through a glossy magazine opened on the table.

It reminds me of a 1980 Mahotella Queens cover (*Tsamaya Moratuoa*), which makes me think of *Garden and Home* magazine, which my mother used to subscribe to in the suburbs. The four Queens, all dressed alike in starch-white pantsuits, pose around a white, wrought-iron garden table placed in a shaded, suburban, garden alcove. They lean on the table in choreographed formation. Pink fuchsias cascade from a hanging basket.

The Queens remind me of Zesimanjemanje in red pantsuits and boots, swiveling their hips in a row as they sing into microphones. Mike lines tangle up the 1981 cover photo's foreground (*Umahlongwane*). Then there are the swinging bellbottoms, platform shoes, and gigantic Afro hairdo covers, like Zesimanjemanje's 1976 *Isitha Sami Nguwe*; and the Airlight Swingsters posing in shiny, floral shirts and tight, white trousers in front of a two-person prop plane and, on the back of the sleeve, captured in midair, out of focus, jumping in choreographed flamboyance onstage.

Deep, gritty sixteenths pulsate at the bottom of the mix.
"Ngigibel'ipanoyi, ngigibel'ilaksari," sing Sibusiso Mbatha
nabangani. "I'm riding on a plane, I'm riding in a luxury vehicle,"
they sing in sweet, close-harmony soul vocals.[24]

Wrapped in blankets and wearing grass Swazi hats, the Mahotella Queens pose serenely outdoors in 1983 (*Khwatha O Mone*). In a dusty Johannesburg park they sit on grass mats and a blanket with the band. With outstretched arms they offer communal beer in decorated drinking pots to their fans, the viewers (Amaqhawe Omgqashiyo 1983).

If I have a favorite, it is the first Zesimanjemanje LP jacket, from 1967. The young women wear Smokey Robinson and the Miracles black-and-white checkered vests, crooners' smiles, and slender black bow ties. Sporting black, peaked caps and CBS logo badges on their vests, they click their fingers. Janet was not with Zesimanjemanje then. Now, in the rehearsal room she puts on the smile, does the finger click, and laughs, remembering the times, the sound, and their youthfulness.

Jane smiles with the detachment of gazing back nine years at their LP *Zenda Zangishiya*. I tease her about her proper pose in the coffee-table photo. "In those days we were very decent, expensive ladies!" she quips. She chuckles at her younger self while she straightens her jacket and skirt and knots her glossy scarf before leaving for home after rehearsal.

Tracks Mixed *Liveness Particularized*

The tension between the "authenticity" of performance and the "falsity" of mediated sound is a discursive one. In popular music discourse, especially about World Beat, and in "First World" ideology about the "Third World," authenticity is encoded in music making as an idea about sounding live. The idea of sounding live is a trope of authenticity in both recorded musics and in African music making. The privileging of liveness

Isigqi Sesimanje on stage, George Goch Stadium, Johannesburg, 6 October 1991. Left to right: Bheki Mthembu, Jane Dlamini, Janet Dlamini. *Photo by TJ Lemon.*

Izintombi Zesimanjemanje on stage in the Super Star Studio, Salisbury, Rhodesia, March 1975, dressed to sing their song "Ukulunga kwami" (My Kindness). Left: Lindiwe Mthembu; right: Jane Dlamini. *Courtesy Jane Dlamini.*

Izintombi Zesimanjemanje posing in one of their performing outfits, Noord Street rehearsal rooms, Johannesburg, 1970. Left to right: Thoko Khumalo, Jane Dlamini, Sana Mnguni, Nunu Maseko, Thobi Mnguni. *Courtesy Jane Dlamini.*

Izintombi Zesimanjemanje on stage at the Rio Bioscope, Market Street, Johannesburg, 1974. Left to right: Nobesuthu Shawe, Lindiwe Mthembu, Jane Dlamini. *Courtesy Jane Dlamini.*

in each of these expressive domains corroborates with and enhances that in the other.

In the case of South African mbaqanga the tension between authenticity and falsity and between "African" and "mediated" musics encodes sociopolitical discourse about social difference. Specifically, discourse about liveness in the studio shapes and expresses a particular Africanness. The aesthetic desire for live-sounding production is refracted through different nostalgias about blackness and nativism. This creates a trope of authenticity that shapes contemporary mbaqanga production. One nostalgia remembers a moment in mbaqanga studio practice in which technology enabled the voice of live musicians. Another nostalgia remembers and retells a moment in which mbaqanga musicians embodied that voice in staged display. Another imagines a moment in which African music making was unmediated, intuitive, and integrated into the practice of everyday life.

This discursive configuration of nostalgia and authenticity is the mediating form through which mbaqanga style is shaped by social practice and social practice is reproduced in the production of mbaqanga. The production and distribution of ideas and values of African musicality and African Otherness are exponentially intensified by the technology and institution of the music industry, as are the power differentials between owners of production and musical laborers. Furthermore, in mbaqanga the materialization, integration, and circulation of this Africanness wholly concerns, speaks to, and speaks about technological mediation, as it does about mediating social difference. In so doing, it renegotiates the dialogue over its authenticity as African in relation to the dialogue about the authenticity of mediated music.

Unpacking the components of liveness opens up a theoretical passage into the complexities of mediation and into the analysis of its forms. It suggests that links between discourse and practice, institution and individual, and market, politics, and performance are deeply embedded in the creative participation of technological forms.

The idea that Africans "know" something different and differently, that they have a knowledge that is sensed, felt, and lived, is articulated through the sounds of blackness and Africanness. These sounds and discourse about them can be positioned within the sociopolitical debates about race, class, and ethnicity in South Africa and within the socioeconomic packaging of race, class, and ethnicity in the World Music market. The whole discursive configuration is played and played out in mbaqanga music production. It is reproduced in technological practice in the recording process, in studio social practice, in the shaping of mbaqanga style over time, in shifts in forms that constitute the genre/marketing category, and in the local and global marketing arenas within which mbaqanga is positioned.

Blackness/Africanness, liveness, and authenticity are negotiable, provisional notions that are dialogically refigured in socially and formally reconstituting moments. These moments are wholly aesthetic and deeply political. They hold within them the possibility for artistic and social renewal precisely because they are concerned with images of race, class, and ethnicity and with the experience of personhood.

The First World preoccupation with authenticity—a spin-off from global commodity production[25]—produces Africanness as a particular idea of liveness, as a groove and sensuality that enables certain kinds of flow of products, sounds, images, people, and wealth. Yet even as this global flow genericizes the idea of Africa into a singular sensibility, which readily diffuses further into an idea of the nonwhite or non-Western or non-First World or noncosmopolitan Other, it arises out of cultural production in a state-based social, and specifically racial, hierarchy. This apartheid hierarchy is in transition. While South African social and moral positionings are deeply rooted in decades of apartheid history and insidiously conscientious ideological production, they are currently up for grabs. Africanness—that is, the reshaping of a local aesthetic in the encounter with global commodity production—participates in reconfiguring local ideas of personhood and local social relationships, in and out of the studio. It facilitates moving beyond the local, and it reproduces local senses of difference.

The South African case offers a look into a uniquely positioned relationship between the racial politics of music capital and apartheid state as it is refracted through the discourse of authenticity. As Feld writes, "As the discourse of authenticity becomes more militant and nativistic, more complicated, and more particularized to specific interest and taste groups, the activities of appropriation get more overt and outrageous, as well as more subtle, legally sanctioned, accepted, and taken-for-granted" (Keil and Feld 1994, 272). In this process, he continues, the owners of the means of cultural production become one and the same as the guardians of authenticity. In this way, the apartheid state accumulated power through the construction and maintenance of a kind of authenticity. For the state, that discourse of authenticity was one about ethnic purity and racial difference, an idea shaped and sustained largely through the exploitation of the media and popular expressive forms.

Deconstructing the idea of Africanness as it is constituted and constituting in mbaqanga production reveals conceptual pathways through style into an intricate discursive web. Exploring the significance and forms of Africanness demands simultaneous unpacking of other subtropes, the meanings of which are always emergent, always negotiable, and variously invested.

Playback

July 1989

Alton Ngubane and his band are recording a cassette of Inkatha Freedom Party songs with instrumental backing. In the first session in a small studio in town, Tom, the engineer, sets up the mikes, prepares the console for the backing tracks, and programs a drum track.

The musicians banter. They warm up for the session. The keyboard player sets up on the outboard effects console. Rim-shots and bass beats pop from the big speakers. Next comes the lisping hi-hat. The lead singer practices in the vocal booth. The guitarist gets his fingers running up and down the guitar strings.

Tom can't hear himself programming, he says, please.

Next he picks a channel on the console for the bass guitar. Bongani lugs the amp into the little booth. He starts to plug in.

No, says Tom, holding down the talkback button.

Bongani looks up. He plugs in anyway. He starts twisting the amp controls.

No, says Tom.

Tom calls Bongani back into the control room. The bass must go directly into the console. Much cleaner sound, he explains. Sorry, no half-assed sound is going out of this studio.

The band wants the bass amped and miked. Period.

We're dedicated to sound quality in this studio, Tom insists.

The band wants the bass amped. Period.

They all try to explain, they talk, they listen.

Look, I'm always open to suggestions, but I know it's not gonna work, Tom says.

He shrugs.

Ngubane lights up and takes a puff.

Tom bends over the console and sweeps his forearms over the faders, pulling them down to zero. He switches off the controls.

The band watches.

No one says anything.

They pack up their instruments.

That man doesn't know our music, Bongani grumbles to me as we leave. He doesn't even like it.

Sounding Figures

Guide Vocal

31 March 1992

In the sixth of seven studio sessions, producer West, engineer Neil, and the musicians are programming a synthesized flute riff to overdub onto their title song, "Lomculo Unzima." Musicians, singers, and production team are crowded into the control room. Some squeeze together on the couch at the back, behind all the recording equipment; others cluster around the keyboard. They smoke, listen, chat, throw in their takes on the problems with the sound.

Tefo plays the DX7 that sits on top of the outboard effects rack. He's trying to play a riff that West has requested. Tefo's struggle with a seemingly easy task is dragging the session down; his reams of mistakes stretch the day into a longer one. West rocks and swivels, rocks and swivels in his producer's chair behind the console. He listens and corrects Tefo. He sings the flute line, over and over. Tefo plays along, trying to match West's melody and chords. Hansford picks the part on his acoustic guitar, while singing the notes Tefo needs to correct.

Gesticulating musicians chip in, in Zulu, "It's wrong—the top note."

"Here's the space where you enter."

"We need two notes here."

"Maybe he'll get it right when we join him."

West keeps singing the riff for Tefo, over and over. He whimsically slips a word or two between his vocables and soon he's made up a whole line of lyrics for the second half of the riff.

He sings in English, "If we're together today, love me now and forever."

He peals into laughter. Others chuckle.

Tefo Sikhale, Johannesburg, 2002. *Photo by Brett Eloff.*

"You're composing!" teases Jane. (They are all speaking Zulu; Neil doesn't understand their conversation.)

"It's very easy to make up whitey bubblegum songs," West replies. "I can make twenty in one day!"

"Hey! It's very easy!" agrees singer Joana, overlapping with his talk.

"Twenty! I can make you twenty!" boasts West. "All I need is two words, only three words."

Jane chips in, "Ja, you just lay down doh what what what what."

"Then the song is done," concludes Joana.

Tefo is still struggling to get the riff into his fingers. Hansford strums the chord progression to help him while West chats on about composing what he calls whitey bubblegum music.

"Ja, [two or three words, and] then you just leave out the guitars and play the drums." He plays an imaginary trap set in front of him while vocally imitating a drum pattern in time with the flute phrase. Hansford joins in, strumming his guitar, as if he were a singer-songwriter or country musician. (He loves Dolly Parton.)

To this guitar accompaniment West spontaneously composes a verse:

My final romance is for you, my love.
I need you too badly, forever, my love.
My final romance: I'm gonna get you tonight;
I'm gonna kiss you now and forever anytime.

He performs his hyperbolic love-text with parodic playfulness, deliberately enunciating "gonna," singing in a flat, distanced voice and just under pitch at the peaks of his phrases, and pedantically adhering to the beat. Hansford enhances the whimsy of the moment with his guitar strumming and by slipping in a run up to the first beat of the second verse and as a coda.

Hansford keeps up his strumming pattern as Tefo repeats the flute line —he has almost figured out the notes now. West adds an impromptu vocalized percussion line, matching Hansford's strumming pattern. The three of them groove through the riff together while Neil starts up the click track, synchronizing it with their beat and tempo.

As the riff ends, Neil asks West, "Can we take it?"

"Let's try," he answers.

"Let's go for it," suggests Neil.

This playful moment—a moment of disintegration of the studio session, a hiatus in productivity—rests on particular musical and metamusical discourses. Here I scrutinize this foundation in order to provide concrete instances of image-making and expressions of subjectivity in the constitution of musical experience for music-makers in the studio. How is musical experience figured? What are the relationships among playing with stereotypes, innovating by manipulating socially marked sounds, and shaping subjectivity in the process of making music?

My task is to integrate historical analyses of the political life of stereotypes with ethnographic interpretations of the work stereotypes do in shaping embodied identities, full of feeling, in contemporary practice. In particular, I use Taussig's thoughts on the peculiarities of colonial contexts and Robert Thornton's discussion on the South African/Zulu historical case. Concerning image and feeling, the Bakhtinian work of Kathleen Stewart (1996), Susan Lepselter (1998), Benjamin Feinberg (1998), and Erica David (1998) informs my analysis. While cut 3 also presented types in action, here I develop the ways in which, as objectified as they might be, social types can be productive of deeper experiences of identity and of collective and personal voices.

What is a figure? I am thinking concurrently of two concepts, one derived from social theory and the other from music theory. First, a figure is a socially constituted type, or icon, presented and recognized through style. Figuring, then, becomes an ongoing process of elaborating, reworking, recovering, and "trying on" social types.

Second, a figure is a repeating motive or pattern. Here I borrow the musical term to refer to a recurring timbre or sound quality, rather than to a harmonic/melodic or rhythmic motive. A specific usage of the term couples the figure with a concept of a ground. The figure is a motive that is subject to ornamentation, to variation in repetition, over a more or less steady (bass) line, termed the "ground." At times, the parts can exchange their roles of figure and ground.

In combination, figuring is the process of realizing abstract tropes into particular voices and as specific experiences (Fox 1995). In a sense, it is a process of arguing musically, by means of repeated and varied motives, over ideas about social relations.

Track I *Playing the Stereotype*

take 1 : figuring whiteness

"It's easy to make up whitey bubblegum songs!" says West. "Just two or three words—"

"Ja, you just lay down doh what what what what," chips in Jane.

"Then the song is done," concludes Joana.

In their parody West and the musicians are mimicking mainstream international pop. They are mimicking the music that dominates the global market. Since particularities are glossed over in an essentializing process, it is no surprise that this is an undifferentiated global category for them at this moment. The lack of differentiation also resonates with the marketing discourse around World Musics, from within which they speak. World Music is marketed as a celebration of diversity and cultural rootedness, and it is contrasted with mainstream popular musics on this basis.[1]

From West and the musicians' perspective, this music is inferior be-

West Nkosi's control-room
improvisation, "My Final Romance,"
31 March 1992. *Transcription by
James Harkins.*

cause its guitars merely strum, its drums dominate the mix, its vocal delivery is disengaged, and its texts are inane. It is music without swing or groove or "participatory discrepancies" (Keil 1987). It is dead in tune and dead on time and, hence, "white." The musicians communicate their take on this music in considered talk about it, as well as musically through performance. West's vocal timbre, rhythmic delivery, the exaggerated emphasis on the first beat, his emphatic "gonna" marking white slang, his deliberately flat intonation, and his improvised hyperbolic text all pass judgement on its artistry.

In addition to mimicking international pop, West is also joking about the musicality of the genre that dominates the domestic market. He is laughing at local township pop, the music pejoratively and affectionately called "bubblegum." "Twenty! I can make twenty in a day!" he boasts. Bubblegum is the hit-oriented, keyboard-based music of the urban black South African youth market that evolved out of disco in the mid-1980s and remained popular into the mid 1990s. In practice, this style takes no less time to produce than mbaqanga does and its stars and consumers are not white.

So why is he calling township pop stylistically white?

Text, music, production techniques, and marketing all support his argument. That township pop songs are sung principally in English, with repetitive lyrics about love, lust, longing, and betrayal, earns them West's label.

Dan Tshanda's "bubblegum" voice sweeps out over a punchy buoyant groove. "Your smile / cannot confuse me by the look / in your face," he sings.

"Face face face face," mimics his chorus, filling in more notes of the chord with each repetition.

The precision of sequenced articulation reigns in the immanent energy of the groove.

"I can see that your eyes are full of jealousy . . ."

"Jealousy."

". . . when we are facing each other / you are smiling interest in passing."

"Eya eya oye," cruise the chorus, "la la la. . . ."[2]

Some bubblegum texts describe the violence and commodification of fast urban life, but these are generally also dismissed by mbaqanga music-makers as superficial textual treatments.[3]

In contrast to the failings of bubblegum lyrics, mbaqanga artists consider contemporary traditional and mbaqanga lyrics to be poetic. They are predominantly composed in Zulu. Composers select their images and words with care, tell stories in their texts, and include cultural referents. In addition to singing about their musical prowess, romantic relationships, and urban and work-related issues, the musicians sing about social problems (especially about struggles with poverty), rural living, and traditional custom.

Musically, township pop is white because it shares formal characteristics with particular popular styles that black South Africans in the early 1990s identified as music produced and consumed by white people, namely, intensively produced studio music that grew out of a rock tradition. The approach of Dan Tshanda, bandleader and producer of Splash, the leading township pop band in the early 1990s, serves as an example. "Musically, it's quite innovative," Neil reckoned. He was programming a new release for Tshanda. "Dan likes new and different sounds—it's a really big sounding project. The music's a kind of mixture between 'Oxygène' and Alan Parsons—and some black stuff, so it's gonna be interesting."[4] Tshanda and other township pop composers exploit the studio's means to vary the positioning of sounds in acoustic space. They play with depth, height, breadth, timbre, and textural density in order to bring interest to a usually repetitive harmonic, melodic, and rhythmic architecture.

A tight, almost reedy bass riff popping on the left; tsk tsk tsk tsk steadily pricking on the right; a tight, almost reedy counterpoint fed to both sides in the middle range.

A hard bass drum with a click to its attack and almost no sustain bounces from underneath. Snare, slap, scraper, wooden block, and a bass line jostle the groove. "Your smile . . . ," sweeps in Tshanda's reverbed, double-tracked solo over a lush brassy-string bed. Men's reverbed voices hang under his voice in the second part of his phrases.

A triple-tracked women's chorus overlaps the "eya eya oye" of the triple-tracked men while steely offbeat chordal punches bounce through the mix. Immanent energy is reigned in by the tantalizing precision. Echoed phrase endings grow into fuller chords. The brassy-string bed envelops the action. A drumroll, way in the back, and a cymbal crash. Gasp, for but a second, while the women's echos fade. Tsk tsk tsk tsk pricking on the right,

an almost reedy bass popping a little differently in the left,
the contrapuntal line rides up front in the middle range.
"Your smile. . . ."

Township pop is keyboard and drum based with short call-and-response vocals. It is largely programmed and sequenced—and meant to sound that way. It uses a lot of absolutely electronic, contemporary-sounding timbres, created as themselves rather than designed to represent amplified or acoustics instruments. Signal-processing effects such as reverb, chorus, and echo are self-consciously added to the recorded voice to make it sound miked and manipulated. Similarly, those programmed sounds that reproduce timbres of other instruments sound like electronic reproductions. This is partly because they are coupled with a metronomic obsession, partly because each repeated tone or sequenced phrase is identical in terms of sound quality, partly because of the processing effects that are added so obviously to the basic source sound.

"Passing passing, face face face face," sings the chorus, fading
into echo while their sibilance turns to electronic sizzle, paused,
repeated, panned, repeated, dropped out.

By exploiting the newest technology in shaping its style, township pop is produced to sound state-of-the-art, highly mediated, urban, in control, at the edge, and faddish. It embraces modernity and youthfulness, much as mbaqanga did in the 1970s.

West is calling township pop white because it sounds highly mediated. The way he expresses his distaste for the music draws on the ideological, discursive dichotomy between rationality and intuition, West and the Rest: technical wizardry, science, rationality, and mind are linked with white people; blackness is associated with body, beat, and expressivity. When West mimics the musical limitations of whiteys in his sung parody, he mimics their lack of feel for the beat; when he dismisses township pop as white, he is casting it aside because it does not sound as though it grows out of an essential Africa.

In terms of its status in the early 1990s music industry, township pop held the equivalent position locally to mainstream pop internationally. It dominated the market. This was, of course, a coveted status. Its key musicians and producers gained the kind of control over time and space in the studio that white musicians enjoy and that trad and mbaqanga artists who only have a local market don't. (The Mahotella Queens are the exception, but their product is geared primarily to an international market.) The most successful male township pop producers like Dan Tshanda and Sello Twala have come into their own as all-round pop stars, producers, composers, band managers, programmers, and label owners, and they have accumulated substantial wealth in the process.

At the 1992 Gallo Gold Awards ceremony, Dan Tshanda leaps onto the stage, a tight, almost reedy bass riff popping from the stage speakers on the left; tsk tsk tsk tsk steadily pricking on the right; a tight, almost reedy counterpoint fed to both sides in the middle range. He thanks his band, his engineer, his record company, his mother, his fans. He hoists Splash's framed platinum disc above his head. He bows again. The diners add whistles to their ovation.

Whiteness in West's impromptu song "My Final Romance" is singular, simplistic, and hyperbolic. It unambiguously represents the "not Us." It is a stereotype, viewed from a distance, judged from a disengaged stance. "White" signifies something culturally inferior, artistically compromised through mass marketing, and historically ungrounded. The particular features the musicians exaggerate in their parody are the unfeeling, unsensuous ones. They exaggerate what they view as the constraints of the style, which the performed stereotype represents as limitations of the social group.

The stereotype is itself a reduced form of its signified (white people and pop music), but when seen as an articulation within a field of images-in-process, with which agentive and imaginative individuals play, its productivity and inherent tensions come to the fore.

Whitey bubblegum musicality and ethos are ridiculed because they are undesirable. Yet the music and musicians are recognized as being powerfully situated as a mainstream product. The music-makers' parody contains and plays out this tension in productive ways. On the one hand, they take on the dominant and shatter its image. But this is a momentary discursive play that has no effect on the dominant in itself. On the other hand, they draw some kind of power from the stereotyped original in the process of imitation (Taussig 1993). The parody mobilizes their resources: they get the session going again; they claim control over the process of imaging; and they are collectively affirmed in their Alterity as African.

playback

Neil Kuny is also a drummer. He has overdubbed a steel-pan part for Isigqi's "Lomculo Unzima" by playing electronic drum pads and shaping the timbre at the desk. West and the musicians are decidedly pleased. Now Neil is programming percussion overdubs. The session is cruising; the sound is happening.

"Oh! This is a man who knows things of the Zulu!" nods Hansford in Zulu, as he ducks his head in Neil's direction and raises his eyebrows to show that he's impressed.

"UngumNguni lona" (He's a Zulu, that one), agrees West seriously.

"Ja, indeed, I'm noticing him," chips in a musician in Zulu.

"Kenu Koni!" (He's a Zulu!) cheers Tefo in Sotho.

Then West turns to Neil, switches into English and wordplays. "Are you Koni or Nguni, Neil?" he demands.

"Nguni," replies Neil without missing a beat or stopping work on his conga sound.

The control room erupts into laughter.

"He's Nguni!" cackles a musician through his laughter.

take 2 : figuring South Africa

Tefo is struggling to get the riff into his fingers. Hansford strums the chord progression to help him, while West chats on about composing what he calls whitey bubblegum music.

"Ja, you just leave out the guitars and play the drums." He plays an imaginary trap set in front of him, while vocally imitating a drum pattern in time with the flute phrase. Hansford joins in, strumming his guitar, as if a singer-songwriter or country musician.

Township pop usually leaves out guitars while emphasizing the rhythm tracks built up from the MC500 or some other drum machine—another reason why West accuses it of being as white as international pop. He regards the absence of the guitar and what that absence signifies about style to detract from the genre's identity as a local African music, that is, as a South African sound. "Our guitars keep the natural feel," he explained to me when describing how he shaped the music of Mahlathini and the Mahotella Queens for international consumption. "If you play acoustic guitar alone, it doesn't appeal to the young people. They are now used to the big sound—bang! bang! bang!" We'd been talking about the house bass sound in dance clubs that West had checked out in the U.K. He continued, "So we put those keyboards in to make it a little bit stronger and to the young people's taste. But the guitar is there to keep the originality of the South African sound. If you take that guitar out, it is no longer a local sound and people will easily pick that up."

Steel strings. Acoustic guitar. A Zulu trad introduction: Marks Mankwane ripples down from the upper ranges, down onto the lower tonic, with some twists and turns along the way. His thumb parallels the line in the bass. The tonic rings alone. Then he plucks the band into a groove.

The Mahotella Queens enter. "Come everybody and learn from us," they sing. They elaborate the story in verse and chorus over a mbaqanga backing.

Up comes Marks's electric guitar: up in the mix, up the guitar neck, up into the higher registers. Its acoustic partner picks a sweet counterpoint in the middle register, sitting secretly in the mix on a breathy accordion bed. Mahlathini interjects his bass drama. ("Bon Jour," Mahlathini and Mahotella Queens 1991b)

The guitar style, as West notes, distinctly flags the sound as South African in the World Music market and as a local production in the domestic market. This is not only an issue of instrumentation. It is also about the timbre, playing style, sound balance, and formal function. In township pop, if guitars are ever present in the mix (and this is rare), they are blended into the rhythmic and textural backing. Whereas in mbaqanga and Zulu trad, the guitar is conversationally partnered to the voice and other lead instruments (bass and organ), and mixed up alongside them.

"To us, [the guitar] must get that click," explains Jane to me as she sings a simple repeating riff, imitating a sharp percussive attack and tight timbre. "Ti ti ti de, ti ti ti de," she sings with a leap down to the last note to which she adds a little sustain and glide. She sings the riff almost monotonally, omitting melody to emphasize the timbral features. From this first premise, she goes on to explain that the sound implicates a playing style, played high up on the neck and taking over the role of the voice in breaks between the vocals, "so that when you sing, the voices must be clear; when you leave singing, [the guitarists] will run all over the guitar strings" to fill up the texture. Acoustic guitarists bring out the stridence of their instruments by using cheaper steel strings and by means of their picking techniques. Historically, mbaqanga has used electric instruments only, but West combines electric and acoustic in his contemporary version of mbaqanga. The inclusion of acoustic sounds is a move to traditionalize mbaqanga sound and thereby emphasize that it is African and local.

Whether electric or acoustic, mbaqanga guitar is recorded and manipulated to make it cut through a busy mix. "You want to take *all* that warmth out of it," engineer Lee Short explains to me. "They don't like it, because it starts clashing with the bass. They like it hard. Hard and tight and *nasty!* It's got to be nasty! It's actually got to ring. It's got to scream out at you. If it's not *screaming* out—" He pinches his fingers together, wincing. I laugh at his pain. "Look I mean, if you look at the musical content, it's quite busy. It's full. There's a lot of notes. And if you don't have that guitar hard and nasty, it doesn't actually cut through, so you can't really hear it. It's got to twang away—put a bit of a flange on it, so that it even makes more of a statement, you know, so that you can really hear it between all the other instruments—because you're fighting up against them. [In Zulu trad] you've got the guitar which is screaming, you've got the accordion that's screaming, you've got the hi-hats that are also screaming away. So you're looking for lots and lots of brightness, and you've got to try and get that guitar to stand out." Most basically, a sound engineer takes the warmth out of the guitar sound by boosting the upper frequency range and cutting the lower midrange. He produces a sharp attack by adding very little predelay and brightens the sound by exciting it with flanging, chorusing effects, and phasing. He gives it presence by using little reverb.

The latest mix of Isigqi's "South Africa" rains down into the control room from the large monitors. "Bring up the guitar, the small one which cries up top," calls out Hansford over the playback.

Well, shrugs West, nowadays "you don't have to squeeze [the guitar sound] hard," because stereo and multitracking make it possible to give a sense of more room. You can make the guitar clearly audible by placing it in a three-dimensional space. "It's got to sound nicely so that people can follow it, you see." So that the sound might appeal better to consumers who are not accustomed to listening through a thick local mix, West takes some of the harsh edge off the guitar sound and sweetens it. In doing so, from his point of view he doesn't compromise the South Africanness of the sound—conceptually it is the original sound, reproduced within the means of contemporary technology. Characteristically, West qualifies the argument by bringing some historical specificity and (by implication) some political realism to it: the guitar sound was necessarily strident in earlier recordings because the studio lacked the technological capacity to separate sound. Not only this, of course, but black music was not always given sophisticated technological workovers.

West's pinpointing of the guitar as the sonic icon of South Africa makes historical sense. Indeed, the guitar sound carries a long South African musical and colonial legacy into contemporary music. The instrument was brought to the region by Portuguese explorers and traders in the sixteenth century and has probably been available in trade stores from the time such stores were set up by European settlers. Allingham records the availability of cheap, locally made instruments as beginning in the 1930s (1999, 646).

In various parts of Africa musicians have transferred playing techniques and musical styles from indigenous instruments onto the guitar.[5] Among southern African peoples, it is only the Zulu, Tsonga, and Ndebele of Zimbabwe who thoroughly and early on integrated the guitar into their "traditional" musical repertoire. (Allingham also makes this point [1999, 646].) Traditional Zulu guitar music (maskanda) draws most notably on the formal structure and harmonic pattern of the Zulu musical bow as does its accompanying vocal delivery on the singing style of bow players (Rycroft 1977).[6] The harmonic progression alternates between two fundamentals, usually a tone apart, in cyclic rhythmic patterns, with parts of the vocal line and plucked melodic fragments formed by selecting upper harmonics. Performances open with a florid, plucked display of the key and scale of the song. In the late 1960s strumming was replaced by picking—an innovation of the great guitarist Phuzushukela, a star of Hamilton's Isibaya Esikhulu. Phuzushukela also introduced the electric guitar to the style.

Over the decades of the music industry's involvement in local musics, this style has been multiply transformed and has influenced other styles with which it has come into contact. It was most prolifically recorded in the 1970s, along with mbaqanga and isicathamiya.[7] Produced by mbaqanga's producers, engineered by the same engineers, often backed by mbaqanga band members, touring and sharing festival stages with mbaqanga and jive groups, and supported within the same production houses, maskanda (labeled "Zulu traditional" on record) inevitably infused its sound and some of its playing style into mbaqanga.[8]

"To us, [the guitar] must sound the maskandi way" to have an African sound, Jane says. "To us," she specifies. It's not as if all Africans must sound the maskandi way in order to voice their Africanness on the guitar. But when a South African draws on the Zulu guitar style, he or she integrates the most pervasive and prominent local traditional guitar sound into the music. In those songs of Isigqi in which traditional features are foregrounded, "the sound is based on maskanda, but we are singing modern ways. That lead [of the guitar] is still there. . . . It's a new traditional music, it's beautiful!"

Why has Zulu trumped Tsongan guitar as a South African icon? Tsongan music has remained regionally specific—in a relatively small, northernmost part of South Africa. Traditional Tsongan musicians flamboyantly electrified their style and shifted to a keyboard orientation in the wake of disco. To my knowledge, there are very few, if any, contemporary acoustic guitar players playing traditional Tsongan music.[9] In addition, Tsongan musicians' fan base extends more into areas across the border in Mozambique and southern Zimbabwe than into southern parts of South Africa. Tsongan sounds are therefore less readily available and as a sign less easily hitched to the new signified: South Africa.

The modified maskandi presence suggested in the sound quality, position in the mix, and playing style of the guitar on Mahlathini and the Mahotella Queens's "Bon Jour" and on Isigqi's recording brings into the present a South African music heritage. From West's and the artists' perspectives, this brings to the recording a sense of long-standing local specificity.

"Leaving out the guitar," in the way township pop does, leaves out an understanding of history and locality.

On one level, whiteness and Africanness stand diametrically opposed. They arise from the same set of ideological distinctions (mind/body, tone/rhythm, and so forth). Each is fashioned self-consciously at some level. The music-makers understand what their formal options are to achieve the desired sonic and rhetorical effects, and they craft and manipulate them accordingly. Whiteness and Africanness may be diametrically opposed, but they are differently invested. Africanness, for one, is laid to tape. Whiteness and Africanness vary in distance from the subjectivities of the music-makers. While Africanness is modeled as a type, it is a well-elaborated one, sometimes subsumed into a more expansive blackness, sometimes delineated into subcategories—"Swahili" or "East African," "Zaire," "South African." Music-makers identify with these forms variously, albeit with ironic subtexts. Are you Koni or Nguni?

The whitey parody sets up a sound image against which to figure other images and in relation to which individual music-makers can position themselves and their sounds. More specifically, it is against the flatness of the whitey stereotype that an African figure can emerge in all its fullness and grace. This is a critical step toward making the incorporation of an African figure—itself, in effect, a returned stereotype, reclaimed and celebrated for its essentialism—into a nuanced sense of self for musicians for whom subjectivity is, of course, irreducible and multiply contoured.

1 April 1992

"Let's hear something," prompts executive producer Ali Mpofu as he strides into the studio during the final mix of Sesimanje's recording.

"This is a nice one," West tells him as the tape spools to the title track they're about to work on. "It's got reggae, it's got mbaqanga, and wedding song [features], lots of stuff."

Neil's steel-pan pickup joins the conversation through the monitors. Mzwandile's melodic mbaqanga bass dumps itself onto the first beat along with the kick drum while oiled keyboards, rhythm guitar, and percussion set up a reggae beat, and Tefo's synth flute plays in the center front of the mix. A triple-tracked women's chorus introduces the lyrics.

"Wedding song, and also church music, it has variety!" enthuses Hansford adding to the list of black-identified music styles mixed into the song Ali is hearing for the first time.[10]

"Whoaaa!" interjects Bethwell's bass vocal imitating Mahlathini. Steel pans interrupt him with a flourish.

In composing and recording music in the studio, the music-makers are self-consciously fashioning a particular image of themselves for a domestic and world music market. In terms of the desired international market, they are fashioning an image in sound and visual presentation of a African Other. It is an African Other that is emplaced in South Africa. For the domestic market, they are carving out a regional and ethnically specific niche, rather than directing their product at black urban youth. They are also hoping to draw back their heyday fans. The world and domestic regional markets overlap in the way they both nativize contemporary mbaqanga musicians, that is, they highlight their ethnicity and downplay their urbanity; the attempts to reach "overseas" and to regain their heyday listeners overlap in the need to reproduce aspects of their old sound.[11]

The guitar sound, like other stylistic continuities and recoveries, is also an artistic preference for West and the others as individuals. Their choice is socially coherent and ideologically resonant in 1990s South Africa. If there was a promise of the early 1990s transition period, it was that the state would at last recognize all as equal citizens. All would have the same rights and stature, as the South African public. All could celebrate their claim to South African nationality. The criteria of the music industry for marketable product—sounds of local and emplaced Africa—rides easily alongside these artists' musical observation of their new-made citizenship in South Africa.

The specialness of the guitar sound is also the consequence of personal and professional insights and artistic decisions. It is part of a signifying repertoire of sounds the skillful combination of which has catapulted West over other South African producers into the global market. West selects and combines sounds with a locally and globally informed and interpretive ear. In establishing his sound self-consciously as South African, he accumulates a reputation as a distinctly South African producer. It gives him a niche in the market and sustains his brokering position between South African musicians and the market, as well as between local companies, musicians, and the world scene. His creative autonomy and his professional opportunities are mutually enhanced in the process.

The occurrence of the whitey bubblegum mimesis is prompted by the process of African image-making for these markets by these artists. The shape the parody takes is informed by the very figure of Africanness being produced. It is the antithesis of that figure. This is a case, as Taussig writes, of "unsettled and unsettling interpretation in constant movement with itself" (Taussig 1993, 237). There is no "puppeteer of a world system of images" and no determining center in the transnational production of "imaginary landscapes" (though there are, of course, hegemonies) (Appadurai 1996, 31). Distinct landscapes are painted in tone colors by these music-makers as they wonder about, gaze at, experience, and make fun of the world around them from a Johannesburg studio in 1991.

The latest mix rains down into the control room from the large monitors. Bongos, congas, and toms battle out cross-rhythms panned from left to right. Tefo's synth marimba taps out its tune in "South Africa," the "Swahili song"—the song that has power, Bethwell says, because it combines African nations. "Inesigqi!" he says, pounding his right fist into his left palm. "Bring up the guitar, the small one which cries up top [with a high pitch]," calls out Hansford in Zulu over the playback.

Now, "Can we take it?" asks Neil.

Track 2 Realizing Selves

Musicians and singers smoke, listen, chat, voice their opinions on the sound. West rocks and swivels on in his producer's chair, listening, correcting, singing the riff. Tefo is still struggling. I check if my continuously running Sony recorder, set up on the console ledge, has surely run out of the tape by now. The tension rises. "Maybe he'll get it right when we join him," encourages Jane in Zulu, as West sends someone to fetch a replacement. At this moment when the productive stability of the session is threatened, the musicians collectively parody whiteys. Nothing gets laid onto tape, but the foolery produces sociability among them. The process of parodying as much as the form the parody takes restores the session to progress.

On the level of studio practice, the mimetic play has an immediate effect. The professional relations between producer and musicians are resettled. By othering white people and township pop musicians, these mbaqanga music-makers affirm their mutuality; by doing so collectively they momentarily also level the professional hierarchy among producer, lead artists, and session musicians. This happens at a decisive moment when the difference in their professional status is exacerbated by the exposure of Tefo's seeming musical incompetence.

In terms of the musical task at hand, the foolery takes the attention off Tefo, who continues to work at getting his riff right while West sings "My Final Romance." The spontaneity and playfulness with sounds in the control room loosens up a space for experimentation. Under these conditions, Tefo quickly gets the riff into his hands.

There are aspects of the process of parody that are not about constructing appropriate sonic images for the market or about making strong identity statements by drawing on typed characters that have a charged presence. They are about finding ways to make music well and to negotiate real human relationships among colleagues and friends within the confined and pressured context of a studio session. Similarly, when musicians praise their engineer (unbeknownst to him—but this is another issue) by describing him as a Zulu, they collectively affirm themselves as Zulus/Africans for their knowledgeability, expertise, and sense of style.

West has called Hansford Mthembu into the studio. Hansford is a veteran guitarist originally from Isibaya Esikhulu and a member of West's current band. West needs him to help out on this session for Isigqi with a couple of acoustic guitar overdubs. The song "South Africa" is one of them.

"I'm not going to give them our sound," he assures Hansford in Zulu.

Hansford interrupts, "No, you should never give it away!"

Jane starts to protest.

West tries to pacify her. "No, it'll be the same, sister." He addresses her as *sisi* (sister).

But she is not convinced and neither is Joana.

"You might think you're killing someone else," Jane warns, "only to find you're killing your own sister." She substitutes West's urban, anglicized *sisi* with the Zulu form *dadewenu* (your sister), thereby intensifying his implied obligation as musical kin to help her out.

"Someone of your own blood!" adds bass player Mzwandile in the background.

Jane and Joana don't let up.

West starts to explain, "No, the sound, you see, it's the sound of the guitar, you see—"

"You'll put me back where I was [when we were stars if you give me your guitar sound]," persuades Jane.

West won't budge.

"You mess me up and mess me up"—he's been changing their songs, arrangements, lyrics, and beats—"and then you just leave me!" she complains.

West is "lending" Isigqi the guitarist from his own band. He also lends his beautiful acoustic guitar bought in London. His guitarist contributes the same basic playing style to both projects, though in a less elaborated and improvisatory form in Isigqi's overdub. But West won't share his band's recorded guitar sound. The distinction lies in its miking, recording, and mixing. For this Isigqi production, Neil sets the sound parameters on Hansford's miked amp. But Hansford changes them when Neil turns his back. The engineers are left to manipulate the sound from the console and the effects units. West and Hansford pay scant attention to the sonic result. The main distinction they reserve for their own record-ings lies in the presence they achieve through setting the chorus effect on the pickup and amplifier itself, in a particular (undisclosed) way.

The chorus effect is an electronic setting that triggers a series of milli-second delays. These get blended into the sound, surrounding the pres-ence and clarity of the actual playing with a warm ambiance. On West and Hansford's internationally released CD, this effect is enhanced by miking the amp so that a little of the room ambiance is also picked up.[12] In Isigqi's recording, on the other hand, West and Hamilton afford the chorusing little attention. As a result, the guitar lacks the clear presence of their international release. Because the chorusing is not as tightly calibrated, the guitar's timbre is brassier, murkier, and more submerged in the mix.

Thomas Chauke, the glittering star of Tsongan music, has his own drum sound, "especially the raw snare drum sound—it's a special way of doing it," explains Lee Short who engineered his one hundred thousand seller.[13] "I keep those sounds very guarded."

"I'm not going to give them our sound," West assures Hansford. West and Hansford distribute and perpetuate the idea of the guitar as represent-ing a local collective sound. But within the pool of mbaqanga artists, they are delineating difference, reserving their personal artistic distinction, and exerting control over the management of Africanness. This is both an artistic and professional choice made by individuals who are working within the star system as it intersects with the World Music market.

Jane and her co-singers really want Hansford and West's sound. It's like their own "but even better." Nobody plays like Hansford, Jane says. "They can't reach his hand!" She describes his sound as very rich and sweet, and his playing style as tastefully unflorid. And then she adds, "I don't know how he controls his guitar [sound]."

The tension between image management and expression of person-hood is tangible in this studio moment, as are competing investments in the cultivation of stardom and of a collective identity. These tensions get worked out through another set of relations: West and the musicians—Jane, Joana, and Mzwandile—attempt to negotiate the use of the guitar sound by metaphorically extending their system of kinship obligation. "One of your own blood!" remarks Mzwandile pointedly.

These musicians view extended kinship obligations as well as the practice of extending kinship obligation as an African discourse. (I have contacts, they have kin.) In the case of Jane and West, the metaphoric brother/sister is lent additional weight by their shared history in the music industry as prominent storied figures in mbaqanga's history, though from rival productions houses. Now, however, as Jane's producer, West has gatekeeping power over her career. He enacts this professional power by withholding the guitar sound distinctive to him and Hansford as artists rather than choosing to acknowledge the "African" kin obligations that Jane presses on him. For electric guitarists the distinctions of their sound are the most private domain of professional talk. This is certainly part of the industry lore about guitarists (Jairo Moreno, personal communication). When virtually identical instruments and amplifiers can be purchased, a performer's unique sound setup on the instrument is his or her signature. In retaining a distinctive musical feature—"it's a special sound that one"—West protects both his own musical sensibility and signature sound, and his position as performing star. From the moment of his denial, the tone of their talk shifts from speaking as old colleagues to speaking as authorial producer and recording artist.

This contestation over the guitar sound in the studio exemplifies how a set of invested professional, social, and personal relationships may be unsettled by momentary transgressions. These relationships are reworked in the process of shaping ideas and sound images. A maze of intersecting dialogic trajectories comes into play. First, there's the tension between the management of image and the production of personhood in the making of music stars. Then, in the World Music market, the fashioning of Africanness as the means to stardom and the production of personhood are dialogically entangled. This tension is mediated by delineating a unique African sound—a South African version—for the market while figuring out a personal relationship to South African citizenry and to musical colleagues and friends within the context of renewed geopolitical ties across the south and central parts of the continent.

rewind

Thomas Chauke, the glittering star of Tsongan music, has his own drum sound, "especially the raw snare drum sound—it's a special way of doing it," explains Lee Short who engineered his big hit LP, which sold one hundred thousand units. "If I was doing a M. J. Hlongwane or an Elias Baloyi [Tsongan artists], I would never rip off those sounds. I keep those very guarded, and the next time Thomas comes in, I've got that saved onto cartridge and onto the stiffy. It's not guarding me as an engineer, it's guarding the artist as an artist. It happened yesterday, in fact, on Elias Baloyi's session. He wanted the exact Thomas Chauke drum sounds. No way, I'd never do that! It's like Thomas Chauke's thumbprint. It's just ethical. Now Hlongwane is competition to Chauke. I'll give him his own thumbprint."

From Lee's point of view, this withholding practice is a professional service and courtesy. (It works out also to be a personal marketing device that is intended to entice innovative rather than imitative artists to work with him.) In making a distinctive timbral feature exclusive, he protects Chauke's position as a recording artist and his own as a sound engineer while he rarefies the sound. From his point of view, he gives these artists their thumbprints. The aesthetic sensibilities, the sounds by which recording artists remain true to themselves, are co-constructed signatures that are taken up as unique, embodied identity markers of the individual artistic self. Yet they also remain—without contradiction—as images necessarily performed within a field of other images and in encounters with other music-makers. Performativity is a feature of the irreducible self.

rewind again

The session is cruising; the sound is happening.

"Are you Koni or Nguni, Neil?" West demands.

"Nguni," replies Neil without missing a beat or stopping work on his conga sound.

The control room erupts into laughter.

"He's Nguni!" cackles a musician through his laughter.

The joke is multifold: Koni and Nguni are the same word in two different languages (Sotho and Zulu), so West isn't giving Neil a real choice; Neil probably doesn't know what Koni means, so he picks the term also used in English and the joke is on him; of course, he absolutely isn't Nguni, except within the discursive context of having been named thus on the basis of delivering the sonic goods within a Zulu-identified style— the blatant disjuncture is funny; and West's Koni/Nguni wordplay cleverly implicates Neil's last name, Kuny, into a triumvirate.

What is pertinent here is the demonstration of the movability of sign and its signifier. It is with the knowledge of the performativity of identity and the constructedness of racial and ethnic categories that the joking musicians can so flippantly loosen the sign from its signified and hang it on other forms. They do so without compromising their sense of their own African-centered identities, and in the process of getting a pleasing African sound laid to tape, in part by their white engineer. "It's a nice one, this one," West tells Ali, the executive producer.

This fashioning of identity in mediated sound evolves through a creative play with images upon images, grounded by individuals making choices and finding sense in their lives. Clearly, identity, to quote Taussig, "has to be seen not as a thing-in-itself but as a relationship woven from mimesis and alterity within colonial fields of representation" (1993, 133). That is to say, the historically saturated, mutual but unequal gaze of self and colonial Other is implicated in the imaginaries from within which identities emerge. But identity is also woven by moving between expediency and feeling, and among a critical distance, playful engagement, and a naturalized performativity of the socialized self.

West's critical stance against whitey bubblegum music is not only an expedient and political one. He has little personal investment in the style; it doesn't come from his feeling. His racialized discursive distancing is also a sensually detached dismissal of the sound. "I don't enjoy recording it in the studio," he tells me in an interview. "I always like more traditional music—I have the feeling of that. [With more traditional music] I can help where there is something wrong. I can add more ideas. But this bubblegum music they're doing, it doesn't get into my feelings so much. Despite his personal taste, he has successfully produced some township pop "for the sake of the groups." It is not as if he really dismisses the people who create and enjoy it. But "it's not my line, I don't have the originality of that music. [To arrange and produce it] I've got to take from somewhere—take a few bars, bass lines, or keyboard lines and put them together. That's a heavy job, because it doesn't come from my feeling. But [producing the kind of music that] I've got from my feeling—in the middle of the night you can wake me up and say, 'Right!' and I can do it anytime."

In the end, it is with great assurance that Jane recounts for me why Zesimanje musicians like all musicians need to retain their own sense of their sound. West's sound may be similar to theirs, in fact, similar and better than theirs, she says, but it is their sonic identity. She desires their quality of excellence, but she doesn't want to be submerged under someone else's signature. "Like I'm telling you, Mahotella has got their own sound. . . . Even before the girls come in, you just hear the 'ti ti ti ti!' [on the guitar]"—Jane sings high enunciating her "t" 's—"ah, those are the Mahotellas! You get it from Marks: he always uses this 'ta ta ta ta ting! ta ta ta ta ting!'—at the end of the bar he puts something up," that is, his characteristic phrases end by leaping up to high notes—or penultimate high notes—with some sustain.[14] Jane lets her "ting" ring and fall. "When you listen you say, 'No, these are Mahotella Queens.'" She pauses and shifts position on her chair. "They've got their own sound, and we Simanje-manje have got our own sound. Even West, he's got his own groups. He knows that he mustn't use the sound he's using on his own groups on us. Because then when you start listening to the record, you'll say, 'This must be West's group.' Then you'll look and see 'No! the people on the recording are Simanjemanje!' That is why you must remain [true] to your own sound."

For these particular musicians, there is a vital but difficult tension between fashioning an appropriate image for the market(s) and expressing their aesthetic preferences. They are caught between the desire for the break and affirmation that following the markets' nativizing thrust promises, and the desire to represent themselves in a way that resonates with their everyday sensibility, modes of living, and musical biographies. They think of themselves as metropolitan residents, South African citizens, African people, and innovative professional artists, and they think of their style as historically urban, though they would not fix their selfhood or their sound unambiguously.

Any sense of stasis that might have evolved in defining the categories of white, African, and South African is upset by the presence of different possibilities for identification, which break through the molds of Other and Self. Social alignments along other axes can and do occur. These alignments can rupture the boundaries of a somewhat settled discursive field and loosen the possibilities for sonic innovation and shifting social relationships.

"Can we take it?" asks Neil as the riff ends.

"Lets try," proffers West, keeping open the possibility for hitches and new developments.

"Let's go for it," agitates Neil in response, as his fingers run deftly over the MIDI clock control pads alongside him.

Tracks Mixed *Creativity and the Figure*

Figures do not exist independently but must be embodied in particular individuals through the performance of sound and the enactment of image. The materialization of figures through performance at once both shapes and articulates an immediate set of social and musical relationships. The fundamentally improvisatory quality of this process guarantees that the forms figures take and the significance they hold remain constantly on the move. This poetic improvisation is an intuitively naturalized communicative process (Jakobson 1960); or an aesthetically self-conscious play, as Berliner's analysis of jazz improvisation suggests (1994); or both, as Coplan points out in deconstructing the ethnic identifications in Sotho migrant miners' *lifela* poetry (1994).

The notion of the figure in this South African case slips easily into a form representing a social type—an African, a white person, or a Zulu. By form here I mean a set of sonic parameters shaped in a particular way and repeated with variations in multiple musical contexts. A technological, measured, and rationalized sound is interpreted as white; some version of a strident guitar sound with percussive attack, strong upper frequencies, flanging, phasing, and chorusing effects to give the sound some exciting impurities, and some reverb to add a bit of ring, is heard as Zulu, or in a broader context as South African.

The most pervasive tropes that emerge in the studio during mbaqanga production represent social categories. Constituted as racialized or ethnic types, they are the most prominent poetic figures that mbaqanga music-makers reference in attempts to discuss and specify sound. "Kenu Koni!" (He's a Zulu, that one!) This contrasts starkly with the country, pop, and rock music sessions documented by Porcello (1996) at the Fire Station in San Marcos, Texas. Porcello shows how musicians, producers, and engineers constantly communicate ideas about the sounds they want on tape by multiply referencing other recordings, artists, and brand names. During all of Isigqi's studio sessions, in contrast, only one album was ever referenced, and only once, in an attempt to describe a preferred sound. In Porcello's case, the studio music-makers share much more in terms of their race, class, and ethnic status and language abilities than do the studio music-makers who are involved in mbaqanga production. Hence, the Fire Station musicians and production team also share more in terms of cultural capital, taste, and listening experience. While the rock, country, and pop studio music-makers at the Fire Station seem to imagine one another as part of the same elaborate fluid musical community, or of overlapping music communities, the South Africans seem mutually to imagine their differences first and foremost and to articulate those differences in racialized terms. This divide goes deep: at least some music-makers assume fundamentally racialized differences in their cultural, sensuous, or even physiological listening experience, not only in preferred listening repertoire.

Contemporary discourses are, of course, historically constituted, and South Africa's colonial and apartheid history must be deeply formative with regard to visions of social difference. Robert Thornton posits convincingly that the unitary essentialism between African and white was distilled over time on "both sides"—African/Zulu and European—out of what were historically far more complex, heterogeneous, and divided representations. He writes that racial difference was most acutely essentialized in dichotomous terms when the Union government introduced "color-bar" segregation. With the dichotomy already well in place in discourse and practice by the time apartheid was legislated by the National Party from 1948, it was certainly further entrenched and horrifically practiced into the early 1990s (R. Thornton 1995, 195).

The urgency and uncertainty of the presettlement moment of the early 1990s heightened the profile and the stakes of racial issues in everyday talk. The instability of social categories was highlighted by the ruptures in social practice. Responding to work by David Coplan, George Marcus writes "that the South Africans' point of conversation or rendering accounts is not necessarily to make conditions transparent or to speak a simple truth clear to any listener. Rather, it is assumed that discussions, testimonies, stories, and the like will at least in part remain stubbornly opaque, and that the point is to establish rapport and connections with interlocutors on the basis of necessarily opaque discourses. Truth-telling versus fiction is not an option in South Africa where there can be no nonracially based discourse—it is impossible to escape such terms" (1993, 10). The issue is not just that these terms are naturalized for many South Africans but that the discourse is perpetuated in specific ways at specific moments in pursuit of particular ends—such as the shaping of a sound—which might have more to do with class or other social issues than with race. While race may be an easy and naturalized gloss for multiple differences and tensions, it is also a rhetorical tool. It provides figures through which mbaqanga music-makers attempt to verbalize and communicate their aesthetic preferences and their sociopolitical perspectives; it is, of course, a rhetoric that can have stringent repercussions as well as make deeply embedded impressions as it circulates in the practice of everyday life.[15]

In the case of the studio, a mbaqanga music-maker may merge with a socially descriptive figure, much like an actor who enters into a theatrical role, lives it temporarily, and makes it distinctly his or her own, then steps out of it again, with a somewhat transformed sense of self. But the figure can be more or less than the equivalent of a theatrical role. It can be experienced as so "real" that it becomes a naturalized aspect of the self and remains so for any length of time. Or a music-maker may retain a figure at a distance, view it with detachment, and manipulate it in music making for rhetorical effect as needed. Such is the range of possibilities when "trying on" a social type.

The figure is also different from a theatrical role, in that it exists at multiple levels of abstraction at one time (Friedrich 1991), with various inflections of mood and point of view and differing degrees of diffuseness and particularity.[16] This fluidity is important, for it facilitates degrees of identification with the figure, ranging from merging wholeheartedly with it, to recognizing its form from a distance. Further, it enables movement through these multiple levels, in and out from deep sensuous embrace of a figure to expedient detached manipulation. This movement also encompasses a range from discursive articulation about form to elusive and feeling experience of it.

Layers of figuring are at play, differently, for each music-maker in the studio. As a black Africa-centered producer working with other black South Africans/musicians/friends, West must negotiate multiple positions. But figuring is no less crucial for others in the session, including the engineer.

The way that the self/figure is played and played out in sound itself is a critical part of a larger package by which styles are shaped. The elaboration of reputation by means of a verbal and visual presentation of self outside the studio operates dialogically with the sonic manipulation of figures inside the studio. The relationship between the performing self and figure performed in sound, talk, and display needs to be seen within the larger and heightened context of which it is a part, namely the market-directed star system.

Figuring is also a formative component in cultural production "for transforming difference into discourse, for making it meaningful for action and thought" (Marcus and Myers 1995, 34–35), since it can fuse ideas with the performing body, making difference into sensual experience. Figuring is a means by which certain sounds come to resonate in certain bodies, generating feelings about themselves and about others. It is equally much a way to make the sense of sounds more intelligent to those who embrace them. Figuring is a way of connecting form out into the world, a way of interpreting the experience of musical sound into language, a way of mediating aesthetic and social experience.[17]

When parodied whiteness interfaces with various forms of Africanness, it shapes the sound on tape, manages studio relations, and generates possibilities for the production of selfhood and social positioning for the music-makers.

Defining whiteness opens up the possibilities for what "not white" can be and how it can sound. In West and his fellow music-makers' song "My Final Romance," "white" is constrained and distanced by the singularity of its form. Constraining a dominant discourse into such a tight frame clears a huge space for other discourses to occupy. It creates "room to maneuver" (R. Chambers 1991). It opens up an expansive field in which the imaging of Africanness can be elaborated not only against ideas of Other or white but also in relation to subtropes within the idea of Africa, specifically in relation to ideas and feelings about citizenship in the early 1990s South Africa. This nuanced imaging, at once affirming Africanness and particularizing it, filling it in with feeling and nuance, is also elaborated dialogically and inconsistently with the sensibilities of the music-makers themselves. In their music, figure and ground shift; the dominance and position of sounds shift in the mix.

The poetic, performative, and unsettled process of imaging in sound is fundamentally formative in music production and challenges any moves toward linearity in the analysis of the production process.[18] It is through these features of production that we can find keys to understanding creativity and its relationship to forms of power. When culturally scripted figures are selected and molded by socially situated individuals, power and expression come to reside formatively but unstably in each other.

Music-makers in the studio struggle for political, professional, and personal voice in the process of shaping style. In struggling for their values, identities, and aspirations, studio music-makers perform their sensibilities in dialogue with the figures and images they capture and create. They thereby rework or reaffirm their personhood and sociopolitical positioning in relation to one another and, in the larger context, in relation to those among whom they live.

Playback

Hansford, a fan of Dolly Parton, strums and picks his guitar on the couch at the back of the studio, waiting for the session to begin. His sweet acoustic country sound floats around the control room. Engineer Neil stops his preparations momentarily. He notices.

"Mmh! Nice guitarist, hey!"

Performing Zuluness

Guide Vocal

Midmorning there was no sign of an event at George Goch Stadium, on the edge of industrial Johannesburg, in September 1991. Noon there was no sign of an event at George Goch Stadium, just a scattering of disappointed fans.

There would be no event at George Goch Stadium today—no festive appearance of Isigqi Sesimanje and Ladysmith Black Mambazo, and a string of other scheduled Zulu traditional and mbaqanga groups. Instead, a full-sun Sunday lull hangs over the stadium, the Zulu male hostel alongside it and the city mine dumps around it.

You just never know, or know why.

TJ, a photojournalist, and I head out to a township where there is an Inkatha Freedom Party protest march in response to an ANC attack on an Inkatha funeral (for victims of prior ANC aggression—itself a response to an Inkatha attack). We are still in the city itself when we run into returning Inkatha ralliers scurrying all over the road. They carry shields, spears, fighting/dancing sticks, and an array of sharpened implements. There are guns. There is frenzy. Three hundred meters down the road a white civilian raises his pistol at the ralliers. Positioned beside his idling truck, he isn't noticed much, except by his son. It is a long moment until police come, then go again as the ralliers rush back into their two minivans. The police don't follow them back to their migrant men's hostel.

TJ notices that the soccer game we pass as we follow them is the next target the ralliers will go for. They do. They kill people. They charge the field. They charge the stands. They charge across the road to the trade store. They frenzy back into their idling vehicles and head back to their hostel. At the hostel women ululate in the courtyard. The band of men sing and dance.

It took two minutes. Done.

Back at the trade store, an army guy with a moustache and a stare stands like a monument to some revolution. He watches over the young man whose shopping bag of goodies lies limp beside him, just where it got dumped when he collapsed. The man's palm lies open, ebbed of its grip; palpable in the dust. A cigarette is wedged between his fingers. I look at his flesh. Spilled blood darkens his shadow.

I can see more army personnel monumenting themselves over the bodies on the soccer field.

The singing and ululating inside the hostel has stopped. It has turned into an ordinary Sunday afternoon. The barber is there; the women selling home-brew are there; people are leaning against walls and sitting on soda crates and ambling down the middle of the road.

We watch a team of ngoma dancers practicing in their regular gathering spot on a sidewalk. The dancers sit in a tight horseshoe. They clap and sing as one by one each virtuoso kicks and stamps and falls to the ground in the center of their horseshoe. Or two by two they display their choreographed body work. "Thisa!" one eggs another on. "You're on fire!"

They sing a slow repeating riff. "Sizogwazana, sizobulala" (We will stab one another, we will kill). "Bathi sizogwazana, sizobulala" (They say will stab one another, we will kill). I can't make head or tail of the lower overlapping vocals. A drummer whacks the marching bass with a length of hosepipe and a wooden slat. An echoing dotted rhythm. *Ka kaa! Ka kaa!*

Acoustically, it is a perfect rehearsal sidewalk. The narrow street is edged by industrial buildings with broad steel doors. The drum beat ricochets back and forth. Back and forth. *Ka kaa!* The sound settles. Another extended dotted sequence, whacking back and forth. You can hear it long before you turn the corner, long before you hear the piercing whistle of the leader and the slow deep vocal riff. Then you see the cluster of peaceful, Sunday afternoon hostel dwellers, dancing.

My intention in retelling this raiding story is not to trace out a linear and causal relationship between the violence of the morning and the performance or performers of the afternoon. This would either trivialize or sensationalize aesthetics. Rather, I am concerned with the roles the studio and creative engagement with recording technology play in making ambiguous the relationship between the event of the raid and the singing and dancing about violent acts, as well as the role it can play in naturalizing that relationship. What is so compelling to me and others about the slow, deep vocal riff and the hostel dwellers' dancing? We will stab one another, they say. I am awed by the seriousness of cultural pro-

Ngoma dancers in the isishameni style outside Jeppe (Wolhuter) Hostel, Johannesburg, 6 September 1992. *Photo by TJ Lemon.*

duction, by the precarious power of music and dance, and by the significance of expressive participation in both the production and destruction of social and personal life.

Ethnomusicology in its encounter with conflict has concerned itself with music's important healing and celebratory capacities and with music's function in the promotion of solidarity and the generation of resistance (Averill 1997; Byerly 1998; Reyes 1999). Scholars have done less critical thinking about the relation of feelingful experience of music making to the production of violence and to intentional acts of injury. While important accounts of the organization, dissemination, and repertoire of music in war, especially the Second World War in Germany, are available (e.g., Meyer 1991; Kater 1992; Kater 1997; Bergmeier 1997), I am concerned more with how to get at that potent yet diffuse nonverbal efficacy of sound and gesture that plays a critical part in the production of difference. However insignificant and harmless each instance may be in isolation, social differences expressed in art can gather momentum as art forms circulate far and wide and in the everyday. These differences can become the basis for social exclusions, of which directed violence is a heightened form (J. Taylor 1998; Appadurai 1998; Daniel 1996; Feldman 1994). I wonder whether song and dance are unique media for rendering differences—and atrocities—as natural, even though these very same art forms have the important capacity to critique the construction of difference. When the embodied aesthetic of song and dance intersects with the reproductive and disseminating facilities of the media, what happens to the sense and significance of those art forms in relation to the social struggles with which they are contemporaneous?

The tradition of Zulu men's dancing called ngoma is a style of competitive display that is danced at homecoming times in rural KwaZulu-Natal and on Sunday afternoons at working and work-seeking men's hostels in Johannesburg, Durban, and on the mines. The hostels house numerous teams, each of which is comprised of migrant "homeboys" from one rural ward in KwaZulu-Natal. Historically, ngoma has been implicated in surges of ethnic hostility and popular violence. In the 1930s, for instance, the Chamber of Mines sought to domesticate the dancing into staged, organized competitions as a means of controlling their labor force (Erlmann 1991). In the 1940s altercations between neighboring Zulu wards over land rights and access to agricultural employment were settled by means of dancing and its related stick fighting (Clegg 1982). In the early 1990s aspects of ngoma dancing were incorporated into the Zulu nationalist Inkatha Freedom Party protests and rallies.

There are three main ngoma substyles: umzansi, isishameni, and ngoma kaBhaca. Each style combines choreographed group work and individual improvisation and is danced to singing, clapping, and a marching bass drum.[1] Dramatic emphasis is added to a continuous dotted rhythmic pattern each time the dancers' feet thunder down into the dust or onto the tarmac or cement sidewalk after a kick. The kick is the focus of the spectacle, though much of the virtuosity lies in its preparation and resolution.[2]

A warrior dressed in skins carries a stick, spear, and a cowhide shield. He is performed as the warrior-dancer who unsettles the dust as he flicks his leg and stamps the ground, or as the dancer who vibrates the stage as he stamps into the rising white smoke. This popular icon of the Zulu nation originates especially in those bloody battles against the British in the 1870s, when the Zulus earned a ferocious and militant reputation. The Zulu fought multiple battles before and after the British annexed part of Zululand as the Colony of Natal. The British suffered heavy casualties, as had the Boers before them (see Lindfors 1999). In the battle at Isandlwana fought in 1879—the most (in)famous of all encounters—the Zulus were victorious. (The British recovered their dominance immediately thereafter, and then deposed the Zulu king [Lindfors 1983, 11].) The

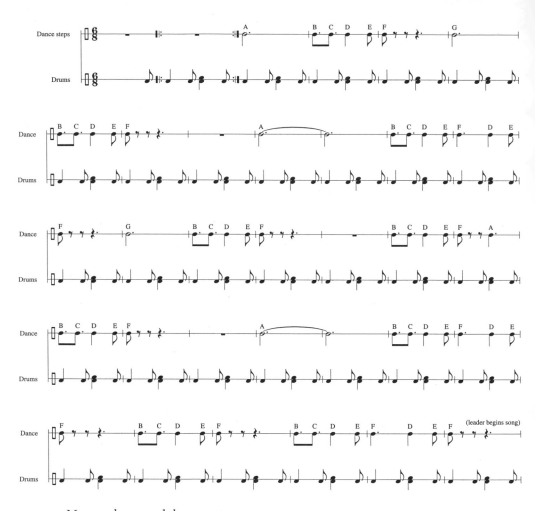

Ngoma dance-and-drum pattern.
Transcribed by James Harkins from *Rhythms of Resistance: The Black Music of South Africa* (Marre 1979).

A: Reaching forward with dance sticks
B: Stepping forward
C: Stepping back
D: Raising sticks over and behind heads
E: Kicking above heads
F: Foot stomps on ground
G: Sticks held horizontally over heads

A South African captures a snap of the "Die Hard Brigade," a British group of history enthusiasts who performed in the reenactment of the 1879 battle of Isandlwana, where Zulu king Cetshwayo defeated the British colonial forces. Isandlwana, KwaZulu-Natal, 22 January 1999. *Photo by TJ Lemon.*

battleground at Isandlwana is now a celebrated Zulu historical marker, where the Inkatha Freedom Party rallied to reenact the battle on 22 January—the day of the battle—in 1992 and 1993. That this was featured in the globally distributed British magazine *Military Illustrated* points to the saliency, precarious aestheticization, and perpetuation of the Zulu warrior image in the contemporary global media (Knight 1994). British enthusiasts have subsequently returned to the battlefield in full regalia to once again replay the historical event.

It is not only stories about Zulus that traveled out of South Africa in the nineteenth century. Even before the mighty battle of Isandlwana, Zulu people were shipped to Europe for display by enterprising Victorian merchants. The first troupe was brought to Britain, France, and Germany in 1853, and others followed in its wake (Lindfors 1999; Peacock 1999). In the United States, Zulus—and local stand-ins for Zulus—were displayed in circus shows from the later 1800s through at least the 1930s. They were also featured at the 1904 St. Louis World Exposition. Bernth Lindfors argues that Zulus enjoyed unprecedented popularity over other peoples on show at these times, such as the "pigmies" and "Aztec Lilliputians," because the Zulus staged dramatic performances (Lindfors 1999). They were presented as wild, fierce, cunning, unpredictable (ibid.). In fact, they became such marked and celebrated icons through their performance that American circus jargon came to refer to any black person who paraded in costume in the grand opening pageant as a Zulu (Lindfors 1983).

A celebrated, dynamic expression of Zulu identity for many Zulus themselves, Zulu men's dancing and warriorship has been championed around the globe, through the century, and in all forms of expressive culture, as an epitome of an "ageless and virile Africa," though with marked differences in the connotations of the shared image (Lindfors 1999; Erlmann 1999). For example, in African American cultural life leading up to and through the era of civil rights, Zulus took on particular empowering significance as a defiant, self possessed, royal, and artful African people. On the other hand, South African proponents of apartheid saw Zulu culture as embodying values antithetical to their own. Zulu performance styles became symbols of Otherness and bodily excess that justified their views on racial difference and on the need for separate development. These and other competing interests have sustained transnational fascination with Zulu performance, of which ngoma is the best known and most commonly imitated dance style.

Countless examples of the performative Zulu icon present themselves: New Orleans's Mardi Gras sports a high-prestige "Zulu float" every year; a hip-hop promotional organization and fan club calls itself the Universal Zulu Nation; rural, white, working-class Texans use *Zulu* as a general term for black people (Aaron Fox, personal communication, May 1996); "tribal Zulu warriors" are sold as leather puppets-on-strings in South African game-reserve curio shops; the Royal Hong Kong Police's tactical unit is called the Z Platoon or Zulu Platoon (Hong Kong's Zulus 1993); the South African rugby team opens its matches with a team of Zulu men posturing on the field in skins, carrying spears and shields. "Dear Siyazi," writes a young British promoter to the leader of Umzansi Zulu Dance in 1999, "I am not expecting to see any unfit warriors with big stomachs when I come to South Africa. Any one who is not prepared to train hard and rehearse will not come on the tour."

"Performing Zuluness" takes the discussion about figuring that I introduced in the previous cut out into the world beyond the control room. As sounds are gathered, built on, juxtaposed, isolated, and reworked into expressive forms in the studio process, so too are figures of ethnic difference overlaid, reconsidered, disavowed, or embraced. Decisions must necessarily be made about the political alignments implicated in those figures. This is a process of engaging with icons in part or wholeheartedly, sometimes casting their political associations aside or into the background, sometimes celebrating them wholeheartedly, at other times refiguring their significance.

Track 1 considers how the image of the Zulu is reproduced in sound. In its three takes I discuss ways in which a song is made to feel like a Zulu song. The manipulation of timbral quality, song form, and lyric content represent degrees of suggestiveness and specificity in the articulation of Zuluness. Tracks 2 and 3 focus on how Zuluness performs in a political context and how it infiltrates the everyday experience of Sowetan living in the early 1990s. The mix blends these tracks into an argument about the overlap in the feeling and form of Zuluness produced for the World Music market and the interests of ethnic nationalism. If it is so that Zuluness is necessarily performed—that it is a form of rhetoric—and intuitively experienced, World Music production may benefit from and exacerbate the politics of difference.

Track 1   *Zuluness as Aesthetic Form*

take 1 : producing Zuluness in timbral manipulation

In 1990 and 1991 West had arranged a ngoma team's songs with additional instrumentation with the intention of international release. He was targeting a gap he saw in the World Music market. After Paul Simon's *Graceland* had opened the way for some South African sounds, two tokens had made it onto the international stage: Mahlathini and the Mahotella Queens in a mbaqanga style and Ladysmith Black Mambazo singing a cappella isicathamiya. West anticipated that if he added more instrumentation to the ngoma team's choral singing and bass drum, he might have a new international success that would fill the stylistic gap between Black Mambazo and the Queens. He wanted to make it possible for foreigners to groove to ngoma in dance clubs while still retaining the rhythmic patterns and feel of traditional Zulu dance. The group he worked with was Umzansi Zulu Dance.

"What [Umzansi Zulu dancers] normally do," says West, "they play drums and dance to the drums only. What I did, I took their singing and I added bass guitar, drums—proper drums [trap set]—and a guitar."

"The guitar keeps a natural feel; if you take the guitar out . . ."

"And a concertina to build up the backing track, so that people abroad can dance to their music. You can change that sound to become a disco record, or to become house music, like rap. It's the same sort of music as Black Mambazo. What is different is that Black Mambazo are only singing the choral part of it. Now I've changed these guys to be on the dance part of it. [Clubgoers can dance to it] on the same rhythm that Umzansi do the traditional dancing. I made it in a way that all musicians can play that music. When they first listened to [Umzansi], I think some of them thought, 'Well, this music cannot be done with any other musicians, like Paul Simon did with Black Mambazo.' So I made it clear to them that this music can be changed. You can play around with it. I put keyboards and guitars in, all sort of congas, plus drums and bass. Then they sing on top. It's super! It's a totally different sound, which I think I'm going to release later this year, for the international market. So it sounds different from Mahlathini and Black Mambazo."[3]

About a year later, 21 November 1991, West is back in the studio. This time he is working with Isigqi Sesimanje—who were to have played at George Goch Stadium that day. He is trying to get the right feel on the drum sound of their new song "Makoti onjani."

He takes the idea of Zulu ngoma dance, represented by its most dramatic moment—the kick, *ka kaa!*—and embeds it in Isigqi's song.

He imports it into the song in the same way he had used it in arranging Umzansi's music. He programs a dotted motive as a drum pattern onto the floor toms, marking each measure. This pattern, which follows the rhythm of the marching bass at the kick points of the dance, was new to the band.

It is interesting that of the three main ngoma dance styles, West works from the umzansi style, which is the slowest and heaviest, has the highest kick, the least "Western" dress, and most bares the dancer's body. Though West reproduces the motive from his earlier Umzansi recording, he does something different with it. He repeats it consistently through the song, pushes it up in the mix, and exaggerates its timbral features at the recording console, adding a lot of reverb to give a sense of space around it, to make it sound big. He experiments with the amount of predelay and decay, and he filters the top frequencies and boosts some of the bottom ones. He wants it big, tough, and "ballsy," in the words of Peter, who is engineering the session.

Kicks are not entirely new to mbaqanga performance. But in mbaqanga's heyday, when the style was considered modern and urban, they were styled somewhat differently. Their preparation step did not extend backward as dramatically and the final landing of the foot was light. In both men's and women's frontlines there was more quick bending and lifting of the knees, without any backward preparatory step. Bass groaners like Mahlathini stamped heavily but without the straight raising of the leg beforehand. Still, today if mbaqanga or rural women kick with a straightened leg, they only raise it one or two feet from the ground; more often they bend the knee instead.[4]

In heyday mbaqanga, kicks were usually glamorously marked by cymbal crashes, and the motif was not consistently present as a sound in the backing tracks. In Isigqi's session, West omitted the cymbal crashes, slowed the tempo down to something more akin to umzansi dancing, and programmed a hard house bass on the first and third beats. He's going for weight and toughness. Into this he programmed the ngoma drum pattern on the floor toms. *Ku dum!*

"The echo is not round, you know," comments West. He vocalizes the sound he wants. "Ku kum! Ku kum!" he says in sync with the toms.[5] "It's got to be a little bit long."

Peter works on, extending the lower frequencies of the decay.

"Why do we have that shshsh?" queries West.

Peter starts to ask for clarification. "Ku kum! Ku kum!" replies West, still in sync with toms looped repeatedly through the monitors. "Not shshsh!"

To get rid of the *shshsh*—the high-end noise—Peter cuts down the reverb. They're back to a dry tom to try again. He pauses to think out a better solution.

West tries another tack to describe the sound he wants. "I'm sure you know that album of *Ipitombi?*"

"Sjoe, West!" Peter exclaims, raising his eyebrows in astonishment.

"*These* are the same tom-toms that we should get, *that* sound," says West, referring to *Ipitombi*. "Not with shshsh! but ku dum!"

This is an incredibly surprising moment in the studio session. Having fully embedded the ngoma sound into the texture, West is going to caricature the idea further by requesting that the sound be tweaked to reproduce the timbre of the drums from the 1970s international hit musical *Ipitombi*. First of all, this is not a reference I would have expected a South African who considers himself progressive to want to reproduce. It was a show written and designed by white South Africans during the height of apartheid. Though they purported to value and promote "traditional culture," their musical was a singularly racist representation that romanticized rural Africa, primitivized African peoples, feared and revered the warrior, and lamented urbanization. In the 1970s it was thunderously ac-claimed in London, on Broadway, in Israel, in then Rhodesia, and in white South Africa. An album that included songs, instrumental cuts (predomi-nantly drumming), and English narration from the show was produced in South Africa and internationally distributed (*Ipitombi* 1975).[6]

Second, naming *Ipitombi* was a surprise also because it was the only reference to another recording called on as a means to describe a desired sound in the entire production of this album. Studio sessions documented in the United States stand in stark contrast, for they are saturated with references to other recordings (Porcello 1996). In the South African studio, in a mbaqanga session, the producer assumes he and the white sound engineer do not share a listening history, except for crossover recordings, which they can draw on to accomplish the seemingly impossible task of talking precisely about timbre.

Peter pauses to think out a better solution.
  West doesn't want what he described as a "krrr" on the drum
sound. He wants the sound to "ring"; he wants a "round echo."
  No shshshsh. No krrr. Ku kum! Ku Kum!
  Peter cuts the sound from the monitors. He's struggling.
  "I'm sure you know that album of Ipitombi*? . . . That sound."*

Third, as Peter said to me on reviewing the sound on a later occa-sion, the *Ipitombi* drum sound is "terrible, awful, it's a really really shit sound—it's all slap, velum, and air, there's no drum."

West's calling on *Ipitombi* is not a request to replicate its precise acous-tic patterns. It is a poetic maneuver to get around describing an ineffable tone quality; it is a strategic way of managing social, historical, and lin-guistic differences that impinge on the work process; and it is an aesthetic choice that carries with it a semiotic package. Aesthetically, West wants the sound of hand-slapping velum, not of a hosepipe whacking the plas-tic head of a marching bass as played by hostel dwellers. He is not after the actual sound of the *Ipitombi* toms, Peter explained, "but I understand the feel he wants in the track." West is evoking the image of a live "tradi-tional" drummer beating a carved wooden "African" drum, no doubt ac-companied by energetic dancing. He wants a feel of "Africa": its passion, its ferocity, its power, its glory and danger, its potential to spill out of con-trol. What better way in this 1990s South African context than to draw on the feeling and form of the warrior-dancer at the moment of his dramatic kick? He is drawing on the globally circulated popular icon of the "great Zulu nation."

In shaping Zuluness into an aesthetic form at this microlevel, West has arrested the sign from its lived reference—recreational dancing outside the hostels—and seamed it to a chronotopic idea of Zuluness—to a time and place that is rural, ancient, tribal. He has created a dramatic, ahistorical, conceptual Zulu figure. The sound of the plastic-headed contemporary ngoma drum has been replaced with the sound of a precolonial equivalent. (Beaten wooden drums were not even traditional to precolonial Zulus [Kirby 1968]; in fact, wooden drums are only traditional to the Venda, Pedi, and Tswana in the northern region of South Africa, and to the Basotho.) West's ngoma drum sound here is more ideally African, more traditional than the ngoma drum as it is heard at the hostels and in rural Zululand today.

To summarize the studio process: A sense of Zuluness as exemplified in the kick is extracted from ngoma in the studio. It is exaggerated, reframed, repeated, and circulated in reproducing versions of itself—a case of what Steven Feld terms escalating "schizophonic mimesis" (1994). As the sound is separated from its source by means of electronic technology and as reproductions are further reproduced in the image of versions of itself already in circulation, the referent becomes increasingly diffuse. Zuluness becomes more and more of a "loosely held suggestiveness," a hard "ballsy" timbre. What carries farthest about the referent is its sensuality and feeling. Though diffuse, difference is made resonant.

The sound of Zuluness here is initiated by a producer who is not Zulu and does not support violent ethnic nationalism. But he likes the drum sound. He wants a tough and powerful effect.

Nevertheless, the suggestion of Zuluness is available to be retrieved by those who say they are Zulus, in moments in which a sense of ethnic identification is salient to them. A "loosely held suggestiveness," as Paul Friedrich says of an efficacious metaphor, may at once become a "deeply held gist" (1991).

take 2 : producing Zuluness in shaping song form

Wedding songs hold the closest equivalent status among women's song and dance forms to the performance of recreational ngoma dancing.[7] This is the women's performance art that draws most public attention to individuals in rural Zulu communities, and it has been popularized in recorded song by the music industry.

In rural KwaZulu-Natal in the Msinga district, the new bride Makoti dances alongside her bridesmaids while the guests look on. She sings a short lead. Her repeated phrase peaks in the syncopated middle of the four-beat measure. She draws out the note and descends, a narrow melodic contour. Her bridesmaids overlap in cyclical chorus. Women ululate. Makoti dances with a carving knife in one hand, a small shield in the other. She points her knife first to one side, then to the other. She steps out from the line of her bridesmaids, dances heavily on her feet. Raising her knife and shield, she lifts a knee and stamps, lifts and stamps, lifts and stamps. She blows her whistle to the rhythm of her stamping. Her leg rattles shiver. Her hips swivel a little to accentuate the syncopation. Men metronomically hit their shields with their fighting sticks to keep the beat.

Young girls take up the pause in proceedings to insert their sound. They dance *mgqashiyo*, beating out foot rhythms with rattles around their ankles, blowing on their whistles, and ending their sequences with a spin of their hips and a jump.

The men from Makoti's family call and chant. Her brother leaps into the open space, hitting his dancing shield with his fighting stick. He stamps. He leaps. He bends to the ground and covers his head with his shield. He stamps again. The men interject exclamatory punches. Makoti's father calls out a phrase. Together they chant a deep response.[8]

Makoti sings over them with her sisters.

Back in the studio, 18 November 1991, West leans back and lights up again. Jane, Joana, Janet, and Michael bustle back into the control room to hear their backing vocals. It's a new recording—perhaps there will be a new hit. The air is sparkling with anticipation.

West launches into his bulldozer explanation about their songs. 'You have to go with the market, you have to go with what's happening now. You'll never make it with this old stuff. You have to do wedding songs. Yes, the whole album.'

These are "noisy" women, to use West's phrase. No, grumbled Isigqi out of West's earshot, this was not "our music," not what we are known for, not what we have rehearsed, and not what we want to do.

The women's sights were set on making an international break with this album, as well as on getting domestic attention. They, of course, wanted to find a gap in the market, but it needed to be one that would not compromise their sense of artistic integrity.

West repeatedly tried to convince the group that they should gear their sound to the big township youth market. He urged that they restyle some of their repertoire to play off the current popularity in the townships of studio-produced wedding songs, as well as off the emerging interest in wedding songs on the Zulu trad market.

Studio-produced wedding songs had caught the attention of the industry by a circuitous route. In a clever marketing maneuver in 1989 Blondie Makhene and his African Youth Band at Hit City Records recorded instrumental versions of protest songs (African Youth Band 1989). These were traditional songs—some of them wedding songs—to which activists had added new lyrics. Using contemporary sound-processing effects and programmed backing, he rendered the implicit rhythms of these a cappella songs in percussion, drum, and keyboard sounds. In recording them as textless instrumental versions, Blondie evaded the censors and produced an instant hit LP among a township public who could sing the traditional or the sloganized lyrics as they listened.

Makhene's success opened a space on the market for other kinds of reworkings of traditional songs, spunked up for the youth. One notable success, produced by Freddie Gwala, was a wedding song single by Platform One.[9] Platform One's sung hit with programmed backing brought wedding songs in popularized form to the attention of the industry. Others followed in her wake.

In the Zulu trad arena, duos or trios of rural girls were newly fronting the established Zulu trad soundtrack (concertina, guitar, bass, programmed drums, and percussion). Ubuhle Bezintombi was electrifying their radio listenership and appearing on Bodloza's music video program on TV 2. They were singing songs from courting parties and wedding ceremonies.

It is the day after Xmas 1992, in Keates Drift, rural KwaZulu-Natal, where the Umzansi Zulu Dance team lives. I trek down to the tea room on the tar road to buy some icy cokes. Music videos air on the store's television, mounted above the door on the hot, still porch. Teenage girls cluster below the TV, entranced. They are dressed for the festive holiday: they have wrapped royal blue cloths from their waists, tied white cloaks around their shoulders, donned long, colored socks and colored sneakers, and decorated themselves with bright-beaded necklaces and belts, rubber bottle seals, and shiny silver watch straps. Xmas tinsel is braided into their wrapped and plaited hair. They are captivated by their

*mirror image in the music video. In royal blue cloth, decorated in
beaded necklaces and belts, the young Ubuhle Bezintombi (The
Beauty of Girls) mime their recorded wedding songs in a TV
studio, with instrumental backing.*

Isigqi Sesimanje were not enticed into trying to reap high sales from the township youth or into succumbing to a genre fronted by rural teenage girls. So West dropped his plug for the high-turnover market that would best benefit the record company, and he persuaded them by playing up the traditionality of the music on which these hits are based. "You'll never find [wedding songs] rotting," he advised.

The next morning they were back in the studio, singing wedding songs. They changed one of their mbaqanga songs to fit the wedding song beat, and Joana composed two new ones, "Makoti onjani" (What kind of a bride is this?) and "Hamba kahle" (Go well).

The lyrics of these three songs address aspects of marriage ritual (bride-wealth in "Phumani," for example), the plights and duties of the new wife ("Makoti onjani"), and the departure for a new homestead ("Hamba kahle"). They are sung with a female lead and chorus. Ululations are interspersed into the instrumental breaks. "Phumani" and "Hamba kahle" take the upbeat tempo of wedding songs. "Makoti" is slowed to correspond with the ngoma drum motive West has constructed and follows the slower pacing of the *ikondlo* (the solemn principal song of the bride) as it is sung in some regions of KwaZulu-Natal. The percussion tracks realize implicit and explicit rhythms in the dance. The rim-shot, for example, metronomically lays out the beat much as hand clapping and shield hitting does at weddings. The syncopated emphasis in the middle of the measure is present, as is the narrow melodic contour.

"Makoti" deviates more from wedding songs than Isigqi's others do. West inserts a Mahlathini-like bass commentary into the song, and he gives the male backing chorus some presence, thereby integrating the idea of the men's wedding singing into the same song. (At weddings, men and women generally sing separate songs, but they overlap in their performance.) The concept of the Zulu wedding is embedded in the composition of "Makoti onjani." Isigqi Sesimanje have traditionalized their song form.

take 3 : producing Zuluness by reworking the lyrics

21 November 1991

Isigqi Sesimanje are recording the vocal overdubs on their new wedding song, "Makoti onjani." Joana, lead singer on this song, and West are to insert spoken interjections between some of the sung verses. They stand side by side in front of a mike in the recording booth. For once, the musicians can hear everything, since they are listening in the control room while West, being cooped up in the recording booth, has to gesticulate through the control-room window at Peter when he wants to communicate if the mike lines are not open. Peter has control over piping music and talk into West's puffy headphones.

West improvises the words and corrects Joana's impromptu responses. Joana and others in the group suggest details back to West. Peter works the console.

Unusual for a mbaqanga song, the story of the lyrics (written by Joana) is set in rural Zululand, where homes clamber over the hills like old, brown women chatting in clumps. Round, thatched houses with dark, low doorways cluster around each family's kraal.[10] The wire-wire doesn't stretch this far.[11] Public sewers don't stretch this far. Litter accumulates, and the river ambling through the valley looks murkier every day. Goats meander, ripping out the last of the yellow grass. Children run in clusters. A battered pickup rattles up the dust road. Men pass the *ukhamba* (earthenware pot), sip the home-brew, pass the pot, sip and pass, in the skinny shade of a thorn tree. Conversation moves with gaps and echoes. Women irrigate their vegetables in slow motion, down near the riverbank.

In the song a new young bride (Joana) has joined such a community. The women (Jane, Janet, Joana, and Michael) criticize her in chorus, publicly. They sneer at her laziness: she is not a good woman, she is not a worthy bride, she won't get up and work for her new family. The men agree indignantly "Ngikhalela izinkoma zikababa, engalobola ngazo lelivila" (I'm crying over my father's cattle that have gone into bridewealth for the lazy one!), they sing.

Her new husband (West), whose family has of course paid *ilobolo* (bride price), expects a dutiful wife to do him proud in return. "Mkhaliseleni ibell, akwazi ukuvuka!" (Ring the bell, she just won't wake up!), he bellows, as if the patriarch of a rural homestead.

But she is awake, and she talks back. "Heyi mina ngifuna impompi

Icilongo player en route to a wedding, Keates Drift, KwaZulu-Natal, 1992.
Photo by TJ Lemon.

angifuni ukuya emfuleni!" (I want a pump, I don't want to go down to the
river!), she cries. The homestead women support their married man. They
reiterate his order, "Vuka uyokhamanzi emfuleni!" (Wake up and go and
fetch water at the river!)

Peter rolls the tape; West has to insert his interjection. He misses. Peter
stops the tape.

"Vuka!" (Wake up!), calls out Tefo playfully at West, as if he were the
producer now. (Tefo's exclamation is not audible to West in the booth.)

West rehearses the line, then they try to put it down again. One more
time. He's having trouble finding the correct moment of entry and meter-
ing out the line to fit with the backing. He asks Peter to repeat it once
again. He practices cold a few times. It doesn't fit. Distracted, he plays
around with the wording. For fun he invents an onomatopoeic alter-
native to *ibell*. He sings, "Mshayeleni *ibell*—/ Mshayeleni *iting ting*
akwaz'ukuvuka, bo."

West's playfulness offers an opening to the musicians to voice their
ideas. Joana corrects his township wording by substituting the Zulu word
for an iron bell into his line—that is, she uses the word for a school or
church bell.

"Mshayeleni *insimbi*," she directs him. No problem. West switches to

"Mshayeleni insimbi" without missing a beat while rehearsing the line with the backing tracks. He laughs, then improvises a Mahlathini-like groan. He sings, "Wo! Mshayeleni insimbi akwaz'ukuvuka, bo."

Joana voices agreement, Peter rolls the tape again. They start and stop, because the timing is still not accurate enough. Tefo leaps into a moment of silence. "Yini yicilongo? Insimbi yicilongo, angithi?" he asks in Zulu. "Why not *icilongo, insimbi* is *icilongo,* isn't it?" *Icilongo* refers to the bugle played at festive events in rural communities. It has replaced the animal horn trumpet. No one answers. Peter starts the tape again. West enters in the right place, but this time he reverts to the original word *ibell*. He sings, "Wo! Mshayeleni ibell akwaz'ukuvuka, bo."

Wrong again, so he practices, changing back to use *insimbi*.

Wo! Mshayeleni insimbi akwaz'ukuvuka, bo.

"It's *icilongo!*" insists Michael.

"Hey?" asks West.

"It's *icilongo!*" he repeats.

West can be stubborn, authoritarian, and provocative. He exacerbates the distance between his and the musicians' positions by replacing the anglicized *ibell* with an Afrikaans version, *iklok,* instead.[12]

"It's *icilongo*—in Zulu it's *icilongo!*" Michael asserts again.

"I can't hear you," replies West from the recording booth.

A chorus of voices in the control room tells him, "It's *icilongo!*"

"Hey?" he asks again. "Just put through those voices, Peter."

Tefo explains to him that it's *icilongo* they want.

"Oh!" replies West, and then he practices his part inserting the right word.

Tefo and Michael voice approval to each other. They are the two band members whose first language is not Zulu, yet they are the ones who are insisting on the insertion of the most Zulu word. (Michael's mother tongue is seTswana, Tefo's is seSotho.)

"Ja, it's not *ibell*" adds Tefo loud enough for West to hear.

West, who has been challenged here, blurts out "Hey! Michael isn't a Zulu!"

Joana aligns herself with powerful West and agrees. "Michael doesn't know the Zulu language!"

West reiterates, "He doesn't know Zulu—he doesn't know these things which are done by you!"

Michael responds to this criticism by asserting the correct Zulu again. Then he marks the performativity of all these positions and the shiftable relationship of ethnic markings to the identities of the speakers by spurting out *icilongo*'s most politically laden opposite, the Afrikaans *iklok*, which West had first introduced. "It's *iklok!*" he exclaims, laughing.

"It's not *iklok*," retorts Tefo, "*iklok* is Sotho, it's *icilongo*."[13]

Now Joana stands by Tefo but she repositions the word association as white rather than seSotho. "It's not *iklok*," she agrees, "*iklok* is white."

Michael turns to me and jokes again by substituting the other white term. "It's *ibell!*"

So I join the performing fray. "It's *ibell*," I joke back, in the spirit of Tefo's assertion of his Sotho ethnicity.

"Bell made in hell!" quips Michael, improvising on its sound in English while suddenly distancing himself from its whiteness and reminding me playfully of my privilege.

West practices singing his lines the Zulu way, and he gets the timing right. "Okay," he says.

They're ready for a take. Peter rolls the tape.

From West's perspective, this substitution was principally a technical one. He was trying to find a word with the right number of syllables to fit the meter of the line. The musicians wanted some authority in the shaping of their song—the temporary inversion of their and West's studio roles and spatial positioning made this possible.[14] That West has momentarily set aside his authority as producer in order to stand behind a microphone lays open the possibility for musicians to renegotiate their professional positions and concerns, which they do in the process of arguing over things Zulu.

But the musicians also wanted something else that got worked out in the process: they were concerned with the authenticity of the Zulu sound image. Their alteration in the interjection is a Zulu-izing substitution in both language (from *ibell* to *icilongo*) and in the object to which it refers (from an iron school/mission bell to the rural bugle), a shift from the colonial closer to the precolonial and deep Zulu equivalent.

takes mixed

The Zulu-izing moves in this song happen on multiple levels: in the timbre of the drum, the insertion of the drum motive, the transformation of the genre to a wedding song, in the poetics and narrative of the lyrics, and in the combination of aspects of different traditional forms (ngoma and wedding song).

The timbre of the drum not only represents an authenticity by sounding acoustic and therefore live, but it also emphasizes this idea by signifying even more authenticity than actual contemporary ngoma practice. By replacing the contemporary version with the sound of the preindustrial equivalent, it is more ideally African, more traditional than the ngoma drum as it is heard at the hostels and in rural Zululand today.

The insertion of the ngoma figure into the rhythm track traditionalizes the programmed house bass version of the wedding song heard on the youth market. West is deliberately drawing on the currency of the wedding song in the township youth and Zulu trad markets and reworking it according to his own production style. The wedding song, in turn, traditionalizes Isigqi's mbaqanga.[15]

It is notable that these moves arise from varying quarters. They are variously motivated by studio music-makers who have differing investments in the project and different projections about its marketability. The reasons by which they argue for these specific changes aren't even necessarily first and foremost about sounding Zulu. Yet the result of all this symbolic and sonic overlay, of the "transformative interaction of the various subtropes" (Fernandez 1991, 6), is an intensification of Zuluness in their mbaqanga.

Zuluness is intensified in two ways in this song. First, the layering intensifies the emotional and experiential potency of the trope. It is at once recognized as a concrete, compact instance or figure and experienced as an enduring sensuous mode of being; it is both a pattern apprehended and an improvisation, a learned form and a felt resonance (Feld 1988; also Taussig 1993). Second, the kinds of overlays and juxtapositions mark and heighten the way that Zuluness is a constructed authenticity. Zuluness is a performance collaged out of multiple versions of itself.

In working Zuluness into their sound, the musicians are looking for appropriate figures and good poetics for the regional domestic market for which they are targeted and for the World Music market they want to reach. The regional market is one that must take into account the ethnic nationalist sentiment raging at the time; the early 1990s World Music market is one that entertains products that contribute to the image of the (ethnic) diversity of the world's peoples that the industry celebrates. While keeping an ear on their prospective markets, the musicians are also working through more immediate, local, and personal concerns. They are building consensus among themselves about what sounds they like as artists. Tefo and Michael cultivate solidarity within the group by voicing a preference for the sounds of the majority ethnicity in the studio, namely Zulu.

In negotiating all these concerns, a take on ethnicity and its relationship to the musicians' sense of self as political subjects emerges. Here, in the domain of semantic referentiality, Zuluness can be named. But it still doesn't get fixed. In fact, musicians seem to work at unsettling it, intuitively, whenever it stands still for too long or consolidates too monologic a voice. "Hey! Michael doesn't know Zulu!" By keeping Zuluness on the move, it stays up for grabs, to be absolutely owned by no one for long. In this way, the musicians know and show that ethnicity is relational. It exists in process. It is performed and recognized as rhetorical.

Track 2 *Zuluness as a Political Position*

Midmorning there was no sign of an event at George Goch Stadium, on the edge of industrial Johannesburg, in September 1991.

Noon there was no sign of an event, just a scattering of disappointed fans.

There would be no event at George Goch Stadium that day—no festive appearance of Isigqi Sesimanje and Ladysmith Black Mambazo, and a string of other scheduled groups. Instead, a full-sun Sunday lull hangs over the stadium, the Zulu male hostel alongside it, and the city mine dumps around it.

You just never know, or know why.

TJ and I head out to Thokoza, a township where there is an Inkatha Freedom Party protest march in response to an ANC attack on an Inkatha funeral (for victims of prior ANC aggression—itself a response to an Inkatha attack).

Inkatha had not always been a violent player nor a political party nor even a presence in the areas around Johannesburg. It was conceived in the mid-1970s by its founding members as a cultural movement, not a political body. But it was puppeteered by the apartheid state into a deadly political program. The strategy was to generate a counterforce to the already broiling internal popular resistance that was aligned with the African National Congress/South African Communist Party-led liberation movement.[16]

In the 1980s, as Inkatha's relationship with the state became increasingly formidable and structurally integrated, and its relationship with the ANC soured drastically, it turned its focus to regional consolidation and the production of Zulu political consensus. Consensus was sought through physical threat at the same time as it was engendered through political rhetoric. Over the course of the decade, the movement became inextricably and violently linked to state security and police organs, among other state institutions. From these covert institutional ties it drew financial support, training, personnel, and protection while its members actively confronted the state's internal opponents.

From the 1980s into the 1990s, Inkatha leaders defined who their opposition was in increasingly ethnic and essentialized terms. Their rhetorical correlation between Xhosas and the ANC was the most prevalent ethnic essentialism. However, the "enemy" named by both IFP leader Buthelezi and the Zulu King included "Zulus" who rejected Inkatha. Zulu Inkatha dissidents were hounded as traitors and witches (Maré 1993). As Buthelezi announced in a speech, "no one escapes being a member [of Inkatha] as long as he or she is a member of the Zulu nation" (ibid., 75). In another instance, the King Goodwill Zwelethini called on his supporters to "eliminate from your midst all those disgusting usurpers of our dignity without one shred of malice in your beings. . . . Go out my people, conquer evil, but never lose your humanity and never degrade the humanity of those you conquer. Rout them out only to make them one of us. Thrash them, if necessary, only to purge them into becoming better Zulus" (ibid., 72–73; see also de Haas and Zulu 1993).

Fueled by rhetoric and backed by deadly state institutions, Inkatha-related violence escalated dramatically. In the mid-1980s the KwaZulu-Natal midlands was the most drastic region of conflict. But by 1990 the worst violence had spread beyond KwaZulu-Natal onto the Witwatersrand, the area around Johannesburg.[17] Here, "the township war," as it was termed, raged predominantly between migrant single male hostels (which had become IFP strongholds) and informal settlements (ANC strongholds). Eventually, it spread right into the city centers of Johannesburg, Durban, and Pietermaritzburg (the latter two being major towns in KwaZulu-Natal).[18]

There are guns, there is frenzy. We are still in the city when we run into returning Inkatha ralliers scurrying all over the road. Between 1991 and 1993 violence on the Witwatersrand is at its most drastic and most complex.

The process of mobilizing Zulus in support of a political program involved a massive and spectacular utilization of cultural symbols and expressive practices, as well as of "traditional" sociopolitical structures. IFP political leaders sought to legitimate and increase their own authority by authenticating their links to the leadership of a tribal and militaristic distant Zulu past. They cultivated a constituency by championing Zulu tradition and performance practices, especially those linked to mighty warriorship (see Mzala 1988; Wright and Mazel 1991; de Haas and Zulu 1993; Harries 1993; Maré 1993; Hamilton 1998). Imagine ten thousand IFP supporters marching through Johannesburg, as happened on 17 October 1992.[19] Throngs of men dressed in skins and carrying shields, sticks, and spears sang and danced in regimental bands through the high-rise city center. Zuluness was enacted. It was presented in living, moving form. Men like these, dancing, singing, parading down the street, came to stand as living representations of the historically deep trope of the tribal warrior. Such striking displays of a contemporary "tribal" ethic were luxuriantly circulated by the news media.

There are two important points to clarify here. First, the cultivation of Zulu nationalism has to be seen within the context of the apartheid state's overall strategy of separate development, whereby the state imposed ethnic divisions on black South Africans as the basis for land rights and labor control. The response by the liberation movement, until well into the 1990s, was to dismiss ethnicity as nothing other than an apartheid construct designed to undergird the state's ideology and all its policies of separate development (see Zegeye 2001). The IFP's violent ethnic nationalism arose like a grotesque phoenix out of the contestation over the terms and "truth" of ethnic identity.

Second, Zuluness was the only black ethnicity mobilized into a political identity that came to be represented by an ethnic nationalist political party during the 1970s through the first democratic elections. The IFP ultimately became a voice to be reckoned with at the negotiating table in the run-up to the first democratic elections in 1994, while it had also developed into a formidable state-sanctioned military force. Over six million Zulu-speaking South Africans were faced in the early 1990s with having to decide whether and how to align themselves politically. They simply had to refigure their sense of self in relation to a dramatically charged and mobilized Zuluness.

At its broadest, the ideological climate impinges on the course of artistic expression and the tenor of its reception. But the political and aesthetic realms are also inextricably linked at the level of institutional organization and social practice. The effects of political policy and campaigning can be seen in action in the musicians' changing strategies for securing performance opportunities. When I first met Isigqi in early 1991, they said they were no longer performing in townships or in the rural areas, except if they were part of a festival, because it had become too dangerous. They were also becoming frustrated with the small returns and unpredictability of their weekend shows on the mines. Besides, the shows had become too difficult to organize. They had to rely on the entertainment corps of particular shafts at particular mines to promote their show on the intercom and to put up posters; they had to schedule their appearances to coincide with payday weekends, or the turnout would be too small. Mining officials were not often cooperative in either regard. Additionally, the musicians had problems with transport and in hiring an adequate sound system. They tried to get a Sowetan taxi owner to sponsor them by loaning them a vehicle, but his promise never materialized. And whenever there was any potential for union-related "unrest" or any "ethnic violence" at a shaft, officials canceled their shows without notice.

Jane traveled to Zimbabwe to set up contacts for a tour. They hoped to collaborate with the Red Cross as they had in the 1970s. But the Zimbabwean officials couldn't arrange for work visas or ensure them payment in the form of a contract before they embarked on the tour. They also participated in some one-day music festivals in KwaZulu-Natal and Johannesburg, played occasional hotel gigs, and played at the Indlamu Cultural Festival, which had a dismal advertising campaign and a disastrously feeble turnout at a facility between Soweto and Johannesburg.

These kinds of performance possibilities dwindled as the violence continued to escalate in the early 1990s and the economic situation deteriorated. So, toward the end of 1992, Isigqi and a few other traditional and mbaqanga groups sought out a new performance space: the migrant men's hostels in and around Johannesburg. They arranged concerts through IFP representatives in the hostels. At that time, anyone known to be unsympathetic to the IFP could not perform in these hostels in safety. Isigqi Sesimanje made a distinction between IFP ideologues and ordinary people like themselves. Isigqi Sesimanje do not support violence. They do not necessarily support the IFP and, to my knowledge, did not attend political rallies.[20]

Track 3   Zuluness as Everyday Experience

Tuesday morning, 31 March 1992

Isigqi is back in the studio. While waiting for the session to begin, the singers chat about the weekend, ambling from one topic to another. The talk spins around to their latest dangerous township moments and then to the bigger, scarier picture of Soweto in the making.

Over the weekend, Joana and Michael were visiting hostel dwellers at a hostel in Soweto. This was nothing out of the ordinary for mbaqanga musicians who have fans living in these decrepit overcrowded residences.[21]

"And you would hear the sound of guns," recounts Joana, as she leans on the recording console. "We ended up staying at Dube hostel [in Soweto], and we said 'Heyi! Somebody announced this on the news this morning! Things are getting wrecked all over!' We woke up, dressed the kids. I was too scared to go out, but they warned me, 'Hey, come out or you will die inside.' The shooting didn't stop, guns were sounding dwang! dwang!"

"They were exchanging fire like firecrackers," exclaims Michael in alarm, snapping his fingers like gunshots. *Ka! Kaa! Ka! Kaa!* "Sister Joana!"

Having started off by recounting an event in which Joana and Michael inadvertently became subjects in a life-threatening story, the conversation moved on to everyday talk about other everyday people, all of whom witnessed violence during the course of their township living in the early 1990s. But in no time these musicians' storying is taken to a level of abstraction at which subjects become objects, individuals become types, real becomes figure, experience becomes reworked into an idea about social organization and moral practice.

Let me explain.

Migrant male hostels are positioned at the edge of residential areas in Soweto. They take their names from the areas adjacent to them (Dube, Orlando, Mzimhlophe, Jabulani, and so forth). In many cases, informal settlements have been constructed adjacent to hostels.

The Isigqi musicians live or have lived in the matchbox houses of the township itself. Sisters Jane and Janet lived together with their children, Jane's partner, and other extended family members in a residential area in Soweto. They grew up in a predominantly Zulu township outside Durban in Kwazulu-Natal but moved to the ethnically diverse Johannesburg area twenty-five years ago in order to work as professional recording artists. Janet recently moved into a flat in town. Joana moved in 1972 from KwaZulu-Natal to the city, similarly driven by the city's promise of fame and fortune—or at least in the hope of making a living by making music. For years she lived with her daughter and grandchildren in Soweto; recently they moved into a crowded high-rise in Johannesburg's city center. Michael is also a longtime urbanite from residential Soweto, though he has moved to Thokoza, another township in the area.

Township residents, hostel dwellers, squatters: these are three modes of being Sowetan. They represent three distinct living places around which volatile tensions erupted in the early 1990s.

Tape rolling: the conversation continues.

"They have those hostels on the other side. People are dying in the township just like that—and they are blaming the people in the hostels," comments Janet. By her accusatory tone she derides those who cast blame for the killings in the wrong place. From her point of view, the hostels do not house murderers.

"There is this white man who said on Saturday that the hostels must be demolished. Why?" asks Michael brusquely and rhetorically. "Because it's a hiding place for criminals—the ones who are friends with the hostel dwellers. They bring back weapons and leave them there."

As the IFP worked its influence up from KwaZulu-Natal into the Johannesburg area, South African Defense Force-and IFP-trained and -armed cohorts—or at least cohort trainers—were bussed up and housed in the hostels. The distinctions between who was a long-term resident, who was on hire for the weekend, who was trained by the visitors, and who acted as vigilantes became increasingly blurry (Minnaar 1993, 68). The confusion inside the hostels was certainly to the advantage of those who supported or engaged in violent activity, and it was probably deliberately perpetuated by those it served.

They charge the soccer field. They charge the stands. They kill
people. They charge across the road to the trade store. They
frenzy back into their idling vehicles and head back to the hostel.
Later, it has turned into an ordinary Sunday afternoon.

In their Tuesday morning conversation in the studio Michael and Janet distinguish meticulously between perpetrators of criminal violence against townspeople, and hostel dwellers, with whom they feel some allegiance. In enunciating these distinctions they are participating in a raging public debate on the destiny of the hostels and the living conditions of migrant laborers.

The hostels had been part of the backbone supporting the apartheid policy of influx control. Could these decrepit residences now be rehabilitated to accommodate families who had forcibly been retained in rural areas by apartheid legislation while the adult male members had migrated for work? The plight of the hostels in the new South Africa was being debated in political and civic arenas with great passion and volatility. The key issues were whether and how to do away with the single-migrant-male-hostelling system and whether to demolish or restructure the buildings.[22] The terms of the debate had been shifting somewhat in response to the constant eruptions of retaliatory violence in which the hostels were implicated. Four major massacres had occurred in confrontations between hostel dwellers and squatters in 1991 and 1992, and these fueled multiple and multiplying smaller outbursts.[23] Some debaters argued that it was necessary to demolish the hostels and dismantle the migrant labor system in order to eradicate such fatal aggression.

"There is this white man who said on Saturday that the hostels must be demolished. Why?" asks Michael. He positions this spokesperson according to his white privilege. He is an outsider whom Michael grants an ear and some authority on the basis of his South African social status.

But Jane challenges Michael's white author. "You see, when they say the hostel must be demolished, they are going to make things even worse for us!" she warns. The "white man" has no experience of living in Soweto. Jane reminds her fellow conversationalists that he is not one of "us." He has a fragile base for his weighty opinions, and he suffers none of the consequences of his proposal. The white privilege on which Michael grants him authority is the basis for the naïveté on the grounds of which Jane discounts his authority.

At this point, Janet forcefully reenters the discussion. "They are Zulus —they are Zulus who'll come and live in the township," she warns her sister and friends.

Who is a Zulu, then? I'm reminded that Janet had asked me a few weeks earlier what my plans for the Easter weekend were, for perhaps she could take me "ekhaya," to her family in rural Zululand. I think also of Jane telling me about the way they, Zulu people, do this or that, or the way they are. In these explanations to me, she included herself among Zulu people. I think of Joana explaining the deep Zulu meaning of *isigqi* to me. I remember when I asked Jane if she wasn't afraid to go and perform in the hostel so late at night, and she responded, "It's safe if you're one of them." I'm reminded of being complimented that one day I'll be able to speak Zulu "like Inkatha." "Zulu," then, is none of these things for Janet at the moment when she says, "They are Zulus—they are Zulus who'll come and live in the township!" Zulu is a threat, a subject in her story, a character she knows, an indexical icon of township violence.

Tape rolling.

"The white man says the hostels must be demolished and the people placed in houses. Don't you think they—"

"Look Mike," interrupts Jane urgently, "those people mustn't be chased away from their hostel. They'll be a threat to our children."

Janet backs her sister up. "Hey, when a Zulu comes and stays in your yard after he's left the place where he used to live, he'll come and live [at your place] by force!" Most Sowetans rent out tiny living spaces in their backyards for additional income. For many this is a critical source of revenue.

"They must be separate," Michael agrees, clarifying his earlier position. "If he stays, [he stays uninvited], Janet. They don't care."

Cut.

In speaking as Sowetan residents with children and home space to protect, these speakers risk appearing to favor the opposition to the Zulus. Jane swivels her positioning artfully as she continues to passionately shake her index finger and heap up parallelisms that drive home her feeling and her point.

"These kids, they are the ones who are stopping the hostel dwellers from going to work. These kids, they are the ones who are supposed to— it is said that mothers used to stay in the hostels. Isn't it true that there used to be rooms available? It is said that these kids kicked them out. And then when they see that you do not belong there, they kill you."

The other musicians in the studio join her in shaping a picture of their Soweto, in which they are part of a silenced and invisible moral order. Together they represent the youths as central agents in a social world seriously out of control.

"They sell [whatever they get]," claims Michael.

"In Meadowlands [an area in Soweto] they even killed a white lady, they even killed, they even killed a white lady in Meadowlands," relates a horrified Jane.

"( ) and he grabs you like this" explains Michael, thrusting his right arm forward as though hooking an unsuspecting pedestrian around the neck from behind.

When these musicians talk about the kids, they refer to the disrespecting youth, the young street hooligans. In their view of Soweto, there is a blurred division between these youth and street activists. South Africa was rife with labor disputes, strikes, "go slow" actions, and boycotts. The 1980s resistance movement had sought power through rendering the townships ungovernable. With this recent history, by implication "kids" also implies unionized workers and young activists of the ANC.

"I ask you now," interjects Joana, shifting the conversation back into the hostels, "how do these people know each other [in these huge hostels]? Because, you know, you see new faces everyday now. How can they know everyone? If you knew twelve thousand people, maybe—you could never know so many!" How easy it is for criminals to hide in the hostels, she reminds her fellow artists.

"Besides that, Joana," adds Jane, "take for instance the hostel up there, the big one—you've never heard somebody say there's fighting going on. . . . These things are in the middle of the township—"

"—in the middle of the township," Joana insists, overlapping with Jane and nodding.

"It's our kids who are intimidating the hostel dwellers," Jane pronounces.

In the process of picturing this type—"kids"—and standing against it, the musicians foreground the hostel dwellers again, as if a positioning against the kids is a positioning with the hostel dwellers. One subject in the narrative exists in relation to the other.

Janet, who a few minutes ago was threatening that the Zulus would come and take over your backyard by force if the hostels were demolished, now defends hostel dwellers against the kids. "Even in this hostel in Diepkloof you would never hear somebody say, 'These people are fighting.' They are being intimidated!"

Jane disagrees. She doesn't think that the violence is coerced; the responsibility for injury and death cannot be thrust upon shadows and silent forces originating in KwaZulu-Natal. Neither can injury and destruction be excused as fear-driven defensive action forced on citizens by activists threatening violence against scabs and boycott breakers. Aligning herself with the township residents she asserts, "They're killing one another—those ones are not being intimidated, in the true sense of intimidation! If it's said that a person dies in Diepkloof [hostel], they have killed one another, they were not killed by the township [people]."[24]

Janet concurs. "They killed one another."

"If they were to start leaving Diepkloof hostel, those new houses would be finished [burnt down]!" says Jane, bringing the flipside into focus again. New housing projects had been initiated in parts of Soweto to begin to alleviate the burgeoning informal settlement problems.

"You see," Janet elaborates, "if they say the hostels must be stopped [the hostel system eradicated], someone is going to have to leave his or her own house."

"The houses would be finished, they would be finished!" interjects her sister. "Where are they going to build for them?"

Tefo has arrived. He leans against the outboard effects console, on top of which engineer Peter will set up the DX7 for Tefo's keyboard overdubs, and he enters the fray. "Heyi, they would be finished! If it comes to that, they would be finished!"

Jane talks over him. "Our yards are full of our children. Now where are you going to build houses for hostel dwellers? You won't say they should live in shacks."

Michael tries to intervene, but Jane persists. She introduces a new ethnic type, the Xhosa, into the intensity of the moment. "And this thing is caused by the Xhosas who come from the yards."

"Yet that [white] person said South Africa has many colors!" exclaims Michael with exasperation at the naïveté of someone who would unleash more (ethnic) tensions on Sowetans.

Backyard renters, hostel dwellers, squatters; owners, renters, forceful occupiers; Zulus, Xhosas, and a white person championing the country's multiethnic constitution: these are ways of being positioned in Soweto in relation to a matrix of distinct living spaces. Old neighborhoods, new housing, hostels, shacks. Underlying these divisions is an implication of political alignment. The hostels had become IFP strongholds; the informal settlements alongside them supported the ANC and its allies.

We head out to a township where there is an IFP protest march in response to an ANC attack on an Inkatha funeral, of victims of ANC aggression in response to an Inkatha attack. We are still in the city itself when we run into returning Inkatha ralliers scurrying all over the road. There is frenzy.

Jane is the most established Soweto resident of the group, the head of her household, a landlady with renters in her backyard, and a long-standing figure in her neighborhood. She knows every house and backyard is already overcrowded. She does not advocate that anyone should have to live in a shack. She also knows that a hostel dweller would probably not be safe if he moved into an informal settlement, since his party alignment would place him at risk. At the climax of the conversation, when she introduces Xhosas, she designates them in this instance as the apex of dangerous Otherness. Janet meets Jane's upped stakes by reintroducing the Zulus, whom she had first pinpointed as troublesome and different near the beginning of the story. The sisters play out urban tribal warfare—the same battle I see storied in the mainstream media. Though they distance themselves from the aggression, they and Joana position themselves against the Xhosa. As the dialogue progresses, they start to re-place themselves in the story, reposition themselves on the ground by expressing some identification with the Zulu.

Rolling.

"You know, I'm telling you that now these people, the Zulus, they say you can do—they say once the hostels are demolished they are going to get into houses and they won't stay in shacks. They are going to stay in someone's home," says Janet.

"They say if you demolish the hostel, everybody who stays in a shack will have to pack and go. They say the hostels and shacks are alike. [The treatment you get from the people who live in both is the same.] And there are many people who live in shacks. Do you see the trouble hasn't even started yet!" worries Jane.

"The squatters will pack and go, and you just don't know—I don't know what these people are like," answers Janet.

"Don't consent again to take people from the farms [rural people, migrants in the hostels] and allow them to stay in your backyard. Look now, they came out of the house and ululated the other day," says Jane. Women ululate in celebration or to call attention to something of social significance. The practice would here be understood to be associated with traditional ways and hence with rurally oriented people, which in this context would be a reference to Zulus and, by implication, to IFP supporters.

"Out of your house!" exclaims Janet.

"They went all the way to the street, they want to cause us trouble," Jane remembers.

"You know it," agrees Joana, nodding again.

As Zulus themselves in terms of their birthplace and mother tongue (with the exception of Michael and Tefo), as long-term Sowetan residents, and as artists whose fans are mostly mother-tongue speakers of the Zulu language, these Isigqi artists move in and out of the discursive space called Zuluness as they dodge the threat of multifaceted violence that haphazardly comes their way. In the process they figure themselves in relation to Zuluness as they collaboratively position themselves in the place of Soweto. Positioning themselves in early 1990s Soweto, after the resistance movement had strategically sought to render the township ungovernable for a decade and a half, calls for a discursive dancing among the multiple, overlapping, and contradictory categories of political and civic resistance to apartheid. To position themselves in relation to a tribalized Zuluness is a complicated task, for they have to shape their sense of identity in relation to urban spaces and practices, and in relation to urban feelings about rurality. Urban-rural stresses implicate other kinds of tensions—generational, political, ethnic, religious, class, and so forth—which arise from the way the urban-rural divide has been historically exploited by apartheid exponents (see Coplan 1993, 338; Howe 1993, 35).[25]

"They are not scared of firearms," scoffs Michael, "that a bullet will come out of the barrel the wrong way and hit you."

"They must be chased away! They must be chased away! The Xhosas, they must go! They must be chased away, because they want to cause us trouble!" cries Janet fiercely.

"They are practicing [to shoot]," Joana warns. "They are already here at Mlamula-Nkunzi station, [their guns] sounding there already. You hear them say, 'Hey! hey!' One brother said there's nothing happening. That means these people are just practicing. They are just warning you, 'Hey, you!' Today there were ambulances and police helicopters."

"The trouble is going to start now," predicts Michael somberly.

At the taxi ranks and the train stations, daily Sowetan commuters may be caught in the haphazard crossfire of intraethnic faction fights, of political fraction fights, of intercompany taxi wars, of a ready police force, of petty criminals, of a combination of any of these overlapping and contradicting. The tensions of one conflict are exploited to further the interests and empires of another.

Next Michael shifts into a new, concrete introduction to a story in which he figures as a subject again. "You know, on Saturday, there was a car at our place, if you heard its sound—its like a motorbike, sister," he says as he starts to tell about a drive-by shooting at a local drinking spot near his mother's home.

In their conversation, Jane, Joana, Janet, and Michael say there are Zulus in the hostels, non-Zulus in township and squatter camps. "They are Zulus who'll come and live in your yard by force!" So their story goes. But Joanna, Jane, and Janet are Zulus by birth and often identify themselves as Zulus. They say there are criminals in the hostels, citizens in the houses. So their story goes. But many hostel dwellers are law abiding citizens. "It's a hiding place for criminals, the one's who are friends with the hostel dwellers," they qualify. They say there are fighters in the hostels—"No, its the kids out of control in the streets, intimidating the workers in the hostels." IFP warriors. ANC kids. So their story implies. No, many hostel dwellers do not participate in IFP violence; card-carrying IFP members are not necessarily supporters of IFP ideology;[26] many residents are not vocally ANC; many activists are mature adults; many residents,

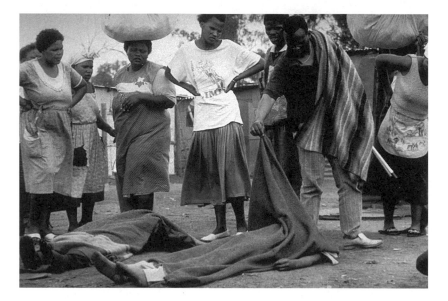

Fleeing with their possessions, residents of Phola Park pass an elderly couple killed in an overnight attack by Inkatha. East Rand, Johannesburg, December 1990. *Photo by TJ Lemon.*

like themselves, are not activists. "You see, if the whites demolish the hostels. . . ." "Everybody who stays in a shack will also have to pack and go." "The Xhosas, they must be chased away." "They are not scared of firearms, that a bullet will come out of the barrel the wrong way and hit you." "Do you see, the trouble hasn't even started yet!"

It is at this level of abstraction, where the musicians have removed themselves as individual characters from the discourse and imagine categories of difference, that they actually (re)orient themselves in the real world, as they collaboratively position themselves in the place of Soweto. In talk about types, hearsay, objects, and figures, they realign their relationships to one another and to their ideas of how the material world functions. A relationship to the social world is fashioned in this story world, which in turn is fashioned from (but not identical to) the social world.

In the story world these social types play against one another. As the story leans into the picturing of one type, the other type fades to the background; as the foregrounded type begins to crystallize, it momentarily freezes the alignments of the speakers in relation to one another right in the studio and in the larger world of sociopolitical relations. Then, another backgrounded type shifts up to the foreground again. The manifestation of these types is fluid and the musicians' alignments to them shifting because they are fundamentally performative, rhetorically charged categories. Furthermore, their constitution is predicated on a tumultuous sociopolitical history in which repressive state policies have been based around irrational social distinctions.

Isigqi's studio conversation exemplifies their undecidability about the agency entailed in the category of Zuluness even as they identify with specific Zulu aesthetic practices and forms. They move between ideas of the Zulu as victim and perpetrator of violence, Zulu as of object and subject of death, Zulu as themselves and as Other, Zulu as difference with which they identify, and Zulu as rhetorical category. From the broadest level of state policy to the smallest instance of identity politics, social categorization as "Zulu" is experienced as fundamentally performative at the same time as it is recognized as having real effects.

In its form this conversation replicates the ibell/icilongo discussion. Speakers in each conversation shift positions that link ethnicities to objects, spaces, behaviors, or social position. What is Zulu and what is not is determined though their interaction, though it is easily and quickly redefined. Both conversations express an approach to ethnic identity as relative and performative. However, in the Sowetan civic realm, the life-and-death stakes of being identified as Zulu are exposed. This latter talk reveals the level of vulnerability that confronts these musicians and others like them in claiming or rejecting a Zulu identity in the early 1990s.

It is not only by iconic repetition that the two conversations are meaningfully linked. Operating as a discourse about culture and cultural ownership, the ibell/icilongo conversation informs and prepares the terms for the Soweto/hostel conversation, which operates on the level of everyday experience of the political realm. The vulnerabilities associated with Zuluness in the civic realm unnerve the distinctions delineated in the aesthetic realm. The aesthetic feeds back into the civic and political: it provides expressive forms with which to mark, live in, reflect on, and shape categories of the difference. The artistic arena and the poetics of metacultural discourse keep the boundaries blurred in the everyday. Expressive practice marks the categories it draws into its forms as performative in and of themselves, even in the civic and political arenas.

On the politicians' playing field, Zulu nationalism is cultivated, legislated, and administrated. In everyday practice and in ordinary language, Zuluness as a precarious political position is refigured in the process of socially repositioning individuals and social groups, in and out of the studio. In this domain, Zuluness is a shifting figure—sometimes a political position, sometimes an endangered civil identity. It is felt and imagined in relation to other possibilities or in relation to threats. It is expressed through talk about political action. Such talk is dense with emotions: anxiety, anger, passion, concern.

Shifting into the domain of aesthetic form, Zuluness is self-consciously shaped into an expressive motif. It is fashioned during Isigqi's Sesimanje's production by rewriting lyrics, changing the song form, and by manipulating the tiniest details of timbre. That is to say, Zuluness is embedded in poetic language, and it moves away from semantic referentiality through the pragmatics of talk outward into Zuluness as a sound. This is a move away from prescription toward feeling, away from the defined toward the ineffable, from the articulated to the sensed. As Zuluness is increasingly aestheticized in this way, as it moves out of the realm of argument and into the body, it ensures that the possibilities remain open for experiencing or interpreting Zuluness in nonnationalist and deeply personal ways, just as it offers party activists a reservoir of already feelingful suggestiveness to draw into their nationalist project. The instability of the political alignment of Zuluness overlaid with the ambiguity of signifying through sound and movement transforms what could be a straightforward, surface understanding of a sign as communication into a deeply felt experience of its significance.

The political, the everyday, and the aesthetic are mutually saturated on the level of sense, beneath and around the articulated and the obvious, in that naturalizing realm where tropes reside. Zuluness is at once a deep organizing trope or "gist" elaborated into the poetics of expressive forms, and a loosely articulated "suggestiveness." As Paul Friedrich writes, the "extraction of gist and the maximization of suggestiveness . . . are in fact mirror images of each other: an aptly stated gist will give off many reverberations, whereas rich suggestiveness necessarily implies a deep core" (1991, 41, 42). Participating in difference by performing or feeling Zulu can reconfigure how South African artists imagine their difference.

Zuluness is brought to life and brought into question by iconic sub-

PLATE 1. Bafana Mdlalose, a ngoma dancer at Keates Drift, KwaZulu-Natal, 25 December 2000. *Photo by TJ Lemon.*

PLATE 2. Ngoma dancing at Keates Drift, KwaZulu-Natal, 25 December 2000. *Photo by TJ Lemon.*

PLATE 3. King Zwelethini's new bride, Nompumelelo of Mzinkhulu, dances at her wedding, Royal Palace of KwaNongoma, KwaZulu-Natal, 25 July 1992. *Photo by TJ Lemon.*

PLATE 4. Dancing at the wedding of King Goodwill Zwelethini at the Royal Palace of KwaNongoma, KwaZulu-Natal, 25 July 1992. *Photo by TJ Lemon.*

PLATE 5. Inkatha Freedom Party supporters en route to a rally. Alexandria township, 1992. *Photo by TJ Lemon.*

PLATE 6. Inkatha Freedom Party
march, Johannesburg, May 1993.
Photo by TJ Lemon.

PLATE 7. Residents of an informal
settlement rescue their belongings
after a raid by Inkatha supporters
from a neighboring hostel, 1992.
Photo by TJ Lemon.

PLATE 8. Inkatha Freedom Party funeral, Sebokeng, 1993. *Photo by TJ Lemon.*

PLATE 9. Isigqi Sesimanje and Abashayi Bengoma choosing their own pose for a promotional photograph, Johannesburg, 1992. Left to right, back row: Nhlanhla Qwabe, Derrick Dlamini, Bheki Mthembu; front row: Jane Dlamini, Joana Tango, Pauline Nkosi, Janet Dlamini. *Photo by TJ Lemon.*

stitution—that is, by the accumulation and overlaying of repeated but variegated versions of it, and by people sometimes taking its representation for real. Zuluness is also brought to life through indexical relations, facilitated by technological reproduction and distribution. That is, the direct link from the ngoma drum sound in Isigqi Sesimanje's song to the Umzansi Zulu Dance recording, which in turn links to the drumming of ngoma dancing outside the hostels and in rural KwaZulu-Natal on the one hand and to the *Ipitombi* romanticization on the other, brings the power of Zuluness into Isigqi's expression. The blurred and potential associations between ngoma dancing and violent IFP raids by assumption of their coexistence as hostel activities further loads the drum sound with potency and questions.

Tropes upon tropes, wedding songs, ngoma beats sometimes overlap isomorphically; at other times, they interface in part or merely intersect in passing. In shaping, juxtaposing, isolating, reworking sounds into expressive forms, ethnic difference and its political alignment is reconsidered, disavowed, or embraced. It is engaged with in part or wholeheartedly. Its politics are cast aside or into the background, or refigured in relation to other terms of significance. Political restructuring and realignments of social differences could not happen without this circulation, spiraling, gathering momentum; this connecting of the everyday to mediated images and experience from the outside; this bringing of larger, more encompassing, and powerful other worlds back home.

July 1992

"The South African Broadcasting Corporation presents the royal wedding of King Zwelethini Goodwill ka Bhekuzulu, king of the Zulus!" announces Bhodloza Nzimande, host of TV2's music video program, in his reverbed, bantering DJ voice. Zwelethini married his fifth wife, Queen Nompumelelo of Mzimkhulu, in Ulundi, KwaZulu-Natal. TV2, the Zulu and Xhosa television station, was on site to document it.[27]

As Bhodloza introduces the special feature in Zulu, Isigqi Sesimanje's newly released wedding song "Hamba Kahle" starts up in the background.

Cut to the bride's white satin wedding dress modeled on its stand. Isigqi's first verse plays. Zoom in to the chunky rhinestones and silver beads glinting on the bodice and trail. Cut to the poised bridal party getting into their early 1980s brown Cadillac. A cluttered shot of photojournalists with elbows and straps and lenses all over the frame. A long shot of a dry and dusty Zululand valley with milling crowds and a striped tent for the dignitaries in the valley's hollow belly. Isigqi's singing continues. A shot of a huge crowd of men dressed in skins and headdresses. They are seated on the ground in the hot dust. The first close-up of the king himself. He is dressed in imperial military regalia: peaked cap, white gloves, gilt tresses on the shoulders, sword at his side. Cheers and ululations from the crowd overlay Isigqi's song as the bride arrives on the dusty scene. The soundtrack fades. Cut to youths in skins dancing in formation to a cowhide military bass drum. The first portrait of Chief Gatsha Buthelezi, leader of the Inkatha Freedom Party. He is arrayed in the chiefly Zulu ceremonial dress and seated with foreign and white dignitaries. Cut to the bride dancing and singing now in traditional style and dress in a circle of young women and girls. She carries a knife and small dancing shield; a skin partly covers her chest; stranded beads hide her eyes. The second close-up of Zwelethini, this time in his Zulu royal dress, watching the dancers with his paramount chiefs. Bhodloza narrates. More traditional dancing and singing of the *amabutho* (military cohorts). Shots of visitors: a woman dozing off in the second row; the Swazi party wrapped in red Swazi cloths. The older amabutho perform. More visitors, in serious suits and snazzy shades. A speech over the loudspeakers. More Zulu dancing by men and young women. Crowds watch. A posturing warrior dancer rushes into the arena center for a solo display. Lines of choreographed dancing youths unsettle the dust as they kick their legs up and then stamp the ground. Zoom into a shield. Cut to the white wedding–style reception and the wedding couple slicing a six-tiered cake with Zwelethini's sword. A close-up of Gatsha Buthelezi in bow tie and olive-green suit, seated alongside the king himself in his satin-collared dress suit. Then the guests clap while Zwelethini and his new wife jive to African jazz.

Cut to the music video program logo and to Bhodloza seated in the television studio as he sums up the feature over the organ introduction to Isigqi's song "Hamba Kahle." "Hambani kahle" (Go well), he greets his viewers as Isigqi's video fades in, and we see them miming their wedding song in the midst of dry-ice smoke in the studio. Their song airs all the way through.

Cut. Commercial break. A leopard chases across the screen in slow motion, advertising gasoline.

In this video coverage of King Zwelethini's wedding, which was broadcast to the nation, visual and aural relationships are drawn between the traditional ritual of the historic Zulu figurehead, Inkatha's political representative, a version of ngoma dance in its most "authentic" redressing (skins, feathers, hide drum heads), and Isigqi's mbaqanga rendition of a wedding song. It is as if by rubbing shoulders with one another, these versions of Zuluness, which are learned from one another, reinvigorate one another by their co-presence in the same frame. They each become larger than their single lives. Similarly, though less directly, the video itself rubs shoulders with Sesimanje's released recording and with performances, rallies, and violent eruptions.

Through the mediated contiguity of forms of Zuluness, performers may at once exchange, extend, and gather a sense of Zuluness for themselves as artists and persons. Did I see Bhodloza's program? Jane asked me. "It was very, very beautiful. The wedding was beautiful, and they played 'Hamba Kahle' with it." Jane was very, very happy, she said. So were Joana, Janet, Michael, and the members of their band.

For listeners, the process of figuring out their relationship to Zuluness through mediated expressive culture may be similar. For example, when rural teenage girls are captivated by Ubuhle Bezintombi singing the kinds of wedding songs on television that the girls themselves sing while dancing with a bride who carries a knife and dancing shield, they are processing a relationship between a ritual and aesthetic practice they participate in and its circulation through the media to and from domains and Others outside the girls' immediate experience. Each encounter with a wedding-song performance resonates with a sense of Zuluness, on some level. In relationship to one another, each version participates in production of Zuluness.

Mediation facilitates the popularization and distribution of Zuluness. Mediation also escalates the flow of Zuluness through technological facility and market-driven principles. It can intensify that feeling of being Zulu by compacting, juxtaposing, and overlaying multiple features into a figure like the drum sound, which then indexes a world of Zulu-identified worlds and suggests connections to them.

Similarly, a situation of conflict like that in South Africa, like that in the KwaZulu-Natal region, like that in the Witwatersrand, like that in the townships and the hostels promotes, quickens, and directs the flow of Zuluness. But such conflict also heightens the passions and raises stakes of participation. It intensifies the sentiments and the stakes embedded in a figure like the drum sound and the mbaqanga wedding song.

Mediation and sociopolitical conflict each excite the feeling of Zuluness set in motion by the other. Each prompts the other into gathering more momentum around Zuluness. The potential offered by the media industry for the reproduction and circulation of ideas did not pass IFP politicians by. Through mediated expression, Inkatha was able to reach and extend its constituency very self-consciously.[28] Less directly and perhaps more significantly, it could convince its supporters of their Zuluness and give their Zuluness form by passionately embracing some aspects of Zulu expressive culture. And from there, by stylistic association, other expressive forms fall into an ethnic patterning in their production and consumption, some more closely than others. Zuluness as a representation becomes believed, sensed, felt, and experienced through discursive forms. It becomes lived in the everyday through the consumption of popular forms, like mbaqanga with its contemporary Zulu-ized ethos.

In its post-*Graceland* domestic revival and international visibility, mbaqanga's local stylistic features have been increasingly foregrounded and marked as Zulu features. This traditionalizing thrust plays into and participates in the production of the heightened ethnic consciousness evident in South Africa of the 1980s and especially of the 1990s. Of the multitude of South African ethnicities, Zulu ethnicity underwent the most dramatic and thorough politicization. It became the most self-consciously marked black South African ethnicity. This occurred at the same time as politically motivated violence escalated with unprecedented intensity and ever-increasing complexity in South Africa, especially in KwaZulu-Natal and on the Witwatersrand.[29]

The changes in mbaqanga sound and ethos also coalesce with and reproduce stylistic shifts that are amenable to the World Music market. When mbaqanga traditionalizes, it moves specifically toward a Zulu bracketing. There are multiple reasons—stylistic, historical, political, economical, domestic, and global—for privileging this particular ethnicity.

In the national and global marketing arena, as well as from the point of view of Isigqi music-makers, to sound Zulu is to sound live in various ways, and to sound Zulu is also to sound deeply African. Zulu is a living epitome of African participation as "tribal" in the world. This is a representation that is actively present regionally, nationally, and globally, and it has a long history. It is a quintessential manifestation of the trope of authenticity in African music.[30]

In politicizing this chronotope of tribalism, the stakes in claiming or rejecting what it represented were intensified for everyone who evoked it, not least for music-makers. An increasingly aestheticized Zuluness was coupled with an intensifying politics of violence and, often, with death. The ambiguity about Zuluness as an identity of difference facilitated its aestheticization into a trope of African "liveness" in some moments, while in others it played into the deadly politicization of Zulu ethnicity as a form of violent nationalism. These two trajectories are importantly linked. Zulu nationalism persuades through images of the performing Zulu body and the poetics of talk; "liveness" on the World Music market draws potency from the presence of icons of authenticity in the everyday ordinariness of 1990s South Africa as experienced on the street and represented in the media.

The arenas of World Music and ethnic nationalism play off and into each other. World Music's contemporary, partying, tribal image may be ethnic nationalism's political display and some Africans' lived identity. Both the discourse and practice of World Music and ethnic nationalism hold the dynamics of globalization and (re)tribalization in tension. Mbaqanga's mediated liveness emerges from and reproduces this tension.

The ambiguity around the meaning of Zuluness that this tension creates on the ground and in the studio is knowingly and necessarily performed by Isigqi musicians and others like them, as they make sense of their lives, engender and situate their personhood, and produce records. Such ambiguity is essential to music's precarious power, gathered between the stage, the studio, and the street, between pleasures of play and acts of injury.

They sing a slow riff. "Sizogwazana, sizobulala" (We will stab one another, we will kill). "Bathi sizogwazana, sizobulala" (They say will stab one another, we will kill). A drummer whacks the marching bass with a length of hosepipe and a wooden slat. An echoing dotted rhythm. *Ka kaa! Ka kaa!*

A virtuoso arches back in a steady pick-up to his kick. As if a spring suddenly triggered, he kicks into the sky, thrusts his foot above his head, holds it there. He snaps, thunders his sole down onto the sidewalk's asphalt. "Thisa!" they exclaim. Thisa! *Ku dum! Ka kaa!* The drumbeat ricochets back and forth. You can hear it long before you turn the corner, long before you hear the piercing whistle of the leader and the slow, deep vocal riff. Then you see the cluster of peaceful Sunday-afternoon hostel dwellers dancing, on that day when there was no event at George Goch Stadium at the edge of industrial Johannesburg.

Playback

16 October 1992

Bongani and Sicela, two young Zulu entrepreneurs who live in the inner city, have organized a gig in Wolhuter hostel—the hostel where the ralliers returned that day. Isigqi and a few other mbaqanga and traditional groups are to appear. Bongani and Sicela have negotiated with leaders of the Inkatha Youth Brigade who live at the hostel.

But tonight there are problems. First, Isigqi's amplifier is broken. They hire one from a fellow musician at a steep price. Next, we are stuck without transport. I take Bongani to the hostel to try to borrow a minivan. After being cleared by the hostel's security official at the gate, we walk into the large courtyard enclosed by decrepit four-storied, red-brick living quarters. The courtyard bustles. Vendors sell fruit, jewelry trinkets, boiled eggs, or porridge and meat. A man waits alongside his handcrafted Zulu sandals, all laid out in a row. Friends drink bottled beer. Radios play. Shouts echo inside the buildings. Here and there a woman mills among the men. In the center of the courtyard, an IFP meeting is in session—tomorrow the IFP will march through Johannesburg's city center down to the prison to protest the proposed fencing of hostels and ban on the carrying of traditional weapons in public. Men gather in the meeting circle, some holding their fighting/dancing sticks and their *knopkieries* (round-headed clubs). The icilongo player swings his bugle at his side. A man with a stare clasps an ax. Splashes of red mark the group's IFP affiliation: red T-shirts, a red armband, a red headband or two. Those on the edge size us up. Themba, Bongani's Youth Brigade contact, leaves the group to greet us and takes us inside a hall. I notice the red graffiti: "IFP RULES." In the hall, the leadership is having a meeting around a table. We whisper. We are in the innards of an institution. Themba negotiates the use of a truck.

Eventually we return to Downtown Studios where we lug all the equipment downstairs and wait on the sidewalk for the hostel's truck to arrive. We wait until after 10 PM. We make three stops and two trips. By 11:30 PM we are back inside the hostel. The musicians decide to perform despite the hour, just to uphold their reputation—the gig had been announced at the IFP meeting in the courtyard, and a banner hangs across the hostel's entrance. Isigqi Sesimanje! Umfazi Omnyana! 16 October, 7 PM–12 AM.

Much later into the night the gig gets postponed anyway. The artists will return next Friday. On Friday it gets postponed to next Sunday; on Sunday it gets postponed to the next Friday.

'There was a war in the hostel,' drummer Mandla explained to me.

A young man lies slumped in a boggy hostel gutter in Thokoza.
Unclaimed, unnoticed, lying there dead among the litter until
photographer Martin Pope spots him through a toilet window. It is
a cramped shot from above.

Isigqi are third in the lineup.

The Travelers perform first. A young soul-mbaqanga group, they have their disco and break-dance moves down. Their keyboard riffs, their soft soul close-harmony vocals, their flamboyant soul mbaqanga synchronized leaps, and their metallic gold overalls draw a crowd into the low ceilinged basement hall.

Next Abashayi Bengoma, Isigqi's backing singer-dancers take to the "stage."

Joana has sewn Isigqi new outfits for their first set: short, shiny, yellow skirts and black lacy shirts, black hose, and white sneakers. Isigqi squeeze through the listening bodies to reach the diminishing clearing in the hall. The audience whistles as the women dance through to their microphones while Tefo, Bethwell, Mandla, and their new guitarist get the groove going for their title track, "Lomculo Unzima."

Listeners sit cramped on the floor and on benches and a few chairs. They crowd around the pillars, all the way around the performance spot, and behind the seated people. The only electric cord runs through a high, tiny window of this basement up to a hostel room on the third floor. Men block the window on the outside, trying to get a peep at the show. The organizers hang a blanket over the opening. Yet another hand appears from the outside to part it a little. Bongani prods the blanket with a broomstick from the inside. 'Ngenani!' he calls to the outsiders. 'Come in [and pay]!'

Isigqi take tiny steps. They shuffle a few steps back, a couple forward, as they dance their otherwise usual sequences, extending the instrumental breaks on their recording. Isigqi's performance is like their other appearances I have attended at George Goch Stadium and in halls or outdoor arenas on mines around Johannesburg. The emcee announces their songs, hypes up their reappearance for their second set (for which they wear their traditional beads and headdresses), and eggs on the clapping. Isigqi doesn't posture differently here. They don't mention the IFP, or talk about things Zulu. The emcee reminds the audience of Isigqi's latest recording.

"Traditional" guitarist Nogabisela follows Isigqi. He stamps and kicks in his skins between verses to the cheers of the crowds, many of whom know him. He is an impressive performer. Finally Umfazi Omnyama, the new, hot, young Zulu traditional guitarist, entertains with his virtuosic antics and fast-paced jokes.

It is late. We pack up. The door takings were reasonable—better than other times, Jane tells me. At R5 a head and five groups of performers and two organizing entrepreneurs, their returns could not have been much.

In the courtyard an old drunkard with a face like a drought-stricken floodplain hobbles towards me. Cataracts cloud his vision; a bloodshot tear-bag waters and pusses. He holds a blackened, dustbin-digging hand out to me.

"Siyabonga" (Thank you), he says.

"Ngiyabonga, baba," I reply as we handshake.

"Abantu bahlala nabantu" (People live with other people), he says of the hostel dwellers. "Izilwane zihlala zodwa" (Animals live alone).

I return to the hall to carry out more clunking equipment.

A radio still blares from a window ledge upstairs. Outside a hurried siren cries.

As we reverse out of the courtyard, our headlights glare onto a sleeping man wrapped up in cardboard for the night. He stirs.

cut 6

Imagining Overseas

Guide Vocal

1987. Mahlathini and the Mahotella Queens are back in demand. They're on record with Virgin, and even on CD with new releases and re-releases. They're on the stage; they're in the studio in Paris. They're recording for Celluloid direct. They're in London playing to a massive Wembley Stadium crowd at Mandela's seventieth birthday concert, broadcast live to some sixty countries (1988). Next they're in a London studio collaborating with Art of Noise on the song "Yebo" (1989). They're touring in the United States and Canada (1989). Now they're licensed for international distribution to Shanachie (1990). They are wowing the crowds at the twenty-fifth anniversary of the Montreux Jazz Festival, at the invitation of the famous Quincy Jones (1991). Five hundred thousand people dance to their music in New York's Central Park (1991). Soon their circuit expands eastward, to Tokyo, then to Australia en route to Japan, back to Europe, to Canada, to the United States, to the Caribbean, then to Fiji via Australia again, en route back to Japan.

In 1991 while Isigqi worked in the studio downtown, Gallo sent artists crisscrossing across the globe. It was a year rich in promise and artistry. While Mahlathini and the Mahotella Queens toured to Australia, Japan, North America, Guadeloupe, and France, isicathamiya choir Ladysmith Black Mambazo toured the United States. The African Jazz Pioneers played jazz in the style of the 1950s and 1960s in London, then appeared with the Elite Swingsters and Dolly Rathebe in France. Lucky Dube and his reggae band, Slaves, played in Australia, Japan, Europe, the United Kingdom, the United States, and Canada, and they made their debut at the Reggae Sunsplash in Jamaica. O'Yaba, West's young reggae band, played on the Cape Verde islands. And township pop star Yvonne

Chaka Chaka performed to great acclaim in Nigeria, Malawi, Uganda, and Tanzania. A few artists signed to other domestic companies also toured internationally, though the Gallo artists were by far the majority and their tours were given the highest profile by the local press.

1991. Mahlathini and the Mahotella Queens are back from overseas for a while, in between traveling east to Australia and Japan, and west to North America and Guadeloupe. They are to rehearse in their room upstairs at Downtown Studios, alongside Hamilton's room, catty-corner from Isigqi Sesimanje. They will record at Downtown Studios, just like other Gallo artists, only they will be mixed at the even classier Bop Studios and released overseas.[1] Mahlathini smokes on the street, in the sun outside, like those who haven't left. Yet. Joseph alights from a minivan with his bass in a case splattered with stickers. Phillemon arrives in a new-looking leather jacket, Nobesuthu in a T-shirt with places and dates running all the way down her back. Lucky Dube is back from Jamaica's Reggae Sunsplash. He drives up in his shiny Benz, parks in the garage, and cruises on upstairs.

Stories get told in the sun, in the elevator, in the passages of the rehearsal space, in the press, in the rehearsal rooms and around the recording studios.

Musicians listen to the stories told.

Standing around in the studio reception area, West's young reggae group, O'Yaba, listen reverently to Lucky. I linger, listen, greet from the edge. Lucky speaks. Irene, brothers, Irene. Sunsplash. Yeah, Sunsplash was magic. It was happening, man! The crowd went crazy—they just wouldn't stop cheering. The stage manager kept beckoning to us to keep on playing. (Lucky gesticulates like the manager.) Playing and playing. The people loved us. You see, because everything was live. What the people heard is what they got. You didn't hear a whole choir when the women sang their choruses. You heard three. Three good ones. You didn't hear fancy programmed effects. The only percussion and drumrolls you heard were the ones you could see being played on the sets. No, we were all live. And the dancers, man, they could move better than anyone else at Sunsplash. The people wouldn't stop cheering.

Heyi! exclaims O'Yaba's lead.

Upstairs bass groaner Dingane Skosana is preparing for rehearsal with Hamilton's new mbaqanga group. I introduce myself to his frontline singer Gugu. She tells me that she was once one of the Mahlathini Girls. And me, I used to sing reggae backup for Lucky Dube, adds Connie, who now sings alongside Gugu.

The Mahotella Queens on stage, Ellis Park Stadium, Johannesburg, 1991.
Left to right: Nobesuthu Shawe, Hilda Tloubatla, Mildred Mangxola.
Photo by TJ Lemon.

Mahlathini on stage,
Ellis Park Stadium,
Johannesburg, 1991.
Photo by TJ Lemon.

On the second floor, Mzwandile swings into the studio. He has toured overseas with Mahlathini and the Mahotella Queens. He slides his Yamaha keyboard onto the outboard effects console to prepare for the session.

"Bonjour!" he greets the assembled artists.

"Eita, snawu-snawu!" (Yo, King of the Streets!), replies guitarist Hansford in local street language.

"Yebo!" (Yes!), exclaims another casually in Zulu.

"Bon voyage!" offers Siyazi playfully. Like Mzwandile, he has performed in France.

"Comment ça va?" Mzwandile quips back.

"Prego!" bursts out West, laughing. Then he turns to Peter with whom he usually speaks in English, and says in Afrikaans, "Okay, bra Peter, laat ons nou werk" (Brother Peter, let's get to work).

A thing called "overseas" implicitly permeates music-making processes and the musical imaginations of mbaqanga musicians in the early 1990s. It is present in the studio, even when making a low-budget domestic recording. Mbaqanga artists do not expound on its constitution during recording and mixing, but their ideas and aspirations are sounded in their musical utterances.

How is "overseas" imagined by mbaqanga musicians? Scholars have paid detailed attention to local articulations of place within the context of globalizing markets, information networks, and traveling populations. How do local visions of the world out there coproduce local articulations of place and contemporary mbaqanga sound? How does the global, as it is imagined, play a part in local struggles? For mbaqanga musicians who wish to participate in a global network, there is a fundamental tension. On the one hand, they desire to participate in the world as cosmopolitans who can move with social ease across geopolitical divides, unfettered from nation or locality as a primary source for identity. On the other, they face a pressure to metaculturally mark their global participation as ethnically specific and emplaced. When the processes of imagining the global and fashioning sounds that might enable access to its stages are situated within the context of local struggles, processes of mediation and commodification become analytically inseparable from conceptions of culture and musical experience.

21 November 1991

On this third day in the studio, Isigqi Sesimanje is laying down the vocals. The backing men crowd round a microphone in one booth, the frontline women in the other.

"You're right, bro, put it in," says Jane to Bethwell in Zulu before they slide the door closed between them.

"Help us out," prompts Janet.

"Give it some nice kick!" entices Michael.

Bethwell nods back.

In the control room, Peter starts up the already-recorded backing tracks for "Lomculo Unzima." They play through the large monitors in the control room. The women and Michael sing their verses over the instrumentals.[2] The backing men add their choruses. Suddenly, on the repeat of the first verse, Bethwell's voice cuts through the women's harmonies.

"Waaa!" he belts out in the gap between the women's phrases. His neck and shoulder muscles strain taut. He focuses his gaze fiercely ahead of him while he sings from the chest, swooping up to a note near the top of his throat register, holding it over four, gritty, rasping counts, then gliding back down again. His glide extends way over the next beat as he descends through his bass vocal range until he has expelled the breath out of the very last pockets in his lungs.

The women and Michael sing on and over him.

He picks up the end of their phrase and sing-speaks it back. "Shwele!" he cries. Them, him; them, him, overlapping, echoing.

On the final line before the flute break, he tucks in his chin, raises then lowers his heels as his voice glides down deeper than I thought he could. It is an impressive *ibhodlo* in pitch range and stridency. I had not heard him do it before—not at any festival appearance, not on a Saturday afternoon at a mine gig, and not in rehearsal.

"Imitating Mahlathini!" chuckles West from the producer's chair.

Blues and "honky"-style polka musicians in the 1950s emphasized those stylistic features of their music that had come to stand as stereotypes for working-class black and Polish American sound for the (white, middle-class) mainstream. This mainstream had exploited the music and musicians over the two prior decades. In embracing and reasserting those stereotypes, working-class black and Polish Americans reclaimed those

Bethwell Bhengu,
Johannesburg, 2002.
Photo by Brett Eloff.

sounds as their own (Keil 1985). They brought their sounds home again. In
the wake of glasnost, Bulgarian folk-orchestra musicians reclaimed their
right to creative musical mixing and assertively reincorporated ethnic
musical features in the rediscovered spirit of the freedom of expression
and in the hope of reaching the World Music market (Buchanan 1995).
Country musicians in a Lockhart honky-tonk resocialize the alienated
high-tech music commodity through talk and song about the ordinary,
the low tech, the outmoded, and the repaired (Fox 1997). Bethwell roars,
more Mahlathini than Mahlathini himself, grittier, raspier, dirtier than
1990s Mahlathini. He growls like the "Lion of Soweto." He brings home
the lion in celebration of what it represents and in the hope of riding the
beast back overseas, back to its den.

Prior to his international breakthrough, Simon Nkabinde was known
in South Africa as "Indoda uMahlathini" (Mahlathini the Man) and as
"Indlov'uMahlathini" (Mahlathini the elephant) (Allingham 1999, 643;
see also Indoda Mahlathini 1975). It was on his first international re-

Bethwell Bhengu's ibhodlo for
"Lomculo Unzima," 21 November 1991.
Transcription by James Harkins.

lease, which featured him alone, that he was marketed as a wild, roaring, dangerous, and respected African king of the beasts. On the 1987 Virgin compilation of reissued songs entitled *The Lion of Soweto* (Mahlathini 1987), his co-artists do not appear in name or image on the cover.[3] They are mentioned only in passing in the liner notes. Mahlathini is photographed for the cover in his slick street style: tipped porkpie hat, shiny shirt, dark trousers, necklace, chunky ring, and a sauntering stance. The liner notes highlight his association with the defiant working-class street life of Soweto. It is only in closing that the iconicity of the lion is elaborated: "Here the Lion of Soweto is captured in full roar and it's the defiance and resilience characterizing these songs which helped Mahlathini survive those bleak and barren years [when disco trumped mbaqanga and Mahlathini refused to commercialize]" (McRae 1987).

The lion image reappears in the title to the next international release, which features him over the Mahotella Queens, although the women are also listed on the jacket sleeve. This 1991 Shanachie recording entitled *The Lion Roars* likewise has a street image of Mahlathini as its front jacket illustration. On the back, Mahlathini poses in full skin regalia and a leopard-skin-patterned tank top. The queens appear behind him in beads and traditional head gear. The scanty liner notes pit Mahlathini's "gritty low-registered roars" against the "spirited, open-throated harmonies" of the Mahotella Queens.

Subsequent international releases paint Mahlathini and the Mahotella Queens as an integrated unit and present them all in traditional-looking clothing, with Mahlathini in skins. Some refer to his voice as a "roar" but no longer is there a rhetorical need for a direct reference to the lion. The association has been sufficiently cultivated to stick. Furthermore, by moving Mahlathini's image closer to a tribal one, an association with the wild is implicated. The image of the lion continues to be elaborated by critics and promoters in the popular press. For example, Jonathan Pepper, writing in *Rhythm Music Magazine,* which is published in the United States, and Bruce Elder, reviewing a concert in the *Sydney Morning Herald,* both typify Mahlathini by collapsing the icons of him as tribal chief and as king of the beasts. "Mahlathini, the 'Lion of Soweto,' stalks the stage dressed in a lion skin, feathers, and furs, growling and roaring his way through another tune. The interplay and verbal sparring between Mahlathini and the Queens is non-stop, Mahlathini boasting and strutting his stuff, the Queens laughing him off and taking him down" (Pepper 1994, 14).[4] Or, "Mahlathini, dressed like some tribal chief in strips of animal skins, plays out elaborate and amusing charades with the three women like some old lion being kittenish with his pride" (Elder 1991). Neither of these voices are eccentric in their descriptions.

It is tempting to read into Elder's cuddly and cutesifying image of Mahlathini at the least a patronizing emasculation and infantalization of the then fifty-three-year-old artist, and at most a recognition of the way in which the world system of cultural production disempowers even those "Third World" artists who reach the international stage. Whatever the case may be, Mahlathini the lion is, of course, a representation of Africa that is compatible with the commodification of the subcontinent as a place of savanna and safari, of its indigenous people as closer to nature than Westerners are, and of Zulu's (or South Africans more generally) as strong, proud, aggressive, and posturing.

The successive lionizing of Mahlathini has been coupled with some shifts in his stage performance and vocal contribution to the group's songs. Whereas the earlier local celebrations of the singer as "indoda" (the [big] man) and "indlovu" (the elephant) are equally much about power and authority, they foreground somewhat different characteristics. Mahlathini's participation in earlier recordings was sustained through a much greater portion of each song. He often sang along with the women's chorus and even carried entire songs without vocal backing (see, for instance, the 1970s re-releases on *Putting on the Light* [Mahlathini and the Mahotella Queens 1984]). In his stage shows of the late 1980s into the 1990s, he worked the crowd with dramatically petulant or defiant gestures and seemingly unpredictable behavior. He was the lion. This stage persona was part of Mahlathini's image in heyday mbaqanga, but it probably was not his dominant performance mode. In the internationally released recordings from the 1980s and 1990s, his vocal contribution is similarly "unpredictable": while doing less sustained singing, he interjects strident commentary, overlapping with the Mahotella Queens's melodies, and he makes more use of vocables and vocal effects, leaving the presentation of the majority of the lyrics to the Queens.

The more recent exotic characterization of his bass groaning voice as a "roar" marks the shift in the role he is seen and heard to play in the group, as well as in the particular features of the sound its nomenclature marks. In South Africa the sound is talked about in English as a "goat voice" by musicians such as Aaron Lerole, who was the first to sing in this bass style (called *ibhodlo* in Zulu) in the early 1960s.

Mahlathini himself is quoted as saying in an interview, "I have been a street singer for more than twenty six years but my voice grows stronger all the time. When people say to me 'Ai! Mahlathini! How is it that your 'ukubodla' [*sic*] never dies?' I just smile. They are asking me how it is that I can go on singing with my deep goat's voice after all these years. But my voice keeps on because it comes out of everything going on around me. As long as I live on in White City, [a residential zone] in Soweto, I sing on" (quoted in McRae 1987). His own identification of his voice with the gruffness of a goat slips by unnoticed in the international marketing arena, as to a lesser extent does his identification with the urbanity of his Sowetan neighborhood. Goats are commonplace domestic items in rural South African homes. They are slaughtered for parties and on ritual occasions at rural homesteads and in townships. They are also included in bridewealth payments. All rural families I know keep and cultivate them.

The "goat voice" is a referent that makes less comment than the lion's roar does on the register of the sound, the unpredictability in the moments of utterance, and the range in volume and pitch, while it gives more significance to timbral features—to the gruffness, to its deep-throated vocal production, which produces a feeling of pitch distortion and a constrained resonance, resulting in a pulsating effect. The metaphor also comments on the repetitive presence of the utterance.

I think of the record player needle. I wait for its jump.

Bethwell's groan was a reach for the world-stomping footsteps of Mahlathini. He roared more Mahlathini than Mahlathini himself. In reproducing the star, Bethwell made his sound wilder to fill an anticipated overseas expectation, to meet the imagined and reflected desires of overseas.

playback

Bethwell groaned on a recording by Thoko Mdlalose in 1997. "I groaned and I groaned and I groaned. They bought lots of copies overseas. When I arrived in Holland on tour with her, someone said, 'He's the one who groans.' 'Hawu! Yo! It's you there?' they exclaimed. Heyi, those white people were happy! They loved it too much. *Too* much! They made a film—a white woman with a camera—I groaned and I also danced [Zulu kicking and stamping]. They loved it!"

"Waaa!" roars Bethwell in the gap between the women's phrases. His neck and shoulder muscles strain taut. He focuses his gaze fiercely ahead of him while he sings from the chest, swooping up to a note near the top of his throat register, holding it over four gritty, rasping counts, then gliding back down again. His glide extends way over the next beat as he descends through his vocal range until he has expelled the breath out of the very last pockets in his lungs.

The women and Michael sing smoothly on and over him.

He picks up the end of their phrase and sing-speaks it back. "Shwele!" he cries. Them, him; them, him, overlapping, echoing.

Bethwell's groan was grittier, raspier, dirtier than 1990s Mahlathini. While an image of native wildness is cultivated internationally in the figure of Mahlathini, the sound of his voice has, in fact, been smoothed out and sweetened for international consumption. This is evident on both new recordings and, to the limited extent that it is possible, on the remastered reissues of songs originally produced in the 1970s and early 1980s.

The difference in Mahlathini's voice on the new recordings from the mid-1980s and especially the 1990s is effected by two related phenomena, the second compensating for the first. First, Mahlathini's lung capacity had indeed changed since his youth, especially given that he was a long-time smoker and suffered from tuberculosis. As West put it, Mahlathini was no longer able to "hold the wind like he could hold it in the early days" when his singing style was marked by long, sustained notes that often began with a vocal glide onto the tone and ended with a descending glide and the rasp of a last spurt of breath. He sang loudly. He sang stridently. He didn't let up the physical tension in his vocal performance until after that last spurt of breath ended each phrase with a raspy percussive hook. He exploited his wide vocal and expressive range and wallowed in his extraordinary chest register. He held his longest notes mostly at or near the top and the bottom of his throat and chest registers respectively. Furthermore, he sang long lead vocal parts, frequently paralleled the singing of the women's chorus, and recorded numerous solo vocal cuts with backing band. Altogether, his was a strenuous vocal delivery style, which to some extent has taken its toll.

Well, says West, "We do not want him to go deeper like before, because we are looking [after] his age. As long as he can push his normal voice, then its fine. Only in some places he can go deep [where he is still able to], not too much like before. You have to work according to what he's got now."

So in the 1980s and 1990s studio and on the stage, something different is made of his performance. Onstage he interjects more vocables, banters and charades comically with the Mahotella Queens, and gives over significantly more of the singing to the women's chorus.

In the studio, aural focus is placed on the qualities of his "normal voice." Recording techniques are exploited to bring out the richness of his baritone register, thereby highlighting the contrast between his voice and the sweet close harmonies of the Queens. The contrast between the vocal blending and instrumental percussiveness is also brought out. Percussive effects are left up to the instruments to a greater degree than in the earlier recordings, and programmed percussion is added. West explains the changes to me in terms of Mahlathini's aging and the changes in the aesthetics of studio production. "In the old days we put a lot of echo [on his voice], to sound bigger. Now you pick up some distortions if you put too much echo on him because of his voice—he hasn't got the same volume that he used to have when he was still young. That is the problem." However trickstering this response to me might be—it is at the least only a partial technical explanation—it is notable that West should guard against "picking up distortions"—that is, he is concerned with smoothing out some of the noise that was part of Mahlathini's earlier distinction.

This smoothing out is compatible with a production aesthetic enabled by multitracking and digitalization of studio equipment. Sound separation and processing techniques enable the engineer to manipulate the quality of sounds in order to give an impression of aural three dimensionality. With this facility, sounds do not necessarily have to be made to stand out in a mix by loud or harsh or bright playing.

This studio-sound aesthetic is also compatible with an international dance music aesthetic of the late 1980s into the 1990s. Foreign dance clubs and their clientele were the principal consumers West was targeting with his productions of Mahlathini and the Mahotella Queens. ("Traditional collectors" were his secondary projected market.) He considered these consumers to be refined in terms of their timbral preferences and to value clean, fine production quality.

"Well those days [of recording prior to the twenty-four track console], we were supposed to make the sound bright because people, our audience, they were the audience that likes rock-and-roll music, like the Beatles—they were so bright! So in the market those days, every record should be bright because the audience wanted bright things, because the style was bright.

"Now time has changed. Now you will have very few people who buy that. We've got to work according to the audience that we're performing for. And then also with the technology, with the equipment that is being used today. It also plays a very important role.

"So you cannot just brighten it, it loses the feel. You can make it hard, but with a very good sound, nice level sound, which doesn't bend people's ears. Take for instance the white—the rock music, they don't make it bright like the old days. It's still the same—it's not as bright as they used to do, like 'ka yunng!'—they don't do that. They keep it very smooth. It appeals. It gets into somebody's feelings nicely, you know. The audience is different."

Advances in technology and the more-or-less parallel fetishization of these advances in the form of an aesthetics of refinement (clean, smooth sound, clarity of separation, unmarked processes of mediation) are also evident in the remastering of reissued recordings. On some re-released Mahlathini songs, for example, more reverb has been added and mid and upper-mid frequencies boosted in a re-equalization process in order to compensate for the cutting of some of the high frequency bands in the cleaning up process. (Cutting higher frequencies reduces the hiss and noise of older recordings.) The resulting sound is sweeter and more blended.[5]

When Bethwell "overdoes" the pitch inaccuracy and rough timbral quality of the ibhodlo, he compensates for these changes in an effort to deliver according to another value that musicans understand that overseas wants: an "old sound."

Bethwell's groan undomesticated Mahlathini in two ways. First, like Mahlathini, who in turn was probably prompted or inspired by his international promoters and foreign reception, Bethwell was reproducing the image of an untamed animal—an image that originates overseas. In reproducing the star, he exaggerated the wild and strident features of his interjections. Second, in attempting to retrace Mahlathini's footsteps, he produced a grittier, less-controlled-sounding timbre than the old master singer in his contemporary performance. He sounded closer to the younger, earlier voice of Mahlathini in terms of its sound quality.

That the outmoded and the old were prized aesthetic qualities among musicians, and that they anticipated that their foreign audience would value it as well, is expressed in Marks Mankwane's narration of mbaqanga's origins to the foreign press at the time he was spokesperson for

Mahlathini, the Mahotella Queens, and the Makgona Tsohle Band. He delineates a mbaqanga history controlled by mbaqanga musicians and independent from foreign inspiration.

"While similarities exist between mbaqanga and Western pop, Mankwane says that the group was unaware of Western music until well after the sound had been formed. This can be partly explained by the fact that the musicians had grown up under governmentally-enforced racial segregation, which allowed only thirty minutes a day for township radio service. And phonographs were beyond the financial reach of most blacks.[6] 'We were just domestic servants—garden boys,' said Mankwane." (Elder 1991, 14)

Mbaqanga could not have been conceived without an ear and a gaze directed across the ocean, especially at African America. Yet Mankwane insists on a particular kind of musical integrity. He suggests that an unavoidable naïveté and parochialism of mbaqanga artists makes mbaqanga a special kind of creolized music: it is domestically hybrid but not contaminated by external influences. Its singularity is the product of tradition retained in the township ghettoes and by the isolation of black musicians during apartheid. Mankwane downplays the musicians' transnational aural experience and mbaqanga's historical connections outside South Africa. In his representation, the isolation apartheid enforced on music-makers in the 1960s and 1970s adds additional spatial distance to the time separation implied in the idea of the outmoded.

Take 3 *The Revitalizing Lion Returns from Overseas*

If the reach for overseas is carried in the processes of undomesticating the ibhodlo, the return resides in the redomesticating moves of that same moment. Mahlathini is reclaimed from the sophisticated global arena for local consumption and as a local identity marker.

Bethwell is back in the booth to add more bass interjections to the second verse. His voice and the already-recorded tracks of "Lomculo Unzima" play back through the large monitors. Isigqi Sesimanje and their backing band listen in the control room.

"Kodwa ngeke iphele," sing the women on their already-recorded track. Bethwell repeats the end of their phrase, "ngeke iphele." The beginning of their next line overlaps with the end of his; he copies and overlaps their next line; them, him; them, him, until he swoops down deep into his chest and Peter cuts the instrumental break.

"Let's go again," says West in Zulu.

"It's coming, it's coming," replies Peter, fiddling about on the console.

"Ngeke iphele!" sings West at the back of his throat, deep in his chest, exaggerating the distorted, gritty aspect of Bethwell's imitation of Mahlathini and playing jokes while he waits for Peter.

"Hayibo, mfo!" exclaims Jane. "You can groan better [than Bethwell]!"

West does it again. He laughs. "It's fine as it is, man!"

Jane protests. She wants West to erase Bethwell and overdub himself. She wants his version of the groan because it will maximize the effect and because his would be more skillfully rendered.

West refuses.

Isigqi didn't retain the ibhodlo figure and sound when they performed live subsequent to the release of the recording. This was partly because Bethwell was needed on the bass guitar where they benefited from his playing skills and musicality, and partly because they anticipated that his vocal intonation might sometimes disrupt the flow of the song. Of course the group could have replaced him with a more experienced singer. They chose not to do so even though they usually strove to reproduce their recorded sound as accurately as possible on the stage, with extended instrumental dance breaks. For Isigqi the inclusion of the groan voice in the studio was principally a reach toward the international stage.

Joana is sure they will be overseas by next year.
Maybe—but I think so, she says.

One performance a few years later in which they did reintroduce a powerful male figure on stage is informative: it was in 1998 at the Windybrow Arts Festival in a Johannesburg theater, which Jane correctly anticipated would have a crossover audience. Even more to the point, tourists and foreign promoters were to be in attendance. Though not a groaner, the singer they used was a strong, wealthily paunched man who sang in the style of Zulu traditional singers. He wore skins and a magnificent headdress with curling cattlehorns that spiked the air as he danced. He carried a traditional knopkierie and postured about on the stage.

While the group made nothing further of the groan in the promotion of the recording it appears on, they did experiment with the idea in subsequent productions.

Two years later they featured a guest groaner, David Jozini, on their next release, *Sebenza Ntokazi* (Izintombi 1994). On the basis of the interest that Jane felt Jozini lent to their sound, the variety his inclusion offered, and the pleasure it gave her and her fellow singers, Jane had plans of recruiting one of the former Isibaya Esikhulu groaners to her band. While their primary motivation for Bethwell's groan had to do with cultivating an internationally enticing sound, there was also a musical payoff for the artists. The experiment opened up sonic possibilities for further consideration. In the longer run, then, the ibhodlo on "Lomculo Unzima" did do some work in revitalizing the band's style.

Keil argues that the acceptance and transformation of a sound stereotype—like those in his case studies in blues and polka—can be a reinvigorating celebration of those shared local musical features that a dominant faction has valued and acclaimed. By reclaiming these features local music-makers reassert their identity dialectically against the dominant (Keil 1985). In Isigqi's play with the sound on locally released cassettes, Mahlathini's groan returns home, reinvigorated for the musicians through its overseas acclaim. In their case, however, overseas is not viewed as an oppressor regulating their modes of behavior and exploiting small-time musicians. Isigqi do not see themselves as having to resist an onslaught. In part, overseas is a key to their liberation from national constraints. They see themselves in dialogue with something beyond the nation, even though through their engagement they know they are still caught up in asymmetrical power relations.

Mahlathini's groan returns home. In the process of its reinvigoration, the fact is affirmed—if not established—that the groan belongs to mbaqanga musicians, that South Africa is the home of the groan. This claim is also worked in the foreign press. For example, Elder reports in the *Sydney Morning Herald* that although (foreign) critics often compare Mahlathini's use of his voice to that of blues singers like Howling Wolf or John Lee Hooker, Marks Mankwane insists at the time he was spokesperson for Mahlathini, the Mahotella Queens, and the Makgona Tshole Band that "the voice was Mahlathini's since his teens" (1991, 14). In a different discursive climate, mbaqanga musicians might milk the connections their sound makes to American music styles, but here Mankwane's official position is that Mahlathini is not a mimic of sounds developed elsewhere. In the ensuing interview, Mankwane goes on to situate Mahlathini in a traditional South African cosmological and familial world: Mahlathini's parents, suspicious that their young son's unusually deep voice was the work of "witchcraft," consulted a traditional healer before they would accept that the voice was indeed Mahlathini's. "Mahlathini then relaxed and used the sound to his advantage, creating a vocal style all of his own" (ibid.).

Take 4 *The Lion Made Ordinary*

From another perspective, Bethwell's ibhodlo is the local version of Mahlathini: unglamorous, gimmicky, skimpily budgeted, reaching for the elusive overseas, and bursting with optimism and affect, yet rendered with lesser skills than the vocal master and unattended and constrained by the limited investment in it by the production team and record company. The vision and emotional intensity of the singer is compromised by the small prospects for profit that the company expects from his singing.

1 April 1992

Peter is rewinding and readying the tape and MIDI units for recording. Hansford is just hanging out in the studio, listening, bringing joviality to the session. He intercepts the mixing from behind the outboard effects console, in Zulu: "Hey, S'bhu"—he often uses this nickname for West, his longtime friend—"listen to this young man, he's out of tune!"

"Well," acknowledges West who wants to get the project done, "he's out of tune. He doesn't know how to sing."

"Just in one place," modifies Hansford kindly.

"He doesn't know how to sing," repeats West.

"Ja," acknowledges Hansford. "It's like the soup gets spoiled when he enters."

West shrugs. "Hey! He's just like that, you see, but we can sell this one as it is."

Hansford, a perfectionist, is still unsettled about it. He persists. "But there's a part where he goes very out of tune, hey S'bhu, you must take him out on that small part—you'll hear it [on the recording]."

Laughing lightly, West sets the suggestion aside.

But Hansford insists. "Where he says 'shwele'—there where he says 'shwele'—it's there that he's badly wrong, just in that part. Leave him in the other places—[take him out] only on 'shwele,' because he can really be heard there."

West points to the monitor through which the already-taped male chorus (which includes Bethwell) had played back. He is frustrated by the time expended in laying down sufficiently accurate tracks and is not very impressed with their intonation. "Those are Abafana Bengoma, Young Men of the Song!" he quips, calling them by the name he had in fact suggested to them himself. Hansford laughs at West's irony.

"They think that singing is [as everyday as] porridge, you see," West explains.

Jane is concerned about the quality of her recording and her artistry, and with realizing her best potential for success. Not only is her local reputation on the line, but she does not want to compromise the opportunity that this production with an internationally connected veteran mbaqanga producer promises. In this moment she is faced with an impossible choice: inserting an imperfectly rendered exotic stylistic token—the lion's roar—into their sound, or omitting it in order to produce correctly standardized pitch.

"Can't you throw them out and let us sing it alone," she suggests to West. "You see, when they sing together, they're right on. But this one"— she means the ibhodlo—"no!" She wants it erased, and if West won't do the overdub himself, she wants it omitted. "Heyi! It doesn't go anywhere!" she complains in exasperation.

Another musician supports her quality call, but West brushes the idea aside. "He'll surprise you," West says of Bethwell. "It's a thing for the market, they'll like that part. Really, I'm telling you!"

Peter rolls the tape for one more playback before they record the group's next overdub. The song blares out of the wall monitors. After the instruments, the frontline voices enter precisely in tune and in time. Bethwell's recorded goat-voiced groan cuts through their sweet close harmonies. "Shwele!" he bellows in the gap between their phrases.

West does not want to bother with improving the interjection for local working-class listeners who would probably be listening on small, cheap music systems or cassette recorders. The sound is good enough for this market, he says. As a producer responsible to a record company, he does not want to extend the project over the budgeted studio time. Neither is he invested in the project enough to exceed his own contract for the work or to aggravate his already tight time constraints.

West hears no lion in Bethwell's ibhodlo. It is a comical market gimmick from his perspective. The ibhodlo is de-exoticized. It is made ordinary by a producer who is familiar with local listeners and listening practices. He regularly attends festivals and visits kin and acquaintances in peri-urban areas, and he has lived in townships around Johannesburg for many years.

In accepting a compromise on the quality of pitch, of all possible sonic parameters, West is bringing the ibhodlo home in a thoroughly informed way.

"It's fine as it is, man!" he says. "They'll like that part. Really, I'm telling you!"

In the studios perfect intonation is a preferred but not prioritized musical quality for local releases. This matter confounds the sound engineers. "Tuning and sound first," say the engineers. Good tuning—meaning correct intonation—and clarity of sound are the foundation of a quality product. They struggle to maintain the standards they believe in while they voice frustration at having to become pitch police and quality controllers—a responsibility they say the producer should uphold. Their explanations generally begin by deferring to the professional division of labor in the studio, undergirded by an understanding that there are different ways of listening. As Dave Segal, a Gallo engineer and A&R person, explained to me, "Even if you think the mix isn't great, you have to have faith in your producers and think, 'Well, that's how they intended it to be,' you know, and 'Maybe that's what the market wants.' Sometimes if the tuning's a bit, uh, strange, I think 'sjoe!' (yikes!), but then that's what your producer wants, so you have to have faith in them." By deferring to the producer, he adheres to the standard protocols for engineers in studios. In representing himself this way in an interview with me, he rhetorically distances himself and his reputation from lower local standards of production and presents himself as a member of an imagined community—an ideal and a global one—built around shared sound-quality values and professional work ethics.

The process of accounting for discrepancies in professional standards and coming to terms with local limitations is sometimes elaborated into a view that acknowledges that there could be different aesthetic principles at work. As Neil Kuny discussed with me, "The blacks seem to have a different concept of tuning. I think in a lot of black traditional music, out of tune is not out of tune. Out of tune is in tune, as far as they are concerned. Whereas to the whites, who've got their tuners and their thises and their thats, it's either a hundred percent in tune or it's out of tune. That's my ear. A lot of the black producers don't hear when something is out of tune—and often when they think it's out of tune, I think it's in tune. I don't quite understand how they hear their tuning. Some of the guys who've got a more sophisticated ear will know what's in and out of tune. But especially in the traditional stuff, they don't really care. I mean if the guitar's totally out of tune, it adds spice to the music. In that case, if I know that it's going to pass [the record company's postproduction A&R committee], then I won't correct the tuning."

Neil's explanation hits on key timbral features of Zulu traditional and mbaqanga sound and echoes the viewpoints of other engineers. First, the favored guitar sound has some percussive edge, some grit, buzz, and stridency. This can be rendered through exciting the principle frequencies by building in slight pitch discrepancies—tuning the strings just out enough to still be sufficiently "in tune" will add a little rub or distortion. The stridency is enhanced by making the sound incredibly bright, by boosting the upper frequencies, the treble. While the engineers most frequently remark on tuning differences in talk about recording guitars, these same aesthetic values are applied to other instruments. The overall sound can be similarly "spiced up." Historically, these styles have been recorded in the studio with the instruments and voices pushed up right to the front of the mix. What Neil is remarking on is a different aesthetic approach to timbre and sonic experience, in which pitch discrepancies play an important part in producing an expressive-sounding sound.

Darryl Heilbrunn recorded "a bunch of [African] kids that Peta Teanet had found on the street, and their vocals were out of tune completely, but they were used as an effect, not as good young lead singers." Not long after that he heard a young, white girl, "and I said 'Bang! This is it—superstar!' This girl singing with this voice, crystal clear, perfectly in tune, thirteen years old, really pretty!"

When West dismisses Bethwell's inaccurately pitched ibhodlo with a "they'll like it—really, I'm telling you!" he is not suggesting that the ibhodlo is "in tune" in a different system. To West and Hansford and Jane and Peter, it is definitely out of tune. That's their ears. In other circumstances West would certainly stop to correct it.

West is acknowledging that (1) the passion and expressivity with which Bethwell's ibhodlo is delivered and (2) its timbral grit are musically important in the domestic market, with the local listeners to whom it is targeted. Within limitations, if need be, for this market, he will prioritize these features over absolute pitch accuracy because he knows that many local listeners will do the same on playback. He domesticates Bethwell's ibhodlo according to the aesthetic priorities of local listeners.

playback

"Me? Is it me who's playing out of tune?' gasps a concerned Mzwandile in the recording booth. He's been called into the studio to assist with some overdubbing for Isigqi's production. He joins West and Hansford in the control room to hear the track. They reminisce about touring overseas.

"In Paris, we did some backup singing for the O'Jays," recounts West. He was on tour as saxophonist with Mahlathini, the Mahotella Queens, and the Makgona Tsohle Band at that time. "They wanted men's voices, not the women, so three of us did it. But one couldn't sing in tune. We left him out."

"And remember when you called me to New York," delights Mzwandile. "You were going into the studio to record and one wasn't playing in tune. You said to him he was fine at the shows, but in the studio you needed me. Heyi! He was suffering when he heard that!"

Peter isolates the bass track to listen more carefully.

"Mzwandile, he's a maestro!" exclaims Hansford as he listens.

"His hand is tight!" West enthuses back.

Mzwandile listens as if casually to the playback of the track.

Mix *Forms of Flow*

Bethwell's groan was grittier, raspier, dirtier than 1990s Mahlathini, though lacking some of Mahlathini's masterful vocal control. It was Mahlathini undomesticated—that is, 1990s Mahlathini made wilder to fill an anticipated overseas expectation, to meet the imagined and reflected desires of overseas. It was also Mahlathini redomesticated—that is, it was a local imitation of Mahlathini, shaped as much by domestic production constraints as by the stories returned about overseas. Bethwell's groan was both a reach for the world-stomping footsteps of Mahlathini and Mahlathini's return to the level of the local. Both the reach and return are encapsulated in the same moment and performed in the same sound.

Much debate in music scholarship, popular discourse, and promotional rhetoric presents the local and the global as a somewhat transparent dichotomy: as though each is represented in music by a sonically distinct sign, or as though this dichotomy is a difference between here and there, or now and then, between the particular and the general, the grounded and the ephemeral, between a set of practices and a system, a point of cultural production and a world of consumption. In Bethwell's gesture, the local and global are not discreet entities, separating a lived sensibility from an apprehended system. The local and the global are not represented or indexed by separate sounds, heard at different moments or in different registers. Neither are overtly articulated, though both are implicitly present in the moment of performance. Here is an utterance that at once replicates a generalized sound image that has entered into a commodity state and expresses the struggles of the singer's apartheid-derived professional experience.

Because the return and the reach are encapsulated in the same sign, in a discursive moment the one may easily come to stand for the other. When the utterance that makes Mahlathini's ibhodlo ordinary is experienced as a moment of matching the marketable exoticism of the star, a circulation of generated expectations and desires is put into motion. Similarly when the moment of return becomes another reach for overseas in the process of storying about the sound and its practitioners, those expectations and desires are further fueled, elaborated, and accorded additional substance. Story further mediates the return into a reach. Story takes the sounded material moment and travels with it into the musicians' imaginations about overseas. Story opens up promise by making narrative connections seem like material ones. It makes fantasy possible. It traces pathways in the artists' imaginations to the global stage, to foreign adulation, to expanded musical conversations, to new leather jackets and T-shirts with place names streaming down their backs, to the comfort of better, safer living and of brighter, safer futures—away from waiting, waiting, hoping, working, waiting. Toward rest. "One day," says Jane, "I will be able to rest."

In the case of Bethwell, the distance between singing the groan in the studio and performing it in Paris—that is, the distance between striving to follow in Mahlathini's footsteps and actually being in them—is enormous. Interventions by people cultivating markets, manipulating technologies, managing studio relationships, and telling stories must occur for that distance to be traversed and for the motivating fantasy about the process and possibility of an overseas break to be sustained, thereby motivating new reaches for the experience.

The men have been recording, doubling and triple-tracking their chorus parts. Bethwell sang the bass.

"The O'Jays!" jokes West sarcastically from his producer's seat as the three men huddle around a microphone recording their close-harmony vocal backing.

They struggled to get their tuning right. Now Peter is overdubbing strings played by Tefo on the D50 keyboard.

Bethwell returns from the booth to the control room. The struggle in recording these vocals accurately has unsettled the atmosphere. Not getting sounds right quickly can feel humiliating. It's time for West to rectify things after his reprimanding tone of management.

"I want to teach you to sing," West says to Bethwell in Zulu. "Your voice is right. Your problem is you have no idea how to sing. If I train you well, you won't—you know you have a really grand voice."

Michael, Mkhize, and Joana echo West's affirmation, enthusiastically tumbling over West's and one another's voices.

West continues, "You're being defeated by this singing, you see, but you could blow many people away!"

"No, it's just a matter of rehearsal—" begins Bethwell, when West interrupts.

"Ja, somebody must teach you, you see. You see Madondo, I taught Madondo—he was just like you.[7] I found out that his voice is good, and I said, 'No, Madondo, come here, the idea of singing should be like this,' and he learned."

Bethwell is encouraged. Madondo had become a local Swazi traditional celebrity in the early 1980s under West. "Ehe! Help me rehearse, and help me sing!"

"Play the keyboards please!" calls out Peter. Tefo strikes a couple of wheezing electronic-strings chords.

West chats on. "No, I must teach you because when you are on your own, you can never learn this thing, you see—"

"Ja," listens Bethwell.

"—because it has parts, you see."

"Ja!" he says again, tuned into West's promise.

"You see, it's like Mahlathini. Mahlathini is aging and now he can't sing."

"Ehe!" (Yes!), urges Bethwell.

"No, I see this Mahlathini case," explains West. "Mahlathini has got a problem. He can't sing! No, he can't sing at all! He knows how to sing this thing *his* way but if you were to take him now and say, 'Right, I'm asking you to come and sing with the three of us,' he won't [be able to] sing. Even you will—"

"Oh!" nods Bethwell. "He wants to play by himself!"

"He's used to playing alone!" adds Michael.

"And now he's sick, so he can't start [learning] now," says West.

The sound of organ strings merges into their conversation. A "cello" bows its way into the bass line. Tefo plays another chord. Violins. Viola. He punctuates the viola line.

By what means does this conversation facilitate imaginative leaps overseas? First, West offers practical help to Bethwell to improve his singing skills. He offers him mobility toward stardom. Then he iconically links this promise to others whom he has helped to success, each more famous than the last: West helped Sipho Madondo (who was killed in a car accident at the height of his career). West helped Mahlathini into the international arena (though he was not successful in helping him sing in a chorus).

An indexical connection between the former and current star weaves the characters together more intricately. Mahlathini sang with Madondo under West's direction before getting his international "break." Additional iconicities, inverted, close the gap between Mahlathini and Bethwell: according to West, Mahlathini needed the vocal coaching West is offering Bethwell. Bethwell is promised better success and offered mobility toward stardom, while Mahlathini's aura is diminished by foregrounding his weakness (from West's perspective) and suggesting that his singing and career peaks have passed. These narrative features elevate Bethwell, while they bring Mahlathini into ordinariness, if only for a moment. This facilitates metaphorical conflation of Bethwell with the star, enabling Bethwell to leap imaginatively to overseas.

Lastly, the story's coda points out that Mahlathini's professional days are diminishing, that there will be a gap on the market to be stepped into. A gap will have been prepared for someone else to make a break.

While West's talk is aimed at rectifying unsettled social relations in the studio after the struggle of capturing a good enough version on the tape, its logic readily stimulates fantasies about international success and imaginings about foreign experience, though West does not train Bethwell in the end or take him under his professional wing.

In imagining overseas the way they do in sound, the music-makers are responding to foreign representations of themselves and to foreign senses of their place. The image of the lion and of African culture as tribal thrusts South African musicians outside modernity. This image is then mapped onto a second idea, which situates them remotely from cosmopolitanism: they sound outdated, as though they were stuck in the late 1960s or 1970s.

These ideas that the musicians replay are ideas about mbaqanga sound and South African ethnic identities already out in international circulation, spinning on the rhetoric of journalists, promoters, and musicians themselves. For example, Mankwane's version of mbaqanga's history appeared in the *Sydney Morning Herald*, which in turn had taken the story from an interview Mankwane gave to the *Boston Phoenix*.

The concepts of reach and return, as spun out from the performed gesture in the studio, captures the local-global relationship relentlessly in process. The to- and fro-ing has a trajectory and propulsion: it is a reach *for* and a return *to*. The concepts of reach and return also capture the constant and necessary movement between the material and ephemeral, the sound and imagination, the sign and its interpretation, and between a generalized commodity status (here, of blackness) and the depth and struggles of the actual experience of race and racism behind it.

The reach and return are discursive moves that produce a sense of the local in the face of the idea of overseas. While they absolutely cohabit, residing in the same sign, they produce a dichotomy of imagined place: the local, this side, at home, *ekhaya*; and the global, on the other side, overseas, *phesheya*.

Ikhaya (home) from the point of view of overseas (as it is imagined by mbaqanga musicians) is constituted as African, as South African, as Zulu, and as a musical heritage developed out of the experience of apartheid, urbanization and proletarianization, township living, and the modernities of the 1970s. In other words, it is a specific version of blackness.

At its least elaborated, *phesheya* means "the other side" as opposed to "this side." *Phesheya* in Zulu refers to any other place (over the river, the other side of the mountain). Even at its most basic, phesheya has form. Joana talks in English about having music in Africa that they don't have "in overseas." She wishes to go "to overseas."

Overseas is given form in the imagination. A material, social, and subjective relationship to the global is cultivated on the basis of that form. As Susan Stewart writes in another context, the imagination turns the local-global "flux into form" and "infinity into frame" (1993, 76). It tames the overwhelming "out there" and gives social shape to this desired arena.

Overseas is the gaze of Others onto blackness. It is crowds of fans. It lends mbaqanga musicians a sense of owning and presenting something unique, and it offers them a space to be heard by Others—by others who are similar to those who have historically denied them a voice. "Audiences would love to see us, because they don't know us," Joana reckons. "It would be the same as when Diana Ross, Donna Summer, and Michael Jackson came here. We were happy to see them because they brought things we didn't know before." It is names—brand names, place names, people's names, companies' names; it is brushes with famous people, contacts, ins, and hard work with rewards. It is the latest in technology. It is expertise and opportunity. It is new musical experiences. It is meetings and exchanges with foreign musicians, especially with other like musicians (Africans, African Americans, marginalized and minority artists) at festivals. It is direct encounters with exotic and new music styles. It is inspiration. Joana says she and her fellow artists would "gain more knowledge. When you arrive elsewhere, the mind works, because it's different to South Africa. Here we see one thing, one road, one building. It's not the same when we go out, so our minds would be running. We would be able to create more things."

Overseas also signifies material wealth and possibilities for greater creative control and unhampered professional performance. That is, it is as much about access to capital as it is about the affirmation of having an audience. It is a place of plenty (languages, currencies, people, goods, venues, distances, possibilities, sounds). It is a place that values excellence. It attends to the artist and fixes its consuming gaze on the dramatized African. Within its industrial power structure, there is an idealized moral order.

Like entry into the recording studio, a break overseas is a means of access to plenitude. Like the studio, overseas is idealized as a place of resources and hence a source of power that enables the realization of creative potential.

The appeal and fantasy of the place overseas is heightened by the lived conditions of music making at home. Viewed, imagined, and desired from the postcolonial, postapartheid, and professional backwaters, overseas becomes idealized as everything the local is not. It is the antithesis of the dysfunctional local conditions of music production. In addition, it is desired and envisioned as the way out of these local constraints and exploitive conditions of music making and living. Overseas takes on specific characteristics as an ideal type and as a shared community: it facilitates creative inventiveness; it insists on high technical and musical standards; it demands peak performance and values excellence; it provides the necessary material backing (budget and promotional support); it operates on the basis of nonracial professional relationships; and it rewards with reputation and returns. Overseas is about flow, not isolation. That is, once inside, pathways open up, whereas being inside here at home is a feeling of entrapment. Overseas is an enterprise that is free from state politics and much closer to being rid of contemporary racial prejudices.

Remix *Forms of Struggle*

Mbaqanga music-makers do not idealize the international arena as equitable, egalitarian, and easy. They know exploitation is inevitable in the age of the multinational music corporation. However, they argue that in the international arena, exploitation is at least globally shared and not figured on the basis of race. The distinction (black) mbaqanga music practitioners make between the power centers overseas and at home resonates with Robert Thorton's articulation of the "two forms of a single [nineteenth-century Zulu] reification of the European—on the one hand as a generalized source of goods and moral authority, and on the other hand, as a form of virulent Otherness and violent exclusiveness" (1995, 204). This conceptual polarity "between the white power of the 'outside,' generalized as a form of occidentalism, and the white power of the 'inside,' generalized as a form of racism" is still crucially operative in contemporary South Africa (ibid., 203–4). It undergirds mbaqanga artists' conception of overseas and hence their efforts to engage with it.

In the experience of South African music-makers, phesheya is not just any and all space off the African continent. It is specific pinpoints on the map. It is metropolitan centers; it is sites of advanced, rapid, technological reproduction and outstanding industrial design. It is New York, Paris, London, and, more recently, Tokyo. It is Japan and Australia, the United States, Britain, and Europe. For artists it is venues that host touring African bands, like s.o.b.s in New York City and the Town and Country in London. It is the Montreux Jazz festival, Reggae Sunsplash, and the New Orleans Jazz Festival. For sound engineers and some producers and musicians, it is studios in Los Angeles, New York, Paris, and London. It is the ssl and Neve consoles. Overseas is good instruments in stores stocked with ample variety.[8] For company executives and marketing personnel, it is media industry expositions like MIDEM (International Record, Music Publishing, and Video Music Market). Places like Mauritius or Fiji or Cape Verde islands or Zambia are more like stepping-stones to overseas than part of the category itself. These places are either stopovers en route to a major venue, a dress rehearsal for the major centers, or a litmus test of newer artists. In and of themselves, these in-between places promise relatively small returns.

Stories from and about returning artists are crucially motivating in home musicians' drive for international exposure, but stories are not synonymous with direct experience. The effects of the poetics of the tellings and of translation of others' experiences are not lost on musicians at home. "When you go outside over there [overseas], you meet other musicians. You see exactly what people want on that side," Jane says. "This is different to when someone comes back this side and says, 'Heyi, people like music like this, they do this and that.' We want to see for ourselves *exactly* what is happening and how those people feel when they see you. It's our wish just to see them."

In the studio itself, there are key sonic features that make or break access to the global market. For an international release, "tuning and sound" is the bottom line, insist the engineers. Without consistently correct intonation and clarity of sound, a 1990s production cannot hope for success in the international market. Even an inspired performance badly recorded and mixed or poorly rendered in terms of its tuning will flop, they say. "Now, we [at Gallo] know there's a lot of interest in the Elite Swingsters overseas, and, sjoe!, the tuning was bad, the guitar was totally out of tune, the drum sound was very bad. So then [remixing it] was basically an A&R decision." Then A&R person Dave Segal, himself an accomplished sound engineer with some experience behind the console in foreign studios, draws a distinction between those South Africans who are participants in a global music community (that is, those who can hear right and deliver consistently on pitch, like good musicians from overseas) and those who will remain in the backwaters. Segal and his A&R team take their fine ears as the standard for cosmopolitans.

When West smoothes out Mahlathini's sound for an international listenership, "to get into their feelings nicely," not like in earlier times when the aesthetic was a "bright" sound that rock and rollers liked, he is following similar principles. He is striving for a sound clarity for which he is prepared to compromise his simulation of an older African sound. With an international consumer in mind, he prioritizes production quality.

It is against the backdrop of an understanding of a globally shared value of consistent intonation and good sound that Bethwell's ibhodlo relegates the production to a low-income domestic market when his "shwele!" exceeds the limits of pitch accuracy. In other words, when West decides to retain the ibhodlo as is, he indicates to the musicians that this is not the production that will catapult them onto the international stage.

Correct intonation is thought of as a principle that is outside politics and outside culture. Ideally, it would be the basic leveling device for everyone in a professionally uncompromised system. However, in practice, politics and histories are certainly implicated in issues of "tuning and sound." In moments when leniency is accorded to intonation, like in Bethwell's ibhodlo recording, music-makers recognize that they are working in the backwaters of an international industry and within a social system still burdened by unequal access to resources. Such recognition often comes with a sense of resignation. In some cases it reveals a tolerant understanding of the nation's history of race and class. When guitarists come into the studio with battered instruments and old strings because that is all they have and all they can afford, "You try and tune the thing, and after one song it goes out of tune and eventually you just kind of give up," Neil says. "Because you'll be there all day trying to tune the thing." But in other cases deep-seated prejudices surface, refracting issues of inconsistent intonation into racist criticisms about different tuning systems and about different levels of sophistication in listening and thinking.

Of course, at one level, pitch precision and sound clarity are simply issues for all accomplished musicians, wherever their product is directed, whatever style they might perform or record, whatever the tuning system they use, and whatever their aesthetic approach to timbral principles might be. "Tuning and sound" are also just matters affected by limitations in studio time and budget in many of these run-of-the-mill projects.

In the case of South Africa, the degrees of attention paid to tuning and sound rest in part on the production team's assessment of what playback technologies the targeted consumers are likely to own. If they anticipate low-fidelity equipment, then the audibility of pitch inaccuracies and sonic nuance will be diminished, as will the attention afforded to fixing them during a recording session. Sometimes inaccuracies are tolerated by musicians, producers, and engineers because circumstances dictate that they do so, as in the case of performers playing on battered instruments and with old strings.

Whatever their politics and their social positioning, everyone in the studio seems to agree that the maladies of apartheid have constrained the creative flow within and out of South African studios and have held back the market potential of South African studio production. Struggles over tuning and aesthetically appropriate but technologically refined sound, for all of them, bare the skeleton of the problem. In their approach to other musicians' intonational difficulties and sound preferences, mbaqanga music-makers express something about how their own capacity to participate in a global studio-produced music community is hampered by the currents against which they struggle.

Overseas as it is articulated by mbaqanga musicians is all of a place or set of places, a network of highly powered relations, a market, and a trope of a creative practice first and foremost organized around excellence rather than race. To access overseas is to tap into a source of power. Overseas is laden with potential within a context in which professional potential is constrained by the regiments of home. Its elaboration on a meta-cultural level is at the same time avidly attended to and worked at. These two levels connect, on the one hand, through the circulation of products, symbols, and people between geopolitical nodes in a global network—between South Africa and large, wealthy metropoles off the African continent—and on the other, through the circulation of stories told during the course of that process, connecting sound events to international experiences.

The reach and return, epitomized by Bethwell's studio performance, must be seen in the integrated context of escalating investments in studio production and international success. Access to overseas and entry into the studio—each ups the stakes on the other. Entry into the studio ups the fantasies and expectations about overseas and mobilizes music-makers toward its realization. Overseas and the studio as fetishized spaces are each infiltrated with the other and always present in the constitution of the other. Together they produce, perform, and commodify an identity that is ethnically specific and emplaced, as a means of developing for South African musicians access to the prosperous cosmopolitan world in which they also wish to participate.

The reach and return call attention to the processes of mediation that reproduce, distribute, translate, and indeed formulate ideas of "home" and "overseas" for musicians and consumers. Media and "culture" are totally integrated (Lysloff 1997). Though only partially represented in the commodity form, the experience of musicians on the ground is analytically inseparable from the circulation of essentialized ideas about that experience through the media industry.

Janet, Paulina, Mandla, Bheki, Bethwell, and Joana rave noisily outside their rehearsal room. Assertive interjections punctuate the thickly textured stream of their voices. International promoters are in town. Two *abelungu* (white people) are looking for African talent—some think maybe one German, one French; Joana thinks one German, one local. No one can say for sure. No one knows their names or what company they represent. All Isigqi knows is that the abelungu are working with or through an independent local promoter, one Madela, an herbalist consulting on the fifth floor of a city-center high-rise down the street.

The problem is that these promoters want singers (the women's frontline, fine) and dancers (their vocal backing, fine), but they have to be traditional. That is to say, they have to be accompanied solely by an array of bongo drums. The women are to do a drama: Joana explains that they are to come down to the river to wash clothes like dutiful Zulu maidens costumed in traditional beads. There they are to sing about working, love, and the hard life. That's fine, we can do that, she says. It wasn't their thing, but she can handle the concession in order to get overseas. Their drummer, Mandla, will be able to join in: he can just leave the trap set and rejoin the male backing line. But what about Bethwell, Tefo, and their guitarist? Don't worry, goes the solution raised initially by Paulina, who has recently joined the frontline. You three will just have to dump your electric instruments and learn to play the bongo drums quickly.

I worry that this ploy will not produce a performance tight enough to get them the gig, and I hate the concessions that the group is prepared to make. 'Don't worry,' Jane assures me. 'There's no problem, it will be beautiful. It's pure tradition.' I protest. She concedes that their music is beautiful, too, and explains that they will insist on presenting it in the audition—just so that the abelungu will know what they can really do. Perhaps in the final show they will be able to include a couple of their songs with guitars.

This is to be their magnificent break. First they are to warm up in a hotel in South Africa. The brand-new Lost City is being negotiated as a preliminary venue. Part of the extravagant Sun City complex, Lost City is an international tourist hot spot, the latest casino resort of South Africa's foremost millionaire. After a run there, Isigqi will head out to Australia and on to France (or Germany, but they think France). The musicians understand that an extended European tour is to follow. At last, they say, after two years of struggling, things are coming right. Very right.

Through Madela, Jane learns that the abelungu want a team of seven male dancers along with their frontline. Dancing is to alternate with the dramas. Jane approaches Siyazi, lead of Umzansi Zulu Dance, to provide her with three from his team. Not only will the umzansi dancers fill out the numbers, but they will be able to train and polish her young township singer-dancers in the genuinely traditional Zulu moves.

Now, Umzansi has given up waiting and rehearsing, day after day, for the tour to Japan that West has for months been telling them is imminent. But Siyazi doesn't take to Jane's proposal on three counts: he can't break his group (who were all from his home community) nor break away himself, even for this opportunity; the dancers won't even be carrying their own name overseas; and Jane's young dancers don't dance "the traditional" properly, and he feels it inappropriate to train someone else's group when his own, already-skilled dancers are relying on him to open up opportunities for them.

Well, the warm-up round at the Lost City never materializes. Instead, the musicians are to get a run, with Umzansi Zulu Dance, at a local, low-key holiday resort, and perhaps at a small hotel in ritzy Sandton. They have already planned a tour of their own to KwaZulu-Natal that will leave them no rehearsal time. Now, how can they disappoint their local fans when even the posters and radio advertising is out? asks Jane. How can they let uTisha down when they'd roped in his mbaqanga group to tour with them because the popular guitarist Umfazi Omnyama has dropped Isigqi at the last minute for a better tour?

In the end, their self-organized local tour gets cut short due to circumstances not tied to Isigqi's international prospects. They also refuse a spot at a festival in the city of Durban, even though it promises a large turnout, for they feel they must remain in Johannesburg to fulfill their engagements for the overseas abelungu.

None of these engagements happen.

I never discover if these promoters exist in the flesh. Madela, the herbalist-promoter, evades my requests for their names, their whereabouts, or a way to contact them: 'They're visiting Durban'; 'They'll be back tomorrow'; 'Lovey, come again on Tuesday.'

Isigqi dumps Madela and the abelungu once they figure that there are, in fact, no returns to be had, and besides, they won't be able to use their own name. They will have to perform under the direction of Madela as

Vuka Afrika! (Wake up, Africa!) They decide to wait for another opportunity.

They know it will come.

Joana says, "There is a beginning. When is the beginning? We know it doesn't go smoothly the first time. One day it's good; one day it's bad. But as long as we remain healthy, we've got that hope that one day we'll make it. Things will come right. Yebo."

The abelungu are still hanging out on the beach.

A Final Mix

Mediating Difference

May 1992

I am at the South African Broadcasting Corporation with Isigqi Sesimanje for the filming of a music video. Four of their newly released songs are to be aired on TV2's and TV3's weekly music programs.

The studio stage is ablaze with a neon orange, blue, and white set. Cameramen wheel equipment into place and zoom in for close-ups. As the musicians dance and mime their wedding songs, as well as "Lomculo Unzima" and "South Africa," clouds of artificial smoke spew periodically from spigots on the stage. The women look magnificent jiving in their brightly beaded skirts, beaded halterneck bodices, beaded headbands, white crocheted and fringed leg and arm garters, and white sneakers, the soles of which enable them to swivel easily on toe and heel. I glimpse their fancy footwork as their sneakers peak out of the billows. They mouth their triple-tracked verses, translating the narrative into choreographed hand gestures, while their recording plays out from the studio's sound system. Mandla, Bheki, and Nhlanhla, the backing dancer-singers, posture youthfully on the set in their animal skins and headdresses. Michael drums while miming the lyrics into the space between his crash cymbal and hi-hat. Tefo is absent, but his stand-in fingers the keyboard chords to a tee. Bethwell seesaws his bass guitar to the beat. He thwacks his fingers onto the strings with a vigor that would have made for messy playing in live-sound performance. Guitarist Mkhize bobs to Bethwell's bass beat.

Next, the women swish in their beaded traditional getups down the corridors to the dressing room. White women packed into suits clip-clop past. Some smile, some greet Isigqi in English or Afrikaans.

There is bustle and excitement. Isigqi know they are poised at an edge, that the broadcasting of their videos might bring them an opening that would boost their careers again. They are hoping to be thrust into a prosperous future by performing their remembered and imagined pasts. In the dressing room Janet and Joana break into their jubilant wedding song. They sing in a perfect blend while dancing in their beads in front of the huge mirror glitzed out with its string of seventy-five-watt light bulbs.

Mix On Producing a Voice

In reflecting on the studio talk during this production, I am struck by the fact that there was so little discussion of the sound of the front-line voices, especially considering that the band formed around the vocal quartet. Neither musicians, producer, nor sound engineers talked about the qualities of the women's voices despite their striking contribution to the mbaqanga sound. How to record and mix the vocal choruses and overlapping solos was taken for granted.

Unlike the group's male chorus, which had been recently constituted, the women were thoroughly experienced in singing together. Their veteran excellence made close-harmony singing seem quite automatic. Their intonation was always faultless. The length, pace, and position of the vocal glides and phrase breaks was perfectly, effortlessly synchronized. Their timbral sonority and registeral balance were consistent. In the rehearsal room and studio they would stop to teach one another melodic lines. They would talk about vocal arrangements but not about timbral qualities.

"Izwani, iyenyuka! Angithi sengifun'ukujoina i-alto yakho" (Listen, the melody is rising! I want to fit with your alto), advises Jane, interrupting her friends who are hum-singing on the couch at the back of the control room. "Two, three, *dumela wena,"* they continue singing while Jane adds another part.

That the singers and instrumentalists did not argue over the sound of the women's voices doesn't mean that enchanting voices were not noticed and prized. To the contrary. "Mahotella!" exclaims Jane. "Those women can sing! If you are going to sing with Mahotella, you must prepare yourself, because those ladies put note to note [precisely together]."

The silence on vocal production in the mbaqanga studio can be attributed in part to the naturalness of the vocal instrument and to the naturalization of multipart singing among black South Africans. The act of singing and the ability to sing are taken as unremarkable by mbaqanga artists, although, of course, some voices excel and others don't stay in tune. Singing is present in the everyday lives of all the mbaqanga artists. Children sing multipart songs a cappella. Protesters and ralliers sing in parts. Church-goers sing in harmony. Party revelers call and respond, overlap, and add higher and lower voices.

*"Dumela wena" (Hullo to you), sings Joana again, musing while
waiting for Peter to cue the next song.*
   *"Dumela wena wena, dumela wena," respond Jane, Michael,
Tefo, and Nhlanhla in a closeharmony hum.*
   "Tsotle di siame" (Everything is all right), Joana sings.
   "Tsotle di siame."
   "Dumela wena."

Electronic instrumentalists must delicately manipulate their controls in order to produce a trademark sound. They take ownership of the sound by withholding from others the calibrations and details of the electronic settings of their factory-produced instruments, amplifiers, and mixes. "I'm not going to give them our sound," West assures Hansford. Instrumentalists articulate their musical character even at the level of timbre. Vocalists start with the grain of their voice. Its basic timbre is what they have to work with, and it is unique to each singer. They own it wholly.

In the studio, mbaqanga singers—especially female singers—are less adept at electronic manipulation than instrumentalists. They don't consider it their domain of expertise. "That is not my job," says Jane. "That is not what I listen for." Clearly she does listen acutely to timbre in order to blend her voice evenly with the others in the vocal quartet, but she does not consider the aspects of electronically reproducing that timbre on tape her responsibility or something within her domain of control.

Joana similarly thinks of singing as transparently natural. For her, it is implicitly Zulu. Instrumentation is a self-conscious addition that overtly articulates the rhythms implicit in singing as well as provides a rhythmic counterpoint to the voice. Hence, it is the instrumentation—the arrangements, the sounds, the mix—that is subject to debate, not the voices.

From the point of view of the producer and sound engineer, recording vocal choruses is a daily chore with standard practices involving close miking, triple tracking, some reverb, some flange, and so forth. West says his trick in recording the vocals of the Mahotella Queens and Ladysmith Black Mambazo was "to add a shadow." He blended a track that was recorded fairly dry with a second that was recorded with more reverb. He added the second to the first with a minute delay to produce the "shadow." While West devoted more attention and more studio time to getting timbral shadings just right for his productions that targeted an international audience, he used the same basic techniques for domestic vocal groups. He judged Sesimanje's vocal sound to be adequate for local consumption; he did not afford their voices special attention.

The production approach to vocal choruses is not peculiar to mbaqanga. Many South African recorded musics include triple-tracked chorusing. Mbaqanga's particular, soft vocal blend draws influence from the sound of soft soul groups like the O'Jays and smooth R&B backing choruses. Where mbaqanga differentiates itself from soft soul and R&B, and shows stylistic connections to traditional Zulu singing styles is in its highly developed synchronized gliding up to held tones and in its pitch falls coupled with sound decay that end most musical phrases. On the other hand, mbaqanga's singing contrasts with the stridence and nasality of Zulu traditional singing. The differences between soul, mbaqanga, and Zulu traditional styles lie more in the singing than in their electronic reproduction. In other words, while the frontline singing style is a notable feature of mbaqanga as it is performed, its studio practitioners do not consider its timbral quality and blend as it is achieved by technological means in the studio to be unique within South Africa or more broadly.

"The O'Jays!" jabs West sarcastically.

Metacultural markers are particularly apt to appear in the production of artistic expression in situations of political and economic domination, for it is in these situations that cultural "identities" are challenged or awakened and that having culture is explicitly useful (Samuels n.d.). So, too, do such markers become critical in moments of turmoil and transition, for metacultural discussion comes markedly into play in figuring out if and when culture matters, what it is, and how its expression can be harnessed to the concerns of an individual or collectivity.

The mbaqanga women's frontline sound does not operate on its own as a marker of place, nation, or ethnicity in the early 1990s production of *Lomculo Unzima*. From the perspective of some, like Joana, it is so transparently Zulu that it is simply not up for discussion. From the perspective of others, like Jane, its manipulation is not an issue, because its technological procedure is naturalized. For others, it lacks the local distinctiveness that would make it worth further highlighting and foregrounding in the mix.

It is in the context of an abundance of other metacultural markers of Africanness, South Africanness, and Zuluness that are specified in relation to ideas about technology that the timbral qualities of the women's frontline pass by without debate in the studio. While the singers have ownership over their voices and little concern with the details of technical reproduction, the instrumentalists work their musical character in part through manipulation of their sound. They, as well as the vocalists, are more invested in the studio manipulation of the instrumental sounds. It is the instrumental work along with the distinctively mbaqanga ibhodlo that is subject to debate.

Instrumental work in the studio brings analytic attention to the importance of timbre in the production of feeling and significance. Timbre has been understudied, partly because it seems so indefinable, unquantifiable, and intuitive. Yet music-makers and listeners talk about it all the time—or at least we talk around it with elaborated poetics, usually tying it up with equally unquantifiable feelings. Feeling is crucially captured in and transported through timbre. The ineffability of musical timbre and the indeterminacy of feeling are both analytical problems and key theoretical points, for it is because of the ambiguity and indeterminacy of both that the one can house the other. It is critical to our sonic experience. Timbre matters because it houses debates that are articulated as a feeling about things—a "Zulu" guitar, a "ballsy" drum sound. Because timbral qualities are about feeling, they are deeply invested but never fully defined or finally fixed. That is why timbre is so crucial to the contingent production of meaning.

Remix On Commodifying Ethnicity

I am at the South African Broadcasting Corporation with Isigqi Sesimanje for the filming of a music video. The musicians dance and mime their wedding songs. Their brightly beaded clothing looks magnificent against the neon orange, blue, and white set. The youthful backing singer-dancers posture in animal skins. Afterward, there is bustle and excitement. Isigqi know they are poised at an edge. They are hoping to be thrust into a prosperous future by performing their remembered and imagined pasts.

In performing Africanness, South Africanness, and Zuluness, mbaqanga artists' metadiscourse on overseas and on the studio also take form.

Markers of home and self are shaped in relation to local visions of overseas. In some ways, the principles of overseas reproduce those of the studio: access is exclusive and thoroughly desirable; a music-maker needs a break to get into the studio, just as he or she looks for a break to get out overseas. In other ways, overseas represents the studio's inversion. Whereas the studio takes music-makers to the worlds "within," overseas takes them to the worlds "without." Whereas the studio is imagined and experienced as a site of production, of interiority, as private and intensive, overseas is exterior, extensive, public, a site of consumption, spectacle, and display.[1] Both overseas and the studio are idealized as separate from the local and everyday, as having worlds within worlds, as places of flow despite the boundaries to be traversed, and as transformative spaces that rework ideas concerning the constitution of the local. In tandem, discourses about overseas and the studio intensify the production of the local as an idea divorced from actual conditions of the present and here.

Music and ethnic identity are global commodities that share the same space in the studio, where they are blended into one groove. In the process of crafting ethnicity into a reified concept, some realms of experience (a history of subjugation, for example) are cast into the background while others (bodily expressivity, for example) are overgeneralized in a celebrated public display.

That race, nation, and ethnicity are the qualities of identity that are marked and commodified in a South African music of the 1990s speaks to the country's history of racism, racialization, denial of full and equal citizenship, and politicization of ethnicity. However overgeneralizing the ethnic image might be in commodity form, beneath it there lie the deep experiences of people who are at work and at play in the studio. That the terms of the debate shift position in the commodified mix in the 1990s— albeit that they remain the same terms—is synchronized with the political transition from apartheid to democracy, to the reentry of South Africa as a leading state and nation into continental African politics and into the world market.

Music-makers in the studio struggle for political, professional, and personal voice in the process of shaping style. In struggling for their values, identities, and aspirations, they perform their sensibilities in dialogue with the figures and images they capture and create. They thereby rework or reaffirm their sociopolitical positioning in relation to one another, and, in the larger context, in relation to those among whom they live.

The early 1990s were years during which (South) Africa enjoyed a marked presence in global cultural production. These years also stand as an emergent moment in the South African struggle. Such dramatic events made clear how important to the theorization of expressive form were issues of technology and the media, diaspora, transnational flows, class, gender, generation, race, ethnicity, and nationalisms. The integration of these issues in mbaqanga production absolutely forges together the studies of World Music production, South African popular culture, political formations, forms of knowledge, and contemporary social life.

Final Mix   On Mediating Difference

On the studio stage at the SABC, Isigqi Sesimanje dance their songs. They mouth their triple-tracked verses and translate the narrative into hand gestures, while their recording plays out from the studio's sound system. Cameramen wheel their equipment into place and zoom in for close-ups.

The technological means of production, the corporate structures that house the technology, and the labor relations that organize the practices around that technology are critical forms of mediation that "intervene" in the participatory experience of music making. In commodity production, these forms of mediation are mutually supportive.

In terms of its material process, mediation is a technological manipulation of one kind of matter with another (sound and image, for example), from one location and one media to another—say, cassette tape in a music studio to videotape and television broadcasting. Mediation captures face-to-face experiences and disseminates them, making other new face-to-face experiences possible.

In terms of labor relations within the workplace, one might think of mediation as a kind of arbitration. Laborers, technicians, and artists interface in negotiations in the workplace. The investments of business executives, employees, freelancers, and clients are thrust together in the control room. Vocalists, instrumentalists, producers, and sound engineers rework sounds. Arbitration aims at changing a dissatisfactory status quo in order to make sound happen, music move, and products popular.

Labor relations in and around the studio are represented and discreetly negotiated through the performance of language difference. As Isigqi swish down the corridors in their beaded getups back to the dressing room, white female office workers greet them in English or Afrikaans. Isigqi say, 'Good morning.' They resume their Zulu conversation. Code-switching virtuosically between different languages, shifting stylistically between different kinds of talk, and drawing from different technical lexicons all offer speakers ways of bonding and opening up access to others while these linguistic arts also offer ways to mark the speakers' exclusivity or to pull a punch.

1 April 1992

White session musician and drummer Kevin Kruger strides into the studio.

"Yes! Kevin Kruger National Park!" greets West raucously.[2] Kevin knows the greeting.

"Country and Western Music!" he retorts exuberantly, imitating a black South African accent.

"Howzit, Kevin," greets West again, in South African English slang.

"Howzit," he replies. "How're you doing?"

"Ah, not too—" begins West.

"Number the *first!*" (I'm one hundred percent fine!), interrupts Kevin, switching back into a black accent.

"Yes," confirms West. Pause. They catch each other's eye.

"Country Westernkosi!" bursts out Kevin again.

"Ja. Kevin Kruger National Park!"

"Kruger National *Perk*," corrects Kevin.

"Ja."

"Not Park—"

"Kruger National *Perk!*" they chant together, both caricaturing a black accent.

They laugh loudly.

"I want to book you for percussion," begins West seriously.

Sounds themselves are shaped and reshaped in relation to talk about them. Technical lexicons about sound production and reproduction, theoretical discussions about form, and expressive evaluation of performances are all featured aspects of the poetics of talk about music that crucially effect the outcome of sound on tape as well as its socially salient interpretation. Poetic language mediates different worlds. That is to say, it brings them into contact through refracted lenses. In the mbaqanga studio, the starkest disparities brought into contact are between the worlds of "black" and "white," historically the oppressed and the oppressor, and between the worlds of sound and technology.

The poetics of talk about music flow in performance between song and speech. The deployment of vocables, for example, constantly mediates between the intelligibility of referential language and the communication of feeling and texture.

"Now here the hi-hat is going to go like tshiki tshik tshiki tshik tshiki tshik tshiki tshik!"

Peter gets to work, programming in an imitation of West's sung-spoken hi-hat pattern, which communicates a rhythm, a basic timbre, and a playing technique alternating open and dampened cymbal hits.

"Tshiki tshik tshiki tshik tshiki tshik tshiki tshik tshiki."

In South African studio talk, the difficulties in describing something as ineffable as sound are overlaid onto shifting debates about the social values of those sounds. This layering is situated within a highly politicized history of racialized talk. The transitional, early 1990s sensitivity to the perniciousness of racial prejudice embeds talk about Otherness discreetly in terms of other discussions, such as ones about aesthetic preference. Technical and stylistic discussions in the studio present heightened scenarios in which these tensions are played out.

In the SABC studio an official with a nametag prevents me from taking a photograph. I argue that I am with the group that is performing on the stage. Regulation, he replies, sorry no photography in here. He won't bond with me as a fellow onlooker and let me take one anyway.

In social practice just as in studio practice more specifically, mediation is a negotiation of social positioning within a system of power. In art worlds, cultural brokers negotiate cultural value into exchange value (Steiner 1994; Marcus and Myers 1995; Lutz and Collins 1993). Glossing the experiences of one "culture" for another, brokers are also pivotal in establishing categories of Otherness and facilitating their interpretation.

In the music industry, music producers are critical gatekeepers into commodity production because they are institutionally positioned to negotiate between laborers (musicians) and management (the record companies) and between aesthetic and market concerns. In the South African case, especially historically, producers are also structurally positioned to broker black cultures for largely white capital and industrial executives, as well as for crossover and foreign consumers. In other words, producers hold the responsibility of mediating between blackness as a fiction, rhetoric, and commodity on the one hand and blackness as sensibility and experience on the other. Sound engineers are mediating figures in other ways. At the console, they convert performed sounds, as well as poetic expressions about timbre and feel, into scientific calibrations of soundwaves to be recorded onto magnetic tape.

In the South African mbaqanga case, struggles over positioning and expressions of difference work themselves out through a process of figuring social types in the creative process. These struggles principally concern racial representations, but they are also engaged with issues of class, ethnic, generational, and gender differences. That is to say, these are mutually mediating discourses that get formed through and in relation to one another.

As Goffman and de Certeau's attention to the interactional practices of everyday life has suggested, the microdynamics of personal relationships are both expressive and productive of larger social configurations (Goffman 1959; Goffman 1967; de Certeau 1988). While social practices are conventionalized, they are also unpredictable and improvised. Modes of improvisation and modes of being, appropriate to the habitus (Bourdieu 1984), are worked out through metacultural figuring, through poetic representations of the self and others in relation to one another. Social configurations, such as class fractions, maintain their instability because ideas of taste can and do shift (Bourdieu 1984).

As an expressive symbolic process, mediation transfers meaning from one kind of interpretive domain to another. Interpretation is conditioned by the constant interaction of values, settled though never resolved at the moment of an utterance (Bakhtin 1981). Mediation is explicitly named in semiotic theory as fundamental to the process of meaning production: the sign mediates between its object and its interpretant. Signs are concrete, compact instances that are inherently unstable because they exist in the context of other polysemic signs. Chains of semiosis set multiple possible pathways of inference into motion. In other words, there are multiple ways of tracking sounds, musical experiences, commodity circulation, and their mutual significances. I take symbolic mediation to be both a mediation of images and of sensibilities, just as it is individual and collective, personal and social. It is a mediation of fictions while it is also a mediation of lives lived in struggle.

The years 1991 and 1992, during which *Lomculo Unzima* was produced, were times of excitement, danger, promise, and volatility in the struggle for liberation. With Mandela and his comrades released, organizations of the liberation movement unbanned, and their leadership back in the country, the Convention for a Democratic South Africa (CODESA) convened in Johannesburg. At CODESA's meetings, South African politicians negotiated the terms of transition to a new constitution and form of governance, which was institutionalized through national elections in 1994. The enormous historic political mediation for which CODESA was one of the final large-scale organizational meetings shifted the terms of the South African liberation struggle from revolution to negotiated settlement.

Transition on the grandest scale was replicated in debates in smaller, specialized arenas: housing, land, education, employment, language policy, the future of the single men's hostels, restructuring of the SABC, minimum airtime quotas for South African music, and so forth. Transition also implicated changes in relations to and shifts in the relative power of music corporations. National, foreign, multinational, and independent companies vied for a slice of the musical pie and of the more open market.

The consideration of the political struggle as an arena of mediation interlinked and operating with other kinds of mediations challenges us to recognize the centrality of aesthetic production to processes of resistance, to the voicing of oppositionality, and to processes of empowerment. Struggles over musical style implicate and promote struggles over circumstances of subsistence and democratic rights. The musicians involved in the production of *Lomculo Unzima* empower themselves by means of the loopholes that poetic ambiguity and play produce. They resist being fixed and placed, and they creatively exploit the slippage between different kinds, modes, arenas, domains, and levels of mediation.

A sense of authenticity—here, of forms of blackness—is often a critical element of cultural expression, for it provides a discursive link between sound and sentiment. Authenticity is a key mediating figure in the shaping of style. Two systems of value converge in this concept and are relationally negotiated through it. Both are concerned with what is good, true, natural, and coherent according to culturally specific codes. Both are always provisional. The first is concerned with human dignity and personhood. It is a system of social ethics. The second is concerned with poetics and form. It is a system of aesthetics. In Bakhtin's terms, in expressive culture "the image of man" converges with the poetics of form in an instance of mutually constituting heteroglossia (Bakhtin 1981). Feld writes similarly about aesthetics as the iconicity of style (Keil and Feld 1994). Style presents instances in which the meaning of personhood is distilled.

Mediation is at once an intervention and a means of contact. It is a form of insertion, which is integrally part of social experience and of the commodity state. It inserts a frequency band into a timbre, a tone into a tune, a solo into a soundtrack. It transports a musician into a performance, a listener into a distant world, a reader into a happening. Mediation blurs the boundaries between theory and story, theory and practice, imagination and experience. It injects rights to ownership into creative practice, and questions of politics and ethics into aesthetics.

Mediation embeds layers and layers of experience in the expressive commodity form, and it opens up multiple possibilities for interpretation of those embedded experiences. Mediation operates in different arenas, such as commodity production, social practice, and political struggle; in different communicative modes, such as poetics and semiotics; in different expressive forms, such as music and dance, spoken and written narrative, visual representation, display on the body; and at different levels, such as the material, the cultural and metacultural, the micro and the macro. It is in the convergence of these forms of mediation that social difference is produced and variously made powerful. Such processes lie at the heart of the production of music style in the South African recording studio and of social life in and around artistic practice.

Final Playback

May 1992

After dancing and miming on the stage, the women swish down the corridors back to the dressing room where Janet and Joana break into their jubilant wedding song. They sing in perfect harmony while dancing in their beads in front of the huge mirror glitzed out with its string of seventy-five-watt light bulbs. Joana dance-kicks, mbaqanga women's–style, with her usual strength and dignity. Her elbows pointing out sideways, hands forward at shoulder level, and palms inward, she prepares for the upbeat with an upward flick of her arms: fingers leading wrists leading forearms. On the upbeat she raises her left knee and drops her forearm. Then down stamps her foot and up flick her forearms. She catches her vigorous action just at the point of its completion: a silent landing, like a gasp. She holds her poise in tension for a moment. Then she interrupts her celebratory performance to explain to me, "Now this is really isigqi!"

They had previously glossed *isigqi* for me as meaning "something like sound." It also refers to a heavy step or a dignified gait, to mixed elements coming together, and to something that they said was too deep to translate. Isigqi for Joana in the dressing room was a moment of coherence. It was something stylistic and contemporary, worldly and African, aesthetic and ethic, that their group had got exactly right. Isigqi affirmed Zuluness. It expressed dignity. It generated potential. It encapsulated the perfect dance step, the anticipated hit, the pulsing wedding song, the potency of West's production, the promise held in the dressing room of a TV studio.

Print-Through

*print-through: Sonic resonances bleed through layers
of a wound tape, to be heard as a trace on another track.*[1]

It is with sorrow I record the passing of some of
the musicians who bring grace to the grooves of mbaqanga
and to the pages of my text.

JANET DUDU DLAMINI (1952–1993) died of illness.

WEST NKOSI (1942–1998) died from injuries sustained in a road accident
while speeding home from the studios in his Mercedes.

MARKS MANKWANE (1939–1998) and **MAHLATHINI SIMON NKABINDE**
(1938–1999) both died of illness, reported in the press as diabetes and
"complications from a long-standing diabetic condition" respectively.

Guitarist **ROBERT MKHIZE** died in a taxi crash in 1992 while scouting for
gigs for Izintombi Zesimanje in Zimbabwe.

ISAAC LUVUNO, Isibaya Esikhulu's road manager and subsequently a
sales representative for Gallo died similarly while visiting distant retail
outlets in 1996.

Zulu traditional musician **MSAWETSHITSHI ANDRIES ZAKWE** (1962–2000)
sustained gunshot wounds when trying to mediate an altercation.

UMFAZI OMNYAMA MPHATHENI KHUMALO died of illness that same
year. His kidneys failed, they said, in the street.

Tsongan artist **PETA TEANET** (1966–1996) was hit by a stray bullet
from a policeman's gun outside a bar.

Downtown's engineer **HUMPHREY MABOTE** fell ill and passed away in 2002.

The memory of these artists lives on in the creative work
of those who remain.

After a hiatus, the Mahotella Queens resumed their international touring and recording, opening their shows and ending their latest CD with a tribute to West, Marks, and Mahlathini (Mahotella Queens 2000). They are working with a new young backup band. The music industry has showered them with accolades since the deaths of their colleagues: in 1999 the South African Music Association recognized them with a Lifetime Achievement Award; in 2000 WOMEX World Music conference in Berlin named them "Artist of the Year," and the American World Music Awards acknowledged them as "Best Vocal Artist."

Hamilton Nzimande remains active as a producer. In 1999 he moved out of Johannesburg, away from the eye of the industry. He scouts and records around East London in the eastern Cape, focusing on black church music.

Downtown Studios remains active and up-to-date. They are recording plenty of Zulu traditional artists and "the top mbaqanga acts in the country," Darryl Heilbrunn reports. The company no longer retains in-house engineers. Of those who worked there in the early 1990s, Darryl has become Downtown's general manager; Lee Short left the business to pursue interior design work; Richard Austen returned to England; Lance Longley also left the country and currently works in Florida.

Peter Pearlson keeps busy as a freelancer in Johannesburg, working especially at KD Studios. Neil Kuny has set up a new studio, Music Master Studio, where he both works as an engineer on others' projects and creates his own music.

Having split from the group after recording *Lomculo Unzima,* Joana and Michael continue to record together under the band name Isigqi Sesimanje. With a new line-up, they have released two recordings through a small black-owned enterprise, TK Productions (Isigqi 1999; 2001). These releases followed their appearance at the televised All Africa Games in Johannesburg in 1999. There, out of one hundred and eighty bands and dance troupes, they took home a third-place trophy for their choreographed rendition of the All Africa Games theme song. Joana says a promoter could help solve their difficulties in securing other paying performance spots. She is still hoping to tour overseas. She reckons the mines and hostels at home are no longer viable options. Michael continues to sew and tailor to generate additional income.

Like Michael in 1994, Bethwell and Tefo traveled to Holland to perform with Thoko Mdlalose in 1997. Intermittently, both musicians play as sidemen for a variety of traditional and mbaqanga acts.

Derrick Dlamini and Nhlanhla Qwabe, two of Zesimanje's backup singer-dancers, joined the cast of the revised *Ipitombi* musical. After performing in theaters in Johannesburg and Cape Town, they toured Australia with the company in 1998.

Jane Dlamini continues to scout for local performance venues for her group. With the exception of the state- or city-sponsored events (such as Mandela's birthday concert in 1996) and occasional arts festivals (such as at Johannesburg's Windybrow Theatre in 1998) in which Zesimanje participated, performance opportunities have been sparse for all mbaqanga and traditional music artists during the last few years. At the same time, Zesimanje have continued their studio work. The group followed the release of *Lomculo Unzima* with a self-produced cassette in 1994 and a CD in 1999.

At last, in 1999, Zesimanje traveled to the United States, where the city of Middletown, Ohio, hosted the group. That year city officials chose to feature South Africa at Middfest International, an arts festival and "international outreach effort" (Middfest 1999) that promotes the city's economy and enhances their citizens' experience of diversity.[2] The Zesimanje artists were happy to visit for a week, to appear at a beautiful festival, to meet Americans, and to be treated with gracious hospitality.

Middletown invited Zesimanje back to the twentieth anniversary of their festival in 2002. Jane tried to persuade the National Arts Council in Johannesburg to sponsor the plane tickets. Maybe a promoter or a producer would hear them on stage or TV over there, Jane said, God willing. In addition to this, a promotions company overseas had shown interest in adding them to their roster. This would include performing in London for six weeks in 2002, they told her. Word has it that the same company is drawing Hamilton back to Johannesburg to revitalize Isibaya Esikhulu under their auspices.

2002 will be a new year, Jane said. She titled her freshly composed promotional autobiography "Despite Years of Struggle," and she ended it by affirming that "it is through music, dance, and other forms of art that we can learn from one another. Through music we can be better understood, and remembered by those who will follow us: the next generation. May we all put our differences aside and become Africa-focussed. LET US EMBRACE OUR UNIQUE CONTINENT, our diverse cultures, our languages, and our people. May we unite and continue to play music."

Notes

Demo Tape

1   Downtown Studios purchased DAT recorders in 1991–92. In 1992 Gallo companies, like domestic companies in general, pressed a few vinyl albums principally for promotional purposes on radio. Most mbaqanga sales were on cassette. Only productions anticipated to have a crossover or international market and productions of musicians who already had an enormous employed urban following were released on CD as well as cassette. Isigqi's *Lomculo Unzima* was certainly not counted in either category. The first South African CD plant, Gallo's Compact Disc Technologies, opened in South Africa in 1992 (*Newsbeat* 1992, 3).

2   Sale of fifty thousand units in the year of release earns music-makers a platinum disc. In South Africa gold status represents sales of twenty-five thousand units.

3   The 1992 Goldstone Commission, which investigated covert security operations, was referred to informally as the "truth commission." This is different from the later Truth and Reconciliation Commission.

4   When Gallo became a subsidiary of the Premier Group in 1980, it acquired full control of RPM Record Company and RPM Studios (renamed Downtown Studios in 1991) (Al Jolson's *Sonny Boy* 1991, 9). Three years later the Gallo Group and CNA merged to form CNA Gallo Ltd., which was listed on the Johannesburg Stock Exchange (*Gallo Newsbeat* 1989, 6). This happened when Premier combined its interests in Gallo with Argus Printing and Publishing Company's 52 percent interest in CNA. So now Premier and Argus share control of CNA Gallo with a joint 66 percent holding (Al Jolson's *Sonny Boy* 1991, 9).

5   KwaZulu and Natal were reamalgamated in 1994. Henceforth I refer to the region as KwaZulu-Natal (KZN), in accordance with current provincial divisions and nomenclature.

6   Musicians use the phrase "deep Zulu" to describe those values and beliefs that they consider most culturally specific, most "traditional," and least reproducible by non-Zulus.

7   For examples of interpretive symbolic anthropology applied to music systems see Keil 1979; Feld 1990, 1988; Roseman 1991; and Rice 1994. For class conflict and resistance models see Gramsci 1971 and Williams 1977. For anthropology of the senses see Stoller 1989; Howes 1991; Seremetakis 1994; and Jackson 1996; and for its application to sound see Feld 1996b. For analyses of global cultural flows see Goodwin and Gore 1990; Barber and Waterman 1995; Marcus and Myers 1995; and Erlmann 1999. For sound technology consumption see Frith 1986, 1991, 1996; Théberge 1993, 1997; Chanan 1995; and T. Taylor 2001. For commodity fetishization see Sayer 1987 and Taussig 1993. For the colonial and apartheid state's participation in the construction of ethnicity, see, for example, Marks and Trapido 1987; Tomaselli, Tomaselli, and Muller 1989; Vail 1989; Maré 1993; Wilmsen, Dubow, and Sharp 1994; Mamdani 1996; Wilmsen 1996; Hamilton 1998; and James 1999.

8   The ballad "Ukuhlupeka kwami" [My suffering] was also among her favorites. She identified with the Christian message and hymnal sound of song, though she did not consider it necessarily to be commercially enticing. My analysis therefore does not explicitly encompass it.

9   Jazz studies have perhaps pushed timbral notation furthest. See, for example, Paul Berliner's transcriptions in *Thinking in Jazz*, which detail technical effects and timbral changes in improvisations (1994).

cut 1 Mbaqanga

1   RPM House, Gallo's downtown studio and rehearsal venue, changed its name to Downtown Studios during the course of my research.

2   In turning down the tops of his bass guitar, Bethwell cuts the amplification of the instrument's upper frequencies, thereby toning down its brightness. Boosting the lower frequencies lends more weight to the sound. For explication of subsequent in-house terms and of studio technology, see the glossary.

3   Interview by author, 20 August 1998, Johannesburg, in English. This and all subsequent single voices presented in double quotation marks or as block quotes are excerpted from interviews with me, unless otherwise noted. See bibliography for full references.

4   In my experience, Hamilton actually appeared less frequently than twice a week.

5   Pretoria was the administrative seat of the apartheid government, as well as the location of the headquarters of the defense force and the Dutch Reformed Church, the biggest Afrikaans church, which aligned itself with the apartheid state.

6   The article fails to note Rupert Bopape's co-directorship of Mavuthela that preceded West's executive success.

7   Rehearsal rooms were financed by record companies such as CBS. Hamilton was different from his early competitors in that he bought instru-

ments to equip his rooms and to enable musicians to perform shows. Other producers relied on the publishing divisions of the companies that employed them to supply instruments, as well as a "mobile" (a minivan equipped with a megaphone) for promotion. It was only in the late 1970s that they stopped depending on their publishers for these services and like Hamilton took more control of the showbiz for themselves (Albert Ralulimi, personal communication, August 1997).

Gallo continues the practice of providing rehearsal space (as do some other companies), but the company no longer supplies instruments for use by their contracted musicians. Some producers own equipment, which is stored in their rehearsal room, used by their artists, and hired out to others for performances. In 1996 Gallo changed its policy and began to rent out its rehearsal space to producers.

8 See, for example, the cover of *Aretha in Paris* (Franklin 1968) and of *Reflections* (Diana Ross and the Supremes 1968).

9 *Isidudla Sika Josefa* (Izintombi Zesimanjemanje 1967a).

10 Ivor Haarburger, executive director of Gallo Music International (personal communication, 21 August 1997).

11 Rob Allingham, manager, Gallo Music Archives (personal communication, 9 June 2000).

12 For valuable ethnographic treatments of reputation building by musicians see Waterman 1990; Barber and Waterman 1995; Gerstin 1998; Erlmann 1999, 214–33. Gerstin includes a review of ethnomusicological literature that treats reputation building. He writes that representations of tradition play a part in the informal negotiation of positions of authority among performers of bèlè music in Martinique, French West Indies.

13 While in jazz circles musical literacy was championed as a sign of advancement, mbaqanga practitioners played by ear.

14 Isibaya Esikhulu toured what was then Rhodesia first in May 1968 and a number of times subsequently. They performed in Zambia in 1969, 1979, 1980, and 1981; Mozambique and Malawi in 1974 and 1977; and the Ivory Coast in 1982. Towns in Botswana, Namibia, Lesotho, Swaziland, and South Africa were regular performance destinations. (Moses Dlamini, personal communication, August 1997).

15 "Vala Nzimande" is also the title of a 1969 hit single of Isibaya Esikhulu's sax jiver Bra Sello. Bopape had moved from EMI to Gallo in 1964.

16 Splash's first recording, a 12" single titled "Mr. Tonny," was marketed as a "pop vocal" in 1985. Their first hit, released the following year and titled *Peacock*, was marketed as "soul" though it differed distinctively in style from earlier soul recordings (Splash 1986).

17 GMP's other producers were West Nkosi, Richard Siluma, Dan Tshanda, Lucky Monama, and Bhekinkosi Ntuli. GMP was established in 1989.

18 First, in 1989 he and sound engineer Peter Ceronio started an enterprise that took on the name Isibaya. Later, he joined Stanley Nkosi and his pressing and distribution company, Phoenix Records. Hamilton's two explorations into independent production are multiply storied mo-

ments. Here I reproduce information offered by Peter Ceronio (interview by author, Johannesburg, 9 January 1992) and producer Koloi Lebona (interview by author, Johannesburg, 17 May 1991) respectively. Ceronio recorded most of Isibaya Esikhulu's GRC productions.

19 The Pretoria Tower Boys were produced by Cuthbert Matumba at Troubadour Records and released on the Hit label. I compiled West's early professional history from his press biographies (Mahlaba 1982; Musician 1989; Thema 1983; Gallo n.d.) as well as with information provided by Rob Allingham (personal communication).

20 Bopape had a number of production assistants who were also exceptional performing members of his roster. Mavuthela included most notably Rupert Bopape (producer, co-director with Peter Gallo and David Fine), Shadrack Piliso (Bopape's principal assistant), Ntemi Piliso, Elias Mthembu, Elijah Nkwanyana, Michael Xaba, Chris Songxaka, and Wilson Silgee. Other key artists, who did less arranging and assisting than those above, included Marks Mankwane, West Nkosi, Joseph Makwela, Lucky Monama, Lemmy Special Mabaso, Roger Klizane, Simon Nkabinde (Mahlathini), and the Mahotella Queens. The Makgona Tshole Band (basically Mankwane, Nkosi, Makwela, Monama, and Vivian Ngubane) was Mavuthela's massively popular instrumental group. Sam Alcock talent-scouted and promoted the roster. (Albert Ralulimi, personal communication, November 1992.)

21 Recordings made noncommercially by and for the SABC for broadcast purposes. SABC did not copyright any of the material, though they did press records. While the SABC instituted this practice to generate material for programs for its rapidly expanding ethnically specific stations, producers and musicians used the service to test the potential popularity of new songs before producing them commercially.

West's discovery of Ladysmith Black Mambazo is a multiply storied moment, as is Bopape's retirement. This version is based on my interview with Albert Ralulimi (Johannesburg, November 1992).

22 Makgona Tsohle Band drummer, Lucky Monama, and bass player, Joseph Makwela, also became producers for Gallo at a later stage, though Makwela only briefly so.

23 From 1964—Mavuthela's beginning—the members of these groups were not consistent, though the Makgona Tsohle Band was remarkably stable. Neither was the Mahlathini-Mahotella Queens-Makgona Tsohle Band combination a stable threesome.

24 *Mathaka vol. 1 and 2* (Makgona Tsohle 1983), *Utshwala Begazati* (Amaswazi Emvelo and Mahlathini 1985), *Ejerusalema Siyakhona* (Mahlathini Namatshezulu 1986), *Thokozile* (Mahlathini and Mahotella 1987), *Melodi Yalla* (Queens only, Mahotella 1988), *Rhythm and Art* (Mahlathini and Mahotella 1989), *Music of our Soul* (with Colin Smith; Mahlathini and Mahotella 1990a), and *Paris–Soweto* (with Philippe Groux-Cibial; Mahlathini and Mahotella 1990b).

25 LPs at this time were principally intended for promotional purposes, as the market was singles oriented.

26 Their LP releases included *Izintombi Zesi Manje Manje* (1967b), *Kajeno* (1968), *Laduma Zesi Manje Manje* (1971), *Nomali* (1974 [1993]), *Umun'othulile* (re-released, 1993b), *Ho Buoa Morena* (1976), *Isitha Sami Nguwe* (1976 [1992]), *Ujabulisa Abantu* (1978 [1992]), *Boraditaba* (1979a), *Ha ke Dikela* (1979b), *Makoti wakena* (1980), *Umahlongwane* (1981), *Zenda Zangishiya* (1983), *Sematsatsa Sane* (1984), *Ke Lorile Balimo* (re-released, 1993a). The group enjoyed so much public attention that Zulu and Tswana versions of a number of their records were released. The release of different language versions of hit group recordings was an industry practice at the time.

27 Zesimanjemanje sings alone, without horns or male vocals, on side B.

28 Other artists and groups in Isibaya Esikhulu between 1966 and 1979 include mbaqanga frontlines Izintombi Zentuthuko, Amakhosazana, Amatshitshi, Amajongosi, Izintombi Zesibaya, S'Modern Girls (some of which were nontouring studio regroupings of others); backing and instrumental bands Abafana Besimanje, Nzimande All Stars, the Goldfingers, the Inn-Lawes; groaners Mthunzi Malinga, Mabhawodi Ndlovu, uSizwe, and Dingane Skosana; soul bands Amatayitayi, Abafana Bama-Soul, the Creedence Solid Quintet; sax jivers Hosia Moshupye and Jerry Mhlanga (also one of Isibaya's drivers); organist Solly Rametsi; violinist Noise Khanyile; emcee and announcer Nana Chiliza, and others. Some of these groups shared a pool of musicians. Various Zulu guitarists were also recorded during this time, but they were overshadowed by Phuz'ushukela.

Of Hamilton's 1970s GRC pool, three artists are internationally successful today: Izintombi Zesimanjemanje's Nobesuthu Shawe and Hilda Tloubatla are two of the current three Mahotella Queens and Abafana Bentuthuko drummer Phillemon Hamole played with the Makgona Tsohle Band. Other artists have struggled to maintain a musical career and livelihood part-time, or have returned to it full- or part-time: Jane and Janet Dlamini who sang as Isigqi Sesimanje in 1991–1992 were frontliners in Izintombi Zesimanjemanje from 1969 and 1987, respectively; groaner Dingane Skosana was trying to make a comeback with Nzimande in 1992, though his demo never materialized as a commercial product; unemployed bass player Moloi Lameke returned to the rehearsal rooms and studio to participate in Nzimande's 1991–1992 revival attempts; Isigqi's bass player, Bethwell Bhengu, played lead guitar with Isibaya 1972–1977 and bass with them again briefly in 1984.

29 Other mbaqanga groups with female frontlines rehearsing intermittently at this time include the Super Queens, Dingane Skosana's frontline; Amagugu AkwaZulu, who perform with Noise Khanyile; and later the group formed by Joana Thango who left Zesimanje in 1993 and took their reformed name, Isigqi Sesimanje, with her.

30 Zesimanjemanje's first two singles, "Pendula magwala" and "Uyawuz umoja makoti," were recorded in October 1967. They were marketed as "African Jazz Zulu Vocal" on GRC's AB label.

31 Other mbaqanga women singers and their producers likewise developed romantic relationships. Rupert Bopape married then–Mahotella Queen Irene Mawela; Isibaya's guitarist Hansford Mthembu married singer Thopi Mnguni. Mthembu and Mnguni eventually left Nzimande's production house and formed a new mbaqanga frontline, Amagugu Esimanjemanje, which Hansford produced.

   The professionally and socially gendered power play between celebrity mbaqanga producers and key female performers resonates structurally with similar relationships in the international female pop star arena. The risk that a producer and patriarch's sense of authority might spill over into domestic life, especially if the woman involved is significantly younger than her artistic boss, manager, and husband, is certainly present. The public image of these married singers as feted but controlled and artistically molded by their producer-manager-husbands further suggests that local mbaqanga practices emulated the styles of American girl groups, female soul stars, and foreign celebrity producers of the 1960s and 1970s.

32 In the 1960s, 1970s, and into the 1980s mbaqanga frontlines were all produced and managed by men. Now Jane is one of a few women who lead and manage their own groups. Nomsa Nene of the Super Queens, Thoko Mdlalose, and Joana Thango (from 1993) are others. I constructed Jane's biography from multiple conversations with her.

33 The five Mahotella Queens were Hilda Tloubatla, Mildred Mangxola, Nobesuthu Shawe, Juliet Masamisa, and Ethel Mgomezulu. On 1990s releases, Nobesuthu is listed as Nobesuthu Mbadu.

34 Rob Allingham provided the information on the Gallo party (personal communication, 9 June 2000).

35 *Mathaka*, Volumes One and Two (Makgona 1983/1990), *Utshwala Begazati* (Amaswazi 1985), *Ejerusalema Siyakhona* (Mahlathini Namatshezulu 1986), *Thokozile* (Mahlathini and Mahotella 1987 [1988]), *Melodi Yalla* (Mahotella 1988, Queens only), *Rhythm and Art* (Mahlathini and Mahotella 1989 [1990]), *Music of our Soul* (Mahlathini and Mahotella 1990a, coproduced with Colin Smith), and *Paris–Soweto* (Mahlathini and Mahotella 1990b). "Yebo" was a song collaboration with Britain's Art of Noise (Art of Noise 1989, mbaqanga remix by J. Jeczalik).

36 *Mbaqanga* (Mahlathini and Mahotella 1991b), *Women of the World* (Mahotella 1993, without Mahlathini, coproduced with Mike Pilot), *Stoki Stoki* (Mahlathini and Mahotella 1996), *Umuntu* (Mahlathini and Mahotella 1999a, produced by Moses Ngwenya), and *Sbai Bai* (Mahotella 2000).

37 Mahlathini, the Mahotella Queens, and the Makgona Tsohle Band did not burst onto the international scene out of the blue. Like most breaks that the industry and popular discourse sensationalize in this way, their

appearance on the stage and on new recordings was preceded by the international release of numerous compilations of South African musics, a number of which featured them. One such compilation, *The Indestructible Beat of Soweto* (1985), made it onto Billboard charts. Others that feature some or all of these artists include *Rhythm of Resistance* (1984), *Soweto Never Sleeps* (1986), *Thunder Before Dawn* (1987), *The Heartbeat of Soweto* (1988), *Freedom Fire* (1990), *The Kings and Queens of Township Jive* (1990), and *From Marabi to Disco* (1994). One CD entirely of Mahlathini et al. re-releases, *Putting on the Light* (Mahlathini and Mahotella 1984), was issued in the United States by the independent Rykodisc as early as 1984. Another, *Phezulu Eqhudeni* (Mahotella Queens, Mahlathini, and Other Stars 1984), which was released by Earthworks that same year, presented various lineup combinations of the Mahotella Queens, Mahlathini, and others with whom they recorded, as well as a track from the Mthunzini Girls.

Once Mahlathini et. al. had made an impression through their performances and new products, a number of compilations from their older albums were re-released on CD and distributed internationally, mostly through Earthworks and Shanachie. These include *Izibani Zomgqashiyo* (Mahotella 1989), *The Lion Roars* (Mahlathini and Mahotella 1991a), *King of the Groaners* (Mahlathini 1993), *Sixteen Original Sax Jive Hits* (Nkosi 1991, licensed through Sterns), and *Young Mahlathini: Classic Recordings with the Mahotella Queens 1964–1971* (Mahlathini and Mahotella 1999b).

Since then, other old mbaqanga songs and groups have also been collectively reissued on such CDs as *Phezulu Equdeni* (Mahotella 1984), *Soweto Never Sleep*s (Soweto 1986), *The Kings and Queens of Township Jive* (The Kings 1990), *Flying Rock* (Flying 1990, cassette issue only), *Dark City Sisters and Flying Jazz Queens* (Dark City 1993), *From Marabi to Disco* (From Marabi 1994). These groups include the Flying Jazz Queens, the Dark City Sisters, Irene and the Sweet Melodians, the Mgababa Queens, Izintombi Zomgqashiyo, and the Mthunzini Girls. None of these groups have (been) re-formed to record new products in the wake of these re-releases. Neither have they been recruited for foreign festival appearances, to my knowledge.

The market for re-releases and "roots" and "old" sounds expanded further with the issue of mbaqanga "predecessors." The most notable and famous among them, the Skylarks, which included the young Miriam Makeba, has appeared on compilations (e.g., *Township Swing Jazz! Vol. 1* [n.d.], *From Marabi to Disco* [1994]) and as a single issue, *Miriam Makeba and the Skylarks* (Makeba 1992). A cut from another "predecessor," Nancy Jacobs and Her Sisters, is included on *From Marabi to Disco*.

Izintombi Zesimanjemanje is starkly absent from the list of international mbaqanga rereleases—just one song appears on *From Marabi to Disco*—though GMP did reissue seven of their hit albums on cassette in the early 1990s for the domestic noncrossover market. These included *Isitha Sami Nguwe* (Izintombi 1976 [1992]), *Ujabulisa Abantu* (1978 [1992]), *Nomali* (1974 [1993]), *Umuntu'othulile* (1993), *Ke Lorile Balimo* (1993). Khanyile, jive violinist and Zulu guitarist, supported by the Jo'burg City Stars and his women's frontline Amagugu AkwaZulu, toured in Europe following the international release of *The Art of Noise* through Globestyle (Noise Khanyile 1989), although no further international releases followed this one.

38 "Lovely Lies," recorded in 1956 after Makeba's addition to the group, was the first South African entry onto the Billboard Top 100 (Allingham 1992).

39 Jane Dlamini, personal communication, August 1998.

40 Peter Ceronio, interview with me, January 1992, Randburg. Words enclosed within parentheses represent likely but uncertain transcriptions here and elsewhere in the text. Empty parentheses on the transcript mark inaudibility here and elsewhere.

41 Moses Dlamini speaking about the 1970s in an interview with me, 14 February 1992, Johannesburg.

42 The scene that follows is described, transcribed, translated, and edited from a fieldtape, 18 November 1991, Downtown Studios. All subsequent studio session conversations are likewise worked from fieldtape recordings made in 1991 and 1992, though they will not be cited.

43 These restrictions were specified by the Group Areas Acts. These acts, along with the Land Acts, which prohibited black ownership of land outside the "homelands," and the Registration of Voters Act, which prohibited black persons from voting, formed the central tenets of apartheid legal policy.

44 Detentions without trial, disappearances, torture, and police brutality are but some of the forms of violence that escalated dramatically with the intensification of the resistance within South African borders.

45 Radio Bantu had expanded to ten stations by the early 1980s (Hamm 1995, 230). Television was only instituted in South Africa in 1976. Radio access percentages quoted in the text originate in *A Study in Bantu Radio Listening* from 1974, quoted in Hamm 1986.

46 Isicathamiya recordings also proliferated during this era (Erlmann 1996b, 252–60).

47 The others were Strike Vilakazi, who worked for Trutone between 1952 and 1970; Cuthbert Matumba, who worked for Troubadour Records until 1965; and David Thekwane at Teal (1972–1984) (Allingham 1999, 640). The next generation of distinguished producers included West Nkosi, Marks Mankwane, and Lucky Monama, who all began by assisting Bopape; Moses Dlamini, who began by assisting Nzimande; Hansford Mthembu, originally an Isibaya Esikhulu artist who has produced for a low budget indie; Koloi Hendrik Lebona, who has successively freelanced for most of his production career; and Jimmy Mojapelo who produced for RPM Records. Since the mid- to late 1980s, the number and array of producers has increased along with the proliferation of small

recording studios and independent recording companies. This is in part due to changes in recording technology, as well as being a consequence of the post-*Graceland* promise of South African success, the breakdown of the cultural boycott, the explosion of the World Music market, and the presence of a developing local, black, professionally experienced, entrepreneurial class.

48   Elite Swingsters 1992. For their older sound, listen, for example, to the Air Light Swingsters's LP *Umhlobo'mdala* (Air Light 1981).

cut 2   The Recording Studio as Fetish

1   I translate *abelungu* (white people) as *whiteys* although this difference is not articulated in the Zulu utterance. *Whitey* in South Africa is similar in tone and positioning to gringo/a or honky in the United States. The idea of whitey is tinted with a naïveté that is assumed necessarily to be a consequence of white privilege.

2   *Via straight* is street language for "go directly."

3   Here I present a part of Allingham's memorializing narrative by foregrounding the history of the Gallo studios in his mix. The story of the studios is intricately tied to competition between record companies in Johannesburg, to the global expansion of multinationals into South Africa and domestic responses to their presence, and to advances in recording technology.

In 1912 Britain's Gramophone Company Limited sent the first portable field-recording unit to South Africa. At much the same time, commercial recording had also begun in other parts of the world in which European and North American powers had a colonial history or an entrepreneurial foothold (see Gronow and Saunio 1998).

Throughout the ensuing decades market developers weighed the efficiency of recording in situ against the sound quality they could achieve by recording in more technologically advanced centers. Though sound quality would be sacrificed, local recording meant a quicker release. From the 1920s into 1930s it was common to ship South African musicians back to the company's motherland for recording. This was true even for the Gramophone Company, which had its field-recording unit at hand. Recordings were shipped back to South Africa for sale (Allingham 1992).

The second mobile unit arrived in South Africa in 1930. This equipment belonged to Columbia Records, which by then was a chief rival in South Africa to HMV, a label owned by the Gramophone Company.

Foreign investors were fast laying claim to local spoils. In their midst, there was only one fledgling domestic wholesale music enterprise: Brunswick Gramophone House. Eric Gallo had opened this retail business in 1926 to distribute records from overseas. In the early 1930s he shifted into wholesale. Like his competitors, he sent musicians to

London to record. First, he shipped Afrikaans musicians to record for his new Singer label. Prompted by Columbia and HMV's successful activities in the African market, he soon expanded to include African musicians. Within two years, his company was forced to change its London-based recording practice, for the British enterprise with which it had a recording arrangement folded. In a savvy move, Eric Gallo recruited the now unemployed engineer of the company, John Hecdt, to come and build a studio in Johannesburg.

Here, in 1932, begins Downtown Studio's lineage. Allingham writes that Gallo's first studio was housed "in the basement of the Embassy, a 'bioscope-cafe' located around the corner from the Rissik Street post office on President Street. This was the first permanent recording facility in sub-Saharan Africa and possibly the first on the entire continent. Unfortunately, it proved impossible to properly isolate heavy traffic noise from the street outside so a second, more successful studio was built at 160 Market Street the following year. In 1938, a third, improved studio was built on the sixth floor of the new company premises on the corner of Troye and President Streets. This would remain in use for the next three decades producing thousands of recordings by the famous and obscure alike" (Allingham 1992).

By the late 1930s, the Gallo company was recording prolifically. But it did not remain free from domestic competition. In 1939 an entrepreneur named Llewelynn Hughes constructed a studio and two record presses in Johannesburg. These facilities gave Hughes an immediate advantage over Gallo in terms of production time, for Gallo was still shipping its masters off to Decca in the U.K. for pressing. Gallo, however, had the upper hand in terms of sound quality. This market rivalry continued to spur industrial development for both companies through the 1940s. (Though Hughes was a significant industry figure in the later 1930s and 1940s, his company did not grow into a huge multifaceted music business like Gallo's did.) Hughes sold La Fayette in 1945; Arthur Harris, its new owner, hired a trained sound engineer and constructed a new studio and manufacturing plant; within four years the quality of their product improved tremendously. Under the name of Trutone Industries—a name change effected in 1949—Harris's operation became a formidable competitor to Gallo, until in 1962 Gallo incorporated Trutone as a subsidiary (ibid.).

Throughout the 1950s, with Trutone as a vibrant competitor, Gallo's Singer label maintained its dominance and the company worked all possible corporate strategies to hold its position in the market. It cultivated loyalties with its smaller competitors; it matched its major rivals' innovations; it expanded its scouting and distribution area; it integrated related enterprises; and it restructured its corporate identity.

For example, when GRC, a family-owned retail business, moved into production in the 1940s, Eric Gallo provided some financial assistance in return for which GRC recorded most of its product at the Gallo studios.

When in 1947 Trutone began to dispatch field-recording units into rural areas, Gallo followed suit (ibid.). Gallo's field-recording efforts were decidedly lucrative. First, the company headed into the Rhodesias, then into Mozambique and Angola, and eventually it reached as far north as Uganda.

The key to success lay in the company's association with ethnomusicologist Hugh Tracey. Tracey's personal scholarly interest lay in documenting and preserving the subcontinent's traditional musics. Gallo lent him financial support for his archival work, with the understanding that Tracey would act informally as a talent scout for the company. Under this mutually beneficial arrangement, Tracey undertook numerous trips north over several years. Tracey's extensive recording for his own research purposes formed the basis for the International Library of African Music sound archives, now housed at Rhodes University in Grahamstown, South Africa. From Gallo's point of view, the arrangement generated such commercial success that the company eventually built permanent studios in Bulawayo and Nairobi. These were the first in then Southern Rhodesia and Kenya (ibid.).

In the midst of these market expansions, Gallo (Proprietary) Limited became a public company in 1946. With the increased financial base of the new Gallo Africa Limited, various capital improvements could be effected. The old direct disc-mastering system was replaced by tape-mastering machines, which enhanced the flexibility of their recording. Gallo constructed its first pressing plant that same year (1949) and soon started pressing long-playing vinyl discs (1952), which improved their reproduction. (Shellac discs had been introduced into the South African market by the American Columbia label in 1948.) By 1953 Gallo was issuing as many as one-and-a-half million discs of local music annually (ibid.).

Gallo Africa's studio facility had become a crucial cog in a burgeoning corporation that integrated production, manufacture, and distribution to form the leading music enterprise operating in Johannesburg in the mid-1960s.

4 One of EMI's local subsidiaries, Teal Records, was a prominent player throughout the 1950s and 1960s (Allingham 1999).

5 Calculation based on approximate exchange rate in 1992.

6 By the end of the decade, the Bop studios lay dormant.

7 Videolab was originally named Videosound when Teal, its parent company, moved out to this Randburg location. It became part of the Gallo group when Gallo bought Teal Trutone. Gallo also owns a tape-manufacturing plant (GIM), a videocassette-reproduction company (VCR), and a CD-manufacturing plant (CDT).

8 Some women apprentice at the South African Broadcasting Corporation and work as sound engineers there. None had moved into commercial recording by the early 1990s, though some of their male counterparts had, such as Downtown engineer Lee Short.

9 The studios are all fitted out with Dolby SR/A, JBL monitoring, and Studer A 827 tape machines. They have soft-front/hard-back acoustic design. The three main studios house different consoles: an SSL4048 G Series, a Sony, and a Harrison. A TS 12 Soundcraft console is installed in the sixteen-track Fostex studio. The digital editing suite features an Apple Mac and Digimix software.

10 Among the prized old equipment retained by the studio are Pultec EQPIA valve equalizers, a Manley variable MU stereo compressor, a Focusrite stereo equalizer, Neuman U67s, and AKGC12 valve microphones.

11 The South African Broadcasting Corporation was the second to install an SSL, although its use was restricted to the SABC until the late 1990s when producers began to book it on a freelancing basis.

12 Tom Porcello, personal communication, January 1995.

13 Low studio budgets range from approximately S.A. R4,500–14,000 (U.S. $1,500–$4,700). In contrast, West's prize domestic projects in 1991, reggae group O'Yaba and soul singer Walter D, each enjoyed R20,000 ($6,600) of studio work. The production budgets for Mahlathini and the Mahotella Queens would have been much higher than this. (U.S. dollar equivalents are based on the approximate currency exchange rate in 1991, the time of these productions.)

14 The red warning lights above the double studio doors are rarely used. The lights nevertheless mark a boundary. Porcello suggests that these lights are a holdover from an earlier recording era when sound editing was less sophisticated and interruptions could more easily ruin a take (personal communication, January 1996).

15 See T. Taylor 2001 for a fascinating look at the discursive and technological interfaces between music and the military-industrial complex in postwar America. While much postwar technology developed out of military research and design, it was first and foremost space research that captured the imagination of the public and that was used in advertising campaigns for music technologies of the era.

16 Howard Becker's *Art Worlds* (1982) foregrounds the interconnectedness of institutions involved with art production. Here I extend his idea.

17 *Rhythm of Healing*, Virgin Records (U.K.) and Earthworks (USA), Carol 2427-2, mastered in the British Chop 'em Out Studios, released 1992 "overseas" and at home.

18 Walter Benjamin (1968) means something different by *aura*, although my thinking is prompted by his work. Aura, for Benjamin, emanates from the actual physical presence of an original artwork. It is that presence and the time/space situation it brings to the artwork that compels attention to the artwork. I use the term more loosely to represent an unspecifiable but compelling quality of an object. That quality appears to be natural or spiritual. This is perhaps closer to Robert Plant Armstrong's "affecting presence" (1971). The monetary expense of studio technology also contributes to its aura.

19   For description of the structural details of soundproofing, see Munro 1994; Burd 1994; Huber and Runstein 1995; and Nardantonio 1990.

20   See again Munro 1994; Burd 1994; Huber and Runstein 1995; and Nardantonio 1990 for technical specification. The amount of leak-through is also affected by the choice of microphone and the settings selected on it, which determine the shape and dimensions of its pick-up pattern.

21   There are, of course, variations in the ideal specifications of the acoustic environment of recording booths versus the control room in terms of ambient noise, sound isolation, absorbency, and acoustic character. Additionally, those specifications are also in part determined by the type of recording project for which the studio is principally constructed. However, preference for a dry environment holds as a general principle, especially for productions and musics that are aesthetically engaged with the technological manipulation of sound (see, e.g., Burd 1994, 112–16).

22   Here my generalization glosses over the differences in aural skill of different kinds of music-makers. Sound engineers' ears, for example, are trained and developed in a particular way, notably to listen analytically to the minutiae of timbre and separation, whereas musicians often do not pick up these differences per se. Tensions over discrepancies in aurality do arise during studio sessions. They are often expressed as judgments of another's musicality. Tom Porcello's recounting of a troubled wind quintet session in a studio in San Marcos, Texas, illustrates the communicative complexities and value judgments that arise from discrepancies in aural points of reference (Porcello 1996, 191–228). *Golden Ears* (Moulton 1995), an eight-CD ear-training program designed to develop the aural acuity engineering requires, lays out timbral nuances in fine detail.

23   In most mbaqanga and trad sessions I witnessed, two bass lines were recorded simultaneously: a DI line inserted directly into the console and a mike line set up at the bass amp. The two were either combined in the mix or the miked track was discarded. The mike line could be used as a backup while it acted as a means of reassuring bass players, used to recording their music via their amps, that the sound engineer knew what was appropriate to the music.

24   He is referring to a demo cassette. Isigqi had given him a copy of a tape I recorded during rehearsal. Few groups have the opportunity or budget to produce professional demo tapes of their songs.

25   The tension is further troubled by the difficulties of rendering matters of musical hearing and sound into speech.

26   Composition of his own work is qualitatively different from production, in terms of his desire for protection and privacy. West was altogether more hesitant about my taping in the control room than other producers I asked. He deferred to Isigqi's executive producer, Ali Mpofu, when I

requested permission to tape Isigqi's production—the only studio production I taped with West, although I was present at many of his other sessions.

27 Despite their creative significance to twentieth-century music, technological gear, technological engagement, and studio production practices have rarely been addressed in music scholarship in any detail. In the 1980s when interest did begin to pick up, technology was lamented as a contaminating presence. A more positive, often celebratory discussion was first stimulated by the work of sociologists (Kealy 1979; Bennet 1980; Frith 1981) and culture and media studies scholars (Frith 1986; Hennion 1989; Théberge 1989). Keil's seminal thought piece, "Music Mediated and Live in Japan" (Keil and Feld 1994), originally published in 1983, is the single ethnomusicological voice directly addressing the issue in the early 1980s.

Ethnomusicology has been particularly slow to recognize the creative potential and semiotic nuance of technology in music making and to include its analysis within the field's interpretive frameworks. This is in part an outcome of the facts that ethnomusicologists have privileged live performance, expected technology to take away from both creative processes and from the experience of music, and have focused historically on musics that have, or seem to have, a life of their own outside the music industry. In recent years ethnomusicologists have acknowledged the presence of technology, and scholars have begun to adopt a more agent-centered approach to technology's processes by looking at how music practitioners make, manipulate, understand, and experience technology.

Most of this new work (which claims ethnography as fundamental to its approach) has examined the engagement with technology at the moment of staged and public performance or of "reception" (Waterman 1990; Manuel 1993; Walser 1993; Fox 1992; Fox 1996; Sutton 1996; Rasmussen 1996; Gay 1998; Lee 1999; Greene 1999; Greene 2001; and others). These discussions focus especially on issues of distortion, amplification, the juxtaposition of styles facilitated by electronics, and the technologies of reproduction and circulation. Moments of recording have been less considered. Part of the problem is that the studio—a critical compositional site—has historically been treated as the black box in analyses of production. That is to say, its popular representation as secret, magical, and unknowable has been taken at face value. As long as the studio was thought of as a site into which creative agents and compositional ideas would go, get compromised by technological manipulation there, then emerge packaged for consumption, there was little need for detailed analysis of its processes.

However, there are important texts that carved a way into the studio from different angles. Robert Faulkner's work (1971) on Hollywood studio musicians situates session musicians within the institution of the industry and nuances issues of power and control over music making in studio environments. Edward Kealy's paper (1979) recognized the sound engineer as an artist in his own right and tied this new status to technological evolutions. Herman Gray (1988) entered the studio as a media and popular culture studies scholar. Though he does not address issues of style or unpack technological processes during the recording procedure, his work introduces the studio as a socially constructed space. Keith Negus (1992, 1999) lays out the nonlinearity in the organization of music production and discusses the interplay of creativity and market management in the industry. Norman Stolzhoff (2000) articulates the studio as a primary site in the production of Jamaican dance-hall culture. Thomas Porcello (1996, 1998) details studio discourse and artistry with a focus on sound engineers in the first extended and ethnographic study of the studio. Writing as a linguistic anthropologist, ethnomusicologist, and audio engineer, he develops an anthropology of production that places issues of music style and language poetics at the center of the study of the relationship between power, technology, and creativity. Along with Paul Théberge (1997), Porcello argues for a focus on sound, socially situated, rather than music, more narrowly conceived, as the object of study. He shows the studio to be at once a mundane workspace for sound engineers and a rarefied entity in the popular press. Sound engineers have also been recognized for their artistry in the popular press, with publications such as Richard Buskin's series of interviews (1991), and those by Terri Stone (1992).

While the scholars above began to develop ethnographic treatments, others such as Michael Chanan (1995), Théberge (1997), Mark Cunningham (1998), and Timothy Taylor (2001) have reexamined music histories, introducing technologies as a crucial component in the theorization of music styles and practices. Taylor combines field research and historical work. He argues for a practice-theory approach, with a focus on the relationship between people using technology for expressive purposes and the shifts in technological design and organization. While not studio-specific themselves, these works collectively contribute to studio research in their sophisticated theoretical thinking about technology and by drawing attention to a different way of listening to sound at the level of timbre.

28 Rainbow Records folded in 1993–94.

29 As Porcello has commented, this exacerbation is in direct contrast to the popular rhetoric that celebrates the new MIDI-based studio technology as a democratizing move (personal communication, January 1996). As the prices of the equipment drop, the rhetoric hurrahs that now anyone can have a studio in the backyard.

For other discussions of how access to technology is empowering (or lack of it disempowering), see, for example, Frith 1991; Jowers 1993; Keil and Feld 1994; Fox 1996; and Samuels 1998.

30 The recording became *Buyisani Lomswani* (Ntuli 1991). Ntuli performs under the name Unganeziyamfisa Ntuli. Mhlongo is not credited as the

assistant producer on the album, although he worked in this capacity to some extent, and sat in the producer's chair throughout recording.

31 This was being recorded onto a two-inch analog master tape, so bringing the pitch register down to facilitate the recording process was not a viable option.

32 Hierarchies also exist among sound engineers. They celebrate and admire the top sound designers overseas as they do their most virtuosic colleagues who can "get any sound out of that desk!" The best technicians are stars within the world of engineering. Studying in the U.K., "You actually see the guy who made an SSL, actually teaching you how to work it! He'll teach you major major big problems that you can encounter on an SSL and he'll tell you straightforward, 'I made *this* to correspond with *that.*'" Engineer Humphrey Mabote breaks from his customarily calm posture to gesticulate *this* and *that,* here and there. "And the guys who made the Mitsubishi digital machines, they are all there!" His forearm sweeps across an imaginary crowd of celebrities. "You know, actually I'm talking of the big guys."

33 At any one time a large percentage of the adult male population of the independent kingdom of Lesotho is working in South Africa as migrant labor, mostly on the mines. By saying that the musicians come "straight from the hills," Peter is referring to the fact that Lesotho is a small mountainous predominantly rural country. By *kraal*, he means a rural African homestead; this Afrikaans word literally refers to a cattle and goat pen, usually a centrally located feature of a rural homestead. The blankets he refers to are patterned blankets wrapped around from the shoulders, which mark a popularized image of the Sotho, coming from the cold, rural highlands. The walking/fighting stick, often decorated, is another "tribal" marker, one that is shared with other ethnic groups.

34 *Nê:* Afrikaans question form implying a positive response is anticipated.

cut 3 Producing Liveness

1 By asking for a sequenced riff he is asking the sound engineer to program a short rhythmic-melodic motive to repeat itself successively.

2 See Erlmann 1996b on the preponderance of the bass in Zulu music.

3 Lindemann engineered three hit albums for Thomas Chauke: *Simatsatse no.7, Simatsatse no.8, Simatsatse no.9,* Tusk Records.

4 In the rural KwaZulu-Natal midlands, for example, fans listen to music on radios, cassette players, and on decks hooked up to car batteries. There are occasional festivals in the district, usually in nearby townships. Here and there televisions are to be found—for example, in trade stores along the main road.

5 Max Weber ([1921] 1958), Eric von Hornbostel (1928), and Curt Sachs ([1961] 1965) are famous and striking proponents of this theory.

6 West's replacement of the Korg organ sound with synthesized marimba is not without precedent in Isigqi's sound repertoire. On Izintombi Zesimanjemanje's 1985 disco maxi single, a song celebrating Africa, "The Biggest Show in Africa," uses synth marimba (Izintombi and Seoka 1985). Other groups likewise had begun to integrate the marimba sound into their tracks. Toms and congas had started to appear with the use of drum machines.

7 Their social difference is never fully erased. During the entire production, Tefo and Janet never directly address Peter and rarely express themselves in a language that he can understand and participate in.

8 Similar riffs appear on songs of Mahlathini, the Mahotella Queens, and the Makgona Tsohle Band recorded after their international break, though the sound is softened, warmed, and buried in the mix: "Won't you please sing along" (Rhythm and Art, 1989), "Vuya" (Mbaqanga, 1991b), "Sibali" (Stoki Stoki, 1996), and "Malaika" (Women of the World, Mahotella 1993).

9 The encounters that "liveness" proposes as somehow "real" lend the recording a peculiar property. When the relations of production are no longer transparent, the aura of the commodity itself is enhanced, for the commodity takes on some of the significance that would have been placed in the relations themselves (Tim Taylor contributed this point). For Marx, the social relations of production are increasingly obscured in the march toward modernity (see Sayer 1987); in the studio, such relations are additionally masked through creative technological manipulation by means of which face-to-face encounters come to be represented.

10 West is referring to the LM-1 drum computer designed by Roger Linn.

11 The LM-1 was followed by two new designs—the LinnDrum and the Linn 9000 (a sequencer/drum machine)—before Linn was bought out by AKAI in 1986. (See M. Vail 2000 [289–93] for further details on Linn gear.)

12 Peter reports that Isigqi's recording was the last project on which he worked with West using the original Linn. It had been on loan to the studios. When its owner retrieved it, West moved on to using more updated equipment.

13 West is not alone in prizing the LM-1 and dismissing the Linn 9000, though his reasons for valuing the instrument are somewhat eccentric. Mark Vail opines that the LM-1 had a feel that later machines have not equaled. He places its unique quality in its shuffle feature, which seemed to give tracks better swing than other drum machines could. The Linn 9000, he says, was "forward-looking but ill-fated" (M. Vail 2000, 291–93).

14 For example, minute headphones replace clunky monitor speakers and cordless mikes or headmounted mikes replace meters and meters of cable and microphone stands across the front of the stage.

15 Here popular and scholarly discourse reproduce the authenticity debate in 1970s folklore theory, epitomized by Richard Dorson's distinction be-

tween "folkore" and "fakelore" (1976). In his view, "fakelore" character-izes expressive practices that are contaminated by their interaction with the market and with hegemonic forms.

16 See T. Taylor 2001 for examples and discussion of electronica substyles where authenticity is simply not an issue associated with creative engagement with technology.

17 The assumption behind being from a place like Swaziland in the context of Darryl's talk is that the musician is rurally located, therefore more "tribal" and "traditional" than he or she would be were he based in Johannesburg.

18 Not all sound engineers would agree with him. Some of those that do might disagree with the extent to which he is prepared to push the point.

19 He is referring to the mbira or kalimba, various versions of which are played across the continent. It is also known by other names (see Berliner 1981). It is not an instrument traditional to the Zulu.

20 Similar patterns may well be apparent in other recording situations in which the social discrepancies between studio music-makers are stark, especially in other places outside the main centers of production (Wallis and Malm 1984) or in places with a history of colonial racism, for example, Australia and the Western/Central Pacific (Breen 1992; Hayward 1998; Hayward 1999).

21 Looking to African Americans and the United States for stylistic innovation has a long history. See Erlmann 1991 for meticulous documentation of the intricacies of the historical link between African Americans and black South Africans in choral music. See Ballantine 1993 for connections in terms of marabi and early jazz recordings and metadiscourse.

22 An array of MIDI keyboards has followed the popular DX7.

23 Here he means that the styles differed in performance practices.

24 Tefo Sikale and Bethwell Bhengu, personal communication, July 1998.

25 See Feld 1994, Erlmann 1996a.

cut 4 Sounding Figures

1 This is an image of diversity rather than diversity itself (Erlmann 1994; also Feld 1994).

2 "Jealousy" on *Eye for an Eye* (Splash 1991).

3 Mbaqanga musicians do appreciate the exceptional township pop musicians, singers, and songs. For example, singers Brenda Fassie and Yvonne Chaka Chaka invariably elicited admiration. Chaka Chaka's lyrics were also singled out as exceptional.

4 "Oxygène" is a recording by composer, producer, and electronic keyboardist Jean Michel Jarre. The original work (1976) was later remixed. Oxygène is a large-scale work that combines ambient and orchestrated-sounding electronic music. In his public presentations of his work, Jarre

often combines soundtracks with laser- and fireworks displays in huge open-air performances.

Alan Parsons was an in-house engineer at Abbey Road Studios, who engineered the Beatles and Pink Floyd. He later became a recording artist himself, recording with the Alan Parsons Project. See Cunningham 1998 and Buskin 1991 for interviews with him about his sound and recording procedures.

5   There is an expanding literature that notes or discusses the stylistic transference from indigenous instruments onto the guitar in southern, west, and central Africa. See, for example, Rycroft 1977; Low 1982; Waterman 1990; Brown 1994; wa Mukuna 1994; Davies 1994; Schmidt 1994; Kaye 1998; Charry 2000; and Turino 2000.

6   The musical bow, such as the *umakhwenyana*, is a one-stringed bow with a resonating calabash attached. The string is either struck or bowed. See Impey 1983 for stylistic exegesis.

7   That these styles were so prolifically recorded in the 1970s is in part due to the proletarianization and urbanization of South Africa's massive labor force that, in a sense, defined the decade (Moodie 1994).

8   See Davies 1994 for an explication of maskanda's musical features. For discussions of contemporary maskanda see Olson 2000 and 2001. For a broad view that positions maskanda in the industry, see Allingham's overview of "neotraditional" styles in Allingham 1999, 646–47.

9   Tsongan music in South Africa has thus far remained scantily researched and documented.

10 The influence of church music is prominent on "Ukuhlupeka kwami," the second track of the album. This ballad follows hymnlike chordal progressions and a churchlike choral singing style. A largely homophonic organ part, played with wide vibrato, is prominent in the accompaniment. The lyrics express suffering.

11 The international and local markets of course do not overlap in terms of production quality and studio time afforded them.

12 *Rhythm of Healing* (Nkosi 1992).

13 *Simatsatse No.10* (Chauke 1990).

14 Jane notes that another marker of Marks's guitar style is that he plays a busy lead.

15 Forms that instantiate blackness and whiteness in sound are multiple and varying. In British dance clubs, white youth interpret music and dance styles as black if they appear to be grounded in a place and centered on the body and the voice, whereas white styles are those that celebrate and feature hi-tech sound and minimize the presence of the person or place. This discursive distinction bears little resemblance to who the artists actually are, where they are produced, what the style is, or where its history lies (S. Thornton 1995, 71–76).

16 A theatrical role could be developed out of multiple figures.

17 Ethnographic analyses linking music discourse and sense owe much to

the interpretive anthropological work on music of the 1980s. I think especially of work that considers relationships among music, language, thought, other aesthetic domains, and experience (Feld 1990; Roseman 1991; Seeger 1987; and others). Earlier philosophical work considering "meaning" and symbol in EuroAmerican music, such as Zuckerkandl 1956 and Schutz 1967, has also offered important insights.

18 Scholars are well on the way to dismantling the theoretical models of production and consumption as discreet entities and of the production-consumption process as a linear one (e.g., Frith 1991; Negus 1992; Porcello 1996; Théberge 1997; Negus 1999; Mahon 2000; T. Taylor 2001). In these mbaqanga studio sessions, there are multiple instances that demonstrate that practices of consumption are integrated into moments of production. For one, artists imagine their listeners while recording. At times they anticipate the moment of dance while they shape the music. They also weigh up the "tastes" of their target market constituencies. More subtly, bringing figures garnered from the street and the media back into studio sound plays a part in blurring the theoretical boundaries between pre- and post production and among the conception, recording, and consuming of music.

cut 5   Performing Zuluness

1 Percival Kirby documents that a double-sided, cyclindrical drum, which had thongs lacing the skin heads together, was played in the Zulu Rebellion in 1906. It hung around the drummer's neck and was played with padded drumsticks. He calls this drum *isigubu* and convincingly argues that it was an imitation of the British military bass drum (1968, 44–46). The idea of the bass drum has been integrated into Zulu dance for a century.

2 On ngoma style see Tracey 1952; on the organization of its practice see Thomas 1988; on its domestication by mining and municipal officials see Erlmann 1991; on its history, military associations, and class and ethnic divisiveness see Clegg 1982; la Hausse 1984; and Marks 1989.

3 West produced three Umzansi recordings, though in the end they were only released on the domestic market (Umzansi 1988; Umzansi 1991; Umzansi 1994). The group has subsequently released three more, produced by team leader Siyazi Zulu (Umzansi 1997; Umzansi 1998; Umzansi 1999).

4 Once married, women in rural KwaZulu-Natal no longer dance in public.

5 He uses the rounded vowel sound /u/ to perform the roundedness of the timbre. He frames the vowel with a hard initial consonant, a velar stop /k/, to give it a sharp attack and a nasalized /m/ to imitate an extended delay and a scoop at the bottom of the sound. Later in the discussion he substitutes the voiced dental /d/ for the /k/. "Ku dum!"

6 *Ipitombi* was produced by Billy Forest and Lofty Shultz. In London the show played at the West End for over a year (September 1975–November 1976) and in New York on Broadway for several months in 1977. Though hailed inside the theater in New York, it was met with vocal criticism from anti-apartheid picketers outside (Lindfors 1999). See Coplan 1985 (217–19), Anderson 1981 (100–101), and Lindfors 1999 for further information. In the late 1990s *Ipitombi* was revived and played in Australia. A CD and video of this production has been released.

7 *Amahubo* (clan praises sung by men) are regarded as the highest prestige form of Zulu performance arts (see Joseph 1983). Within the wedding song repertoire, the *ikondlo* is the principle form in which the bride sings about her lineage and about leaving her home. This most-rehearsed moment of the wedding is a "subsidiary" of the *ihubo* genre (Xulu 1992). Joseph gives a more detailed account of the types of wedding songs within the ceremony. After the solemn ikondlo, other, more playful dance songs follow in which contentions over *lobola* (bridewealth payments in cattle) are a major subject of the parties' jesting (Joseph 1983).

8 There are regional distinctions in how weddings are conducted, and there is a range of blended traditional and Christian ceremonies. Simultaneous competitive singing between the bride's and groom's parties is widespread. The songs popularized in the music industry take their name from what Musa Khulekani Xulu calls *izingoma zemishado* (modern wedding songs). These, he says, are the wedding songs sung in the townships, where traditional and Christian ceremonial practices are usually mixed (Xulu 1992).

9 *Isencane* (Platform One 1990). *Vaal Express* (Makoti 1991) was another, produced by Koloi Lebona and Mduduzi Masilela. In addition to opening a space for wedding-song music on the youth market, Blondie and African Youth Band's success also spawned other *mzabalazo* (protest song) releases after the unbanning of the organizations of the liberation movement and the release of Mandela in 1990. The post-1990 timing of these releases made overt alignments to political platforms and the addition of lyrics possible—for example, Amaqabane 1990 (ANC), Mayibuye 1990 (PAC), and Inkatha Youth Band 1991 (IFP).

10 Kraal: cattle and goat pen (Afrikaans).

11 Wire-wire: power lines (black South African colloquialism).

12 West hitches a grammatically appropriate Zulu prefix onto the Afrikaans word *klok*.

13 The Afrikaans word for a bell is *klok*. Predominantly Afrikaans-speaking regions in the north and central part of South Africa overlap with predominantly Sotho-speaking regions; hence the conflation for Tefo. Additionally, Afrikaans is used over English in the multilinguistic mines where code switching and mixing of languages is pervasive and complex.

14 Note that this negotiation is over a question of representation and form

in the lyrics. It is not an altercation over the manipulation of the sound itself. Isigqi—especially the women—neither intervened so vociferously and directly on microlevel issues concerning the timbre, texture, balance, and mix, nor were they granted the same space to do so. To effect sonic/technological changes, they worked indirectly through persuasion—"You'll put me back when we were stars"—or by simply playing the way they wanted it to go, as Nogabisela did when he reset his guitar amp after Lee took control at the console.

15 It gambles with the market of the youth at the same time.

16 This did not proceed without power struggles internal to the IFP.

17 The Witwatersrand is the major industrial and mining region of the country. It includes Johannesburg and Soweto. The majority of Zulu migrants who do not work within the KwaZulu-Natal province migrate to the Witwatersrand to work.

18 For documentation of conflicts in Natal, 1986 into the early 1990s, see for example Aitchison 1989; Osborn 1991; Louw 1991, 1992; Minnaar 1992; and Howe 1993. For documentation of the violence on the Witwatersrand in 1990–1992, see for example Minnaar 1992, 1993.

19 On this particular march they were protesting the planned fencing of the all-male Zulu migrant residential hostels and the then recent ban on the carrying of traditional weapons in public.

20 Based on their research in KwaZulu-Natal, Mary de Haas and Paulus Zulu report that the IFP's appeals to Zulu ethnicity in the 1980s and early 1990s were not wholeheartedly embraced. Some people who identified deeply with a sense of Zuluness distanced themselves from the IFP for various reasons. De Haas and Zulu highlight the following reasons: (1) that the IFP was regarded by some as an arm of the apartheid state and even as having administered the system's policies particularly badly; (2) that violence, including that inflicted by the KwaZulu police, alienated some potential IFP supporters; (3) that Buthelezi was regarded by some as having illegitimately usurped the position of the Zulu king (1993).

21 See Segal 1991, Minnaar 1993, and Sitas 1996 for details of how hostels developed from relatively cooperative and peaceful multiethnic residences into single-ethnicity barracks, predominantly for Zulus. See James 1999 for the impact on Pedi male migrants and their *kiba* performance practice. See Chimeloane 1998 for a firsthand account of hostel life.

22 See, for example, Minnaar 1993 and Segal 1991.

23 Forty people were killed in an attack on a funeral vigil in Sebokeng (12 January 1991); twenty-eight were killed in an attack on the Swanieville squatter settlement (12 May 1991); twenty-one at the Crossroads settlement outside Cape Town (3 April 1992); and thirty-nine at the Boipatong massacre (17 June 1991). The Boipatong incident provoked enormous outrage on the Witwatersrand. Vigilantes originating in KwaMa-

dala hostel went on the rampage in the ANC-aligned squatter camp alongside it. These are only the deadliest of a host of attacks during 1991 and 1992. (Minnaar 1993, 63).

24 Diepkloof hostel was razed to the ground in a violent confrontation.

25 Let me stress that this conflict is historically situated and not an onto-logical condition of black South Africans, who experience these multiple tensions largely as haphazard or gratuitous violence in their everyday lives. I emphasize this in order to clarify that I am reporting on local violence here in order to demonstrate how aesthetic production can amplify or diminish conflict and asymmetrical relationships of difference.

26 See de Haas and Zulu 1993 for elaboration on some reasons for their IFP membership. See Minnaar 1993 (63, 66) for elaboration on how various Zulu-speakers and hostel residents become implicated in violence without being IFP-ideologues.

27 Aired on Ezodumo, the weekly Zulu music video program. At this time, TV2 was one of four language-specific television stations. The SABC subsequently restructured and increased the number of channels after the elections in 1994.

28 One example: a cassette of Inkatha songs, *Theleweni*, was released (Inkatha Youth Band 1991). The song arrangements are styled similarly to the ANC-aligned *Ntate Modise* (Amaqabane 1990) and the PAC-aligned *Thina Maqabane* (Mayibuye 1990), cassettes that preceded *Theleweni*'s release.

29 See Minnaar 1993, Howe 1993, and Louw 1992 for overviews of the violence in these regions.

30 Belief in the primacy of Zulu ethnicity is shared by many who identify with Zuluness themselves, as well as by those distanced from it. Jane explained to me once that of all people in the world, Africans know best how to dance. But among Africans, none dance as well as Zulus. She referred in this instance to Isigqi's dance style as Zulu. For her, Zuluness is the epitome of Africanness.

cut 6 Imagining Overseas

1 Mahlathini and the Mahotella Queens's 1991 recording *Mbaqanga* occurred before the SSL console had been installed at Downtown Studios.

2 Michael sings a second alto part, which is usually sung by a woman. He originally joined the band as the drummer but switched into the frontline when one of the singers left.

3 Mahlathini does not sing with the Mahotella Queens and the Makgona Tsohle Band on *The Lion of Soweto* (Mahlathini 1987), because he had broken with Gallo at the time of the original recording (1970s) and hence did not work with Gallo artists. Instead, a frontline called the Queens and a backing called the Mahlathini Guitar Band accompanied him.

4　The "lion skin" that Pepper refers to is the *ibheshu*, a Zulu man's cow-hide apron, which hangs from the waist down over the buttocks, and the *isinene*, a frontal loin covering.

5　For example, compare the versions of the song "Mahlalela" on Indoda Mahlathini 1975 and on Mahlathini 1987. This is only one possible step in a complex remastering process.

6　For an explication of the rapid expansion of radio services and the presence of rock-and-roll and jazz recordings in South Africa, see especially Hamm 1986, 1988, 1991. See also Coplan 1985.

7　Sipho Madondo was one of the lead singers of West's popular Swazi traditional group, Amaswazi Emvelo, which recorded in the 1980s.

8　Among more widely traveled artists, this is a distinction especially of the United States.

Final Mix

1　I draw here on Susan Stewart's contrast between the miniature and the gigantic (1993), though the contrast between the studio and overseas do not bear much further similarity to her discussion.

2　The Kruger National Park is the largest wildlife reserve in South Africa. It is owned by the state and named after Paul Kruger (1825–1904), president of the Transvaal Republic (1883–1900).

Print-Through

1　Print-Through is titled with reference to Porcello 1998. (See also my glossary for his articulation of the concept.)

2　Given the currency of new-age notions of multiculturalism and musical universality, one needs to be concerned about unexamined issues of exploitation that creep into international music exchanges, whether through calculation or naive oversight. I am troubled by the lack of sensitivity on the part of Middfest to the circumstances of many of their foreign artists, and indeed, by the organization's reluctance to remunerate artists who perform at Middfest International. A volunteer explained that the organization operates under the assumption that the states of those countries featured at the festival will support the artists who represent them. However, not all artists who appear are invited through state channels, and therefore not all artists are remunerated for their professional services at the festival.

Glossary

amabheshu   Zulu men's cowhide aprons worn over the buttocks. (ibheshu, sing. Zulu)

cans   headphones, in studio talk.

chorusing   "an effect where the audio signal is given multiple delays so as to sound like several instruments playing at once. The delay times are short, typically 20–45 milliseconds, and each delayed signal may be pitch-shifted. The effect is similar to hearing a 'chorus,' where everyone is singing the same thing but at slightly different times and pitches." (Bohn 1995)

click track   an electronic metronome track. A steadily repeated, high-pitched "click" is piped into the recording musicians' headphones to keep them playing absolutely in time with the previously recorded and programmed tracks of the song.

compressor   "a signal processing device used to reduce the dynamic range of the signal passing through it. . . . Sound engineers set a threshold point such that all audio below this point is unaffected, and all audio above this point is compressed by the amount determined by the ratio control. . . . Applications have evolved where compressors are [also] used in controlling the creation of sound. For example when used in conjunction with microphones and musical instrument pick-ups, compressors help determine the final timbre by selectively compressing specific frequencies and waveforms. Common examples are 'fattening' drum sounds, increasing guitar sustain, vocal 'smoothing,' and 'bringing up' specific sounds out of the mix, etc." (Bohn 1995; see also G. White 1991)

converter box   instrument that enables the synchronization of analog and digital devices by converting voltage fluctuations into digital information. It is hooked up to a MIDI clock.

decay   refers to the "manner in which a sound ceases" (Huber and Runstein 1995, 40). It is one of four points in the duration of any audio signal, which comprises an attack, decay, sustain, and release. Thus, decay (or initial decay) refers to the rate of reduction of the signal from the peak level of the attack to the sustain level. The release can also be termed the final decay. There are three variables that can be manipulated in shaping a decay: the time duration, amplitude, and amplitude variation with time. The character of an electronically produced sound is shaped in part by controling these features. (See Huber and Runstein 1995)

delay   an exact replica of a signal is added to its original, played simultaneously but with the onset of the replica milliseconds behind that of the original. The timing of the delay can be set by the sound engineer. Delay circuitry is built into most effects units and is fundamental to reverb, echo, flanging, phasing, and other processes. (See Bohn 1995)

dolby   a noise-reduction system developed by Ray Dolby that has become the international standard for master-tape preparation. There are four system types: Dolby SR and A are used in professional production facilities; Dolby B and C are for consumer systems. (See Huber and Runstein 1995)

drum box/drum machine   a computer designed to reproduce drum and percussion tracks electronically. A number of basic sounds are preset by the manufacturer. The sound engineer selects and combines the sounds, manipulates their timbres, programs rhythms, and synchronizes them with other recorded and programmed tracks using MIDI technology.

echo plate   the analog echo plate is comprised of a large steel plate suspended in a cabinet (usually eight by four foot). An audio signal drives an element attached to the plate, that in turn sets the plate in motion. The plate's motion is picked up by contact microphones. Because the plate's reverberation time after a signal is several seconds long, unless dampened mechanically, it adds a warm, metallic echo to a sound signal. The analog echo plate is almost obsolete. It has been replaced by an "echo plate" setting on a digital reverb unit.

echo unit   an electronic unit that adds the effect of an echo or of repeated echoes to a sound. The length and decay of the echo cycle, and the time between each repeat playback is programmable.

EQ   in-house abbreviation for "equalization." When a sound engineer EQs a sound, he or she boosts and/or cuts the volume of selected frequency bands of that signal as it travels through the recording console, thereby changing the shape of the composite signal and the timbre of the sound.

exciter/enhancer   "a term referring to any of the popular special-effect signal processing products used primarily in recording and performing. All exciters work by adding harmonic distortion of some sort. Various means of generating and summing frequency-dependent and amplitude-dependent harmonics exist. Both even- and odd-ordered harmonics find favorite applications. Psychoacoustics teaches that even-harmonics tend to make sounds soft, warm and full, while odd-harmonics tend to make things metallic, hollow and bright. Lower-order harmonics control basic timbre, while higher-order harmonics control the 'edge' or 'bite' of the sound." (Bohn 1995)

expander a device that complements compressors. It is used to increase the dynamic range of a signal. A threshold point is set by the engineer so that only sounds below that threshold are affected. (See Bohn 1995; Huber and Runstein 1995)

faders the sliding controls on a recording console with which the sound engineer adjusts the volume of each recording channel or recorded track.

flanging a process that mixes a direct audio signal with one or two de-layed replicas, and continuously varies the time relationship between them. This effects continuous timbral changes in the sound, creating a "shwooshing" effect. Flanging was popularized in 1960s pop music. (See Bohn 1995; G. White 1991; Huber and Runstein 1995)

graphic equalizer, parametric equalizer a graphic equalizer uses slide controls to adjust the amplitude of frequency bands. It is "named for the positions of the sliders 'graphing' the resulting frequency response of the equalizer" (Bohn 1995). With a parametric equalizer, which uses rotary or slide controls, more features of the equalization process can be controlled. In addition to manipulating the amplitude, the engineer can select the size of the bandwidth to be equalized at one time and shift its center frequency. (ibid.; see also G. White 1991)

ibheshu see *amabheshu*.

ibhodlo (n.); ukubhodla (vb) to bellow, roar, burp. Local Zulu term for the vocal delivery style of Mahlathini and other mbaqanga bass lead singers like him.

isicathamiya Zulu choral music sung by migrant and working-class men. The central performance practice consists of all-night competitions. (See Erlmann 1996)

izidwaba women's short skirts, traditionally pleated leather kilts. (isidwaba, sing. Zulu)

izigqoko married women's wide, flat-topped, brimless hats. (isigqoko, sing. Zulu)

kwela South African pennywhistle music of the 1950s. (See Allen 1999)

limiter "a device used to keep signal peaks from exceeding a certain level in order to prevent the clipping or distortion of amplifier signals, re-corded signals on tape or disc, broadcast transmission signals, and so on" (Huber and Runstein 1995, 475). Limiters can also be used to create special effects, especially in the recording of vocals. (See G. White 1991) *marabi*   urban music style developed in the 1920s and 1930s. (See Ballantine 1993)

maskandi   singer-instrumentalist who plays in the traditional Zulu style (omaskandi, pl.). Male maskandi most usually play guitar, concertina, or violin. Women play the mouth-organ or musical bow in the same style. The music they play is termed *maskanda*. (See Davies 1994; Allingham 1999, 646–47; Olson 2000; Olson 2001)

MIDI   Musical Instrument Digital Interface. "A digital communications language and compatible hardware specification that allows multiple electronic instruments, performance controllers, computers, and other related devices to communicate with one another within a connected network." (Huber and Runstein 1995, 475)

MIDI *clock*   an instrument that synchronizes sequencers, drum machines, and outboard effects.

multitracking   the division of magnetic tape into separated synchronous bands enables the recording and playback of different sound sources onto isolated tracks. This means that different instrumental or vocal parts can be recorded individually, that they can be individually examined in playback, and that they can be re-recorded without affecting all the other already-recorded parts.

ngoma   Zulu male competitive dance, in part choreographed and in part individually improvised. The central feature is high kicking and heavy stamping. (See Tracey 1952; Clegg 1982; Thomas 1988; Erlmann 1991)

noise gate   a type of expander that is "used extensively for controlling unwanted noise, such as preventing 'open' microphones and 'hot' instrument pick-ups from introducing extraneous sounds into the system" (Bohn 1995). The sound engineer sets a threshold point above which the gate "opens" and below which it "closes," thereby shutting out extraneous noise. Noise gates operate between incoming signals and the console. In addition to diminishing noise, gates can be used to enhance the percussive effect of a sound. "Judicious setting of a noise gate's attack (turn-on) and release (turn-off) times adds 'punch,' or 'tightens' the percussive sound, making it more pronounced." (ibid.)

noise-reduction machine   system that minimizes noise produced by analog tape, amplifier self-noise, and extraneous noise from long-distance transmissions. It does so by compressing a signal before recording and expanding it on playback, thereby suppressing background noise while keeping the signal unaffected. DBX noise-reduction units are fitted between the console and the tape machine. Dolby systems operate on the master tape. (See Huber and Runstein 1995; Daniel, Mee, and Clark 1999)

outboard gear   signal-processing and other devices that are external to the mixing console.

overdubbing a recording procedure that "enables one or more of the previously recorded tracks to be monitored while simultaneously recording
one or more signals onto other tracks. This process can be repeated until
the song or soundtrack has been built up. If a mistake is made, it generally is a simple matter to re-cue the tape to the desired starting point
and repeat the process until you have the best take on tape." (Huber and
Runstein 1995, 477)

patcher/patch bay "a panel that, under the best of conditions, contains
a jack corresponding to the input and output of every discrete component or group of wires in the control room. It acts as a central point
where console signal paths, pieces of audio gear and other devices can
be connected." (Huber and Runstein 1995, 477)

phaser/phase shifter "a device which gives an effect similar to flanging
but with less depth. [The delay time is set to be very short, in contrast
to the delay time of flanging.] Phasing works by shifting the phase of a
signal and adding it back to the signal. This causes partial cancellation
at frequencies where the phase shift approaches 180 degrees." (G. White
1991, 244)

pitch shifting changing the pitch of a sound or set of sounds without
changing any other parameters. Thus the timbre, duration, and tempo
remain unaffected.

print-through a "characteristic of magnetic (analog) tape, whereby any
stored signal is transferred through adjacent layers when the tape is
wound on a reel" (Porcello 1998, 485). Traces of the transferred signal
will be audible on playback.

punch-in/punch-out in order to fix a tiny mistake without retaking a
whole track, an artist plays or sings along with the recorded tracks. At
the right microsecond, the engineer "punches" her or him in to record
over the mistake, then punches her or him out again. That is to say, the
engineer activates and then deactivates the record mode.

reverberation (reverb) "the persistence of a signal, in the form of reflected
waves in an acoustic space, after the original sound has ceased. These
closely spaced and random multiple echoes result in perceptible cues to
size and surface materials of a space and add to the perceived warmth
and depth of recorded sound. Reverb plays an extremely important
role, both in the enhancement of our perception of music and in proper
studio design." (Huber and Runstein 1995, 479)

reverb unit an effects unit designed to electronically reproduce the reverberation patterns of various spaces. A reverb unit such as the R7 or AMS
includes a setting for an echo plate.

rim-shot the drumstick hits the rim of the snare drum.

sampler a sampler is a device that digitally analyzes a sound's waveform
and encodes it. That sound can be stored in the soundbank of an elec-

tronic keyboard or another computer for subsequent reproduction or for further manipulation. (See Huber and Runstein 1995)

sequencer "a module in an electronic music synthesizer for generating a repeating sequence of control voltages" (G. White 1991, 295), which produces a repeating sequence of sounds. Sequencing may include the programming of some or all sonic parameters. For example, a repeating series of pitches or a rhythmic pattern or a series of sonorities or dynamic changes, or all or any of these in combination may be electronically generated. Similarly, a single line or multiple parts may be repeated exactly by means of a sequencer.

synth bass, clavi bass in-house abbreviations for synthesized bass and clavier bass, two preprogrammed sound qualities available on electronic keyboards.

tape op/tape operator an apprentice engineer who does most of the manual work of setting up and running a session for the engineer, leaving the engineer free to concentrate on the console. He or she literally operates the tape machine in analog recording set-ups.

tape synchronizer a synchronizer matches and locks the recording and playback speed of a tape recorder with the speeds/time codes of other devices so that they can work together as an integrated unit. (See Huber and Runstein 1995)

thru box a device that can be configured either to retransmit messages received at the MIDI accessory or to transmit messages generated by that accessory. (See Vail 2000, 325)

timbre sound quality, tone color. The timbral character of a sound signal is defined by the frequency spectrum of that sound. The difference between the sound of the same pitch played on different instruments is a timbral difference, as is the difference in the sound two players might produce on the same kind of instrument.

time code "a standard encoding scheme (hours:minutes:seconds:frames) for encoding time-stamped address information. Time code is used for address location, triggering, and synchronization between various analog, video, digital audio, and other time-based media." (Huber and Runstein 1995, 483)

trigger converter a trigger device is programmed to automatically send a signal to initiate an action in some other digital device.

ukubhodla see *ibhodlo.*

VU meter instrument used in the studio to measure volume units. Dials and needles register attack and decibel overshoot. That is, a VU meter measures in a standardized unit the number of decibels that a composite signal deviates from a reference volume.

Zulu trad music industry in-house term for the music that is marketed under the category "Zulu traditional."

Bibliography

Aitchison, John. 1989. Natal's Wastelands: The Unofficial War Goes On. *Indicator SA* 7 (1): 58–61.

Al Jolson's *Sonny Boy* Gave Gallo its Future. 1991. *Gallo Newsbeat* (spring/summer): 9.

Allen, Lara. 1999. *Kwela:* The Structure and Sound of Pennywhistle Music. In *Composing the Music of Africa: Composition, Interpretation, and Realisation,* edited by M. Floyd. Aldershot, England: Ashgate.

Allingham, Rob. 1992. CD sleeve notes to *1992 Gallo Gold Awards: 65 Years.* Compilation CD. Johannesburg: Gallo Africa.

———. 1994. CD sleeve notes to *From Marabi to Disco: 42 Years of Township Music.* Compilation CD. Johannesburg: GMP, CSZAC61.

———. 1999. South Africa: The Nation of Voice. In *World Music: The Rough Guide: An A–Z of the Music, Musicians, and Discs,* edited by S. Broughton, M. Ellingham, and R. Trillo. London: The Rough Guides.

Alten, Stanley R. 1986. *Audio in Media.* 2nd ed. Belmont: Wadsworth Publishing.

Anderson, Muff. 1981. *Music in the Mix: The Story of South African Popular Music.* Johannesburg: Raven Press.

Appadurai, Arjun. 1996. *Modernity at Large: Cultural Dimensions of Globalization.* Minneapolis: University of Minnesota Press.

———. 1998. Dead Certainty: Ethnic Violence in the Era of Globalization. *Public Culture* 10, no. 2: 225–48.

Appiah, Anthony. 1992. *In My Father's House.* London: Methuen.

Armstrong, Robert Plant. 1971. *The Affecting Presence: An Essay in Humanistic Anthropology.* Urbana: University of Illinois Press.

Arom, Simha. [1985] 1991. *African Polyphony and Polyrhythm.* Translated by M. Thom, B. Tuckett, and R. Boyd. Cambridge: Cambridge University Press.

Attali, Jacques. 1985. *Noise: The Political Economy of Music.* Minneapolis: University of Minnesota Press.

Averill, Gage. 1997. *A Day for the Hunter, A Day for the Prey: Popular Music and Power in Haiti.* Chicago: Chicago University Press.

———. 1999. Bell Tones and Ringing Chords: Sense and Sensation in Barbershop Harmony. *World of Music* 41, no. 1: 37–51.

Bakhtin, Mikhail. 1981. *The Dialogic Imagination.* Austin: University of Texas Press.

Ballantine, Chris. 1989. A Brief History of South African Popular Music. *Popular Music* 8, no. 3: 305–10.

———. 1993. *Marabi Nights: Early South African Jazz and Vaudeville.* Johannesburg: Raven Press.

Barber, Karin, and Chris Waterman. 1995. Traversing the Global and the Local: Fuji Music and Praise Poetry in the Production of Contemporary Yoruba Popular Culture. In *Worlds Apart: Modernity Through the Prism of the Local,* edited by D. Miller. New York: Routledge.

Basso, Ellen B. 1973. *The Kalapalo Indians of Central Brazil.* New York: Holt, Rinehart, and Winston.

Bauman, Richard. 1984. *Verbal Art as Performance.* Prospect Heights: Waveland Press.

Bauman, Richard, and Charles Briggs. 1990. Poetics and Performance as Critical Perspectives on Language and Social Life. *Annual Review of Anthropology* 19: 59–88.

Bauman, Richard, and Joel Sherzer, eds. [1974] 1989. *Explorations in the Ethnography of Speaking.* Cambridge: Cambridge University Press.

Becker, Howard. 1982. *Art Worlds.* Berkeley: University of California Press.

Bendix, Regina. 2000. The Pleasures of the Ear: Toward an Ethnography of Listening. *Cultural Analysis* 1: http://socrates.berkeley.edu/~caforum/.

Benjamin, Walter. 1968. *Illuminations.* New York: Harcourt, Brace, and World.

Bennet, Stith. 1980. *On Becoming a Rock Musician.* Amherst: University of Massachussets Press.

Bergmeier, Horst J. P., and Rainer E. Lotz. 1997. *Hitler's Airwaves: The Inside Story of Nazi Radio Broadcasting and Propaganda Swing.* New Haven: Yale University Press.

Berliner, Paul. 1981. *The Soul of the Mbira: Music and Traditions of the Shona People of Zimbabwe.* Chicago: Chicago University Press.

———. 1994. *Thinking in Jazz: The Infinite Art of Improvisation.* Chicago: University of Chicago Press.

Bohn, Dennis A. (compiler). 1995. Rane Professional Audio Reference: http://www.rane.com/digi-dic.html#doctop.

Borwick, John, ed. 1994. *Sound Recording Practice.* 4th ed. Oxford: Oxford University Press.

Bourdieu, Pierre. 1984. *Distinction: A Social Critique of the Judgement of Taste.* Cambridge, Mass.: Harvard University Press.

Breen, Marcus. 1992. Desert Dreams, Media, and Interventions in Reality: Australian Aboriginal Music. In *Rockin the Boat: Mass Music and Mass Movements*, edited by R. Garofalo. Boston: Southend Press.

Briggs, Charles. 1986. *Learning How to Ask: A Sociological Appraisal of the Role of the Interview in Social Science Research*. Cambridge: Cambridge University Press.

———. 1993. Personal Sentiments and Polyphonic Voices in Warao Women's Ritual Wailing: Music and Poetics in a Critical and Collective Discourse. *American Anthopologist* 95, no. 4: 929–57.

Broughton, Simon, Mark Ellingham, and Richard Trillo, eds. 1999. *World Music: The Rough Guide: An A–Z of the Music, Musicians, and Discs*. London: The Rough Guides.

Brown, Ernest. 1994. The Guitar and the *Mbira:* Resilience, Assimilation, and Pan-Africanism in Zimbabwean Music. *The World of Music* 36, no. 2: 73–117.

Buchanan, Donna. 1995. Metaphors of Power, Metaphors of Truth: The Politics of Music Professionalism in Bulgarian Folk Orchestras. *Ethnomusicology* 39, no. 3: 381–416.

———. 1997. Bulgaria's Magical *Mysterè* Tour: Postmodernism, World Music Marketing, and Political Change in Eastern Europe. *Ethnomusicology* 41, no 1: 131–57.

Burd, Alex. 1994. Studio Acoustics. In *Sound Recording Practice,* edited by J. Borwick. 4th ed. Oxford: Oxford University Press.

Buskin, Richard. 1991. *Inside Tracks: A First-Hand History of Popular Music from the World's Greatest Record Producers and Engineers*. New York: Avon Books.

Byerly, Ingrid. 1998. Mirror, Mediator, and Prophet: The Music *Indaba* of Late-Apartheid South Africa. *Ethnomusicology* 42, no. 1: 1–44.

Carrier, James, ed. 1995. *Occidentalism: Images of the West*. Oxford: Clarendon Press.

Chambers, Ross. 1991. *Room for Maneuver: Reading (the) Oppositional (in) Narrative*. Chicago: University of Chicago Press.

Chanan, Michael. 1995. *Repeated Takes: A Short History of Recording and Its Effects on Music*. New York: Verso.

Charry, Eric. 2000. *Mande Music: Traditional and Modern Music of the Maninka and Mandinka of Western Africa*. Chicago: University of Chicago Press.

Chimeloane, Rrekgetsi. 1998. *The Hostel Dwellers: A First-Hand Account*. Cape Town, South Africa: Kwela Books.

Ching, Barbara, and Gerald Creed, eds. 1997. *Knowing Your Place: Rural Identity and Cultural Hierarchy*. New York: Routledge.

Clark, Mark H. 1999. Product Diversification. In *Magnetic Recording: The*

First *Hundred Years,* edited by E. D. Daniel, C. D. Mee, and M. H. Clark. New York: Institute of Electrical and Electronics Engineers Press.

Clegg, Jonathan. 1982. Towards an Understanding of African Dance: The Zulu Isishameni Style. In Papers read at Second Symposium on Ethnomusicology, 24–26 September 1981, Rhodes University, Grahamstown, South Africa, edited by Andrew Tracey. Grahamstown: International Library of African Music, Institute of Social and Economic Research, Rhodes University.

Clifford, James. 1983. On Ethnographic Authority. *Representations* 1, no. 2: 118–46.

Comaroff, Jean. 1985. *Body of Power: Spirit of Resistance.* Chicago: University of Chicago Press.

Coplan, David B. 1985. *In Township Tonight! South Africa's Black City Music and Theatre.* New York: Longman Publishers.

———. 1993. A Terrible Commitment: Balancing the Tribes in South African National Culture. In *Perilous States: Conversations on Culture, Politics and Nation,* edited by G. Marcus. Chicago: University of Chicago Press.

———. 1994. *In the Time of Cannibals: The Word Music of South Africa's Basotho Migrants.* Chicago: University of Chicago Press.

Cunningham, Mark. 1998. *Good Vibrations: A History of Record Production.* 2nd ed. London: Sanctuary Publishing.

Daniel, Eric D., C. Denis Mee, and Mark H. Clark. 1999. *Magnetic Recording: The First Hundred Years.* New York: Institute of Electrical and Electronics Engineers Press.

Daniel, Valentine E. 1996. *Charred Lullabies: Chapters in an Anthropography of Violence.* Princeton, N.J.: Princeton University Press.

David, Erica. 1998. Pancho Villa: King of Durango's Pictorial Vernacular. Paper read at the annual meeting of the American Anthropological Association, Philadephia, Pennsylvania.

Davies, Nollene. 1994. The Guitar in Zulu *Maskanda* Tradition. *World of Music* 36, no. 2: 118–37.

de Certeau, Michel. 1988. *The Practice of Everyday Life.* Translated by S. Rendell. Berkeley: University of California Press.

de Haas, Mary, and Paulus Zulu. 1993. Ethnic Mobilisation: KwaZulu's Politics in Secession. *Indicator SA* 10, no. 3: 47–52.

Dlamini, S. Nombuso. 2001. The Construction, Meaning, and Negotiation of Ethnic Identities in KwaZulu-Natal. In *Social Identities in New South Africa: After Apartheid—Volume One,* edited by A. Zegeye, 195–222. Cape Town, South Africa: Kwela Books.

Doke, C. M., D. M. Malcolm, J. M. A. Sikakana, and B. W. Vilakazi. 1990. *English-Zulu Zulu-English Dictionary.* 1st combined ed. Johannesburg: University of the Witwatersrand Press.

Dorson, Richard. 1976. Folklore, Academe, and the Marketplace. In *Folklore and Fakelore*. Cambridge, Mass.: Harvard University Press.

Elder, Bruce. 1991. Pulsating Life of Soweto. *Sydney Morning Herald*, 20 June 1991. http://www.smh.com.au.

Erlmann, Veit. 1991. *African Stars: Studies in Black South African Performance*. Chicago: University of Chicago Press.

———. 1996a. The Aesthetics of the Global Imagination: Reflections on World Music in the 1990s. *Public Culture* 8, no. 3: 467–88.

———. 1996b. *Nightsong: Performance, Power, and Practice in South Africa*. Chicago: University of Chicago Press.

———. 1999. *Music, Modernity, and the Global Imagination: South Africa and the West*. New York: Oxford University Press.

Fales, Cornelia. Forthcoming. Short Circuiting Perceptual Systems: Timbre in Ambient and Techno Music. In *Wired for Sound*, edited by P. Green and T. Porcello. Hanover, N.H.: Wesleyan University Press.

———. 1998. Issues of Timbre: The *Inanga Chuchotée*. In *Africa: The Garland Encyclopedia of Music*, edited by R. M. Stone. New York: Garland Publishers.

———. 2002. The Paradox of Timbre. *Ethnomusicology* 46, no. 1: 56–95.

Faulkner, Robert. 1971. *The Hollywood Studio Musician*. Chicago: Adline.

Feinberg, Benjamin. 1998. ¿Quiere Hierba? ¿Quiere Hongo? Mushrooms, Commerce, and Identity in Southern Mexico. Paper read at the annual meeting of the American Anthropological Association, Philadephia, Pennsylvania.

Feld, Steve. 1984. Communication, Music, and Speech about Music. *Yearbook for Traditional Music* 16: 1–18. [Also in Keil and Feld, 1994]

———. 1988. Aesthetics as Iconicity of Style, or "Lift-up-over Sounding": Getting into the Kaluli Groove. *Yearbook for Traditional Music* 20: 74–113. [Also in Keil and Feld, 1994]

———. [1982] 1990. *Sound and Sentiment: Birds, Weeping, Poetics, and Song in Kaluli Expression*. Philadelphia: University of Pennsylvania Press.

———. 1994. From Schizophonia to Schismogenesis: The Discourses and Commodification Practices of "World Music" and "World Beat." In *Music Grooves*, C. Keil and S. Feld. Chicago: University of Chicago Press.

———. 1996a. Pygmy POP: A Genealogy of Schizophonic Mimesis. *The Yearbook for Traditional Music* 28: 1–35.

———. 1996b. Waterfalls of Song: An Acoustemology of Place Resounding in Bosavi, Papua New Guinea. In *Senses of Place*, edited by S. Feld and K. H. Basso, 91–135. Santa Fe, N.M.: School of American Research.

———. 2000. A Sweet Lullaby for World Music. *Public Culture* 12, no. 1: 145–72.

Feldman, Allen. 1994. From Desert Storm to Rodney King via ex-Yugoslavia: On Cultural Anaesthesia. In *The Senses Still: Perception and Memory as Material Culture in Modernity*, edited by N. Seremetakis. Boulder, Colo.: Westview Press.

Fernandez, James. 1991. Introduction: Confluents of Inquiry. In *Beyond Metaphor: The Theory of Tropes in Anthropology*, edited by J. Fernandez. Stanford, Calif.: Stanford University Press.

Floyd, Malcolm 1999. *Composing the Music of Africa: Composition, Interpretation, and Realisation*. Aldershot, England: Ashgate.

Fox, Aaron. 1992. The Jukebox of History: Narratives of Loss and Desire in the Discourse of Country Music. *Popular Music* 11, no. 1: 53–72.

———. 1995. Out the Country: Language, Music, Feeling, and Sociability in American Rural Working-Class Culture. Ph.D. diss., University of Texas at Austin.

———. 1996. "Ain't It Funny How Time Slips Away": Talk, Trash, and Technology in a Texas Working-Class Bar. In *Knowing Your Place: Rural Identity and Cultural Hierarchy*, edited by Barbara Ching and Gerald Creed. New York: Routledge.

———. 1999. Vocal Articulation in Country Music: A Micro-Analysis. Paper read at the annual meeting of the Society for Ethnomusicology, Austin, Texas, November 18–21.

Frescura, Franco. 2001. Rural Art and Rural Resistance: The Rise of a Wall Decorating Tradition in Rural Southern Africa. In *Culture in the New South Africa: After Apartheid—Volume Two*, edited by R. Kriger and A. Zegeye, 65–90. Cape Town, South Africa: Kwela Books.

Friedrich, Paul. 1991. Polytropy. In *Beyond Metaphor: The Theory of Tropes in Anthropology*, edited by J. Fernandez. Stanford, Calif.: Stanford University Press.

Frith, Simon. 1981. *Sound Effects: Youth, Leisure, and the Politics of Rock and Roll.* New York: Pantheon.

———. 1986. Art Versus Technology: The Strange Case of Popular Music. *Media, Culture, Society* 8, no. 3: 263–79.

———. 1991. The Industrialization of Music. In *Music for Pleasure: Essays in the Sociology of Pop.* New York: Routledge.

———. 1996. Technology and Authority. In *Performing Rites: On the Value of Popular Music.* Cambridge: Harvard University Press.

Gallo Newsbeat. 1989 (winter) [internal magazine of Gallo Africa].

Gallo Newsbeat. 1992 (spring) [internal magazine of Gallo Africa].

Gallo Records Promotion Department. n.d. West Nkosi: Biography. Unpublished press release.

Garofalo, Reebee, ed. 1992. *Rockin' the Boat: Mass Music and Mass Movements.* Boston: Southend Press.

————. 1993. Whose World, What Beat: The Transnational Music Industry, Identity and Cultural Imperialism. *The World of Music* 35, no. 2: 16–32.

Gay, Leslie C., Jr. 1998. Acting Up, Talking Tech: New York Rock Musicians and Their Metaphors of Technology. *Ethnomusicology* 42, no. 1: 81–98.

Gerstin, Julian. 1998. Reputation in a Musical Scene: The Everyday Context of Connections between Music, Identity, and Politics. *Ethnomusicology* 42, no. 3: 385–414.

Goffman, Erving. 1959. *The Presentation of Self in Everyday Life.* New York: Doubleday Anchor Books.

————. 1967. *Interaction Ritual.* New York: Anchor Books.

Goodwin, Andrew, and Joe Gore. 1990. World Beat and the Cultural Imperialism Debate. *Socialist Review* 20, no. 3: 63–80.

Gramsci, Antonio. 1971. *Selections from the Prison Notebooks of Antonio Gramsci.* Edited by Q. Hoare and G. N. Smith. New York: International Publishers.

Gray, Herman. 1988. *Producing Jazz: The Experience of an Independent Record Company.* Philadelphia, Penn.: Temple University Press.

Green, Paul, and Thomas Porcello, eds. Forthcoming. *Wired for Sound.* Hanover, N.H.: Wesleyan University Press.

Greene, Paul. 1999. Sound Engineering in a Tamil Village: Playing Audio Cassettes as Devotional Performance. *Ethnomusicology* 43, no. 3: 459–89.

————. 2001. Mixed Messages: Unsettled Cosmopolitanisms in Nepali Pop. *Popular Music* 20, no. 2: 169–88.

Groesbeck, Rolf. 1999. Discourse on Timbre among Temple Drummers in Kerala, India. Paper read at annual meeting of the Society for Ethnomusicology, Austin, Texas, November 18–21.

Gronow, Pekka, and Ilpo Saunio. 1998. *An International History of the Recording Industry.* Translated by C. Moseley. New York: Cassell.

Hall, Stuart. 1979. Culture, Media, and the "Ideological Effect." In *Mass Communication and Society,* edited by J. Curran, M. Gurevitch, and J. Woolacot. London: Sage Publications.

Hamilton, Carolyn. 1998. *Terrific Majesty: The Power of Shaka Zulu and the Limits of Historical Invention.* Cambridge, Mass.: Harvard University Press.

Hamilton, Carolyn, and John Wright. 1993. The Beginnings of Zulu Identity: The Image of Shaka. *Indicator SA* 10, no. 3: 43–46.

Hamm, Charles. 1986. Rock and Roll in a Very Strange Society. *Popular Music* 5, no.2: 159–74. [Also in Hamm 1995]

————. 1988. *Afro-American Music, South Africa, and Apartheid.* New York: Institute for Studies of American Music. [Also in Hamm 1995]

————. 1991. "The Constant Companion of Man": Separate Development,

Radio Bantu, and Music. *Popular Music* 10, no. 2: 147–73. [Also in Hamm 1995]

———. 1995. *Putting Popular Music in its Place.* New York: Cambridge University Press.

Harries, Patrick. 1993. Images, Symbolism, and Tradition in a South African Bantustan: Mangosuthu Buthelezi, Inkatha, and Zulu history. *History and Theory* 32, no. 4: 105–26.

Hayward, Philip, ed. 1998. *Sound Alliances: Indigenous Peoples, Cultural Politics, and Popular Music in the Pacific.* New York: Cassell.

———. 1999. *Music at the Borders: Not Drowning Waving and Their Engagement with Papua New Guinea Culture.* Sydney: John Libbey and Perfect Beat Publications.

Hebdige, Dick. 1979. *Subculture: The Meaning of Style.* London: Methuen Press.

Hennion, Antoine. 1989. An Intermediary between Production and Consumption: The Producer of Popular Music. *Science, Technology, and Human Values* 14, no. 4: 400–424.

Hong Kong's Zulus Go Zulu. 1993. *Flying Springbok/Vlieënde Springbok* (October): 19.

Howe, Graham. 1993. The Trojan Horse: Natal's Civil War, 1987–1993. *Indicator SA* 10, no. 2: 35–40.

Howes, David, ed. 1991. *The Varieties of Sensory Experience: A Sourcebook in the Anthropology of the Senses.* Toronto: University of Toronto Press.

Huber, Davied Miles, and Robert E. Runstein. 1995. *Modern Recording Techniques.* 4th ed. Indianapolis, Ind.: Howard W. Sams.

Impey, Angela 1983. The Zulu Umakhweyana Bow. Unpublished honors thesis, University of Natal, Durban, South Africa.

Jackson, Michael, ed. 1996. *Things As They Are: New Directions in Phenomenological Anthropology.* Bloomington: Indiana University Press.

Jakobson, Roman. 1960. Linguistics and Poetics. In *Style in Language,* edited by T A Sebeok. Cambridge, Mass.: MIT Press.

James, Deborah. 1999. *Songs of the Women Migrants: Performance and Identity in South Africa.* Edinburgh, Scotland: Edinburgh University Press.

Jaynes, Julian. 1976. *The Origin of Consciousness in the Breakdown of the Bicameral Mind.* Boston: Houghton Mifflin.

Joseph, Rosemary. 1983. Zulu Women's Music. *African Music* 6, no. 3: 53–89.

Jowers, Peter. 1993. Beating New Tracks: WOMAD and the British World Music Movement. In *The Last Post: Music After Modernism,* edited by Simon Miller. Manchester, England: Manchester University Press.

Kater, Michael H. 1992. *Different Drummers: Jazz in the Culture of Nazi Germany.* New York: Oxford University Press.

―――. 1997. *The Twisted Muse: Musicians and Their Music in the Third Reich.* New York: Oxford University Press.

Kaye, Andrew. 1998. The Guitar in Africa. In *Africa: The Garland Encyclopedia of World Music,* edited by R. M. Stone. New York: Garland Publishers.

Kealy, Edward. 1979. From Craft to Art: The Case of Sound Mixers and Popular Music. *Sociology of Work and Occupations* 6, no. 1: 3–29.

Keil, Charles. 1966. *Urban Blues.* Chicago: University of Chicago Press.

―――. 1979. *Tiv Song.* Chicago: University of Chicago Press.

―――. 1985. People's Music Comparatively: Style and Stereotype, Class and Hegemony. *Dialectical Anthropology* 10 (119–30). [Also in Keil and Feld 1994]

―――. 1987. Participatory Discrepancies and the Power of Music. *Cultural Anthropology* 2: 275–83. [Also in Keil and Feld 1994]

Keil, Charles, and Steve Feld. 1994. *Music Grooves.* Chicago: University of Chicago Press.

Kirby, Percival. [1934] 1968. *The Musical Instruments of the Native Races of South Africa.* Johannesburg: University of the Witwatersrand Press.

Knight, Ian. 1994. Gathering at Isandlwana: Traditional Zulu War Dress. *Military Illustrated* (March 1994): 10–12.

Kriger, Robert, and Abebe Zegeye, eds. 2001. *Culture in the New South Africa: After Apartheid.* 2 vols. Cape Town, South Africa: Kwela Books.

la Hausse, Paul. 1984. The Struggle for the City: Alcohol, the Ematsheni and Popular Culture in Durban, 1902–1936. Master's thesis, University of Cape Town, South Africa.

Lee, Tong Soon. 1999. Technology and the Production of Islamic Space: The Call to Prayer in Singapore. *Ethnomusicology* 43, no. 1: 86–100.

Lepselter, Susan. 1998. The Drifter, the Desert, the Stealth, and the UFO. Paper read at the annual meeting of the American Anthropological Association, Philadephia, Pennsylvania.

Lindfors, Bernth. 1982. Seeing the Races through Zulu Spectacles: Victorian Cultural Attitudes in Modern Times. *Race and Literature* 16, no. 2: 107–17.

―――. 1983. Circus Africans. *Journal of American Culture* 6, no. 2: 9–14.

―――. 1999. Charles Dickens and the Zulus. In *Africans on Stage: Studies in Ethnological Show Business,* edited by Bernth Lindfors. Bloomington: Indiana University Press.

Louw, Antoinette. 1991. Monitoring Conflict in Natal. *Indicator SA* 9, no. 1: 43–45.

―――. 1992. Political Conflict in Natal, 1989–1992. *Indicator SA* 9, no. 3: 57–59.

Low, John. 1982. A History of Kenyan Guitar Music: 1945–1980. *African Music* 6, no. 2: 17–36.

Lutz, Catherine, and Jane Collins. 1993. *Reading National Geographic.* Chicago: University of Chicago Press.

Lysloff, René T. A. 1997. Mozart in Mirrorshades: Ethnomusicology, Technology, and the Politics of Representation. *Ethnomusicology* 41, no. 2: 206–19.

Mahlaba, Martin. 1982. From Herdboy to the Top of the Music Industry: West Nkosi Gets a Seat on the Board at Gallo. *Blackchain Today* (October 1982).

Mahon, Maureen. 2000. The Visible Evidence of Cultural Producers. *Annual Review of Anthropology* 29: 467–92.

Mamdani, Mahmood. 1996. *Citizen and Subject: Contemporary Africa and the Legacy of Late Colonialism.* Princeton: Princeton University Press.

Manuel, Peter Lamarche. 1993. *Cassette Culture: Popular Music and Technology in India.* Chicago: University of Chicago Press.

Marcus, George, ed. 1992. *Rereading Cultural Anthropology.* Durham, N.C.: Duke University Press.

———. 1993. Introduction. In *Perilous States: Conversations on Culture, Politics, and Nation,* edited by G. Marcus. Chicago: University of Chicago Press.

Marcus, George, and Fred Myers. 1995. The Traffic in Art and Culture: An Introduction. In *The Traffic in Culture: Refiguring Art and Anthropology,* edited by George Marcus and F. Myers. Berkeley: University of California Press.

Maré, Gerhard. 1993. *Ethnicity and Politics in South Africa.* London: Zed Books.

Marks, Shula. 1991. Patriotism, Patriarchy, and Purity: Natal and the Politics of Zulu Ethnic Consciousness. In *The Creation of Tribalism in Southern Africa,* edited by Leroy Vail. Berkeley: University of California Press.

Marks, Shula, and Stanley Trapido. 1987. The Politics of Race, Class, and Nationalism. In *The Politics of Race, Class, and Nationalism in Twentieth-Century South Africa,* edited by S. Marks and S. Trapido. London: Longman.

Marre, Jeremy (producer). 1979. *Rhythms of Resistance: The Black Music of South Africa.* Directed by Chris Austin and Jeremy Marre. Videorecording. London: Harcourt Films.

McRae, Donald. 1987. Liner notes for Mahlathini, *The Lion of Soweto.* Earthworks/Virgin Records CDEWV4.

Meintjes, Louise. 1990. Paul Simon's *Graceland,* South Africa, and the Mediation of Musical Meaning. *Ethnomusicology* 34, no. 1: 37–73.

Meyer, Michael. 1991. *The Politics of Music in the Third Reich.* New York: P. Lang.

Middfest International. 1999. Information folder of visitor's package. Middletown, Ohio: Middfest International Foundation.

Miller, Daniel, ed. 1995. *Worlds Apart: Modernity Through the Prism of the Local.* New York: Routledge.

Miller, Simon, ed. 1993. *The Last Post: Music After Modernism.* Manchester, England: Manchester University Press.

Minh-Ha, Trinh T. 1991. *When the Moon Waxes Red: Representation, Gender, and Cultural Politics.* New York: Routledge.

Minnaar, Anthony. 1992. Mayhem in the Midlands: Battle for Bruntville. *Indicator SA* 9, no. 3: 60–64.

———, ed. 1993. *The Dynamics of Hostels in South Africa with Specific Reference to Present-Day Violence.* Pretoria, South Africa: Human Sciences Research Council.

Moodie, Dunbar. 1994. *Going for Gold: Men, Mines and Migration.* Berkeley: University of California Press.

Mudimbe, V. Y. 1994. *The Idea of Africa.* Bloomington: Indiana University Press.

Muller, Carol. 1999. *Rituals of Fertility and the Sacrifice of Desire: Nazarite Women's Performance in South Africa.* Chicago: University of Chicago Press.

Munro, Andy. 1994. Studio Planning and Installation. In *Sound Recording Practice,* edited by J. Borwick. 4th ed. Oxford: Oxford University Press.

Musician with a Midas Touch. 1989. *Club Magazine* (July): 70–71.

Mzala. 1988. *Gatsha Buthelezi: Chief with a Double Agenda.* London: Zed Books.

Nardantonio, Dennis. 1990. *Sound Studio Production Techniques.* 1st ed. Blue Ridge Summit, Pa.: TAB Books.

Negus, Keith. 1992. *Producing Pop: Culture and Conflict in the Popular Music Industry.* New York: Routledge.

———. 1999. *Music Genres and Corporate Cultures.* New York: Routledge.

Nketia, J. H. Kwabena. 1974. *The Music of Africa.* New York: W. W. Norton.

Olson, Kathryn. 2000. Politics, Production and Process: Discourses on Tradition in Contemporary Maskanda. Masters thesis, University of Natal, Durban, South Africa.

———. 2001. 'Mina Ngizokushaya Ngengoma'/'I Will Challenge You with a Song': Constructions of Masculinity in Maskanda. *Agenda* 49: 51–60.

Osborn, Haydn. 1991. The Richmond War: A Struggle for Supremacy. *Indicator SA* 9 no. 1: 46–49.

Peacock, Shane. 1999. Africa Meets the Great Farini. In *Africans on Stage: Studies in Ethnological Show Business,* edited by B. Lindfors. Bloomington: Indiana University Press.

Pepper, Johathan. 1994. Mahlathini and the Mahotella Queens. *Rhythm Music Magazine* (January 1994): 14–15.

Porcello, Thomas. 1991. The Ethics of Digital Audio Sampling: Engineers' Discourse. *Popular Music* 10, no. 1: 69–84.

———. 1994. Unplugging Live Performance: Pop Music's Ironic Retreat from Audio Technology. Paper presented at the annual meeting of the Society for Ethnomusicology, Milwaukee, Wisconsin, October 20–23.

———. 1996. Sonic Artistry: Music, Discourse, and Technology in the Sound Recording Studio. Ph.D. diss., University of Texas at Austin.

———. 1998. "Tails Out": Social Phenomenology and the Ethnographic Representation of Technology in Music-Making. *Ethnomusicology* 42, no. 3: 485–510.

———. 1999. Metaphors of Sound: Structure and Use in Music Production. Paper read at the annual meeting of the Society for Ethnomusicology, Austin, Texas, November 18–21.

Rasmussen, Anne K. 1996. Theory and Practice at the "Arabic Org": Digital Technology in Contemporary Arab Music Performance. *Popular Music* 15, no. 3: 345–65.

Reyes, Adelaida. 1999. *Songs of the Caged, Songs of the Free: Music and the Vietnamese Refugee Experience.* Philadelphia: Temple University Press.

Rice, Tim. 1994. *May It Fill Your Soul: Experiencing Bulgarian Music.* Chicago: University of Chicago Press.

Roberts, John Storm. 1972. *Black Music of Two Worlds.* New York: Original Music.

Roseman, Marina. 1991. *Healing Sounds from the Malaysian Rainforest: Temiar Music and Medicine.* Berkeley: University of California Press.

Roth, Paul A. 1989. How Narratives Explain. *Social Research* 56, no. 2: 449–78.

Rycroft, David. 1977. Evidence of Stylistic Continuity in Zulu "Town" Music. In *Essays for a Humanist: An Offering to Klaus Wachsmann.* New York: Town House Press.

Sachs, Curt. [1961] 1965. *The Wellsprings of Music.* New York: McGraw-Hill.

Samuels, David. 1998. A Sense of the Past: Music, Place, and History on the San Carlos Apache Reservation. Ph.D. diss., University of Texas at Austin.

———. 1999. Icons of Style, Indexes of Identity: Country Singing in San Carlos. Paper read at the annual meeting of the Society for Ethnomusicology, Austin, Texas, November 18–21.

———. n.d. Issues in the Study of Contemporary Native American Music. Unpublished manuscript.

Sayer, Derek. 1987. *The Violence of Abstraction: The Analytic Foundations of Historical Materialism.* New York: Basil Blackwell.

Schmidt, Cynthia. 1994. The Guitar in Africa: Issues and Research. *World of Music* 36, no. 2: 3–20.

Schutz, Alfred. 1967. *The Phenomenology of the Social World.* Chicago: Northwestern University Press.

Sebeok, Thomas A., ed. 1960. *Style in Language.* Cambridge, Mass.: MIT Press.

Seeger, Anthony. 1987. *Why Suyá Sing: A Musical Anthropology of an Amazonian People.* Cambridge: Cambridge University Press.

Segal, Lauren. 1991. The Human Face of Violence: Hostel Dwellers Speak. *Journal of Southern African Studies* 18, no. 1: 190–231.

Seremetakis, Nadia C., ed. 1994. *The Senses Still: Perception and Memory as Material Culture in Modernity.* Boulder, Colo.: Westview Press.

———. 1998. Durations of Pains: A Genealogy of Pain. In *Identities in Pain,* edited by J. Frykman, N. Seremetakis, and S. Ewert. Lund, Sweden: Nordic Academic Press.

Sitas, Ari. 1996. The New Tribalism: Hostels and Violence. *Journal of Southern African Studies* 22, no. 2: 235–48.

Small, Christopher. 1980 [1977]. *Music, Society, Education.* 2nd rev ed. London: John Calder.

Spiegel, Andrew D., and Patrick A. McAllister, eds. 1991. *Tradition and Transition in Southern Africa: Festschrift for Philip and Iona Mayer.* Johannesburg: Witwatersrand University Press.

Spivak, Gayatri Chakravorty. 1988. Subaltern Studies: Deconstructing Historiography. In *Selected Subaltern Studies,* edited by R. Guha and G. C. Spivak. Oxford: Oxford University Press.

Steiner, Christopher. 1994. *African Art in Transit.* Cambridge: Cambridge University Press.

Stewart, Kathleen. 1996. *A Space on the Side of the Road: Cultural Poetics in an "Other" America.* Princeton, N.J.: Princeton University Press.

Stewart, Susan. 1993. *On Longing: Narratives of the Miniature, the Gigantic, the Souvenir, the Collection.* Durham, N.C.: Duke University Press.

Stoller, Paul. 1989. *The Taste of Ethnographic Things: The Senses in Anthropology.* Philadelphia: University of Pennsylvania Press.

Stolzhoff, Norman C. 2000. *Wake the Town and Tell the People: Dancehall Culture in Jamaica.* Durham, N.C.: Duke University Press.

Stone, Ruth M., ed. 1998. *Africa: The Garland Encyclopedia of Music.* New York: Garland Publishers.

Stone, Terri, ed. 1992. *Music Producers: Conversations with Today's Top Record Makers.* Emeryville, Calif.: Mix Books.

Sutton, R. Anderson. 1996. Interpreting Electronic Sound Technology in the Contemporary Javanese Soundscape. *Ethnomusicology* 40, no. 2: 249–68.

Taussig, Michael. 1993. *Mimesis and Alterity: A Particular History of the Senses.* New York: Routledge.

Taylor, Julie. 1998. *Paper Tangos.* Durham, N.C.: Duke University Press.

Taylor, Timothy D. 1997. *Global Pop: World Music, World Markets*. New York: Routledge.

———. 2001. *Strange Sounds: Music, Culture, and Technology in the Postwar Era*. New York: Routledge.

Théberge, Paul. 1989. The "Sound" of Music: Technological Rationalization and the Production of Popular Music. *New Formations* 8 (summer): 99–111.

———. 1993. Random Access Music: Music, Technology, Postmodernism. In *The Last Post: Music After Modernism*, edited by S. Miller. Manchester, England: Manchester University Press.

———. 1997. *Any Sound You Can Imagine: Making Music/Consuming Technology*. Hanover, N.H.: Wesleyan University Press.

Thema, Derrick. 1983. Out of Africa, Always Something New: Now Its Music Will Spread. *The Star* (25 January): 10.

Thomas, H. J. 1988. Ngoma Dancers and Their Response to Town. Master's thesis, University of Natal, South Africa.

Thornton, Robert J. 1992. The Rhetoric of Ethnographic Holism. In *Rereading Cultural Anthropology*, edited by George E. Marcus. Durham, N.C.: Duke University Press.

———. 1995. The Colonial, the Imperial, and the Creation of the "European" in Southern Africa. In *Occidentalism: Images of the West*, edited by James Carrier. Oxford: Clarendon Press.

Thornton, Sarah. 1995. *Club Cultures: Music, Media, and Subcultural Capital*. Cambridge: Polity Press.

Tomaselli, Keyan, Ruth Tomaselli, and Johan Muller, eds. 1989. *Broadcasting in South Africa: Studies on the South African Media*. London: James Currey.

Torgovnick, Marianna. 1990. *Gone Primitive: Savage Intellects, Modern Lives*. Chicago: University of Chicago Press.

Tracey, Hugh. 1952. *African Dances on the Witwatersrand Goldmines*. Johannesburg: African Music Society.

Turino, Thomas. 2000. *Nationalists, Cosmopolitans, and Popular Music in Zimbabwe*. Chicago: Chicago University Press.

Urban, Greg. 1985. The Semiotics of Two Speech Styles in Shokleng. In *Semiotic Mediation*, edited by E. Mertz and R. Parmentier. New York: Academic Press.

———. 1991. *A Discourse-Centered Approach to Culture: Native South American Myths and Rituals*. Austin: University of Texas Press.

Vail, Leroy, ed. 1991. *The Creation of Tribalism in Southern Africa*. Berkeley: University of California Press.

Vail, Mark. 2000. *Vintage Synthesizers*. 2nd ed. San Francisco: Miller Freeman Books.

von Hornbostell, Eric. 1928. African Negro Music. *Africa* 1: 30–62.

Wallis, Roger, and Krister Malm. 1984. *Big Sounds from Small Peoples: The Music Industry in Small Countries*. New York: Pendragon Press.

Walser, Robert. 1993. *Running with the Devil: Power, Gender, and Madness in Heavy Metal Music*. Hanover, N.H.: Wesleyan University Press.

wa Mukuna, Kazadi. 1994. The Changing Role of the Guitar in the Urban Music of Zaire. *World of Music* 36, no. 2: 62–72.

Waterman, Christopher. 1990. *Juju: A Social History and Ethnography of an African Popular Music*. Chicago: University of Chicago Press.

Weber, Max. [1921] 1958. *The Rational and Social Foundations of Music*. Translated by D. Martindale, J. Riedel, and G. Neuwirth. Carbondale: Southern Illinois University Press.

White, Glenn D. 1991. *The Audio Dictionary*. 2nd ed. Seattle: University of Washington Press.

White, Hayden. 1987. *The Content of the Form: Narrative Discourse and Historical Representation*. Baltimore: Johns Hopkins University Press.

Williams, Raymond. 1977. *Marxism and Literature*. Oxford: Oxford University Press.

Willoughby, Heather. 2000. The Sound of Han: P'ansori, Timbre, and a Korean Ethos of Pain and Suffering. *Yearbook for Traditional Music* 32: 15–30.

Wilmsen, Edwin. 1996. Introduction. In *The Politics of Difference: Ethnic Premises in a World of Power*, edited by E. Wilmsen and P. McAllister. Chicago: University of Chicago Press.

Wilmsen, Edwin, Saul Dubow, and John Sharp, eds. 1994. Ethnicity and Identity in Southern Africa. *Journal of Southern African Studies* 20, no. 3. Special Issue.

Wilmsen, Edwin, and Patrick McAllister, eds. *The Politics of Difference: Ethnic Premises in a World of Power*. Chicago: University of Chicago Press.

Wolff, Janet. 1981. *The Social Production of Art*. New York: New York University Press.

Wong, Deborah. 1994. 'I Want the Microphone': Mass Mediation and Agency in Asian-American Popular Music. *TDR* 38, no. 3: 152–67.

Wright, John, and Aron Mazel. 1991. Controlling the Past in the Museums of Natal and KwaZulu. *Critical Arts* 5, no. 3: 59–77.

Xulu, Musa Khulekani. 1992. The Re-emergence of Amahubo Song Styles and Ideas in Some Modern Zulu Musical Styles. Ph.D. diss., University of Natal, Durban, South Africa.

Zegeye, Abebe. 2001. General Introduction: Imposed Ethnicity. In *Social Identities in New South Africa: After Apartheid*, vol. 1, edited by A. Zegeye. Cape Town, South Africa: Kwela Publishers.

Zuckerkandl, Victor. 1956. *Sound and Symbol: Music and the External World, Vol. 1*. Princeton, N.J.: Princeton University Press.

Taped Interviews

All interviews were conducted by the author.

Bhengu, Bethwell, with Tefo Sikale and Lucky Maseko. Johannesburg,
    14 July 1998.
Ceronio, Peter. Randpark Ridge, 9 January 1992.
Dlamini, Jane. Johannesburg, 22 June 1998.
————. Soweto, 20 August 1998.
Dlamini, Moses. Johannesburg, 14 February 1992.
Heilbrunn, Darryl. Johannesburg, 19 November 1992.
Kuny, Neil. Johannesburg, 6 January 1993.
Lebona, Koloi. Johannesburg, 17 May 1991.
Lerole, Aaron. Johannesburg, 14 March 1991.
Lindemann, John. Johannesburg, July 1989.
Longley, Lance. Johannesburg, 8 January 1992.
Mabote, Humphrey. Johannesburg, 3 February 1991.
Mayberry, Tom. Johannesburg, July 1989.
West Nkosi, Johannesburg, 19 April 1991.
————. Johannesburg, 22 May 1991.
————. Johannesburg, 29 May 1991.
Pearlson, Peter. Johannesburg, 15 April 1991.
Ralulimi, Albert. Johannesburg, August 1989.
————. Johannesburg, November 1992.
Segal, Dave. Johannesburg, 26 November 1991.
Short, Lee. Johannesburg, 12 December 1991.
Thango, Joana. Johannesburg, 21 August 1998.

Discography

African Youth Band. 1989. *Thula Sizwe,* produced by B. Makhene. Hit City Records, LEO(v) 069. LP.

Air Light Swingsters. 1981. *Umhlobo'mdala,* produced by H. Nzimande. GRC LSM 566. LP.

Amaqabane. 1990. *Ntate Modis,* produced by B. Makhene and K. Lebona. Sounds of Soweto TWH(EV) 1036. Audiocassette.

Amaswazi Emvelo and Mahlathini. 1985. *Utshwala Begazati,* produced by W. Nkosi. Gallo GRC BL/BC 509. LP.

Art of Noise, with Mahlathini and the Mahotella Queens. 1989. *Yebo!* China Records CHIXP 18. Compact disk.

Belafonte, Harry. 1986. *Paradise in Gazankulu.* EMI P746971-2. Compact disk.

Chauke, Thomas. 1987. *Simatsatse no.7.* Tusk Records. ZQBH 1095. LP.

———. *Simatsatse no.8.* 1988. Tusk Records ZQBH 1109. LP.

———. *Simatsatse no.9.* 1989. Tusk Records ZQBH 1122. LP.

———. *Simatsatse no.10.* 1990. Tusk Records ZQBH 1130. LP.

Dark City Sisters and Flying Jazz Queens. 1993. *Dark City Sisters and Flying Jazz Queens.* Earthworks/Virgin Records CDEWV 31. Compact disk.

Diana Ross and the Supremes. [1968] 1991. *Reflections.* Motown 3746354942. Compact disk.

Elite Swingsters, featuring Dolly Rathebe. 1992. *Woza!* produced by H. Nzimande; executive producer W. Nkosi. Gallo Music Productions MCBL 751. Audiocassette.

Flying Rock: South African Rock 'n Roll, 1950-1962. 1990. Compilation by P. Conte and M. Schlesinger. Global Village C2001. Audiocassette.

Franklin, Aretha. 1968. *Aretha in Paris.* Atlantic SD2-906. LP.

Freedom Fire: The Indestructible Beat of Soweto, Vol. 3. 1990. Earthworks/Caroline 2416. Compact disk.

From Marabi to Disco: 42 Years of Township Music. 1994. Compilation by R. Allingham. Gallo Music Productions CSZAC61. Compact disk.

The Heartbeat of Soweto. 1988. Shanachie SH 43051. Compact disk.

The Indestructible Beat of Soweto. 1985. Shanachie SH 43033. Compact disk.

Indoda Mahlathini. 1975. *Umkhovu,* produced by C. Matiwane. Satbel Record Company KGA 100. LP.

Inkatha Youth Band. 1991. *Theleweni,* produced by J. Ngubane. Sounds of Soweto LA GAZA(EV) 006. Audiocassette.

Ipitombi cast. 1975. *Bertha Ignos and Gail Lakiers' Ipitombi: Original Cast Recording,* produced by B. Forrest and L. Schultz. Satbel Record and Tape Co. ASH-2600. LP.

Isigqi Sesimanjemanje. 1992. *Lomculo Unzima,* produced by W. Nkosi. RPM Records AFRLP 029. LP.

Isigqi Sesimanje. 1999. *Lomthetho,* produced by H. Shange. T. K. Records. Audiocassette. L4(EO)TKP 012.

———. 2001. *Ifa Laphakade,* produced by T. K. Mbatha. T. K. Records. L4 TKP(IK) 100. Audiocassette.

Izintombi Zesimanje. 1994. *Sebenza Ntokazi,* produced by J. Dlamini and M. David. Kariba Records ZERH 2077. Audiocassette.

Izintombi Zesimanjemanje. 1967a. *Isidudla Sika Josefa,* produced by H. Nzimande. Gramophone Record Company AB41. 7″ single.

———. 1967b. *Izintombi Zesi Manje Manje,* produced by H. Nzimande. CBS Records LAB 4003. LP.

———. 1968. *Kajeno,* produced by H. Nzimande. CBS Records LAB4018. LP.

———. 1971. *Laduma Zesi Manje Manje,* produced by H. Nzimande. CBS Records LAB 4027. LP.

———. [1974] 1993. *Nomali,* produced by H. Nzimande. CBS Records/Gallo Music Productions MCGMP 40369. Audiocassette.

———. 1976. *Ho Buoa Morena,* produced by H. Nzimande. Gramophone Record Company LMS 531. LP.

———. [1976] 1992. *Isitha Sami Nguwe,* produced by H. Nzimande. [Gramophone Record Company]/Gallo Music Productions 60 1038. Audiocassette.

———. [1978] 1992. *Ujabulisa Abantu,* produced by H. Nzimande. [CBS]/Gallo Music Productions 60 1039. Audiocassette.

———. 1979a. *Boraditaba,* produced by H. Nzimande. CBS Records MSI95 2947. LP.

———. 1979b. *Ha ke Dikela,* produced by H. Nzimande. LP. Gramophone Record Company LMS 539. LP.

———. 1980. *Makoti wakena,* produced by H. Nzimande. Gramophone Record Company LJD 31. LP.

———. 1981. *Umahlongwane,* produced by H. Nzimande. Gramophone Record Company LZG 49. LP.

———. 1983. *Zenda Zangishiya*, produced by H. Nzimande. Gramophone Record Company HVN NZL 107. LP.

———. 1984. *Sematsatsa Sane*, produced by H. Nzimande. Gramophone Record Company HVN NZL 124. LP.

———. 1990. *Namibian People*, produced by H. Nzimande. Gallo Record Company BL/BC 693. LP/audiocassette.

———. 1993a. *Ke Lorile Balimo*, produced by H. Nzimande. Gallo Music Productions MCGMP 40371. Audiocassette.

———. 1993b. *Umunt'othulile*, produced by H. Nzimande. Gallo Music Productions MCGMP 40370. Audiocassette.

———. 1999. *Ijazi laseZola*, produced by J. Dlamini. Dalom Productions. Compact disk.

Izintombi Zesimanjemanje and Thandi Seoka. 1985. *I Wanna Spend My Life with You*, produced by H. Nzimande. Gallo–GRC 10113. 12″ maxi.

Jarre, Jean Michel. 1976. *Oxygène*, produced by J. M. Jarre. Drefus Records. Compact disk.

The Kings and Queens of Township Jive. 1990. Earthworks/Virgin Records 3-1020-2. Compact disk.

Mahlathini. 1987. *The Lion of Soweto*, produced by C. B. Matiwane. Earthworks/Virgin Records CDEWV4. Compact disk.

———. 1993. *King of the Groaners*, produced by C. Matiwane. Earthworks/Caroline 2428. Compact disk.

Mahlathini and the Mahotella Queens. 1984. *Putting on the Light*. Gallo Music International/Rykodisc HNCD 4415. Compact disk.

———. [1987] 1988. *Thokozile*, produced by W. Nkosi. [Gallo–GRC BL/BC 590] Earthworks/Caroline 2406. LP.

———. [1989] 1990. *Rhythm and Art*, produced by W. Nkosi. [Gallo GRC] Shanachie Records 43068. LP.

———. 1990a. *Music of Our Soul*, produced by W. Nkosi and C. Smith. Gallo Music Productions HUC/HUL 402011. Compact disk.

———. 1990b. *Paris–Soweto*, produced by W. Nkosi and P. Groux-Cibial. Celluloid 66829/Polydor 839676. Compact disk.

———. 1991a. *The Lion Roars*, produced by M. Mankwane. Shanachie SH 43081. Compact disk.

———. 1991b. *Mbaqanga*, produced by M. Mankwane. Gallo Music Productions BL/BC 742/Polygram 314511 780-2. Compact disk.

———. 1996. *Stoki Stoki*, produced by M. Mankwane. Shanachie SH 64068. Compact disk.

———. 1999a. *Umuntu*. Gallo Music Productions CDGMP 40788. Compact disk.

———. 1999b. *Young Mahlathini: Classic Recordings with the Mahotella Queens, 1964-1971*. Compiled by R. Allingham. Gallo Music Productions. Compact disk.

Mahlathini Namatshezulu. 1986. *Ejerusalema Siyakhona,* produced by W. Nkosi. Gallo–GRC BL/BC 562. LP.

Mahlathini Nezintombi Zomgqashiyo and Makgona Tsohle Band. 1983. *Amaghawe Omgqashiyo.* Gallo Record Company. Compact disk. Reissued as Mahlathini and Mahotella Queens with the Makgona Tsohle Band. *Isomiso.* Celluloid Records 66868–2.

Mahotella Queens. [1980] 1994. *Tsamaya Moratuoa.* [Gallo Record Company] Gallo Music Productions BL/BC 226. [LP] Audiocassette.

———. 1983. *Khwatha O Mone.* Gallo Record Company. LP.

———. 1988. *Melodi Yalla,* produced by W. Nkosi. Gallo–GRC BL/BC 617. Compact disk.

———. 1989. *Izibani zomgqashiyo.* Shanachie SH 43036. Compact disk.

———. 1991. *Marriage Is a Problem.* Shanachie SH 43080. Compact disk.

———. 1993. *Women of the World,* produced by M. Mankwane and M. Pilot. Shanachie SH 64047. Compact disk.

———. 2000. *Sebai Bai,* produced by C. Mousset and P. T. du Cros. Indigo and Gallo Music International LBLC 2571 HM 83. Compact disk.

Mahotella Queens, Mahlathini, and Other Stars. 1984. *Phezulu Equdeni.* Earthworks CGCD 4415. Compact disk.

Makeba, Miriam. 1992. *The Best of Miriam Makeba and the Skylarks.* Kaz Records CD 26. Compact disk.

Makgona Tsohle Band. [1983] 1990. *Mataka, Vols. 1 and 2,* produced by W. Nkosi. Gallo Record Company 60 40214 and 60 40215. Audiocassette.

Makoti. 1991. *Vaal Express,* produced by K. Lebona and M. Masilela. Sounds of Soweto L4 SLH(EV) 6036. Audiocassette.

Mayibuye. 1990. *Thina Maqabane,* produced by K. Lebona and M. Masilela. Sounds of Soweto L4 TWH(EV) 1046. Audiocassette.

Moulton, David. 1995. *Golden Ears, Know What You Hear.* KIQ Productions. Compact disk set.

1992 Gallo Gold Awards: 65 Years. Compilation by R. Allingham. Gallo Africa. Compact disk.

Nkosi, West. 1991. *Sixteen Original Sax Jive Hits,* original production by R. Bopape; compilation production by W. Nkosi, A. Ralulimi, R. Allingham. Gallo Music Productions CSZAC 57. Compact disk.

———. 1992. *Rhythm of Healing,* produced by W. Nkosi. Earthworks Carol 2427–2. Compact disk.

Noise Khanyile, with Jo'burg City Stars and Amagugu Akwazulu. 1989. *The Art of Noise.* Globestyle ORB 045. Compact disk.

Ntuli, Unganeziyamfisa. 1991. *Buyisani Lomswani,* produced by M.T. Ntuli. Gallo Music Productions BL 752. LP.

Nzimande All Stars. 1976. *Jacaranda Bump Jive,* produced by H. Nzimande. Gramophone Record Company LMS 519. LP.

Platform One. 1990. *Isencane.* KGM Records 12KGM502. LP.

Rhythm of Resistance. 1984. Shanachie SH 43028. Compact disk.

Simon, Paul. 1986. *Graceland,* produced by P. Simon. Warner Brothers 25447. Compact disk.

Soweto Never Sleeps: Classic Female Zulu Jive. 1986. Shanachie SH 43041. Compact disk.

Splash. 1986. *Peacock.* Gallo–GRC. MCGMP 40353. Audiocassette.

———. 1991. *Eye for an Eye,* produced by D. Tshanda. Gallo Music Productions. Compact disk.

Thunder before Dawn: Indestructible Beat of Soweto, Vol. 2. 1987. Earthworks/Virgin Records 7 90866–1. Compact disk.

Township Swing Jazz! Vol.1. n.d. Celluloid 66893–2. Compact disk.

Umzansi. 1994. *Khuzani,* produced by W. Nkosi. Gallo Music Productions MCGMP 40502. LP.

Umzansi (Zulu Dance). 1997. *Amabhande,* produced by L. Mantate and S. Zulu. Music Team L4 CT138. Audiocassette.

Umzansi Zulu Dancers. 1988. *Bayekeleni,* produced by W. Nkosi. Gallo–GRC BL/BC 618. LP.

———. 1991. *Emzini,* produced by W. Nkosi. Gallo Music Productions BL739. LP.

———. 1998. *Ama Africa,* produced by D. Ngcobo and S. Zulu. VMP Music L4VE (EK) 104. Compact disk.

———. 1999. *Ingculaza,* produced by S. Zulu. Gallo Music Productions CDGMP 40804. Compact disk.

Index

Accordion, 50, 157, 158

Aesthetic evaluation: collective versus individual preference, 162, 165, 168, 171; contingency of principles of, 235; of engineers, 109–10, 156, 163, 167; and market pressures, 169; through performance, 149–52, 261–62; of players, 73, 173, 237, 239, 231, 233–34, 237, 239, 240, 251, 253; and politics, 13, 112, 143, 166, 175–77, 196, 207, 212, 260–61; of productions, 153, 244, 246; of songs, 161–63; of sounds, 109–11, 134, 123, 126, 157, 158, 160, 165, 236; of styles, 147–48, 149–52, 154, 155, 168, 261–62, 286 n.3. *See also* Bass; Drums; Guitar; Isigqi; Keyboards; Percussiveness; Sound distortion; Sound mixing; Timbre; Voice

African Americans: civil rights, 135, 138, 180; style, 13, 31, 122, 135–36, 179, 180, 230, 232, 242, 256, 272 n.31, 285 n.21. *See also* Jazz

African Church of the Nazarites, 117

African National Congress, 5, 59, 135, 174, 194, 201, 203, 205. *See also* Inkatha Freedom Party: tension with ANC; National politics; Political resistance

Africanness, 8, 111–12, 117–18, 155, 241, 247–49, 254; as embodied sensibility, 118–23, 116, 154, 180, 291 n.30; epitomized as Zuluness, 184–85;

historically constituted, 134–38; and ideology of non-mediated sound, 131–34; intellectual history of, 118–19, 171; and kinship, 165–66; as organizing feature in studio sessions, 155; as rhetorical effect, 160, 162, 171; as sound, 111–12, 116–17, 120–22, 168, 226. *See also* Blackness; Ethnicity; Race; Representation; South Africanness; Zuluness

African Youth Band, 186

Afrikaans, 27, 108, 109, 129, 177, 191, 220, 250, 256, 283 n.34, 289 nn.12, 13

AIDS, 5, 263

Allingham, Rob, 35, 76–77, 276 n.3

Ambiguity. *See* Indeterminacy

Apartheid: accumulation of power by discursive means, 143–44; effect on evolution of local studio practice, 103, 132; legislation, 274–75 n.43; music heritage of, 241; restrictions affecting performance and promotion, 58–60, 245–46. *See also* Creative process: under apartheid; Fetishization; Language; National politics; Political resistance; Race politics

Armstrong, Robert Plant, 279 n.18

Arrangement, musical, 55–57, 96, 116, 121, 146–49, 156, 163, 188–92, 221, 227, 233–35, 251, 252

Art of Noise, 217

Audience: choice of repertoire and, 12; crossover, 59, 231; description of, 215;

Kruger National Park, 257, 292 n.2
Kuny, Neil: as drummer, 156, 161,
167; embodied knowledge of, 93–95;
as engineer, 5, 75, 82, 83, 98, 100,
146, 148, 163, 164, 169, 245, 264; on
sounds, 153, 173, 235–36
KwaZulu-Natal, 23, 32, 46, 48, 189, 192,
195, 200; conflict and, 202, 211, 212;
historical, 177; Msinga, 185, 187, 190;
performance and promotion, 248,
267 n.5; rural practices, 185, 204, 208,
209
Kwela, 34, 295

Ladysmith Black Mambazo, 29, 40, 41,
62, 174, 181–82, 194, 217, 252–53
Language, 102, 220, 258; apartheid
policies on, 59–60, 171, 260; in the
control room, 2; English competence,
102, 103; marketing and, 271 n.26;
parody, 148, 152, 257; semantic referentiality, 193; social differences and,
102, 103–5, 163–64, 170, 189–92, 212,
256–57; in the studio, 81, 112, 170,
182–83, 184, 256–58, 280 n.25, 288
n.5; and technology, 98–100, 102, 222,
258, 282 n.27; theoretical approach
to, 11; vocables, 24, 36, 119, 146–
49, 151, 152, 157, 183, 184, 258; Zulu
exoticized, 24, 36; Zulu politicized,
200. See also Afrikaans; Communication; Indeterminacy; Naming
practices; Race politics; Zulu lyrics
Lemon, TJ, 17, 174
Lerole, Aaron, 225
Lesotho, 23, 269 n.14
Lifela, 170
Lindfors, Bernth, 179
Listening, 127, 129, 210–11, 261; musician's sophistication, 93, 230; and
perception, 117–19, 133, 170, 183–
84, 235, 236, 252, 280 n.22, 282 n.27;
playback technology and, 115, 230,
234. See also Audience; Production-
consumption relation
Liveness: as an African aesthetic, 112–
23; contemporary form of, 139–44,

212; historically constituted, 134–
39; as a studio aesthetic, 123–30; as
a trope of authenticity, 112–44, 212,
218. See also Africanness; Authenticity
Lomculo Unzima (album), 5, 7, 11, 122–
23, 253, 259, 260, 265; content, 6, 12;
"Hamba Kahle," 12, 188, 209, 210,
250; "Lomculo Unzima," 12, 98–99,
101, 122–23, 146, 156, 161, 215, 221,
230, 232, 250; "Phumani," 57, 188,
250; "South Africa on Fire"/"South
Africa," 95, 109, 123, 164, 250; studio
bookings, 84; "Ukuhlupeka kwami,"
268 n.8, 286 n.10; "uMakoti Onjani,"
12, 182, 188–92, 250
Lo Six with Thoko Thomo, 54
Luvuno, Isaac, 39, 263

Madondo, Sipho, 239, 240, 291 n.7.
See also Swazi traditional music:
Amaswazi Emvelo
Mafuxwana, Ruth, 46, 56
Mafuya, Mabel, 53
Mahlathini (Simon Nkabinde), 27, 51,
157, 161, 182, 218–19, 224–25, 227–
28, 232, 237, 240, 263, 264, 291 n.3,
295; changes in recordings 1960s to
1990s, 225, 227–29; dance style, 182;
history of image of, 222–26, 229–
30, 232; imitations of, 8, 190, 221,
230–32, 238. See also Mahlathini, the
Mahotella Queens and the Makgona
Tsohle Band; Vocals
Mahlathini, the Mahotella Queens and
the Makgona Tsohle Band, 16, 40–
41, 52, 59, 61–62, 138–39, 157, 224,
232, 237; "Bon Jour," 157, 160; break
with West Nkosi, 62, 264; changes in
members, 51, 52, 271 n.23, 272 n.33;
frontline singing style, 224–25, 251;
history, 51–53, 126, 264, 270 n.20;
international break of, 33, 45, 52, 273
n.37; international renown of, 29,
41, 155, 181–82, 217–18, 228; "Kazet,"
128; Kwatha O Mone, 139; Mathaka,
52; "Mbaqanga," 24–26; Paris-Soweto,

Mahlathini (*continued*)

52, 61, 128; Phezulu Eqhudeni, 52; producers of, 41, 52, 53; production techniques, 126, 156–57, 252–53; *Putting out the Light,* 52; and record companies, 52, 291 n.3; releases, 271 n.24, 273 nn.35–37; as role models, 71, 181–82, 218; sound distinctions of, 168–69, 224; on stage, 23–27, 68, 219, 224–25; Thokozile, 41; Tsamaya Moratuoa, 138. *See also* Izintombi Zesimanje: rivalry with the Mahotella Queens; Mahlathini; Mangxola, Mildred; Mankwane, Marks; Shawe, Nobesuthu; Tloubatla, Hilda

Mahotella Queens. *See* Mahlathini, the Mahotella Queens and the Makgona Tsohle Band

Makeba, Miriam: and the Skylarks, 54, 274 nn.37–38; and the Sunbeams, 54

Makgona Tsohle Band. *See* Mahlathini, the Mahotella Queens and the Makgona Tsohle Band

Malawi, 23, 39, 47, 123, 218, 269 n.14

Mandela, Nelson, 52, 138, 217, 259, 264

Mangxola, Mildred, 23–26, 219, 272 n.33

Manhattan Brothers, 53–54

Mankwane, Marks, 262, 263; on band's history, 229–30, 241; as composer, 51, 270 n.20; as guitarist, 23–26, 51, 157; on Mahlathini's voice, 232; as producer, 41, 51, 53, 275 n.47; signature sound, 24, 168–69, 287 n.14

Mann, Manfred, 132

Marabi, 34, 35, 296

Marcus, George, 171

Marimba, 45, 120–22, 162, 284 n.6

Market: and artists, 192–93; domestic, 6, 44, 57, 77, 83, 154–55, 161; informal sector, 4, 5; international, 6–7, 11, 45, 149, 162, 228, 244; relation between domestic and foreign, 52, 193, 234, 244–45, 253, 286 n.11; targeting consumers, 6, 12, 186–87; youth, 136, 152, 157, 186–87, 192, 289 n.15.

See also Europe; Groaning: global market and; Ngoma: global market and; Overseas: an imagined market; Production-consumption relation; World music

Masamisa, Juliet, 272 n.33

Maseko, Nunu, 141

Maskanda, 6, 36, 286 n.8, 296; basic form, 21; as commercial genre, 39; singing style, 100; stylistic features, 157–60. *See also* Guitarists

Masuka, Dorothy, 53

Mauritius, 19, 22, 244

Mavuthela, 39–41; personnel and artists, 51, 54, 55, 62, 270 n.20; production history, 41, 124

Mawela, Irene, 46, 272 n.31

Mbaqanga, 13, 34–64, 133, 157–58; dance style, 21, 26, 117, 182, 261; dress, 22, 26, 31, 54, 121, 138–39, 215, 224, 250; future of, 397; generic versions of, 6, 19–37, 67–69, 134, 153, 211; and maskanda, 157, 159–60; in 1970s, 31, 37, 54–57, 117, 125, 128, 134–39, 159, 224, 273 n.37; in 1980s, 138; in 1990s, 36–37, 138; reissues, 273 n.37; as a set of historical relationships, 45, 54–62, 71, 135; sociomusical constitution of, 64–69; vocal style, 24–25, 253–54; women's frontline history, 53–54. *See also* Bass; Drums; Guitar; Keyboards; Market; Vocals

Mbira, 285 n.19

McDuff, Jack, 135

McGriff, Jimmy, 135

Mdlalose, Thoko, 49, 226, 264, 272 n.32

Mediation, 8, 11, 129, 211, 259–61; concepts of culture and, 220, 253–54; ethnography and, 14–16, 261; experience and, 220, 238, 256; industrial relations, 256; and the production of difference, 13, 211, 246, 256–61; symbolic, 13, 258–59; technological, 13, 130; theory, 10

Meadowlands, 201

Mgomezulu, Ethel, 272 n.33

Mgqashiyo, 35, 186

Mines (miners), 62–64, 113, 170, 174, 177, 194, 196, 215, 263, 289 n.17

Mkhwebane, Nothembi, 49

Mnguni, Sana, 141

Mnguni, Thobi, 141, 272 n.31

Mnguni, Zodwa, 56

Molifi, Ruth and Doris, 53

Moving Guys, 51

Mozambique, 123, 160, 269 n.14

Mpholofolo, Michael, 57, 96, 110, 112, 186, 189–93, 210, 221, 227, 239–40, 252; biography, 49–50, 198; dress, 19–20; as drummer, 20, 250, 291 n.2; on "Sound of Africa!" riff, 111, 117, 134; on Soweto and contemporary politics, 197–202, 204–5

Msakazo, 34, 35

Msomi, Reggie, 40

Mthembu, Bheki, 250

Mthembu, Elias, 270 n.20

Mthembu, Lindiwe, 46, 56, 140, 141

Musical bow, 159, 286 n.6, 296

Mzabalazo, 144–45, 288 n.9, 290 n.28. *See also* Political resistance: protest songs

Namibia, 23, 45, 269 n.14

Naming practices: in bands, 48, 49, 57; in different languages, 189–91; and engineers, 109, 284 n.7; by ethnic labels, 109, 156, 167, 180, 200–202, 257; by kinship terms, 164–65; in sound processing, 87–88, 98–100

Narrative(s), 199–207, 218–19, 229–30, 237, 238; circulation of, 246; and experience, 244, 261; rectifying professional relationships, 240–41; and reputations, 22, 33. *See also* Overseas: imagined through stories

National Arts Council (South Africa), 265

National Peace Accord, 5

National politics, 5; conservatism, 5, 62; and music production, 5, 232, 256, 259–60; transition to democracy, 5, 7, 79, 162, 259–60. *See also* African Na-

tional Congress; Apartheid; Inkatha Freedom Party; Political resistance; Race politics

Ndebele, 159

Nene, Mandla, 6, 83

Nene, Nomsa, 272 n.32

Ngoma, 185, 188, 208, 210, 287 n.1, 288 n.2, 296; dress, 182; formal principles of, 175–78, 181, 182; global market and, 181–82, 248; history, 177–80; performance practice, 177, 184

Ngubane, Alton, 107–8, 144–45

Ngubane, Vivian, 270 n.20

Nguni, 156, 167. *See also* Xhosa; Zuluness

Nigeria, 218

Nkabinde, Simon. *See* Mahlathini

Nkosi, Stanley, 270 n.18

Nkosi, West, 5, 6, 16, 75–76, 172, 173; and artists in studio, 57–58, 116, 163, 164–66, 186, 188–92, 252; authority of, 66, 83, 98–100, 117, 122, 162, 186, 191, 220; biography, 29, 40–43, 263, 270 n.17; as composer and arranger, 51, 62, 95–97, 146–48, 150–51, 168, 181–82, 188, 280 n.26; as executive, 27, 29, 42; and exploitation of studio's capacities, 55–56, 61, 127–28, 130, 228–29; international interests, 42, 181–82; as manager, 41, 52, 248; as performer, 28, 40–43, 69–70, 188–91, 237, 270 n.20; political position, 27–29, 185; as producer, 27, 41–42, 48, 52, 55–56, 92, 95–97, 109–11, 125, 146, 148, 168, 169, 231, 258, 262, 275 n.47; production techniques, 32–33, 127–28, 156–59, 164–65, 182–84, 227–28, 252–53; sound preferences, 123, 161, 162, 168; talent development, 41, 239–41, 270 n.21; as trickster, 32–33, 58, 60–61, 65, 127, 146–48, 156, 167, 228, 233, 239, 253, 257

Nkwanyana, Elijah, 270 n.20

Nompumelelo, Zulu Queen, 209

Nzimande, Bodloza, 187, 209, 210

Nzimande, Hamilton, 16, 20, 29–32,

Nzimande, Hamilton (*continued*)
50, 51, 159, 218, 264; authority of,
60–61, 66; biography, 30–31, 38, 270
n.17; as celebrity, 47, 55, 69–70, 75;
innovations, 39; as producer, 31–32,
38–40, 43, 48, 55, 71–73, 125; relationship with artists, 21, 45, 46, 54–55;
as trickster, 29, 32, 60–61; views on
overseas, 62, 131; views on race and
technology, 38, 71–73, 104–5. *See also*
Isibaya Esikhulu
Nzimande All Stars, 49, 271 n.28

O'Jays, 135, 237, 239, 253
Organ. *See* Keyboards
Overseas, 217–18, 220, 227–37, 247–
49; and empowerment, 237, 242–43;
engineers' experience of, 81, 131;
as a form of struggle, 232, 243–48;
as a goal, 23, 162, 234; an imagined
market, 131, 220, 241; imagined in
sound, 221, 224–26, 237; imagined
through stories, 218, 237–43; as inseparable from ideas of the local, 241,
254–55. *See also* Audience; Authenticity; Europe; Globalization; Market:
international; Reputation(s): overseas; Sound mixing; Touring; United
States. See also *specific countries*
Oxygène, 153, 286 n.4

Paris, 23, 45, 128, 217, 237, 238, 243
Participatory discrepancies, 152
Parton, Dolly, 148, 173
Payola, 4
Pearlson, Peter, 1, 2, 5, 9, 76, 83, 92; on
sound, 122, 123, 184, 236; in studio
with West Nkosi, 95–97, 109–11, 117,
121, 182–84, 188–91, 221, 230, 233,
234, 237, 258, 264; on traditional
music and musicians, 101–3, 119, 133,
283 n.33
Pedi, 185
Pepper, Jonathan, 224
Percussiveness, 296; in bass sound, 114,
116; in guitar sound, 157–58, 170, 236;
in Mahlathini's voice, 24–26, 226–28;
of organ, 120; vocal, 119

Performance, 11–13, 23–27, 174–
215, 265, 269 n.7, 280–81 n.27; as
articulating musical and social relationships, 169–70, 177–78, 191–92,
213, 238, 255, 260; authority and,
42–43, 107; engineering as, 93–95,
111, 122; as evaluation, 149–52; feeling in, 42, 212, 255, 261; historical
re-enactment, 178; improvisatory
aspects of, 15–16, 66, 169–70; of
knowledge and difference, 98–100,
256–57; negotiating gigs, 62–64, 197,
213–14, 247–49; public, 23–27, 175,
185–86, 209–10, 214–16, 254–55; in
the studio, 124, 126, 130, 146–48, 150–
51; and violence, 196, 197. *See also*
Performativity; Venues
Performativity, 66, 167, 168, 206–7
Piliso, Ntemi, 270 n.20
Piliso, Shadrack, 51, 270 n.20
Pitch. *See* Tuning
Political resistance, 13, 135, 259–60;
artistic expression and, 28, 137, 256;
models of, 10; narrative strategies
and, 32–34; protests, 4, 174–75, 194,
201, 203, 289 n.19; protest songs,
186–87, 252. *See also* African National Congress; Ethnicity; Inkatha
Freedom Party; Mzabalazo; Race
politics; Studio altercations
Polka, 221–22, 232
Poppy Special, 51
Porcello, Thomas, 13, 170, 280 n.22, 282
nn.27, 29
Preston, Billy, 135
Pretoria, 27, 28, 40, 108, 268 n.5
Pretoria Tower Boys, 40, 270 n.19
Producers, 8, 61, 154, 159, 270 n.22,
272 n.32, 275 n.47; authority of, 46,
50, 54–58, 82, 233–34, 269 n.7; "Big
Five," 60, 62; Bopape, Rupert, 38, 39,
40, 41, 51, 54, 55, 125, 269 nn.6, 15,
270 nn.20, 21, 272 n.31, 275 n.47; du
Cros, Philippe Teissier, 53; Groux-
Cibial, Philippe, 61; Gwala, Freddie,
187; in-house, 40; Jila, Roxy, 50;
Jones, Quincy, 217; Lebona, Koloi

Hendrik, 125, 275 n.47; Makene, Blondie, 186–87; Masondo, David, 44, 74; Matumba, Cuthbert, 270 n.19, 275 n.47; Memela, Almon, 50; Mhlongo, Makhosonke, 100–101; Mojapelo, Jimmy, 275 n.47; Monama, Lucky, 270 nn.18, 20, 22, 275 n.47; Motswane, Thomas, 114; Mousset, Christian, 52; Mpofu, Ali, 5, 161, 168, 280 n.26; Ntuli, Thembinkosi, 100–101, 106, 270 n.18; Parsons, Alan, 153, 286 n.4; as powerbrokers, 42–43, 60–61, 162, 166, 258, 265; role in the studio, 12, 56, 133, 235; Siluma, Richard, 270 n.18; Teanet, Peta, 75; Thekwane, David, 50, 275 n.47; Tshanda, Dan, 152, 153, 154, 270 n.18; Twala, Sello, 154; van Wyk, Attie, 50; Vilakazi, Strike, 54, 275 n.47; *See also* Bass guitarists: David, Mzwandile; Dlamini, Jane; Dlamini, Moses; Guitarists: Mthembu, Hansford; Mankwane, Marks; Nkosi, West; Nzimande, Hamilton; Soul bands: Soul Brothers

Production-consumption relation, 74, 115–16, 126–27, 130, 133, 134, 158, 162, 181, 187, 229, 244–45, 253, 281 n.27, 287 n.17

Promotion, 5, 29, 134, 180, 247, 267 n.1; on mines, 63, 264; by performance, 38, 49, 196, 197, 213, 264, 265, 269 n.7

Promoters, 8, 33, 46, 247; Alcock, Sam, 270 n.20; Madela, 247–49

Quad Sisters, 53–54
Qwabe, Nhlanhla, 250, 252, 264

Race politics: conquest and, 72–73, 102, 171; differential forms of knowledge and, 72, 102–3, 170, 256; industry structure and, 60, 66, 78, 243, 246; mixing and, 114, 124–26, 133, 159; in performance and promotion, 31, 62–64; pervasiveness of, 9, 116; privilege and, 78, 191, 199; racial images and, 7, 243, 258; in studio, 9, 11, 122, 125, 168, 235, 243; technologi-

cal control and, 154, 245. *See also* Class; Ethnicity; Political resistance; Representation; Studio altercations

Radio, 5, 29, 34, 37, 41, 115, 187, 213; Radio Bantu, 59, 275 n.44; Radio SeSotho, 49; Radio Zulu, 41; and state propaganda, 59–60, 230, 291 n.6; *See also* Msakazo

Ralulimi, Albert, 35–36, 61

Rap, 181

Rathebe, Dolly, 53, 69, 217

Record companies: BMG, 4; Brunswick Gramophone House, 276 n.3; CBS, 38, 139; CCP Records, 50, 78; Celluloid Records, 52, 53, 61; Columbia Records, 276 n.3; Decca, 277 n.3; Earthworks, 53, 273 n.37; EMI, 4, 30–31, 38, 40, 50, 77–78, 278 n.4; Globestyle, 274 n.37; Gramophone Company Ltd, 276 n.3; Hit City Records, 186; independent companies, 4, 40, 45, 99; Phoenix Records, 270 n.17; Polydor, 53; Polygram, 53; Rainbow Records, 99, 282 n.28; RPM, 5, 50, 57, 77, 78, 267 n.4, 275 n.47; Rykodisc, 53, 273 n.37; Shanachie, 53, 217, 224, 273 n.37; Shandel Music, 74; Shisa International, 42; Sony, 4; Soul Brothers Music, 74; Sterns, 53; Teal, 38, 50, 275 n.47, 278 n.4; T.K. Productions, 264; Troubadour Records, 53–54, 270 n.19; Trutone, 53–54, 275 n.47, 277 n.3; Virgin, 217. *See also* Gallo

Record labels: Blue Note, 136; Hit, 270 n.19; HMV, 276 n.3; ownership of, 154; Prestige, 136; Singer, 276 n.3; USA, 40

Recording industry, 3 4; expansion, 59–60; mergers and buyouts, 40; multinationals, 77; as a star system, 165, 172. *See also* Downtown Studios; Record companies; Studio(s)

Recording media, 283–84 n.4; analog cassette tape, 5, 48, 81, 95, 163, 234, 256; compact disc, 4, 6, 69, 81, 217; digital cassette tape, 3, 81; reels, 73,

Zulu, Siyazi, 74, 220, 248
Zulu dress, 29, 295. *See also* Ibheshu;
Mbaqanga: dress
Zululand. *See* KwaZulu-Natal
Zulu lyrics, 24, 36, 153, 167, 188–92
Zuluness, 7, 156, 167–68, 197–213; as
aesthetic form, 181–93, 207–8, 291
n.30; as affirmation, 164, 210, 262;
global circulation of, 179–80; organizing studio relationships, 188–92,
193, 254–55; and other essentialisms,
111–12, 117, 254; performed on stage,
24, 36, 261–62; as a political position, 194–97; in reworking lyrics,
188–92; shifting positionality of,
156, 167, 200, 208; as a sound, 170,
181–88, 208, 252, 253–54. *See also*
Africanness; Blackness; Ethnicity;
Representation; Race politics; South
Africanness
Zulu Platoon (Z Platoon), 180
Zulu traditional music, 133, 159, 160,
298. *See also* Maskanda; Ngoma
Zwelethini, King Goodwill kaBheku-
zulu, 194–95, 209–10, 289 n.20

Louise Meintjes is Assistant Professor of
Ethnomusicology at Duke University.

TJ Lemon is a photojournalist based in
Johannesburg. His awards include first prize
(arts stories) in the World Press Photo
2001 competition.

Library of Congress Cataloging-in-Publication Data

Meintjes, Louise.
Sound of Africa! : making music Zulu in a
South African studio / Louise Meintjes.
p. cm.
Includes bibliographical references and index.
Glossary and Discography: p.
ISBN 0-8223-3027-x (cloth : alk. paper) —
ISBN 0-8223-3014-8 (pbk. : alk. paper)
1. Popular music—South Africa—Social aspects.
2. Sound recording industry—South Africa.
3. Ethnomusicology   I. Title.
ML3503.S6 M45   2003
781.63'0968—dc21   2002010220